CW00597140

SCIENCE, FORM, AND THE PROBLEM OF INDUCTION IN BRITISH ROMANTICISM

Exploring a topic at the intersection of science, philosophy, and literature in the late eighteenth century Dahlia Porter traces the history of induction as a writerly practice – as a procedure for manipulating textual evidence by selective quotation – from its roots in Francis Bacon's experimental philosophy to its pervasiveness in Enlightenment moral philosophy, aesthetics, literary criticism, and literature itself. Porter brings this history to bear on an omnipresent feature of Romantic-era literature, its mixtures of verse and prose. Combining analyses of printed books and manuscripts with recent scholarship in the history of science, she elucidates the compositional practices and formal dilemmas of Erasmus Darwin, Robert Southey, Charlotte Smith, Maria Edgeworth, and Samuel Taylor Coleridge. In doing so, she re-examines the relationship between Romantic literature and eighteenth-century empiricist philosophy, and forms of art and explores how Romantic writers engaged with the ideas of Enlightenment empiricism in their work.

DAHLIA PORTER is Lecturer in English Literature and Material Culture at the University of Glasgow. Her articles on literature, science, medicine, and visual art have appeared in *Representations*, *Romanticism*, and *The Eighteenth-Century: Theory and Interpretation*, and in essay collections on Samuel Johnson, Charlotte Smith, and *The Afterlives of Eighteenth-Century Fiction*. She co-edited Coleridge and Wordsworth's *Lyrical Ballads, 1798 and 1800* (2008) with Michael Gamer and is a member of The Multigraph Collective, a group of 22 scholars who co-wrote *Interacting with Print: Elements of Reading in the Era of Print Saturation* (2018).

This series aims to foster the best new work in one of the most challenging fields within English literary studies. From the early 1780s to the early 1830s, a formidable array of talented men and women took to literary composition, not just in poetry, which some of them famously transformed, but in many modes of writing. The expansion of publishing created new opportunities for writers, and the political stakes of what they wrote were raised again by what Wordsworth called those "great national events" that were "almost daily taking place": the French Revolution, the Napoleonic and American wars, urbanization, industrialization, religious revival, an expanded empire abroad and the reform movement at home. This was an enormous ambition, even when it pretended otherwise. The relations between science, philosophy, religion, and literature were reworked in texts such as *Frankenstein* and *Biographia Literaria*; gender relations in *A Vindication of the Rights of Woman* and *Don Juan*; journalism by Cobbett and Hazlitt; poetic form, content and style by the Lake School and the Cockney School. Outside Shakespeare studies, probably no body of writing has produced such a wealth of comment or done so much to shape the responses of modern criticism. This indeed is the period that saw the emergence of those notions of "literature" and of literary history, especially national literary history, on which modern scholarship in English has been founded.

The categories produced by Romanticism have also been challenged by recent historicist arguments. The task of the series is to engage both with a challenging corpus of Romantic writings and with the changing field of criticism they have helped to shape. As with other literary series published by Cambridge University Press, this one will represent the work of both younger and more established scholars, on either side of the Atlantic and elsewhere.

See the end of the book for a complete list of published titles.

SCIENCE, FORM, AND THE PROBLEM OF INDUCTION IN BRITISH ROMANTICISM

DAHLIA PORTER

University of Glasgow

CAMBRIDGE
UNIVERSITY PRESS

CAMBRIDGE
UNIVERSITY PRESS

University Printing House, Cambridge CB2 8BS, United Kingdom

One Liberty Plaza, 20th Floor, New York, NY 10006, USA

477 Williamstown Road, Port Melbourne, VIC 3207, Australia

314-321, 3rd Floor, Plot 3, Splendor Forum, Jasola District Centre, New Delhi - 110025, India

79 Anson Road, #06-04/06, Singapore 079906

Cambridge University Press is part of the University of Cambridge.

It furthers the University's mission by disseminating knowledge in the pursuit of education, learning and research at the highest international levels of excellence.

www.cambridge.org
Information on this title: www.cambridge.org/9781108418942
DOI: 10.1017/9781108292412

First published 2018

A catalogue record for this publication is available from the British Library

Library of Congress Cataloging in Publication data
Names: Porter, Dahlia, author.
Title: Science, form, and the problem of induction in British Romanticism /
Dahlia Porter, University of North Texas.
Description: New York : Cambridge University Press, 2018. | Series: Cambridge studies in Romanticism ; 114 | Includes bibliographical references and index.
Identifiers: LCCN 2017058261 | ISBN 9781108418942 (alk. paper)
Subjects: LCSH: Induction (Logic) in literature. | English literature –
18th century – History and criticism. | English literature –
19th century – History and criticism. | Literature and science – Great
Britain – History – 18th century. | Literature and science – Great
Britain – History – 19th century. | Romanticism – Great Britain.
Classification: LCC PR448.I538 P67 2018 | DDC 820.9/007 – dc23
LC record available at https://lccn.loc.gov/2017058261

ISBN 978-1-108-41894-2 Hardback
ISBN 978-1-108-40856-1 Paperback

For Helen and Richard

Contents

Figures

Acknowledgments

I would first like to acknowledge the Internet. In researching and writing this book, I have consulted thousands – if not tens of thousands – of digital facsimiles of books published between roughly 1600 and 1900. I consulted these facsimiles on different commercial and open access platforms, including *Early English Books Online*, *Eighteenth Century Collections Online*, *Historical Texts*, Google Books, HathiTrust Digital Library, archive.org, and the Biodiversity Heritage Library, plus a host of institutional websites and blogs. Between 2005 and 2017, I viewed many of these facsimile editions multiple times, often on different platforms. As you well know, platforms may, or may not, provide information about the specific physical copy or microfilm that was used to produce the digitized copy; and of course, different platforms often supply digital facsimiles of different physical copies. The upshot: I read text, browsed thumbnails, clipped pages, downloaded whole books, etc., from multiple digital facsimiles made from many distinct physical copies over the course of twelve years; many times, including today, I had twenty or thirty digital facsimiles open in a Web browser simultaneously, many of which I neither quote nor mention in this study. The practical consequence? My citations and bibliography do not include copy-specific information for all of the digital facsimiles I consulted in the making of this book.

As a scholar of the book as a physical object, I found this issue deeply disturbing for several years, and I decided to rectify it in February 2017. It became clear very, very quickly that this was untenable – it was not possible to reconstruct which facsimile, or even which platform, I had used on 1 May 2005, 12 August 2009, or 28 February 2014. When you encounter a reference to Maria Edgeworth's *Harry and Lucy Concluded* or Erasmus Darwin's *Loves of the Plants* or Samuel Taylor Coleridge's *The Friend*, bear this in mind: Each citation contains invisible multitudes, the absence of which points to the author's compositional method of extracting – with screen shot, text clip, or page download – bits and pieces of digitized books, building an archive on which to perform her induction.

Institutions, too, deserve acknowledgment. Some – the University of Pennsylvania, Vanderbilt University, and the University of North Texas – I thank for financial support, including teaching release, grants for travel to archives, and research fellowships. Vanderbilt University merits special thanks for a teaching release in 2009–2010, during which I wrote two new chapters and revised existing ones. I also thank the administration and libraries at these three institutions for purchasing subscriptions to commercial databases noted above, without which this book would not exist. The library staff at many institutions enabled this work, including Lynne Farrington and John Pollack at Kislak Center for Special Collections, Rare Books and Manuscripts at the University of Pennsylvania; Courtney Jacobs in the University of North Texas Special Collections; and the staff at the British Library Rare Books & Music Reading Room, the University of Glasgow Special Collections, the Keswick Museum and Art Gallery, the Saffron Walden Museum, The Huntington Library, and the Cullman and Dibner Libraries at the Smithsonian. An Andrew W. Mellon Fellowship of Scholars in Critical Bibliography in 2013–2015 from the Rare Book School at the University of Virginia spurred me to reframe the book substantively. A course on "The Illustrated Scientific Book to 1800" taught by Roger Gaskell and Caroline Dourselle-Melish was particularly inspiring.

A portion of Chapter 3 appeared as "Poetics of the Commonplace: Composing Robert Southey," *Wordsworth Circle* 42.1 (2011): 27–33, and I thank the editor, Marilyn Gaull, for generously purchasing the copyright in my name. I also thank Taylor and Francis, www.tandfonline.com, for permission to reprint "Formal Relocations: The Method of Southey's *Thalaba the Destroyer* (1801)," *European Romantic Review* (20:5): 671–79.

Finally, I come to the multitude of individuals whose generosity cannot be overstated. First, for their unremitting patience, persistence, and acumen, I thank the editorial team at Cambridge University Press, especially Linda Bree and Tim Mason, and the series editor, James Chandler. For comments, questions, provocations, and insights: Kerri Andrews, Alan Bewell, Carol Bolton, Jay Clayton, Meghan Doherty, Jonathan Farina, Geraldine Friedman, Marilyn Gaull, Noah Heringman, Jonathan Hsy, Jacqueline Labbe, Greg Leadbetter, András Kiséry, Arnold Markley, Linda Pratt, Tilottama Rajan, Alan Richardson, Michael Suarez, Peter Stallybrass, Helen Thompson, Alan Vardy, and Mark Wollaeger. For their enthusiasm and engagement with texts and topics central to the book: the students in my spring 2010 graduate class on Print Culture and Literary Production at Vanderbilt- Emily August, Ellie Durham, Heather Freeman, Stephanie Higgs, Amanda Johnson, and Adam Miller. For mind-bending interactivity with people and print: The Multigraph Collective- Mark Algee-Hewitt, Angela Borchert, Thora Brylowe, David Brewer, Julia S. Carlson, Brian Cowan, Susan Dalton, Marie-Claude Felton, Michael Gamer, Paul Keen, Michelle Levy, Nick Mason, Tom Mole, Andrew Piper, Michael Macovski, Andrew Stauffer, Diana Solomon, Richard Taws, Nikola Von Merveldt, and Chad Wellmon. For reading chapters in various states of distress and undress: Gabriel Cervantes, Nora Gilbert, Anne Frey, Scott Krawczyk, Ashley Miller, Jared Richmond, Allison Schachter, Mark Schoenfield, Rachel Teukolsky, and Kelly Wisecup. For editing the full manuscript: Brian Tatum. For agreeing to read chapters on any despicable poet I chose to write about and returning surgically precise commentary on them all: Tim Fulford. For feedback punctuated with exclamations of enthusiasm and innumerable letters in support of this project: Michael Gamer. For starting me down this road in the first place: Stuart Curran.

For helping me complete this book with many, many years of conversation, criticism, commentary, much needed perspective, good will, and love, I thank Gabriel Cervantes.

Abbreviations

BL Samuel Taylor Coleridge, *Biographia Literaria*, 2 vols., James Engell and W. Jackson Bate (eds.), vol. 7 of *The Collected Works of Samuel Taylor Coleridge* (Princeton, NJ: Princeton University Press, 1983).

CIP Charlotte Smith, *Conversations Introducing Poetry*, Judith Pascoe (ed.), vol. 13 of *The Works of Charlotte Smith* (London: Pickering & Chatto, 2007), pp. 59–237.

CL *Collected Letters of Samuel Taylor Coleridge*, 6 vols., Earl Leslie Griggs (ed.) (Oxford: Clarendon, 1956–1971).

EL Maria Edgeworth, *Early Lessons*, Elizabeth Eger, Clíona ÓGallchoir and Marilyn Butler (eds.), vol. 12 of *The Novels and Selected Works of Maria Edgeworth* (London: Pickering & Chatto, 2003), pp. 65–267.

EV Erasmus Darwin, *The Botanic Garden; A Poem, in two parts. Part I. Containing The Economy of Vegetation* (London: J. Johnson, 1791).

F Samuel Taylor Coleridge, *The Friend*, 2 vols., Barbara E. Rooke (ed.), vol. 4 of *The Collected Works of Samuel Taylor Coleridge* (Princeton, NJ: Princeton University Press, 1969).

LC *Life and Correspondence of Robert Southey*, Charles Cuthbert Southey (ed.) (New York: Harper & Brothers, 1855).

LL Samuel Taylor Coleridge, *Lectures 1808–1819: On Literature*, 2 vols., R. A. Foakes (ed.), vol. 5 of *The Collected Works of Samuel Taylor Coleridge* (Princeton, NJ: Princeton University Press, and London: Routledge & Kegan Paul, 1987).

LP Erasmus Darwin, *The Botanic Garden, Part II. Containing The Loves of the Plants, A Poem with Philosophical Notes* (Lichfield: J. Johnson, 1789).

NO   Francis Bacon, *The Great Instauration and the New Organon*, in
       vol. 4 of *The Works of Francis Bacon: Translations of the
       Philosophical Works*, James Spedding, Robert Leslie Ellis, and
       Douglas Denon Heath (eds.) (London: Longman et al., 1858).

PE   Richard Lovell Edgeworth, *Poetry Explained for the Use of Young
       People* (1802), new edn. (London: R. Hunter, 1821).

RS   *Robert Southey: The Critical Heritage*, Lionel Madden (ed.)
       (London and New York: Routledge, 1995).

RW   Charlotte Smith, *Rural Walks*, Elizabeth Dolan (ed.), in vol. 12
       of *The Works of Charlotte Smith* (London: Pickering & Chatto,
       2007), pp. 1–112.

SFE   Hannah More, *Strictures on the Modern System of Female
       Education* (1799), in *Selected Writings of Hannah More*, Robert
       Hole (ed.) (London: William Pickering, 1996).

SL   *Selections from the Letters of Robert Southey*, 4 vols., John Wood
       Warter (ed.) (London, 1856).

T   Robert Southey, *Thalaba the Destroyer*, Tim Fulford (ed.), vol. 3
       of *Robert Southey: Poetical Works, 1793–1810* (London: Pickering
       & Chatto, 2004).

Introduction
Romanticism's Composite Orders

I have bursts of local clarity, frequent access to new evidence, and these I coax to the page eagerly enough. But the backdrop, the larger point of it all, keeps slipping from me. I cannot easily hold the specific and the general in the right equilibrium.

    – Sven Birkerts, "The Millennial Warp," *Readings* (1999), p. 4

– all the knowledge, that can be acquired, child's play – the universe itself – what but an immense heap of *little* things? – I can contemplate nothing but parts, & parts are all *little* – ! – My mind feels as if it ached to behold & know something *great* – something *one* & *indivisible* – and it is only in the faith of this that rocks or waterfalls, mountains or caverns give me the sense of sublimity or majesty! – But in this faith *all things* counterfeit infinity!

    – Samuel Taylor Coleridge, Letter to John Thelwall,
    14 Oct. 1797

I begin with two reflections on modernity. Ostensibly, Sven Birkerts is describing what it was like to write "The Millennial Warp," an essay that attempts to isolate a change in our experience of time. In the passage I've excerpted, he is also introducing the intellectual problem of the essay: he *feels* that the abstract concept of time has shifted significantly in his lifetime because the rate of social interaction, of "life," has gotten faster. For Birkerts in 1999, time was no longer what it had been fifty years before because the basic conditions of life (at least in the tech-obsessed West, if not globally) had been fundamentally altered by the digital revolution. We now live in a world hypersaturated with information, of "data ramified past all true comprehensibility."[1] The reflection above thus serves double duty in his essay: it expresses the condition of living in a digital age, and it reflects the writer's struggle as an analogue of that condition. The problem is how to extract an "incomprehensible totality" from the accumulated examples of lived experience, and how to write about it – the totality as an idea, a condition of existence – in a way that evidences but also reveals it as something more than the accumulation of particular instances.

Birkerts's troubles sound familiar. Clifford Siskin and William Warner have pointed to the end of the eighteenth century as another moment of information saturation, a moment when mediation became overload.[2] Romanticism "happens," as Andrew Piper has argued, when there are suddenly too many books to read.[3] When William Wordsworth complained, in the 1800 Preface to *Lyrical Ballads*, of the "frantic novels" and "deluges of idle and extravagant stories in verse" emanating from the press, he was worrying about new desires, attitudes, and behavior provoked by a "rapid communication of intelligence."[4] The problem was not so much the form of the communication, but the speed and ramification of it, which produced a "craving for extraordinary incident" that was "hourly gratified."[5] As Ann Blair has argued, this reaction wasn't born in the Romantic era: authors in the ancient and medieval world had complained just as bitterly about an overabundance of books and the paucity of resources for dealing with the information they contained.[6] If the "what" continued to shift – manuscript, print, digital – the glut provoked much the same anxiety. In our moment, digital devices and platforms format and mediate our experience; the virtual structures social and object worlds. At the end of the eighteenth century, the Enlightenment project of collecting – artifacts and specimens from across the globe were pouring into European storehouses and museums – seemed, as descriptions piled up in the *Philosophical Transactions*, another iteration of the proliferation of print. As Coleridge complains, rather than a whole integrated by God's plan, nature had begun to look like a heap of minutiae, the totality of which was ungraspable. Faith, the guarantor of oneness, only exposes things dissembling, deceiving by their irreducible particularity – a condition reproduced formally in the string of dashes that punctuate Coleridge's lament.

Conditions may have changed, but the question of how to deal with excess – and the desire to synthesize all the little things – has not. In this book, I'm particularly interested in the writerly conundrum articulated by Birkerts: How does one write in and about a moment of information saturation? What strategies do authors use to deal with and convey the troubling sense of too much, too fast, too many? Like Coleridge before him, Birkerts comes at this problem by quoting. People, he argues, have responded to hypersaturation by "editing," by being selective about what and how much they absorb.[7] Working off this insight, he routes his argument through two long quotations from Arthur Danto's *After the End of Art* and Bill McKibben's *The End of Nature*. The problem of overload calls for

an editorial approach of careful selection, arrangement, and juxtaposition –
not just of examples and observations, but of pieces of other texts. By stitching extracts together, the writer makes something new: he or she produces
a composite that synthesizes various fields of knowledge – in Birkerts's case,
art criticism and climate change – into the expression of a cultural condition. The composite order – a text made by splicing genres and kinds of
knowledge, as well as bits of other texts – fills the gap between particular
examples and a general sense of change.

The book you are about to read is not simply about information saturation in Britain around 1800, a moment that is eerily, pointedly analogous to our own. I am also concerned with the method authors used
to turn a heap of particular instances into the expression of something
larger, and the consequences of that method for books produced in the
Romantic period. In writing this book I wanted to figure out how writers
approached the problem of excess *formally*, and what kind of compositional
strategies they adopted to navigate and capture a seemingly ungraspable
totality. Other recent studies, most pertinently Blair's *Too Much to Know:
Managing Scholarly Information before the Modern Age* and Chad Wellmon's
*Organizing Enlightenment: Information Overload and the Invention of the
Modern Research University*, have focused on genres of information management such as the index, encyclopedia, anthology, and commonplace book.
While I also discuss these genres, I'm particularly interested in how practices of extracting, quoting, and sourcing central to these genres changed
cultural production in the Romantic period. (David Shield's aphoristic,
reference-laden *Reality Hunger* exemplifies this preoccupation in our own
moment of saturation.) The early nineteenth century codified specific formal approaches to sourcing and citation that we retain today: when Birkerts
sets block quotes off from the rest of his text, he follows the citational methods emerging in the late eighteenth century. When he builds an argument
about hypersaturation by collecting, selecting, arranging, comparing, contrasting, differentiating, and synthesizing pieces of other people's texts, he
follows a tried (but not always true) procedure used by the Romantics to
deal with this condition of Western modernity.

The backdrop for my argument is the history of a practice-*cum*-concept:
I argue that the inductive method of seventeenth-century experimental
philosophy became, over the course of the eighteenth century, a template
for producing minds and texts across many fields of knowledge production. Part of this story is well known: propounded in Francis Bacon's
Novum Organum (1620) and codified in the experimental practice of the
early Royal Society, inductive method became the hallmark of legitimate

science well into the nineteenth century, as well as – after John Locke's *Essay concerning Human Understanding* (1690) – the defining procedure of the British empiricist tradition in moral philosophy.[8] In this context, induction is most often understood as a new way – Bacon often uses path metaphors – to study nature by beginning with a "fresh examination of particulars."[9] Bacon wanted to build a databank of observations and experiments that could be arranged, compared, distinguished, and ultimately composed into universal principles. I've chosen the final term in this series carefully: for Bacon and those who took up his method in the seventeenth and eighteenth centuries, induction made experience *literate* – it was a technology for organizing information in writing, as text. Bacon argues that having a "store of natural history and experience" is a good beginning, but new knowledge doesn't emerge from merely contemplating this mass of information: "hitherto more has been done in matter of invention by thinking than by writing; and experience has not yet learned her letters. Now no course of invention can be satisfactory unless it be carried on in writing" (*NO*, 96).[10] What Bacon produced using induction – the example of heat in the *Novum Organum* itself, but also his wide-ranging natural history *Sylva Sylvarum* (1626) – took the form of a collection of aphorisms, signaling the conjunction of inductive method and older traditions of compilation and commonplacing. Induction repurposes Renaissance educational methods; its aim is to produce and manipulate a textual archive, and its product is a composite forged from many sources.

Induction was adopted across eighteenth-century writing about optics, astronomy, botany, chemistry, cognition, emotions, economy, grammar, history, aesthetics, the production of visual art, and literary criticism (and the list continues). Other methodological approaches existed, even flourished, but Baconian induction and the empiricist tradition spawned by Locke's *Essay* underwrote much of the conceptual orientation, if not the practice, of later seventeenth- and eighteenth-century natural and moral philosophy.[11] As inductive method gained prominence and cultural sway, so too did its forms. Induction was not only a procedure for generating knowledge about any particular subject; it also prescribed a set of formal conditions for the presentation of that knowledge. As I detail at length in Chapter 1, these formal conventions were embedded in compositional practice: authors from Robert Boyle to Samuel Johnson to William Wordsworth follow the steps of induction to compile and organize raw materials, with the eventual goal of forging them into a less or more coherent expression of a truth – whether that truth pertained to air, language, or "what is really important to men."[12] What they produced – as Boyle's *New Experiments Physico-Mechanicall, Touching the Spring of the Air*, Johnson's *Dictionary*, and Wordsworth and Coleridge's *Lyrical Ballads* differently attest – were composites. Their sources might include notebooks of first-hand observations or experimental results, stories overheard and noted in passing, records of conversations, commonplace books of textual excerpts, collections of letters or ballads, printed miscellanies, newspaper accounts, or books read and annotated. Whatever combination of sources the authors used, texts made by following inductive method are all products of splicing, grafting, and mixing bits of other written materials onto and into each other.

Some of my readers will be skeptical about this assertion. We feel that Boyle, Johnson, and Wordsworth must have been doing very different things because historical conditions were different when they wrote, they were working toward different ends in different genres, and the works they ultimately produced appear to be radically, even wildly, divergent from one another. Some historians of science might be particularly surprised by the conflation of compiling experimental results and collecting quotations from books, a merger that runs against the story we have told about seventeenth-century experimental philosophy and its break from classical, predominantly Aristotelian, forms of textual authority. While this established narrative remains salient, recent studies have demonstrated the centrality of the commonplace tradition to Enlightenment knowledge making.[13] Aligning Boyle, Johnson, and Wordsworth also pushes against the conventional division in literary studies between Enlightenment empiricism and Romantic organicism. I am obviously not arguing that Boyle and Wordsworth were, in fact, doing exactly the same thing, or that Wordsworth believed he was doing the same thing as Boyle or Johnson. Rather, following recent studies that explore the centrality of Enlightenment science to Romantic literature, I am intent on drawing out the methodological thread that links their practices as writers, a historical continuum that can easily be blotted out by modern divisions of discipline, philosophical orientation, and time period.[14]

In giving attention to compositional practice and the procedures of making texts, I am engaging with various strands of textual criticism. From the description above, my approach seems most consonant with recent work such as Sally Bushell's application of *critique génétique* to Wordsworth, Tennyson, and Dickinson in *Text as Process* (2009). While I share Bushell's interest in authors' compositional processes as they are captured in manuscript drafts and notes, I also focus on how procedures of making texts are manifested in printed books.[15] A number of editors and critics have begun to explore this conjunction. Summarizing criticism about Pierre Bayle, Ephraim Chambers, and other seventeenth-century encyclopedists, Richard Yeo argues that we can often see the ghostly traces of an author's methods of collecting and arranging materials in his or her published books; as Harriet Kirkley suggests of Johnson's "Life of Pope," we can also work in the other direction, unearthing the structure of the published work in the author's compilation and rearrangement of notes.[16] These traces are particularly pressing for the Romantic-era texts I treat here, where the confluence of procedure and form is anything but ghostly: only consider what *Lyrical Ballads* announces in its title, and why the 1800 Preface adds not one but two statements describing compositional process. Through formal choices and paratextual commentary, the texts I examine here insistently draw attention to how they were made, and consequently to their status as composite orders.

My Introduction's title is doubly borrowed. The penultimate chapter of Stuart Curran's *Poetic Form and British Romanticism* is titled "Composite Orders," a phrase taken from Wordsworth's Preface to his *Poetical Works* (1827), first published as the preface to *Poems, by William Wordsworth* in 1815.[17] In the 1827 Preface, Wordsworth defines the "composite order" as a combination of descriptive, didactic, and philosophical–satirical poetic modes, exemplified by Edward Young's *Night Thoughts* or William Cowper's *The Task* – two of the most popular loose, catch-all poems of the mid- to late eighteenth century.[18] In 1815, Wordsworth had used the phrase "composite species," suggesting the botanical and typological roots of his thinking on poetic kinds (in eighteenth- and nineteenth-century botany, the family now designated *Asteraceae* was known as *Compositae*, its flowers being composites of smaller, distinct flowers). When Wordsworth changed the phrase to "composite order" in 1827, he shifted from a taxonomic to an architectural metaphor: Composita (later Composite) is the fifth classical order, being "composed of the Ionic grafted upon the Corinthian."[19] Later technical uses of the term retain this sense of material difference and forced conjunction: composite ships are built of wood and iron, composite photographs superimpose images of two or more people on top of each other. In 1950s engineering, a composite designated "a material made from two or more physically different constituents each of which largely retains its original structure and identity."[20] The "composite order" is not defined by hybridity but by mixture, and an uneasy one at that: like oil and water, the constituent parts maintain a material separation rather than coalescing into a unified form.[21]

Beyond those baggy blank verse poems cited by Wordsworth, eighteenth-century Britain was rife with mixed forms: the novel, the newspaper, the miscellaneous collection, the anthology, the encyclopedia, and the periodical proliferated with abandon – indeed, their spread seemed void of human agency to contemporary critics.[22] Collaboratively written and insistently polyvocal, periodicals announce their varied contents on their title pages; anthologies and miscellanies similarly claim variety as a selling point, whether they collect extracts from the "best" approved authors or compile ephemeral productions of the moment.[23] As these forms blossomed, conventional literary genres fractured and recombined. Pope subtitled *The Rape of the Lock* a "Heroi-Comical Poem"; Fielding called *Joseph Andrews* a "comic epic poem in prose" and cast *Tom Jones* as a "Heroic, Historical, Prosaic Poem."[24] By the time Johnson was canonizing Shakespeare in 1765, "genre salad was fashionable dish," as Barbara Benedict puts it in her discussion of the composite nature of eighteenth-century literary collections.[25] This cornucopia of mixed forms owes its existence to many forces, a number of which appear in Siskin and Warner's account of print mediation as the defining feature of the Enlightenment: the emergence of new networks and spaces of print communication; the much expanded periodical press and the rise of advertising; new forms of association, from social clubs to the Royal Society; and new rules and regulations, including changes in copyright law.[26] Slightly preceding but continuing alongside these mediations, a conceptual revaluation of "mixture" was ongoing. Wolfram Schmidgen has convincingly argued that seventeenth- and early eighteenth-century writers claimed generic, chemical, and political mixture as an unequivocal good, a generative force that supported, indeed produced, England's national genius.[27] Just as Siskin and Warner begin their account of Enlightenment by returning to Bacon, Schmidgen accounts for the eighteenth-century celebration of mixture in the linked scientific and political shifts of the seventeenth century. The seventeenth century's conceptual recasting of mixture materialized in the eighteenth-century proliferation of mixed forms.

What I am designating a "composite order," however, emerges in the Romantic period and is specifically and self-consciously concerned with mixing the oil of verse with the water of prose.[28] In my second chapter, I trace this particular concern back through eighteenth-century aesthetics to the mid-seventeenth-century debates over the constitution and purpose of the Royal Society. These debates centered on questions of style. The capacity to render and convey experimental knowledge was guaranteed by the linguistic precision of clear, transparent, unornamented prose – a kind of prose defined against the figurative play of verse.[29] While this position, articulated most forcibly in Thomas Sprat's *History of the Royal Society of London* (1667), was underwritten by political and religious controversies of the time, over the next century it effectively codified the opposition between poetic diction and the "plain style" of experimental science.[30] So powerful was this binary by the end of the eighteenth century that Erasmus Darwin claimed – in the middle of a poem about Linnaean botany – that "science is best delivered in Prose."[31] Both Coleridge and Wordsworth took up the issue as a problem of definition: In a series of lectures on literature delivered in 1811–12, Coleridge suggested that "[p]oetry is not the proper antithesis to prose, but to science. Poetry is opposed to science, and prose to metre."[32] Wordsworth had made a similar comment in a footnote to the 1802 Preface to *Lyrical Ballads*: "much confusion has been introduced into criticism by this contradistinction of Poetry and Prose, instead of the more philosophical one of Poetry and Matter of fact, or Science. The only strict antithesis to Prose is Metre."[33] These statements attest to the saliency of the distinction wrought in the seventeenth century: even as they attempt to contest the division between prose and poetry, they confirm its foundation. Science was different from poetry, just as prose was different from metrical verse; the difference between fact and figure is analogous to the difference in formal construction between prosaic and metrical language.

In this context, poetic extracts set off from the body of a prose narrative, and prose notes running across the bottom of a printed poem, are an ostentatious display of formal mixture. Like Ionic volutes grafted onto Corinthian acanthus leaves, verse and prose sit atop one another, insistently proclaiming their difference (Figs. 1–4). The space of the page, the way elements are composed and arranged on it, makes it impossible to ignore the composite nature of the text. David Duff has described this peculiarly Romantic proclivity as the "rough mixing" of genres, a "type of generic combination in which formal surfaces of constituent genres are left intact: heterogeneous elements are juxtaposed rather than integrated, thus creating the aesthetic effect of discontinuity."[34] These mixtures can be distinguished from the "seamless fusion of forms" characteristic of Duff's "smooth mixing" or the "blurring of generic lines" between poetry and prose that, Gabrielle Starr has argued, allowed the novel to incorporate conventions and patterns from various eighteenth-century poetic modes.[35] If the eighteenth-century novel could incorporate other genres, eating them up and subsuming them into itself (as J. Paul Hunter's *Before Novels* suggests), this is only one side of the story. Romantic composite orders,

(24)

E'en round the pole the flames of Love afpire,
And icy bofoms feel the *fecret* fire! —
Cradled in fnow and fan'd by arctic air
Shines, gentle BAROMETZ! thy golden hair;   250
Rooted in earth each cloven hoof defcends,
And round and round her flexile neck fhe bends;
Crops the grey coral mofs, and hoary thyme,
Or laps with rofy tongue the melting rime;
Eyes with mute tendernefs her diftant dam,   355
Or feems to bleat, a *Vegetable Lamb.*

Barometz. l. 250. Polypodium Barometz. Tartarian Lamb. Clandeftine Marriage. This fpecies of Fern is a native of China, with a decumbent root, thick, and every where cover'd with the moft foft and denfe wool, intenfely yellow. Lin. Spec. Plant.

This curious ftem is fometimes pufh'd out of the ground in its horizontal fituation by fome of the inferior branches of the root, fo as to give it fome refemblance to a Lamb, ftanding on four legs; and has been faid to deftroy all other plants in its vicinity. Sir Hans Sloane defcribes it under the name of Tartarian Lamb, and has given a print of it. Philof. Tranf. abridg'd, V 2. p. 646. but thinks fome art had been ufed to give it an animal appearance. Dr. Hunter in his edition of the Terra of Evelyn, has given a more curious print of it, much refembling a fheep. The down is ufed in India externally for ftopping hemorrhages, and is called golden mofs.

The thick downy clothing of fome vegetables feems defigned to protect them from the injuries of cold, like the wool of animals. Thofe bodies which are bad conductors of

E   —So,

Fig. 1 Erasmus Darwin, *The Botanic Garden, Part II. Containing Loves of the Plants* (Litchfield, 1789), p. 24. Courtesy of Albert and Shirley Small Special Collections Library, University of Virginia.

19

The BROTHERS.*

" These Tourists, Heaven preserve us! needs must live
" A profitable life : some glance along,
" Rapid and gay, as if the earth were air,
" And they were butterflies to wheel about
" Long as their summer lasted : some, as wise,
" Upon the forehead of a jutting crag,
" Sit perch'd with book and pencil on their knee,
" And look and scribble, scribble on and look,
" Until a man might travel twelve stout miles,
" Or reap an acre of his neighbour's corn.

* This Poem was intended to be the concluding poem of a series
of pastorals, the scene of which was laid among the mountains
of Cumberland and Westmoreland. I mention this to apologise
for the abruptness with which the poem begins.

Fig. 2 Samuel Taylor Coleridge and William Wordsworth, *Lyrical Ballads and other poems by W. Wordsworth*, 2 vols. (London, 1800), 2: 37. Courtesy of University of Michigan Library (Special Collections Library).

expression may be allowed—the matin-bell of a distant convent, the faint murmur of the sea-waves, the song of birds, and the far-off low of cattle, which she saw coming slowly on between the trunks of the trees. Struck with the circumstances of imagery around her, she indulged the pensive tranquillity which they inspired; and while she leaned on her window, waiting till St. Aubert should descend to break-fast, her ideas arranged themselves in the following lines:

THE FIRST HOUR OF MORNING.

How sweet to wind the forest's tangled shade,
When early twilight, from the eastern bound,
Dawns on the sleeping landscape in the glade,
And fades as morning spreads her blush around!

When ev'ry infant flower, that wept in night,
Lifts its chill head soft glowing with a tear,
Expands its tender blossom to the light,
And gives its incense to the genial air.

How fresh the breeze that wafts the rich perfume,
And swells the melody of waking birds;
The hum of bees, beneath the tendril gloom,
And woodman's song, and low of distant herds!
Then,

Then, doubtful gleams the mountain's hoary head,
Seen through the parting foliage from afar;
And, farther still, the ocean's misty bed,
With flitting sails, that partial sun-beams share.

But, vain the fairest shade—the breath of May,
The voice of music floating on the gale,
And forms, that beam through morning's dewy veil,
If health no longer bid the heart be gay;
O balmy hour! 'tis thine love would to give,
Here spread her bloom, and bid the parent live!

Emily now heard persons moving below in the cottage, and presently the voice of Michael, who was talking to his mules, as he led them forth from a hut adjoining. As she left her room, St. Aubert, who was now risen, met her at the door, apparently as little restored by sleep as herself. She led him down stairs to the little parlour, in which they had supped on the preceding night, where they found a neat breakfast set out, while the host and his daughter waited to bid them good morrow.

" I envy you this cottage, my good friends," said St. Aubert, as he met them, " it

K 3

Fig. 3 Ann Radcliffe, *The Mysteries of Udolpho, A Romance, Interspersed with some Pieces of Poetry*, 4 vols. (London, 1794), I: 18–19. Courtesy of University of Glasgow Library, Special Collections.

as far as they are modified by a predominant passion; or by associated thoughts or images awakened by that passion; or when they have the effect of reducing multitude to unity, or succession to an instant; or lastly, when a human and intellectual life is transferred to them from the poet's own spirit.

"Which shadowy to being through earth, sea, and air;"

In the two following lines for instance, there is nothing objectionable, nothing which would preclude them from forming, in their proper place, part of a descriptive poem:

"Behold yon row of pines, that shorn and bow'd Bend from the sea-blast, seen at twilight eve."

But with the small alteration of rhythm, the same words would be equally in their place in a book of topography, or in a descriptive tour. The same image will rise into a semblance of poetry if thus conveyed:

"Yon row of bleak and visionary pines, By twilight-glimpse discerned, mark! how they flee From the fierce seablast, all their tresses wild Streaming before them."

I have given this as an illustration, by no means as an instance, of that particular excellence which I had in view, and in which Shakspeare even in his earliest, as in his latest works, surpasses all other poets. It is by this, that he still gives a dignity and a passion to the ob-

jects which he presents. Unaided by any previous excitement, they burst upon us at once in life and in power.

"Full many a glorious morning have I seen Flatter the mountain tops with sovereign eye."
Shakspear's Sonnet 33rd.

"Not mine own fears, nor the prophetic soul Of the wide world dreaming on things to come— * * * * * * * * * * The mortal moon hath her eclipse endur'd, And the sad augurs mock their own presage; Incertainties now crown themselves assur'd, And Peace proclaims olives of endless age. Now with the drops of this most balmy time My Love looks fresh; and Death to me subscribes, Since spite of him, I'll live in this poor rhyme, While he insults o'er dull and speechless tribes. And thou in this shalt find thy monument, When tyrant's crests, and tombs of brass are spent."
Sonnet 107.

As of higher worth, so doubtless still more characteristic of poetic genius does the imagery become, when it moulds and colors itself to the circumstances, passion, or character, present and foremost in the mind. For unrivalled instances of this excellence, the reader's own memory will refer him to the LEAR, OTHELLO, in short to which not of the " great, ever living, dead men's" dramatic works? Inopem me copia fecit. How true it is to nature, he has himself finely expressed in the instance of love in Sonnet 98.

B b 2

Fig. 4 Samuel Taylor Coleridge, *Biographia Literaria*, 2 vols. (London, 1816), 2: 19. Courtesy of University of Glasgow Library, Special Collections.

novels among them, display their seams and stitchery, the visible imprint of mixture. This mixture of prose and verse has been noted by critics of the "Romantic novel" as defined in the German tradition by Friedrich Schlegel and practiced by Ann Radcliffe, Charlotte Smith, and Walter Scott.[36] Ann Wierda Rowland has argued that the novelistic composite orders of the Romantic period can help us write new "literary histories that describe how the formal and social categories of Romantic literary genre took shape through persistent acts of both differentiation and appropriation."[37] I take Rowland's suggestion quite literally here, while extending it beyond the novel. I argue that the methods of knowledge production and assumptions about genre inherited from the seventeenth and eighteenth centuries do in fact take shape on – and determine the shape of – the pages of Romantic books. This book examines formal mixtures of verse and prose – long poems with longer footnotes, fiction and essays littered with excerpted verse – as products of a compositional method that announces itself in layout and format.

The convergence of process and product thus supplies the book's fulcrum. Induction is a conceptual pivot on which theories and practices of knowledge-making as text-making turn, and the outcome of inductive method is made legible in the physical, material aspect of the composite order. To be clear, I am concerned with both inductive method as a conceptual paradigm *and* how this paradigm determines the *look* or *aspect* of the page. Formal difference is registered in text blocks distinguished typographically by font size, typeface, and indentation; prose and verse are separated by quotation marks (in Coleridge's *Biographia*), a centered, all caps title (as in the Radcliffe example), a single or double line (as in *Lyrical Ballads*), or a swath of blank paper (as in Darwin's *Botanic Garden*). In this focus on page space and layout, my study builds on and speaks to a large and diverse body of work by book historians, bibliographers, graphic artists, book designers, and practicing poets. A group of studies published in the 1980s – including D. F. McKenzie's "Typography and Meaning: The Case of William Congreve" (1981), Walter Ong's *Orality and Literacy: The Technologizing of the Word* (1982), Johanna Drucker's "Letterpress Language" (1984), and Jerome McGann's "How to Read a Book" (1991) – provide the basis for thinking about this issue. In his pioneering work on Congreve, extended in the 1985 Panizzi lectures, McKenzie demonstrated that changes in page design, typography, ornamentation, etc. significantly changed the meaning of Congreve's texts between the seventeenth-century quarto edition and the eighteenth-century octavo. For McKenzie, the case of Congreve illustrates that the "book itself is an expressive means. To the eye its pages offer an aggregation of meanings both verbal and typographic."[38] Writing from the tradition of book design rather than textual editing, Drucker begins "Letterpress Language" with the premise that "writing produces a visual language: the shapes, sizes and placement of letters on a page contribute to the message produced, creating statements which cannot always be rendered in spoken language."[39] In her study of avant-garde art, *The Visible Word* (1994), Drucker further distinguishes between modes of "typographic enunciation": in an "unmarked" text, words "appear to speak themselves," while in a "marked" text, the printer has "utilized the capacity of typographic representation to manipulate the semantic value of the text through visual means."[40] McGann's work suggests the limits of such a strident division: Although some texts, such as Pound's *Cantos*, call out for and dramatize the demands of "spatial reading," it is "a ubiquitous function" of all texts.[41] From advertisements, newspapers, and anthologies to seventeenth-century shape poetry and modern critical editions, the organization of the text on the page – its format and typography – make particular arguments via layout.

Recent criticism has extended these arguments by directing them toward texts and historical moments that are less insistent in their demands for spatial reading, and by emphasizing how layout and typography have shaped the "mentality of the West."[42] As with Ong's arguments about orality versus print, for some modern poets attending to the space of the page constitutes both a practice and a philosophy of *written* poetry, as distinguished from performance art or spoken word (Ong cites the example of E. E. Cummings). Nathanial Mackey, for example, describes his attention to the "graphic amenities peculiar to the page," "to the placement of words on the page (the use of variable margins, intralinear spacing, page breaks, and such to advance a now swept, now swung, sculpted look, a visual dance down the page and from page to page)"; these choices, Mackey argues, can "suggest the unfolding of thought or composition."[43] For Mackey, page space is the poet's tool for meaning making, a position made readily apparent in Tom Phillips's classic *A Humument: A Treated Victorian Novel* and recent experiments with blackout, erasure, and typographical emphasis such as Jen Bervin's *Nets*, where Shakespeare's Sonnet #63 becomes "I am/vanishing or vanished/in these black lines."[44] From the page as a poet's playground it is but a little leap to the page as a site of struggle (or, more generously, transaction) between author, editor, publisher, printer, and reader. Following Ong, critics have considered how "typographic space is present to the psyche" in the literary text or the critical edition.[45] Patricia White uses the Norton Critical edition of Walt Whitman's *Leaves of Grass* to consider how readers

Romantic authors were keenly aware of the outcome of their compositional method, and they tested a variety of techniques for turning a heap of observations and borrowed materials into something more than the sum of its parts. As they pushed back against the methodology they had inherited, these authors as a group began to conceive of the compositional method modeled on induction, and the texts produced by it, as failed attempts at coherence.

In this context, consider for a moment the long-running, pervasive discussion of parts and wholes in twentieth-century criticism of Romantic poetry. These terms have most often been pinned to Coleridge's philosophical pronouncements and his engagement with German idealism, and they remain pervasive in evaluative assessments of Coleridge's less canonical contemporaries and predecessors. I am not interested in debating the relevance of such evaluations here. Rather, I'm interested in how compositional practice and its manifestation on the printed pages of Romantic period books constitute the source of Coleridge's own anxieties and the critical investments he spawned. Even before *Lyrical Ballads* was published in 1798, Coleridge was already insisting that the book was "*one work*, in *kind tho' not in degree*, as an Ode is one work – & that our different poems are as stanzas, good relatively rather than absolutely."[67] The poems in this generically mixed collection, he insists, are of the same essential nature even if they diverge in intensity or extent – and therefore *the book* must be read as a whole work rather than as a collection of disparate poems. Coleridge's concern is with coherence, with unifying formally diverse elements into a literary whole. Two years later Wordsworth added the Preface and its procedural statements to *Lyrical Ballads*, but felt impelled to qualify his compositional theory: habits of mind produced by connecting thought and feeling, he admits, will not yield up connected verse sequences unless the poet be "possessed of much organic sensibility" and the reader "be in a healthful state of association."[68] Without the mental glue that coheres a vast field of feeling and thought into purposive poetic truth, individual poems or the book that contains them might not (as contemporary reviews attested) add up to anything at all.

Coleridge and Wordsworth's proclamations constitute a direct and historically precise response to a shared methodological impasse of induction – an impasse inherited from Enlightenment natural and moral philosophy and the massive eighteenth-century projects of collecting and arrangement they spawned: Carolus Linnaeus's *Systema Naturæ*, Edward Gibbon's *Decline and Fall*, Thomas Percy's *Reliques of Ancient English Poetry*, Samuel Johnson's *Dictionary*, the *Encyclopédie* of Denis Diderot and Jean le Rond d'Alembert, and so on. Coleridge and Wordsworth's shared concern with unity and synthesis derive from the methodological thread that connects these defining Enlightenment projects of information compilation and organization to the literary "experiments" that have long defined early Romanticism. In the book's final chapter (Chapter 5), I read Coleridge's struggles to establish the poet's (and critic's) synthetic mind as a calculated response to the breakdown of an inductive compositional paradigm in his "Essays on Method" in *The Friend* (1818). Locating these theoretical statements as responses to the problem of induction helps explain the tense conjunction of formal mixture and claims for unity that produced *Lyrical Ballads* as a critical litmus for the birth of Romanticism.

By focusing on inductive method, I am entering the ongoing discussion of literature's relationship to "science" in the Romantic period, albeit obliquely. In recent years, numerous studies have investigated how poets or novelists incorporate the ethos, language, and concepts of experimental science, natural history, and a host of narrower fields into their thought and texts, revealing how literature engaged, iterated, and transformed the scientific culture of the period.[69] An anathema to earlier criticism of Romanticism, we have now become comfortable with the "mutually constitutive nature of literary and scientific discourse in Britain during the later eighteenth and early nineteenth-centuries."[70] How, precisely, these broad discursive fields intersect – what the constitutive forces might have been, or what mechanisms enabled their interaction – is by no means firmly established. The essays collected by Noah Heringman in *Romantic Science: The Literary Forms of Natural History* indicate a range of possibilities: professional rivalry between Humphry Davy and Wordsworth, narratives of social progress shared between poetry and geology, or the inclusion of lyric strategies in kitchen garden manuals.[71] Jon Klancher's recent *Transfiguring the Arts and Sciences* extends these and many other local case studies by focusing on the instruments and institutions that "transfigured" the relationship of the arts and sciences in the period. As Klancher argues, Romantic-era arts and sciences were striving for autonomy but also entangled, mutually informing each other while engaged in contentious disputes over authority and priority.[72] The landscape of relations thus looked more like a "crazy-quilt assemblage of unevenly developed crystallizations" than the "grand synthesis imagined by the Romantics" themselves.[73] I certainly agree with this assessment, but want to argue that imagined synthesis was *demanded* by the shared compositional method that produced the crazy quilt in the first place (the metaphor is apt, considering Francis Jeffrey's characterization of Southey's annotated epics – which quote long passages from natural history, travel narrative, antiquarianism, church history, and folk tales – as a "patchwork drapery").[74] One might approach this book as a prehistory for Klancher's argument about the changing relations of the arts and sciences, which he illustrates by contrasting Joseph Priestley's eighteenth-century "commonwealth of learning" and Humphry Davy's competitive, restricted, institutionalized science of the nineteenth century.[75] By focusing on literary works composed before or at the turn of the century, I treat the cusp of disciplinary consolidation rather than its full-blown articulation, although my Interlude, final chapter, and conclusion move farther into the territory mapped by Klancher. In the slightly earlier moment I focus on here, the relationship between "practices and knowledges" was coming to a head: induction's script for knowledge making as text making was under pressure from within even as it was being deployed to authorize the practices and institutional formations that would displace it.

This book also intervenes in a more conventional debate over the Romantic preference for organicism over empiricism, a debate that had gotten a bit stale before two 2009 books – Denise Gigante's *Life* and David Fairer's *Organising Poetry* – revived it. Gigante and Fairer both turn their attention to the relationship between science and literary form, and especially formal coherence and fragmentation.[76] Fairer's study concentrates on ways of "organizing diversity" – on how poetic texts are shaped by an "empirical sensibility" in which knowledge is always a "reconstruction of the scattered materials of perception."[77] In contrast, Gigante sets out to read "certain seemingly formless poems and the symbolic figures contained within them as living forms"; she deploys eighteenth-century "epigenesist" theories of generation to recover an organicist approach to art that valued the "unpredictable vitality" of living forms, Coleridge's unity in multëity.[78] These studies contextualize the problem of fragmentation and unity differently (in empiricist moral philosophy and emerging life science, respectively), generating radically different explanations for what I see as a related set of textual conditions. Induction underwrote both empiricism and organicism as philosophical positions in this period; it directed a way of doing and making, and its ideal outcome was the textual expression of knowledge as totality. As a procedure, it was not the sole property of natural philosophy or experimental science (until, that is, the codification of "scientific method" in the mid-nineteenth century);[79] it was also not reducible to empiricism or mechanistic philosophy, having been taken up and claimed with equal ardor by idealists and materialists alike across the seventeenth and eighteenth centuries. In emphasizing the way authors used inductive method to compile materials and compose texts, I bridge Gigante's argument for unity that expresses itself in fragments and Fairer's counterclaim that diversity would be coalesced into wholeness. The story you will read here, however, is far less triumphalist than either Gigante or Fairer allows. In place of authors actively controlling and molding texts, I describe frustration, flailing, retakes, rejection, doubt, and downright fury. The story of induction in Romantic literature is one of *perceived* failure – authors' responses to their compositional process signal a change in desired outcome, not a change in inductive method or its application. It is this perceptual shift and its material manifestations that define the intellectual core of this study.

In Chapter 1, I provide a history of inductive method as it was consolidated in seventeenth-century experimental philosophy and adapted across a wide swath of empiricist natural and moral philosophy in the eighteenth century. The chapter focuses on key aspects of induction – as a compositional method reliant on the manipulation of a textual archive, and as an internalized map of the mind's faculties – as it was formulated by Bacon and reformulated by his philosophical progeny (Boyle, Locke, Hume, Alexander Gerard, Johnson, Joshua Reynolds, and many others). It also traces the emergence of the problem of induction in the middle of the eighteenth century, as the goal of induction shifted from compilation to synthesis. The chapter concludes by pinpointing how this shift in the desired outcome of induction's scripted procedure generated a new evidentiary status of the textual excerpt or quotation – a shift that produced the prose–verse composites of early Romanticism.

The remainder of the book is split into two parts, each corresponding to a different instantiation of the composite order. Part I examines long, heavily annotated poems, and Part II investigates prose essays and pedagogical fictions rife with embedded verse. The chapters in these sections should be taken as representative case studies, focused on authors who began writing in the 1780s and 1790s: Erasmus Darwin, Robert Southey, Anna Laetitia Barbauld, Richard Lovell Edgeworth and his daughter Maria Edgeworth, Charlotte Smith, and Samuel Taylor Coleridge.

These cases do not suggest the limit of possible authors and texts I might have treated at length in this book. I could also have included chapters on the prose–verse composites of John Thelwall, Wordsworth, Anna Seward, Ann Radcliffe, and Sydney Owenson, among many others. Nor does the composite order fully disappear in the early decades of the nineteenth century, although it is transformed in several significant ways. As I detail at greater length in the Interlude, at the turn of the century

CHAPTER I

Knowledge–Mind–Text
A History of Inductive Method

In 1817, Coleridge contracted with Rest Fenner and Thomas Curtis to compile and edit the *Encyclopædia Metropolitana*. The introduction he wrote would become – after much delay and dispute, many demands for the return of the manuscript, and subsequent rewriting – the "Essays on the Principles of Method" that appear in *The Friend* (1818). Engaging "method" as a topic was for Coleridge an exercise in bridging literary and scientific cultures at an early moment of disciplinary separation: "If in Shakespeare, we find nature idealized into poetry," in modern chemists like Humphry Davy and William Wollaston "we find poetry, as it were, substantialized and realized in nature."[1] This luminous chiasmus was part of Coleridge's larger philosophical project of realigning conventionally opposed figureheads and concepts – Shakespeare and Davy, Plato and Francis Bacon, idealism and experimental philosophy, church and state – through the deft use of quotations.[2] But the "Essays" were equally an exercise in reconstructing a lost text from scraps: John Stoddart (who edited Coleridge's introduction for Fenner) had "cut [it] up into snips so as to make it useless" (*CL*, 4: 860). This literal act of textual dismemberment made Coleridge irate, as he claimed to have spent "four months in the mere arrangement" of the essay, which Stoddart had subsequently reduced to "a heterogeneous mixture of *Contraries*... a compleat [sic] Huddle of Paragraphs, without sub- or co-ordination" (*CL*, 4: 820–21). To write about method involved, for Coleridge, the material and philosophical rearrangement of knowledge, and consequently the "Essays" – indeed the whole of *The Friend* in 1818 – came to be about the path one follows to knowledge and the material conditions of its production and consumption in print.[3]

Coleridge's "Essays on Method" encapsulate several key issues I take up in this chapter. First, Coleridge's comments within and about the essays emphasize that induction is a procedure, a way of getting somewhere, of doing something. As Coleridge puts it, "the Greek Μεθοδος, is literally a way, or path of Transit," a metaphor Bacon had deployed repeatedly in the *Novum Organum* to differentiate his inductive method from the closed systems of "the ancients" and the syllogistic method of Petrus Ramus (*F*, 2: 457).[4] Second, even as Coleridge insists on treating "method" as a philosophical position, he cannot avoid that it is a procedure for organizing knowledge *in and as* text. He implies as much in the very structure of the reconstructed "Essays": Method is first exemplified through a detailed breakdown of passages from Shakespeare's *Henry IV Part 1* and *Hamlet*, and only two essays later does Coleridge acknowledge that method "may be equally, and here perhaps more characteristically, proved from the most familiar of the Sciences... from Botany or from Chemistry" (*F*, 2: 466).[5] For Coleridge, inductive method structured literary texts and the knowledge contained within them as much as it guided the process of scientific enquiry. In this chapter, I consider what it meant for induction to function not only as a template for collecting, organizing, and expounding knowledge of the natural world, but also, and more centrally, as a model for textual production across many diverse areas including natural history, chemical philosophy, history, political economy, education, cognitive theory, rhetoric, and the burgeoning field of literary criticism. How did induction become, in the seventeenth and eighteenth centuries, a widely used and successful procedure for making texts, scientific, literary, and everything in between? And why, in the final decade of the century, did this path – even as it continued to be followed by authors of many stripes – begin to seem less clear, less viable, and more filled with pitfalls, thorns, and impasses than before?

Before tackling these questions, I should clarify what I mean by induction, and distinguish between induction and "method," a term that has figured in both literary studies and the history of science in recent years. For example, in *Romanticism, Nationalism, and the Revolt against Theory*, David Simpson argues that alongside system and theory, "method" fell out of favor conceptually in late-eighteenth-century Britain. During the French Revolution, he suggests, British national culture defined itself against French theorizing, methodizing, and system building; in 1790s Britain, the belief in method as "the progressive application of mental techniques to practical-political ends, comes itself to be regarded as a wild and visionary delusion."[6] A similar perception, grounded in fear of new religious sects, appears more than a century earlier: as J. G. A. Pocock argues, with the debates between Hobbes and Boyle and the consolidation of the Royal Society's experimental program around 1650, it began to seem that "there could be such a thing as a materialist enthusiasm" defined by philosophical rather than theological heresy.[7] By the mid-eighteenth century, the charge of enthusiasm was applied to empiricist data collectors who manifested a kind of fanatical "hyper-rationality," which Jan Golinski labels "an almost pathological concentration on minute incidentals."[8] As these arguments indicate, in the seventeenth and eighteenth centuries "method" referred both to procedures of data accumulation and to the mental operations of sorting and organizing, a point I return to below. For now, I want to emphasize what these studies make clear in aggregate: "method" was an unstable, malleable term that could apply equally to Ramus's syllogistic method and Baconian induction, French philosophy and British empiricism. When used as a standalone noun, "method" is a slippery word, historically and critically, and tracking discursive reactions to "methodizing" does not fully account for how the term (or, more importantly, the procedures it might signal) functioned in the period.[9]

Beyond cameo appearances in literary studies, the procedural aspect of "proper method" has been at the center of modern shifts in the history of seventeenth- and eighteenth-century science over the past 50 years. Beginning in Thomas Kuhn's *The Structure of Scientific Revolutions* (1962) and Paul Feyerabend's *Against Method* (1975), the mid-1980s saw a reassessment of "the scientific method" in two co-authored studies, John Schuster and Richard Yeo's Introduction to the essay collection *The Politics and Rhetoric of Scientific Method* (1986) and, more influentially, Steven Shapin and Simon Schaffer's *Leviathan and the Air-Pump* (1985). Reacting against widespread acceptance of a "single, transferable, efficacious scientific method" and the stories historians had told of its emergence in seventeenth-century Britain, these studies treat the procedures of scientific enquiry – along with truth, objectivity, and "matters of fact" – as historically contingent, the products of specific individual, institutional, political, and rhetorical conditions and practices.[10] By investigating how specific methods of scientific enquiry gained legitimacy at different historical moments, these two books expose how a "scientific method" based on a modified version of Baconian induction became self-evident as *the* routine procedure of scientific enquiry in Britain.[11]

In the wake of these important studies, it became possible to throw off the yoke of scientific method and rewrite the history of experimental science from different vantage points. Historians of science began to investigate what had long been taken for granted, turning their attention to the construction of facts, observations, evidence, objectivity, and so on. In the past 25 years, numerous books and articles have analyzed the ways knowledge was produced, demonstrated, and legitimized from the fifteenth to the twentieth century. These studies have ranged in focus from Peter

Dear's work on the transformation of experience into evidence in mathematical texts from fifteenth-century Jesuits to Isaac Newton; Lorraine Daston's discussion of how evidence became incompatible with intentionality through seventeenth-century shifts in the meaning of prodigies and miracles; Mary Poovey's study of numerical accounting practices developed in the sixteenth century and culminating in the sciences of wealth and economy in eighteenth-century Britain; and, most recently, Daston and Peter Galison's work tracking changes in objectivity and conceptions of the scientific self as they shifted in tandem with technologies and techniques of illustration from the eighteenth to the twentieth century.[12] In these studies, scientific method has shifted from a primary to a secondary focus. Daston's concept of "historical epistemology" provides an explanation for this trend: these are histories of "the categories that structure our thought, pattern our arguments and proofs, and certify our standards for explanation."[13] The mid-1980s focus on process has been replaced by attention to categories. Even so, each of the above studies necessarily engages with induction as a knowledge-making procedure in seventeenth- and eighteenth-century science. As Shapin and Schaffer claim of Boyle's "experimental method," focusing on procedure allows us to see "patterns of doing things."[14] I share Shapin and Schaffer's interest in procedures over conceptual categories. Attending to induction makes explicit how a loosely defined series of steps – observing, collecting, experimenting, comparing, distinguishing, linking by analogy, generalizing, and synthesizing – structured eighteenth-century ideas about how to make texts and the compositional practices that produced them.[15]

Doing and Making

As with the "evolutionary narrative" that, as Gillian Beer has argued, was codified in Charles Darwin's *The Origin of Species*, the procedural model of induction – along with a set of genres, rhetorical techniques, and metaphors – originated with Bacon's *Novum Organum*.[16] Bacon, of course, did not make induction out of whole cloth. Numerous studies have shown that Bacon's inductive method had roots in the judicial practice of common law, the educational tradition of commonplace books, Bacon's political reform agenda, and Aristotelian rhetoric and logic, the target of his most stringent critiques.[17] Baconian induction, however, achieved a kind of saturation from the late seventeenth to the mid-nineteenth century similar to that of Darwin's evolutionary theory in the late nineteenth and twentieth centuries. By the early nineteenth century, it had become commonplace to associate Baconian induction with the rise of modern science. In 1830, John Herschel claimed that "previous to the publication of the *Novum Organum* of Bacon, natural philosophy, in any legitimate and extensive sense of the word, could hardly be said to exist" because "it is to our immortal countryman Bacon that we owe . . . the development of the idea, that the whole of philosophy consists entirely of a series of inductive generalizations, commencing with the circumstantially stated particulars, and carried up to universal laws."[18] As late as 1847, William Whewell proclaimed Bacon "the Supreme Legislator of the Modern Republic of Science" even as he set about renovating Bacon's methodology and putting it to new uses.[19] The process of enquiry Bacon strove to authorize in the *Novum Organum* had become the benchmark of "legitimate science" in the first half of the nineteenth century, even if adherence to it was by and large ceremonial.[20]

Induction's cultural currency did not derive from its ability to produce unassailable, or even believable, results. As early as Thomas Sprat's *History of the Royal Society* (1667), it was already clear that while Bacon's "Rules were admirable: yet his *History* not so faithful, as might have been wish'd in many places."[21] For later generations, Bacon's method provided a "regulative framework for research"; eminently flexible and adaptable, it could sanction widely divergent approaches and objects of study.[22] Case in point: Robert Boyle's experimental chemistry and Isaac Newton's celestial mechanics were both lauded for applying inductive method to practical problems, primarily because both authors aligned their work rhetorically with the Baconian agenda of the early Royal Society.[23] Induction could be claimed and deployed in this way for any number of reasons, but for the purposes of this study, I want to concentrate on what it was understood to achieve and what kind of "doing" it scripted.

I'll begin with Bacon's own prescriptions. After laying out the problems with existing modes of enquiry – the famous discussion of idols in Part I of the *Novum Organum* – Bacon turns in Part II to explaining and exemplifying his new method. To address the limitations of closed, self-referential systems of knowledge – the problem that "what is now done in the matter of science is only a whirling round about, and perpetual agitation, ending where it began" – one must, he argues, open "a new and certain path for the mind to proceed in, starting directly from the simple sensuous perception" (*NO*, 8, 40). Induction is this path, a "scale of ascent" by "successive steps." Beginning with the "fresh examination of particulars," one must proceed to gather observations and experiments into natural and experimental histories. These collections must then be submitted to tabular arrangement – what Bacon calls "Tables of Discovery" – to aid the memory in digesting and comparing the materials of experience. Finally, the understanding must be guided by "another form of induction," the process of rejection and exclusion, which generates successive, increasingly general axioms, each of which undergoes this process in its turn (NO, 91–98). The end result, Bacon avers, will be a "Form affirmative," one of the "laws and determinations of absolute actuality, which govern and constitute any simple nature, as heat, light, weight, in every kind of matter and subject that is susceptible to them" (NO, 146).

I will return to the difficulties Bacon and his followers encountered when using induction to generate synthetic principles or truths; here, I want to call attention to his insistence that induction involves experience being "taught to read and write" and having "learned her letters" (NO, 96). This phrase functions metaphorically, as experience becomes "literate" when the mind is set to work on facts duly arranged and digested by induction. But Bacon also means it quite literally: he insists, "no course of invention can be satisfactory unless it be carried on in writing" (NO, 96). The form of the written text should also mirror the open, accretive process of induction: knowledge should be presented in aphorisms because when "the discourse of connection and order is cut off" the form "invite[s] men to enquire farther."[24] For Bacon, observations are made in the world, experiments in the laboratory, but induction happens in writing (or print), on paper, in books, as text.[25] Induction is a loosely plotted series of steps – observing, collecting, recording, arranging, comparing, connecting, distinguishing, combining, abstracting and composing – that culminates in a textual product. This product reflects, in its form and structure, the procedure by which it was created. Put simply, induction's "doing" is composition; its product is textual.

This aspect of induction is exemplified by Robert Boyle, a figure historians of science have long associated with the cultural ascendance of the experimental program in seventeenth-century Britain. As Rose-Mary Sargent has shown, Boyle's surviving notebooks and "philosophical diaries" reveal the process he followed in collecting, transcribing, organizing, and collating materials for natural histories.[26] Boyle first amassed materials from a variety of sources: his own observations, records of experiments he performed, letters from friends and acquaintances, and extracts from books of travel, history, natural history, and literature. Following Bacon's recommended method, Boyle then compared and collated these materials into categories, using an indexing system to perform the actions of mental sorting, comparison, and connection. For example, to plot the chapters

of his comprehensive history of nature, Boyle compiled the "Promiscuous Paralipomena," 200 pages of material with marginal notations cross-
referenced to an index that indicated which projected chapter each observation would contribute to.[27] Boyle's publications group observations
topically under headings to suggest relations and connections between isolated observations and larger topics. In his published essays, Boyle also
followed Bacon's prescriptions for presenting knowledge in a disjointed
form – he described the design of experiments separately from his theoretical speculations and conclusions – that would provoke further enquiry
and invite interpretation. For Boyle, induction scripted his process of collecting and collating disparate facts and observations from various textual
sources, but it also provided the formal principles for how this material
would eventually appear in print. Induction provided both the method of
creating and manipulating a textual archive, and the generic parameters for
composing texts out of these materials.

The inductive procedure of compiling materials and composing texts
followed by Boyle was taken up by authors in a wide range of fields across
the seventeenth and eighteenth centuries. Although tracking authors'
methods of composing texts is notoriously difficult – even with extant
archives of manuscript evidence – recent bibliographic studies have recovered key examples that indicate the widespread adoption of induction as
a compositional method. Take, for example, one of the eighteenth century's most famous authors, Samuel Johnson. Building on earlier studies
that examined Johnson's processes of reading and collecting materials for
the *Dictionary* and other works, Harriet Kirkley describes Johnson's methods of reading, note taking, and composition for the "Life of Pope."[28]
As Kirkley details, using a notebook Johnson first transferred quotations
from texts onto the recto, later adding related notes from other sources on
the verso. After compiling his notes, he began to assemble and organize
them by underlining, reinscribing, and listing; this allowed him to gather
his notes into topical clusters. As he incorporated various notes into the
manuscript, he canceled them in red ink with a diagonal strikethrough.[29]
Working from a comparison between the notes, manuscript, and printed
text, Kirkley argues we can also infer that Johnson added more material at
the proof stage as he reread the text.[30] Johnson's methods are thus more
accretive than linear; they involve circling back, retracking, and rearrang-
ing in the manner of Boyle's "Paralipomena." As Kirkley suggests, Johnson's methods most directly resemble Locke's model of "inferential reading"
and the accumulative and combinative model that Johnson articulates in
the "Life of Pope," both of which should be understood "in conjunction

with Francis Bacon's model of how empirical data generate new knowledge."[31] Like Boyle's essays, Johnson's "Pope" evolves out of related processes of collection, compilation, arrangement, addition, comparison, and composition.

While Boyle and Johnson's procedure may resemble compositional methods stretching back to Renaissance humanism if not classical antiquity, it is crucial to recognize that authors in this period explicitly understood their methods within the legacy of induction beginning with Bacon and consolidated by members of the Royal Society in Britain in the second half of the seventeenth century. As Kirkley notes, Johnson "originally conceived of the *Prefaces* as one part of a Baconian non-narrative history of modern English letters," and he was not alone in recognizing the methodological roots of his work.[32] For example, in *A Treatise of Human Nature: Being an Attempt to introduce the Experimental Method of Reasoning into Moral Subjects* (1739–40), Hume authorizes his approach with a list of his illustrious forerunners in "the application of experimental philosophy to moral subjects": almost a century after its inception by "my LORD BACON," inductive method entered moral philosophy in the work of "Mr. Locke, my Lord Shaftsbury, Dr. Mandeville, Mr. Hutchinson, Dr. Butler &c."[33] Hume's list runs the gamut of philosophical positions: Shaftesbury's rejection of his tutor Locke's materialism is well known, and his adamant rejection of selfish action and equally resolute endorsement of human virtue as the ultimate public good likewise stands in direct contradiction to Bernard Mandeville's *Fable of the Bees: or, Private Vices, Publick Benefits* (1714), which incorporates an explicit critique of Shaftesbury's position in the third edition of 1724. Francis Hutchinson and Bishop Joseph Butler both penned direct refutations of Mandeville in 1725. In authorizing his text, Hume has implicitly argued for a method of discovery and textual production that transcends seemingly intractable philosophical disagreements.

As Hume's claim suggests, even if authors did not follow a strictly inductive approach in their research or writing, the value of induction for producing knowledge as text remained a salient rhetorical stance throughout the seventeenth- and eighteenth-century natural and moral philosophy. Most famously, Locke's *Essay concerning Human Understanding* (1690) figures the mind as white paper inscribed by experience. In this "slippage from content to method," induction was remade from a procedure for discovering the laws of nature into a way of explaining the structure of human thought and consciousness.[34] This shift appears strikingly in Locke's *Essay*, which opens by aligning his project with the tenets of the Royal Society via Boyle and Thomas Sydenham, as well as an international scientific community via Newton and the Dutch astronomer Christiaan Huygens. Locke's Baconian agenda is reinforced in his methodological statements: he rejects Scholastic philosophy, insists on the primacy of experience, and proposes to follow the "historical, plain method" of collecting, arranging, and giving a written account of his observations.[35] When Locke turns in the primary text to enumerating the faculties "whereby [the mind] makes a further progress toward knowledge," he begins, like Bacon, with sensory perception, "the first step and degree toward knowledge, and the inlet of all knowledge." This first step is followed by a series of mental "operations": accumulation, contemplation, remembering, discerning or distinguishing, comparing, composition (in the sense of putting together or combining), and abstracting.[36] In this progression, Locke translates the steps of inductive method, which Bacon had proposed to guide the understanding, into "operations *of* the mind, which it makes use of *in* understanding."[37] Experience can inscribe knowledge on the white paper of the mind because the mind *inherently* processes sensory data inductively.

The internalization of inductive method as the mind's cognitive script had far-reaching implications in eighteenth-century moral philosophy and aesthetics. Authors from Johnson and Edmund Burke to Alexander Gerard, Hugh Blair, Thomas Reid, Joseph Priestley, Joshua Reynolds, and Hannah More invoke induction as a procedure for enquiry, while also plotting cognitive processes according to the steps of induction. For example, Johnson defined Dryden's poetic genius as "that energy which collects, combines, amplifies and animates," a catalog that Gerard extends into a book-length treatise, his *Essay on Genius* (1774).[38] To produce a work of genius, Gerard argues, the imagination works by "collecting ideas from all the parts of nature," "selecting those as are subordinate to the design," and "disposing them into a consistent plan, or a distinct method," after which the judgment "compare[s] readily the effect of each part in one position, with its effect in another, and from the result of the comparisons, quickly pronounce[s], which is the best arrangement."[39] Applying the same procedure to visual art in his *Discourses on Art* delivered to the Royal Academy between 1769 and 1790, Joshua Reynolds advised the budding artist to take care in observing nature and "digesting, methodizing, and comparing [his] observations"; this will enable him to "make new combinations, perhaps, superior to what had ever before been in the possession of art."[40] By the 1790s, this cognitive model had become entrenched enough to serve Mary Wollstonecraft and Hannah More in the cause of reforming female education. Wollstonecraft deplored that while men were "from their infancy broken into method," the knowledge women acquire is "of a more desultory kind"; as a corrective, More set out a course of study that "will make an exact mind . . . will lead [women] to think, to compare, to combine, to methodize."[41] As More's *Strictures on the Modern System of Female Education* (1799) makes explicit, by end of the century it had become common to align the steps of induction with "that sort of experimental logic . . . compounded of observation and reflection, which makes up the moral science of life and manners" (*SFE*, 227–28).

As these examples indicate, induction is not coterminous with experimental science, nor is it the sole property of "science," even if it would become so by the middle of the nineteenth century. In the eighteenth century, induction had an extensive and varied application. It was used to define fancy, imagination, and the difference between them; scientific, literary, and artistic genius; correct and faulty educational models and cognitive processes; refined taste in poetry, music, and art; responses to beautiful objects and sublime scenes; an educated person's conversational capacities; and so on, virtually *ad infinitum*. Every field of knowledge, philosophical debate, or practical problem was in some way touched by or filtered through inductive method, usually by multiple authors. By the end of the century, induction had become so omnipresent as to become almost invisible, distilled to a set of key words – a mobile, multivalent procedure that functioned to authorize enquiries and define subject areas.

However counterintuitive it may seem, the very malleability and adaptability of induction made it useful for cordoning one subject off from another. Carrying the sanction of a long lineage of famous proponents and the stamp of scientific legitimacy, induction became a tool in the consolidation of modern disciplines. Consider, for example, how Humphry Davy goes about claiming legitimacy for the field of chemical philosophy. In his *Elements of Chemical Philosophy*, Davy defines chemistry's methods as fundamentally inductive: "by observation, facts are distinctly and minutely impressed on the mind. By analogy, similar facts are connected. By experiment, new facts are discovered; and, in the progression of knowledge, observation, guided by analogy, leads to experiment, and analogy confirmed by experiment, becomes scientific truth."[42] This gradual progression from observations to truth is affirmed in Davy's subsequent history of the methodological developments in experimental science. He traces the rise of chemistry as correspondent with the development of modern, inductive methods of scientific enquiry. Rejecting the erroneous ideas of the ancient Egyptians, Aristotle, and Theophrastus, Davy first locates the birth of chemistry in the alchemical works of eighth-century Arabians and the thirteenth- to fifteenth-century Christians Albertus Magnus, Cornelius Agrippa, and Paracelsus.[43] These works were clouded with superstition and thus did not form the basis of a modern science; it was not until Bacon that chemical enquiry began to stand on the solid foundation of observation and experiment. After discussing Bacon, Davy's history describes the isolation, by inductive method, of various elements by an international cast of scientific minds, including John Ray, Boyle, and Hooke in England, Wilhelm Homberg and Étienne François Geoffroy in France, Johann Beccher and Georg Ernst Stahl in Germany, and finally the eighteenth-century chemists Henry Cavendish, Carl Wilhelm Scheele, Priestley, and Antoine Lavoisier.[44] This history of the gradual emergence and application of inductive method provides a platform for Davy's argument that chemistry is a unique, legitimate, and crucially important field of scientific study – a field worthy of institutional recognition and support.

Wordsworth makes a similar claim about poetry in the 1802 Preface to *Lyrical Ballads* by coding the poet's process as the steps of inductive method.[45] He begins with a set of related postulates: if poetry's "object is truth, not individual and local, but general, and operative" and we "have no knowledge, that is, no general principles drawn from the contemplation of particular facts, but what has been built up by pleasure," then "the knowledge both of the Poet and the Man of Science is pleasure."[46] Here, Wordsworth suggests that both poetry and science move inductively from particular facts to general principles, a process that is spurred by pleasure and yields knowledge. Poetry thus shares the procedure and goal of chemistry and mathematics, but it requires a more extensive purview: as Wordsworth argues, "the objects of the Poet's thoughts are every where," guided by the eyes and senses, while the man of science concentrates on "those particular parts of nature which are the objects of his studies."[47] Having posited that induction is fundamentally pleasurable; that the goal of the poet's art is "producing immediate pleasure"; and that the poet's knowledge is more extensive and general that that of other fields, Wordsworth can claim that "poetry is the most philosophic of all writing": "Poetry is the first and last of all knowledge" because "the Poet binds together by passion and knowledge the vast empire of human society, as it is spread over the whole earth, and over all time."[48] With this claim for the poet's unique purview (which happens to be all of moral and natural philosophy) and poetry's status as philosophic knowledge, Wordsworth exemplifies how inductive method became a mechanism for disciplinary division: once it had been applied to everything, induction could be deployed to legitimate any enquiry and enhance professional standing of any field, even a field that defined itself by a *lack* of specialization.[49]

Induction's adaptability and authority at the end of the eighteenth century can account for the apparent tension between the process of disciplinary separation taking place across fields, including literature, around the turn of the century, and the staggering quantity of material from various discursive fields that finds its way into the works I analyze here.[50] Inductive method was, to use Jon Klancher's useful formulation, one of the "instruments" of disciplinary consolidation in the late eighteenth and early nineteenth century. Shared across practically every knowledge domain and undergirding claims to professional status, it allowed profligate borrowing across emerging disciplinary boundaries while also driving the "unintended co-production" of disciplinary formations in the scientific and literary spheres.[51] To extend Klancher's provocative suggestion, induction forwarded the "calibration" of material instruments – whether in printed editions of literary works, catalogs of specimen collections, or descriptions and depictions of batteries – and allowed authors to mobilize the evidentiary work of these instruments to consolidate disciplinary standards, a point I return to in the last section of this chapter.[52]

The trajectory of my examples above – from Bacon and Boyle, to Hume, Reynolds and Johnson, to More, Wollstonecraft, Davy, and finally Wordsworth – suggests that Romanticism shares with its Enlightenment predecessors a fundamental adherence to induction as a template for producing knowledge by manipulating text. This claim is not as radical as it may at first appear. In tracking the intellectual history of induction and its gradual spread across all fields of knowledge production, I've recast a well-known story. The empiricist, experimentalist bent of eighteenth-century moral philosophy in Britain was rehearsed numerous times over the previous century, perhaps most famously in M. H. Abrams's *The Mirror and the Lamp* (1958). His chapter on "The Mechanical Theory of Literary Invention" puts it bluntly: "the course of English empirical philosophy was guided by the attempt, more or less deliberate, to import into the psychical realm the explanatory scheme of physical science."[53] Abrams goes on to give a litany similar to what I have provided above (Locke, Hume, Hartley, Kames, Gerard), ending with James Beattie's claim that the "science of mind" authorizes his rules for composing and judging poems. Abrams follows this litany of quotes with a catalog of "aspects" that define the "mechanical approach." Not surprisingly, Abrams's "aspects" correlate with the steps of inductive method I have outlined above.[54] Abrams, of course, is at pains to distinguish this Enlightenment model from Coleridge's organic imagination, and his chapter replays Coleridge's split between fancy and imagination: The imagination is creative, generative, and vital while fancy, as Julie Ellison puts it, "treats experience as matter that can be manip-ulated but not transformed. It conforms to the process of intellectual sorting – arrangement, classification, and comparison – that constituted the methodological core of the [eighteenth-century] human sciences."[55] And, yes, there is a difference: When Coleridge, Wordsworth, and even Davy early in his career theorized about how the mind works on the materials of experience, their theories privileged an active imagination. This is not, however, because these authors had broken with the empiri-cist tradition or were employing radically different compositional proce-dures than their Enlightenment counterparts. Indeed, quite the opposite. Coleridge's split between fancy and imagination, like Wordsworth's dis-tinction between the poet and the "man of science" in the 1802 Pref-ace, arose directly from the inductive method of textual production they shared with their seventeenth- and eighteenth-century predecessors. What changed was not the method, but the desired outcome – and the difficulty of attaining that new goal of synthetic unity generated the aesthetic theories Abrams associates with Romanticism as a literary movement.

Synthesis and the Problem of Induction

In the seventeenth and early eighteenth centuries, the Royal Society took up the Baconian directive to amass a databank of observations and experiments that could serve as the foundation for induction. In an effort to sweep away the various "idols" impeding the progress of knowledge, Bacon had advocated indiscriminate collecting – everything, and especially instances that deviated from the normal course of nature, might become bricks in the edifice of knowledge.[56] The project succeeded in at least one respect: storerooms, museums, and private houses overflowed with spec-imens and artifacts, and the *Philosophical Transactions of the Royal Society* punctually continued to publish multifarious observations and experi-ments in no discernable order. These disorganized physical and textual collections were subject to criticism almost immediately, which is aptly encapsulated by William King's complaint about the omnivorous collector Sir Hans Sloane, secretary of the Society and editor of its *Transactions* from 1693 to 1713, whose collections would become the basis for the British Museum: "there is not an odd coloured or an ill shapen Pebble in the King-dom, but the Secretary will manage it so as it contribute to the general heap of Transactions."[57] The sheer quantity of stuff – an ever-augmented pile

of textual descriptions of objects, observations and experiments – brought
about the drive to arrangement and classification exemplified in Linnaean
taxonomy. Ordering, in turn, became a target of criticism, leading authors
in collecting-centric fields such as natural history to reevaluate the goals
of induction, tipping the scale toward comparison, linking by analogy,
and synthesis. By the late eighteenth century, Bacon's inductive method,
as Coleridge would later observe, had become a science of relations.

For example, in the Preface to his French translation of Stephen Hales's
Vegetable Staticks (1735), Georges-Louis Leclerc, Comte de Buffon celebrates the method, recommended by Bacon and followed by Hales, of
"constantly collect[ing] experiments" that would serve as the foundation for future knowledge.[58] But Buffon also isolates a problem with this
approach: Hales's work "is a collection of an infinitude of useful and
unusual facts, whose connection is not seen at first glance."[59] In the "Premier discours" to his *L'Histoire Naturelle* (1748), Buffon attempts to correct
this problem. A "new path" for the study of natural history is necessary, he
argues, because there was "a metaphysical error in the very principle of
these [earlier] systems": Taxonomies like Linnaeus's *Systema Naturae* established arbitrary organizing principles that produced textual groupings "so
gratuitous and bizarre that the Author must have made it that way inten-
tionally."[60] Taxonomy might be a useful beginning, but for natural history
to advance, Buffon insisted, "it is necessary to elevate ourselves to something grander and more dignified . . . namely the combination of observations, the generalization of facts, linking them together by the power of
analogies."[61] This process will allow us "to compare Nature with herself
in her vast operations, and . . . open routes to further perfect the different
branches of natural philosophy."[62] As suggested by his eighteenth-century
translator William Smellie, Buffon's work calls for a "philosophy of natural
history" achieved through "the combined force of different minds acting
successively upon the same subject," all working "to mark the distinctions,
to investigate the relations, to ascertain [what] unites the numerous tribes
that people and adorn the universe."[63] Buffon and his English translators
thus shift the goal of natural history from collecting and arrangement to
forging connections, effectively transforming a field defined by classification to one that strove to synthesize not only its own subject matter but
all of natural knowledge. Like the "experiments in 'Connexion'" noted by
Siskin and Warner – Ephraim Chamber's *Cyclopedia* (1728) or Peter Shaw's
new edition of Bacon's works (1733) – this shift was enacted textually: by
packaging knowledge in a new form, natural history was redirected toward
the philosophical goal of synthesis.[64]

As the editor of the first edition of the *Encyclopedia Britannica*, Smellie makes it clear in his commentary that Buffon's vision for natural history fell into line with the encyclopedic projects of the late Enlightenment in France, Britain, and Germany.[65] Eighteenth-century encyclopedias embraced Bacon's mandate for an open, collaborative process of knowledge generation while also striving for both comprehensiveness and unity – a fraught aim in an era defined by heaping up new information.[66] As d'Alembert argued in the *Preliminary Discourse*, the French *Encyclopédie* had two goals: the encyclopedic part, which conveyed "the order and connection of the parts of human knowledge," and the reasoned dictionary part, which contained the principles of each science and art. To achieve the latter end, the *Encyclopédie* was organized alphabetically, allowing the reader to find entries on specific subjects quickly. To achieve the former, Diderot and d'Alembert provided the familiar genealogical tree to show the encyclopedic arrangement of knowledge. This tree placed

> the philosopher at a vantage point, so to speak, high above this vast labyrinth, whence he can perceive the principal sciences and the arts simultaneously. From there he can see at a glance the objects of their speculations and the operations which can be made on these objects; he can discern the general branches of human knowledge, the points that separate or unite them; and sometimes he can even glimpse the secrets that relate them to one another.[67]

Here, induction operates on a grand scale, enabling the reader–viewer to compare and distinguish all the branches of knowledge at a glance – but relations remain ephemeral if visible at all. Like Buffon's grand schema for natural history (which d'Alembert charged with being too speculative, too conjectural in its systematization of nature),[68] the encyclopedic project founders at the moment of synthesis: its form fails to enable the crucial final step of induction. If Bacon had promised that induction would lead out of "the woods of experience and particulars" to the "Forms" of nature, a century later knowledge remained a labyrinth to both eye and mind.

Historians of science have labeled this predicament the "problem of induction" and pinpointed its emergence as a theoretical conundrum in Hume's discussion of causality in *A Treatise of Human Nature* (1739–40) and its revision *An Enquiry concerning Human Understanding* (1748).[69] In the *Treatise*, the problem takes several forms, most directly in the question of how distinct, isolated impressions yield unified experience when the mechanism for connecting them in the mind remains unidentifiable. In the Appendix, Hume comments on his own argument about particular perceptions in the formation of personal identity:

when I proceed to explain [in volume 1, page 452] the principle of connexion, which binds them together, and makes us attribute to them a real simplicity and identity; I am sensible, that my account is very defective, and that nothing but the seeming evidence of the precedent reasonings cou'd have induc'd me to receive it. If perceptions are distinct existences, they form a whole only by being connected together. But no connexions among distinct existences are ever discoverable by human understanding. We only *feel* a connexion or determination of the thought, to pass from one object to another.[70]

In transferring the "experimental method of reasoning into moral subjects" (as he proclaims on the *Treatise*'s title page), Hume is forced to confront a fundamental gap in Baconian induction as it is manifested in the mind's internalized inductive processes: just as induction leaves it open how organized observations of nature will coalesce into synthetic truths, it is by no means clear how heaps of perceptions are connected into a unified idea of self. Hume's "problem" is thus methodological, and like the gap in Bacon's method, it derives from a historical shift in the status of evidence. As Peter Dear argues, before the seventeenth century, singular, historically situated events and observations functioned as illustrations of accepted universals; with the embrace of Baconian induction, particular instances became the foundation of natural knowledge.[71] In posing the question of how perceptions get connected to forge identity, Hume indirectly posed the larger question of how the singular events of individual experience could add up to a universal knowledge claim.

Various of Hume's successors and critics attempted to elide or downplay the problem of induction. Thomas Reid's formulation of "common sense" philosophy in *An Inquiry into the Human Mind* (1765) is an influential instance of this, which provoked a running debate contributed to by Priestley and Dugald Stewart. Like Hume, Reid insists on following an inductive method in his investigation of mind: "The laws of nature are the most general facts we can discover in the operations of nature. Like other facts, they are not to be hit upon by happy conjecture, but justly deduced from observation: like other general facts, they are not to be drawn from a few particulars, but copious, patient and cautious induction."[72] However, Reid also argues that in "the operations of the mind, as well in those of bodies, we must often be satisfied with knowing that certain things are connected and invariably follow one another, without being able to discover the chain that goes between them. Such connections are what we call 'laws of nature.'"[73] Laws of nature, for Reid, are thus the result of inductive method and, simultaneously, an answer to the gap in induction isolated by Hume. This seeming contradiction is explained by Reid's contention throughout the *Inquiry* that the "laws of nature" or "first principles" (which are, as the terms suggests, "the most general facts we can discover in the operations of nature") are also, like the evidence of the senses, a product of "the constitution of our nature"; we know the truth of first principles through "common sense" and do not need to investigate them to ascertain their truth.[74] In other words, Reid gives principles the same status as observations, and allows them to be the starting points, rather than end points, of knowledge production. Here, Reid has reformed Bacon's procedure to solve Hume's problem, a move he legitimizes in *Essays on the Intellectual Powers of Man* (1785) by citing Newton's *regulæ philosophandi* and mathematical propositions.[75] Reid's version of induction, like Newton's, relies on axioms, *a priori* principles present in the mind which supply missing connections. As I discuss in Chapter 5, Coleridge's recourse to Platonic idealism to renovate Bacon's method takes a similar route: for Coleridge, as for Reid, there must be a "mental Initiative" or "leading thought" that precedes and enables induction (*F*, 1: 466, 455).

While moral philosophy tackled Hume's problem by recasting the ground of inductive method, contemporary encyclopedic projects raise the problem of connection as a generic dilemma. As d'Alembert's vast labyrinth suggests, eighteenth-century encyclopedias were spurred by competing drives to survey the content of specific, rapidly differentiating fields and to convey knowledge as a totality. In effect, their sole purpose was to coalesce the heap of particulars into an interconnected whole. The difficulty, if not impossibility, of this generic imperative often ended, as Richard Yeo has noted, in spectacular failures.[76] Marked by a steady decrease in content or cross-references – or left unfinished, abandoned midway through the alphabet – the eighteenth-century encyclopedia materializes the gap in induction in the unfinished serial publication. Further, by instilling the desire for total knowledge while materially projecting its impossibility, the encyclopedia became a site of recognition and response to this dilemma. A working out of this problem underwrites the idealist encyclopedic projects of the turn of the century, from Coleridge's plan for the *Encyclopædia Metropolitana* to Friedrich von Hardenberg's (Novalis's) *Das Allgemeine Brouillon* (1798–99), Friedrich Schlegel's lectures on the *Encyclopedia of Sciences* (1803), Friedrich Schelling's "Lectures on University Study" (1804), and Hegel's *Encyclopedia of the Philosophical Sciences* (1816–32). As August Wilhelm Schlegel's comments suggest – he criticized the empirical, aggregative bent of the *Encyclopédie* while lauding Bacon's encyclopedism[77] – these projects embrace the synthetic endpoint of induction even as they reject its empirical foundation. As Coleridge puts it in the "Essays on Method," a "science of relations" cannot be supplied by a "theory built on generalization" from randomly collected instances; as in Linnaean botany, heaping up instances produces "an enormous nomenclature; a huge catalogue, *bien arrangé*" but not a fundamental "knowledge of LAW" (*F*, 1: 476, 469–70).[78]

The turn to unity through principle was thus a consequence of authors and compilers recognizing the fracture in the encyclopedic project itself: as Tilottama Rajan argues, Romantic encyclopedism entails a perception of the "disseminative interconnectedness *and* incompleteness of knowledge,"[79] an awareness compounded in the first decades of the nineteenth century by a print explosion and the increasing specialization of fields in the process of disciplinary consolidation. As Rajan shows, Hegel attempts to systematize knowledge under the "law of philosophy" by excluding the contingency of experience (i.e., positivist sciences) and metaphorically folding each field into others to achieve the larger progression from nature to Spirit.[80] In this approach, Hegel attempts to overcome the gap between particulars and totality through system, but he cannot entirely sublimate the empirical. Replacing linear steps with arabesque embedding, Hegel seeks unity in progressive interpenetration, but as Rajan argues, this process cannot fully absorb the specificity of pathology – the unity of knowledge achieved by compounding nature into Spirit unravels when confronted with the particular facts of chronic illness.[81] The prickly evidence of bodily experience – its gradual wasting away and ultimate dissolution – derails the synthetic capacity of philosophy.

This wasting condition is endemic to idealist encyclopedias of the 1820s and 1830s, but it is manifested quite differently in earlier, turn-of-the-century projects. While sharing Hegel's goal of synthesis, the work of Friedrich Schlegel and Novalis's *Blüthenstaub* (*Pollen*) and *Das Allgemeine Brouillon* have contributed to making the fragment a hallmark of philosophical Romanticism.[82] Novalis's procedure in compiling his notes for an encyclopedia was implicitly inductive: as with the scientific notebooks he kept during the same period, the *Brouillon* collected, arranged, compared, and (above all) analogically linked a series of reflections and references pertaining to different fields of knowledge. Like Boyle's indexes to his "Promiscuous Paralipomena," Novalis's system of headings in the encyclopedic notebook points to multiple levels of relations and interpenetrations; his labels range from chemistry and philosophy to poetic physiology, organology, and anthropomorphic physics. (Unlike Boyle's litanies of experiments and observations, Novalis's encyclopedia entries rarely include specific details from any particular field – his was an idealist project, not an empirical one.) Novalis's comments on the eventual form of this work are as telling as his penchant for hybridizing nascent disciplines. Labeling and indexing were the precursors to transforming the collection into publishable work, but would the form be "a *recherche* (or *essai*), a collection of fragments, a commentary in the style of Litchenberg, a report, an exposition, a story, a treatise, a review, a speech, a monologue or fragment of a dialogue etc.?"[83] As Chad Wellmon argues, this and other entries reveal that Novalis's encyclopedic project was "obsessed with its own operations and conditions of possibility but also with its own bibliographic form and technologies."[84] Like Coleridge's equally obsessive reorganization of scraps of text in the "Essays on Method," Novalis's collection of fragments poses the question of how to present synthetic knowledge – what form it should take – as a fundamental response to the problem of induction. If induction's "doing" is making texts, the exploration of (and solution to) its procedural rift would, inevitably, be formal.

Striving at once to inventory knowledge and unify it, the encyclopedic projects of this period convey – with an immediacy less palpable in other genres – how authors responded to the problem of induction. The "problem," as I have outlined it here, arose from a shift in the goals of inductive method, specifically in the desire to go beyond the catalog and formulate comprehensive laws or principles. As turn-of-the-century encyclopedic projects indicate, recognizing the gap in inductive method *as a problem* entailed a particular kind of formal response, one that materially heightened the tension between compositional procedure and desired outcome. In the drive to inculcate synthetic principles, the product of induction manifested greater and greater degrees of textual fragmentation. As I detail in the next section, this formal response – like the problem of induction itself – revolves around the status of evidence. While later idealist encyclopedic projects such as Hegel's cordoned off the empirical base of knowledge, moral, philosophical and literary texts multiplied and foregrounded it through practices of annotation, excerpting, citation, and quotation. These practices generated the verse–prose composites of the Romantic period – formal mixtures underwritten by the desire and struggle to coalesce disparate parts into a unified whole.

Literature as Database

The gap between evidentiary base and synthetic principle was not, of course, only registered formally in encyclopedic projects; it emerged forcibly and repeatedly in Enlightenment moral philosophy. Hume's

Enquiry has long been understood as the first work in the British tradition to isolate the problem of induction, but the conceptual crux was forecast by a methodological impasse in his earlier work. In *A Treatise of Human Nature*, Hume authorizes his inquiry with inductive method: the goal of the *Treatise* is to "explain the principles of human nature" on the solid foundation of "experience and observation," which requires that we

> glean up our experiments in this science from a cautious observation of human life, and take them as they appear in the common course of the world, by men's behavior in company, in affairs, and in their pleasures. Where experiments of this kind are judiciously collected and compared, we may hope to establish on them a science, which will not be inferior in certainty, and will be much superior in utility to any other of human comprehension.[85]

Observations and experiments collected and compared will establish the "Science of Man." In the fourth chapter of the *Treatise*, however, Hume strains against his own methodological pronouncements: when he wants to introduce the three "principles" by which ideas are connected in the mind, he inserts a series of disclaimers – "it will not be very necessary to prove," "'tis plain," "'tis likewise evident," and so on – in place of his promised experiments and observations.[86] Here, Hume encounters a fundamental condition of eighteenth-century moral philosophy: he lacks data – the collection of behaviors – that would provide the material foundation for his induction.

When he revised the *Treatise* into the *Enquiry*, he explicitly acknowledges this lack. Again struggling to substantiate the principles of association, Hume suggests that the ideal approach would be to

> run over several instances, and examine carefully the principle, which binds the different thoughts to each other, never stopping until we render the principle as general as possible. The more instances we examine, and the more care we employ, the more assurance shall we acquire, that the enumeration, which we form from the whole, is compleat and entire.[87]

Having again outlined an inductive method, Hume immediately rejects "entering into detail of this kind" and instead chooses to "consider some of the effects of this connexion [between ideas] upon the passions and imagination."[88] The remainder of the section charts the types of connection utilized in histories and biographies compared to those of epic and dramatic poetry. Rather than a catalog of behaviors, Hume's "experiments" consist of distinguishing and comparing generic types; "compositions of genius" stand in for an absent collection of instances, and their "effects" on the passions become the object of analysis.[89]

Hume's *Enquiry* displays an omnipresent strategy of empiricist moral philosophy in the period. As Jules Law suggests, "empiricism does not proceed so much by experiment as by examples and analogies *presented as reproducible experiments*. Thus classical empiricism offers us example and analogy (and thus rhetoric) precisely in the place where modern empiricism would expect experimental procedures."[90] The materials of Hume's induction are metaphors, a recognition that points to Jacques Derrida's analysis of Enlightenment philosophy and metaphysics in "White Mythology."[91] I discuss this condition – specifically the hardened opposition between meaning and rhetoric, between objects of sense and figures of speech – and its formal consequences in the second chapter of this study. Here, I want to point out the implications of Hume's shift of evidentiary base. By replacing observations and experiments with examples drawn from history and epic poetry, Hume's text reveals how and why the tension within inductive method would emerge as a question of evidence by the end of the century.

In the section of the *Enquiry* I have been discussing, Hume goes on to use Aristotelian unities to prove that the operations of the mind depend on the association or connection of ideas – but his argument implies that a ready-made natural history of the mind can be found in the storehouse of its imaginative productions. Textual excerpts, in other words, might become evidentiary. Rather than merely illustrating codified universals or reiterating *sententiae*, textual excerpts could now be imagined as the foundation of empirical theories of cognition, education, genius, and taste, and of the practice of literary criticism. As Hugh Blair put it in 1783, criticism is "founded wholly on experience" and therefore principles such as Aristotle's unities "were not rules first discovered by logical reasoning, and then applied to poetry; but they were drawn from the practice of Homer and Sophocles."[92] The laws of both criticism and cognition could be generated inductively from the existing databank of literary texts.

It is precisely this kind of thinking that fueled criticism of Edmund Burke's *A Philosophical Enquiry into the Origin of our Ideas of the Sublime and Beautiful* (1757). In his Preface to the first edition, Burke articulates his adherence to inductive method. Noting that "the characters of nature are legible . . . but they are not plain enough to enable those who run, to read them," he outlines a necessarily "timorous method of proceeding": we must first "examine every different ingredient in the composition, one by one, and reduce every thing to the utmost simplicity," after which we can reexamine the effect of the composition by comparing and contrasting it with other subjects.[93] "The greater number of these comparisons we make," Burke argues, "the more general and the more certain our knowledge is like to prove, as built upon a more extensive and perfect induction."[94] Despite the import of his extended metaphor, Burke's objects of inquiry are "passions in our own breasts" and "emotion[s] . . . in the human mind."[95] The passage thus figures human nature as an aggregate of elements akin to the words and sentences that comprise a text. Induction, the passage implies, allows us to read people as we would a poem.

This metaphoric transference is hardly surprising: Burke is working in the Lockean tradition of recasting the steps of inductive method as cognitive processes, and he follows Hume in replacing an absent databank of human behaviors with exemplary passages from poets, including Ovid, Homer, Virgil, Spenser, Shakespeare, Milton, Dryden, and Pope. As in Hume's *Enquiry*, a textual archive stands in for observed instances. By scattering illustrative quotations throughout his book, Burke urged his readers to do precisely what would later prove a source of irritation. In the 1759 Preface to the second edition, he complains that rather than disputing his "method," his critics instead "produce as an objection, some poetic passage" that his theory fails to account for. Refutation by example is "improper," Burke retorts, because "the task would be infinite, if we could establish no principle until we had previously unraveled the complex texture of every image or description to be found in poets and orators."[96] In his reaction to critics, Burke isolates the problem of induction as it manifests itself *within* texts. Put simply, Burke discovered that induction is practically untenable: like the natural world or the human mind, the textual archive of literature is infinitely varied and diverse, a prospect of dizzying magnitude and complexity. Procedurally, however, induction demanded that he extract principles from particular instances. Lacking empirical data about the operation of the passions, Burke has implicitly substituted one unmanageable textual archive for another. Even as he insists on applying induction to human "compositions," his induction rests on the evidentiary base of typographically offset textual excerpts from identifiable literary texts. In Burke's text, then, quotations from literature took on the mantle of data and functioned as evidence, despite his strident objections to this approach.

The idea that quotations are evidentiary is recognizably modern. As Margreta de Grazia has argued, the eighteenth century saw the emergence of a new preoccupation with "who spoke what": quotation marks, which had previously appeared in the margins of books to point to important passages, began to signal private property.[97] Passages designated by quotation marks in Renaissance books provided "general truths by which to treat particular cases"; quotations in late-eighteenth-century books were "singular utterances" of an individual author.[98] This shift was bound up with changes in copyright law and the status of authorship in the eighteenth century, but it is most visible in usage. For example, in *The History of Tom Jones*, Fielding inserts a line of verse in his dedication to George Lyttleton, who will "*Do Good by stealth, and blush to find it Fame.*"[99] The line is set off from the main text of the prose dedication and printed in italic font, but it is not enclosed in quotation marks, nor does Fielding provide a citation or indicate authorship beyond ascribing it to "a great poet." In Chapter 8, Fielding again introduces an extract in a discussion of Mrs. Bridget: "*De non apparentibus, et non existentibus eadem est ratio* – in *English*: 'When a Woman is not seen to blush, she doth not blush at all.'" In this instance, the Latin phrase appears in italics and the English translation in quotation marks. In both cases, the quoted phrases function as aphoristic truths by which the character of an individual can be judged – the statements rise above any individual speaker or subject to embody conventional wisdom. Compare this with the quote from Shakespeare that Fielding uses just above the previous example in Chapter 8: listening through the keyhole to her brother's study, Bridget "had sometimes Reason to cry out with *Thisbe*, in *Shakspeare*, 'O, wicked, wicked Wall!'".[100] Unlike the other excerpts, this quotation from *Midsummer Night's Dream* is doubly attributed to a character and an author. The quotation marks display it as a "singular utterance" with a specific context – a farcical play within a play – that is deployed to satirize Bridget's act of eavesdropping. In this instance, Thisbe and Bridget are placed in an analogical relation to each other, and the quotation consequently acts as satiric jab at Bridget more than established nugget of widely applicable wisdom. Fielding's novel signals the emerging break between *sententiae* and the modern use of quotations as evidence – a break that Burke and Hume experienced as a methodological impasse. Coded as the evidentiary base of induction, quotations were no longer clearly illustrative of general truths, as Burke wished them to be treated. Instead, their presence in a text such as Burke's signaled the archive on which induction would be performed, the evidentiary foundation of the more general ideas contained in the text.

The source of Burke's conundrum is clearly registered in the changes to quotation and citation practice across a wide spectrum of eighteenth-century genres. Perhaps most obviously, it appears in Johnson's use of quotations to support each definition in his *Dictionary*, but equally pointed examples abound. The middle of the century saw the beginning of a sea change in historical writing, stemming from a renewed interest in primary sources and archival evidence. Hume's *The History of England* (1754–61) has a lining of annotations along the bottom of each page, referring primarily to earlier histories, topographical works, or antiquarian research; Edward Gibbon's *History of the Decline and Fall of the Roman Empire* (1776–89) includes a massive apparatus, relegated to the back of the book as endnotes. As Peter Cosgrove has shown, Gibbon's annotations were often of the skeptical variety, and frequently act to destabilize the historical narrative being presented in the text proper.[101] Even so, the evidentiary use of notes by Hume and Gibbon anchors nineteenth-century "scientific history," which rose to prominence with the combination of archival research and inductive method practiced by Leopold von Ranke in the 1830s.[102] Similarly, William Jones's antiquarian research in India and Egypt and his studies of ancient languages (especially Sanskrit) are composed of quotations from various sources, documentary and printed, underwritten by source citations that also provide linguistic and cultural information.[103] In Britain and Germany, the antiquarian recovery of folk literature, especially ballads, was also legitimized and forwarded by quotation and citation: Thomas Percy's *Reliques of Ancient English Poetry* (1765), for example, opens with "An Essay on the Ancient English Minstrels" that is by and large a fabric of quotations, extensively annotated, while footnotes for each ballad detail manuscript variants.[104] Walter Scott's *Minstrelsy of the Scottish Border* (1802) and many less well-known literary recovery projects similarly take pains to annotate and authenticate their sources. Taken together, these examples indicate a growing imperative in historically oriented fields to support claims with evidence in the form of quotations and source citations from other works or documents. As with Thisbe's wicked wall in *Tom Jones*, this is only possible if quotations themselves are understood as singular utterances that together comprise a textual archive.

The evidentiary work of quotations was not, of course, limited to eighteenth-century historical and antiquarian writing. Glosses already had a long history in biblical hermeneutics, and extensive footnotes were common in seventeenth- and early eighteenth-century editions of classical works, as the work of the classical scholar Richard Bentley attests. Bentley's overabundant endnotes in his 1711 edition of Horace, which correct supposed "errors" in the text, famously fueled the satirical use of notes in Pope's *The Dunciad Variorum* (1729). Bentley's notes occupy the final 491 pages of the 800-page edition; Pope satirizes this editorial excess by adding so many footnotes to the *Dunciad* that the prose paratext threatens to displace the poem on the printed page.[105] The function of annotations in Bentley and Pope, however, differs from the notes literary authors began to provide for their own works, a practice that can be traced to eighteenth-century scientific poems based on Lucretius's *De Rerum Natura* or Virgil's *Georgics*. The notes for James Grainger's *The Sugar Cane* (1764), for example, record the Latin names of trees and plants he mentions in the verse and detail his observations on topics as diverse as tropical storms and strategies for preserving slaves' health on sugar plantations.[106] Unlike Bentley's corrective emendations or Pope's satirical jabs, Grainger's notes announce themselves as both the evidentiary base for the poem and the material out of which the poem has been made. Similarly, when Thomas Gray added notes to his odes in the 1768 edition of his poems, it was a response to the seeming degeneracy of readers who had failed to grasp his allusions to Virgil, Milton, Dryden, Pindar, Homer, Phrynichus, Cowley, Petrarch, and Lucretius, among others.[107] Providing the passage alluded to along with a source citation, Gray's notes are both explanatory and legitimating; they uphold Gray's poetic practice while also telling readers how to read his poems. By quoting and citing their source material, Gray and Grainger bolster the authority of their verse by laying bare their sources. Implicit in this practice is the understanding of quotations as material that can be collected, sorted, collated, compared, distinguished, combined, and composed into something else, in this case an ode or a georgic. Evidentiary practices of excerpting, quotation, and annotation make visible the authors' inductive method of textual production.

In the final decades of the eighteenth century, the emergent evidentiary function of quotations was taken up in many different genres as a claim to legitimacy and authority. Periodical reviews, for example, regularly quoted passages from the work under discussion, which were inserted, at least ostensibly, to support whatever claims the reviewer felt impelled to make. As a brief survey makes abundantly clear, however, quoted passages seldom directly support the review's overall assessment. Rather than serving as evidence for specific claims, quotations more frequently stand as exemplary instances of the work's beauties and faults, a conventional form of critical evaluation throughout the eighteenth century.[108] Similarly, popular genres comprised entirely of excerpts drew on the new evidentiary status of quotations without using them as evidence or citing sources. As many critics have noted, the eighteenth century saw the publication of an increasing number of miscellanies and anthologies, and the numbers jumped even higher after the 1774 decision in *Donaldson v. Beckett*, which effectively ended perpetual copyright in Britain.[109] Widely reprinted collections such as William Enfield's *Speaker* or Vicesimus Knox's *Elegant Extracts* of prose or verse staked their pedagogical claims on the value of the excerpt. For example, Knox suggests that passages in his collection could be read in private, memorized, copied into a commonplace book, or recited; any of these activities would yield "a great improvement in the English language" as well as instructing readers about literature and taste and inculcating "the purest principles of Virtue and Religion."[110] Grandiose claims of this ilk were both a marketing strategy and a defense mechanism against vitriolic disparagements of the miscellany as a genre: as Hannah More complained in her *Strictures on the Modern System of Female Education*, the "Swarms of Abridgements, Beauties, and Compendiums, which form a too consider-able part of a young lady's library, may be considered in many instances as an infallible receipt for making a superficial mind." More's reasoning: "A few fine passages from the poets . . . are huddled together by some extract maker, whose brief and disconnected patches of broken and discordant materials . . . neither fill the mind nor form the taste" (*SFE*, 166–67). Such criticism draws on a widely held perception of the cognitive dangers of reading excerpts more generally: by jumbling together short, easy passages from many different texts, both miscellanies and periodicals encouraged casual browsing and desultory reading at the expense of logical analysis. As Duff notes, a version of this critique found its way into political debates sur-rounding the French revolution: In *Reflections on the Revolution in France* (1790), Burke characterized Richard Price's *Discourse on the Love of our Country* (1789) as an "extraordinarily miscellaneous sermon" that "mixed up" moral and religious sentiments with political reflections "in a sort of porridge." Stepping off from Price's text, Burke cast the Revolution itself as a mixed genre, a "monstrous tragi-comic scene."[111] In its turn, Woll-stonecraft's *A Vindication of the Rights of Men*, itself structured by carefully chosen quotations and typographically distinct footnotes, took Burke to task for his texts' "mixture of verse and prose producing the strangest incon-gruities."[112] As these threads of critique indicate, even as they deployed the new evidentiary uses of quotations, mixed forms such as the periodical, miscellany, and essay might appear inimical to forming a rational mind and a danger to the body politic.

The turn-of-the-century reaction against the use and misuse of quota-tions was part of a larger uneasiness about the cognitive effects of excerpted passages, explored at length in the second half of this study. If quotations were defined by their evidentiary function, they could no longer stand on their own – they required a context to supply them with meaning and pur-pose. In keeping with this new understanding, by the end of the eighteenth century it was no longer acceptable to treat borrowed material as *sententiae*. As de Grazia notes, the change in how quotation marks were used created a situation where appropriations that were standard earlier in the century started to look more like transgressions.[113] As a consequence, how literary texts were made – and what they were made of – became a topic of intense scrutiny. As Piper suggests, the biblio-literary field of Romanticism was characterized by a "fundamental uncertainty about the control and ownership of communication" so pronounced as to constitute a "persistent sense of a crisis of the genitive."[114] Anna Seward's spirited criticism of Charlotte Smith for plagiarism is a case in point. Seward objects to Smith's *Elegiac Sonnets* (1784) because she does "not find in her sonnets any original ideas, any vigor of thought, any striking imagery – but plagiarism, glaring and perpetual; – whole lines taken verbatim, and without acknowledgment from Shakespeare, Milton, Young, Pope, Gray, Collins, Mason, and Beattie."[115] Seward specifically references the first edition of Smith's sonnets, which did not typographically signal borrowed lines or allusions to other literary works. Where Gray added notes to educate his audience, Smith was taken to task for not citing her sources. In the preface to the second edition, Smith makes a slightly offhand remark about her borrowings: "*The readers of poetry will meet with some lines borrowed from the most popular authors, which I have used only as quotations. Where such acknowledgment is omitted, I am unconscious of the theft.*"[116] In the Preface to the third edition, Smith specifically draws attention to the citations she has added in endnotes: "*I have there quoted such lines as I borrowed; and . . . have restored them to their original possessors.*"[117] Between the prefaces, the sense of what a quotation is and does has changed, a shift materialized in Smith's annotation practices. For example, the final line in "Sonnet I" initially functioned as an established *sententiae* that legitimated the lyric voice – the line reads "If those paint sorrow best – who feel it most!" – but in the third edition Smith inserts an endnote reference "*(a)*" before the line and puts the entire line in italics. The endnote diligently quotes and cites the two lines from "Pope's *Eloisa to Abelard*, 366th line" that supply the sentiment for Smith's line.[118] As noted in the Introduction, in later editions Smith and her publisher experimented with different systems of referencing citations, indicating her continued preoccupation with this issue.

Smith's troubles were hardly unique in the decades around the turn of the century. The charges of plagiarism leveled at Coleridge are infamous in Romantic studies, and Southey was taken to task by Francis Jeffrey in 1802 for creating a poem that was "little more than his common-place book versified" (*RS*, 83). Even modern critics of Johnson have fallen into this trap, casting him as "one who cannibalizes earlier narratives" to support his own conclusions.[119] Such charges of plagiarism make little sense when applied to Johnson, even though they are perfectly in keeping with the climate of criticism in the decades after his death. As Alan Reddick argues of Johnson's *Dictionary*, "at the heart of the work lies a tension between its implicit claims to a unified authority and the presence of other diffuse and disparate – and sometimes competing – authorities."[120] This condition was amplified in Romantic-period formal mixtures – amplified to the point that it became a "problem" demanding attention and resolution. The requirement to quote and cite material borrowed from other sources produced texts whose seams and stitchery were clearly visible to every reader. At a moment when the goal of inductive method had shifted from the accumulation of instances to the expression of synthetic principles, the evidentiary work of quotation and annotation appeared – quite literally in the case of footnotes or typographically offset quotations – to be getting in the way of achieving this higher objective. The more singular utterances it incorporated, the less unified a text looked – indeed, as Jeffrey quips of *Thalaba*, it began to resemble the pattern of a "patchwork drapery" (*RS*, 83) – and this only advertised the disjointed reading practices it encouraged and its potentially damaging effects on readers' cognitive development. In the early- to mid-eighteenth century, building texts by excerpting, sorting, amalgamating, and mixing pieces of other texts was an utterly conventional and common practice, so omnipresent it seldom, if ever, provoked explicit commentary from authors in any field. Even so, Reddick argues that Johnson had no illusions about his monumental work becoming a "fixed, permanent monument": "he thought of his *Dictionary* as organic and growing, striving for fullness and completion yet doomed to failure."[121] Reddick's rhetoric of failed synthesis overcome by a theory of organic growth fills the gulf between Johnson's late Enlightenment project and the formal mixtures of early Romanticism. What had seemed unremarkable in the middle of the century soon proved a source of irritation, a troubling disjunction between the projected goal of compositional process and the textual product that eventually appeared in print. All authors I treat in the succeeding chapters – Darwin, Southey, Richard Lovell Edgeworth and his daughter Maria Edgeworth, Smith, and Coleridge – were more or less ill at ease with the heap of particular instances littering the pages of their books. For authors writing in the 1790s and first decade of the nineteenth century, the problem of induction was writ large in the printed book, and it called for theoretical and practical "fixes" that ranged from Darwin's all-encompassing web of analogical relations to Coleridge's idealization of the poet's synthetic imagination. It is the project of the succeeding chapters to mine the consequences of Romantic authors' bedeviled confrontation with induction as a procedure for making texts and scripting minds.

NOTES

1 Samuel Taylor Coleridge, *The Friend*, 2 vols., Barbara E. Rooke (ed.) vol. 4 of *The Collected Works of Samuel Taylor Coleridge* (Princeton, NJ: Princeton University Press, 1969), 1: 471. Subsequently cited in text by volume and page number. While writing the introduction for Fenner, Coleridge was also giving a series of lectures on the principles of experimental philosophy at the London Philosophical Society.

2 I treat this passage and Coleridge's practice of compiling and deploying quoted material in *The Friend* at length in Chapter 5.

3 It is fitting that you are reading the fourth distinct incarnation of this chapter, it having been recomposed many times using the scraps of its predecessors.

4 Bacon insisted that rather than "going the same road as the ancients," he intended to "open a new way for the understanding" such that by "passing by the outer courts of nature, which numbers have trodden, we may find a way at length into her inner chambers" (*NO*, 41–42). The gendered and imperial connotations of Bacon's metaphors have been widely discussed: see Carolyn Merchant, *The Death of Nature: Women, Ecology and the Scientific Revolution* (New York: Harper Collins, 1980), p. 282; Ludmilla Jordanova, *Sexual Visions: Images of Gender in Science and Medicine between the Eighteenth and Twentieth Centuries* (Madison: University of Wisconsin Press, 1989), pp. 23–25; and Londa Schiebinger, *The Mind Has No Sex? Women in the Origins of Modern Science* (Cambridge, MA: Harvard University Press, 1989), pp. 137–46.

5 Stoddart reversed this order, beginning with Davy and Darwin and ending with Shakespeare – precisely the wrong approach, according to Coleridge, because it gave the sciences ownership over the very concept Coleridge is trying to wrest from its connection to empiricism. For more on this topic, see Chapter 5.

6 Simpson, *Romanticism*, p. 8. Simpson suggests that in the aftermath of the French Revolution, orthodox Baconianism in Britain aligned itself firmly with practice, and "method" either dropped out of the lexicon or survived in less controversial contexts. The nineteenth-century examples of William Whewall and John Herschel, discussed below, put pressure on this claim.

7 J. G. A. Pocock, "Enthusiasm: The Antiself of Enlightenment," in *The Certainty of Doubt*, Miles Fairburn and W. H. Oliver (eds.) (Wellington: Victoria University Press, 1996), p. 126.

8 Jan Golinski, *British Weather and the Climate of Enlightenment* (Chicago and London: University of Chicago Press, 2007), pp. 87–88.

9 Simpson exemplifies this slipperiness when he uses "method" to signify the radical element in Ramism and Methodist doctrine while also aligning it with Baconian induction as a "way of doing things according to a progressive procedure." Simpson rightly notes that in either case "the debate about method is

most often a debate about the relation of such procedures to the true order of things in the world, and about the transferability of any one procedure from one area of the world to others." Simpson, *Romanticism*, p. 7.

10 Schuster and Yeo, Introduction, *Scientific Method*, pp. ix–xxxvii.

11 Steven Shapin and Simon Schaffer, *Leviathan and the Air-Pump: Hobbes, Boyle, and the Experimental Life* (Princeton, NJ: Princeton University Press, 1985), p. 4.

12 Dear, *Discipline and Experience*; Poovey, *Modern Fact*; Lorraine Daston, "Marvelous Facts and Miraculous Evidence in Early Modern Europe," *Questions of Evidence: Proof, Practice and Persuasion across the Disciplines*, James Chandler, Arnold Davidson, and Harry Harootunian (eds.) (Chicago: University of Chicago Press, 1994), pp. 243–74; Lorraine Daston and Peter Galison, *Objectivity* (New York: Zone Books, 2007).

13 Lorraine Daston, "Historical Epistemology," *Questions of Evidence: Proof, Practice and Persuasion across the Disciplines*, James Chandler, Arnold Davidson, and Harry Harootunian (eds.) (Chicago: University of Chicago Press, 1994), p. 282.

14 Shapin and Schaffer, *Leviathan and the Air-Pump*, p. 15.

15 My claim here should not be confused with the line of argument pursued in the essays included in *The Literary Structure of Scientific Argument*, Peter Dear (ed.) (Philadelphia: University of Pennsylvania Press, 1991). Rather than reading "literary" devices and rhetorical techniques in "scientific" texts, I analyze how induction structured – conceptually as well as materially on the printed page – many kinds of texts, from natural histories to essays on taste to dictionaries to epic poems.

16 Gillian Beer, *Darwin's Plots: Evolutionary Narrative in Darwin, George Eliot and Nineteenth-Century Fiction* (Cambridge: Cambridge University Press, 2000).

17 For Bacon's borrowings from common law, see Christiane Schildknecht, "Experiments with Metaphors: On the Connection between Scientific Method and Literary Form in Francis Bacon," *From a Metaphorical Point of View: A Multidisciplinary Approach to the Cognitive Content of Metaphor*, Zdravko Radman (ed.) (Berlin: de Gruyter, 1995), pp. 27–50. For the roots of induction in other seventeenth-century traditions, see Lorraine Daston, "Baconian Facts, Academic Civility, and the Prehistory of Objectivity," *Inquiry: An Interdisciplinary Journal of Philosophy* 8.3–4 (1991): 339–40; Poovey, *Modern Fact*, pp. 10–11, 337–64; Andrew Barnaby and Lisa Schnell, *Literate Experience: The Work of Knowing in Seventeenth-Century English Writing* (New York: Palgrave Macmillan, 2002), pp. 13–44; Joseph Levine, *Humanism and History: Origins of Modern English Historiography* (Ithaca, NY: Cornell University Press, 1987); and Timothy Reiss, *Discourse of Modernism* (Ithaca, NY: Cornell University Press, 1982), pp. 180–88, 198–225.

18 John Frederick William Herschel, *Preliminary Discourse on the Study of Natural Philosophy* (London, 1833), pp. 104–05.

19 William Whewell, *The Philosophy of the Inductive Sciences*, 2 vols. (London, 1840), 2: 389. The value of induction for the discovery of scientific knowledge was hotly contested in the mid-nineteenth century; for a discussion of these debates over Bacon's method, see Jonathan Smith, *Fact and Fiction: Baconian Science and the Nineteenth-Century Literary Imagination* (Madison: University of Wisconsin Press, 1994), pp. 15–20, and Laura J. Snyder, "The Mill–Whewell Debate: Much Ado about Induction," *Perspectives on Science* 5.2 (1997): 159–98.

20 Pérez-Ramos cites Whewell's rejection of Darwin's *The Origin of Species* because it was not based on "inductive or Baconian principles" as a case in point. Pérez-Ramos, *Francis Bacon's Idea of Science*, p. 24.

21 Thomas Sprat, *History of the Royal Society of London* (London, 1667), p. 36.

22 Pérez-Ramos, *Francis Bacon's Idea of Science*, p. 24.

23 Newton's editors and early historians of science proclaimed him a Baconian, and both the *Optics* and *Mechanics* were heralded as the practical consummation of Bacon's inductive method. As Humphry Davy put it in 1808, the "legitimate practice" of science is "that sanctioned by the precepts of Bacon and the examples of Newton." Humphry Davy, "Lecture 1 – Introductory to the Electro-chemical Science," *The Collected Works of Sir Humphry Davy*, John Davy (ed.), 9 vols. (London, 1839–40), 8: 276. As Peter Dear argues, while Newton grounded his work in an older tradition of mathematical science, he rhetorically embedded the *Optics* in the experimental ethos of the Royal Society. Dear, *Discipline and Experience*, pp. 232–43. Dear's insightful analysis explains why Newton was touted by his contemporaries as the culmination of Bacon's methodological legacy even though his procedures were by no means strictly inductive. According to Rose-Mary Sargent, Boyle's references to Bacon "indicate a true allegiance to the latter's precepts," but her study also shows how Boyle expanded and modified Bacon's methodological prescriptions in the formulation of his own experimental philosophy. Rose-Mary Sargent, *The Diffident Naturalist: Robert Boyle and the Philosophy of Experiment* (Chicago: University of Chicago Press, 1995), p. 38.

24 Francis Bacon, *The Advancement of Learning*, vol. 3 of *The Works of Francis Bacon*, James Spedding, Robert Leslie Ellis, and Douglas Denon Heath (eds.) (London: Longman et al., 1857), p. 405.

25 As Pérez-Ramos shows, Bacon's conclusion to his exemplary history of heat, what he calls the "Form of heat," is a descriptive statement that leads to the successful reproduction of the phenomenon it purports to describe. For Bacon, the endpoint of induction is literally the textual articulation of instructions necessary to replicate the observations and experiments by which he reached a specific conclusion. Antonio Pérez-Ramos, "Bacon's Forms and the Maker's Knowledge Tradition," *Cambridge Companion to Bacon*, Markku Peltonen (ed.) (Cambridge: Cambridge University Press, 1996), p. 111.

26 As I discuss below, many of Boyle's project remained incomplete at his death, the material having been amassed and arranged but never brought into a publishable form.

27 Sargent, *Diffident Naturalist*, pp. 140–42. See Sargent, pp. 138–45, for a re-creation of Boyle's index and his comments on how the index was intended to function. As Sargent notes, some of the projected essays in this index were eventually published by Boyle, but most appear again in his final list of unpublished works and (if they were ever written) are now lost. See also Michael Hunter, *The Boyle Papers: Understanding the Manuscripts of Robert Boyle* (Burlington: Ashgate, 2007).

28 Kirkley, *Biographer at Work*, pp. 19–45. On Johnson's reading and note taking, see Wimsatt, *Philosophic Words*; Robert DiMaria, *Samuel Johnson and the Life of Reading* (Baltimore: Johns Hopkins University Press, 1997); and Alan Reddick, *The Making of Johnson's Dictionary, 1746–1773* (Cambridge and New York: Cambridge University Press, 1990).

29 Kirkley, *Biographer at Work*, pp. 30–41.

30 Ibid., p. 44.

31 Ibid., p. 13.

32 Ibid. p. 164. Wimsatt prefaces his study by reproducing a page from Vol. III of Bacon's *Works* that has been marked by Johnson in compiling illustrations for the *Dictionary*. Wimsatt, *Philosophic Words*, frontispiece.

33 David Hume, *A Treatise of Human Nature: Being an Attempt to introduce the Experimental Method of Reasoning into Moral Subjects*, 3 vols. (London, 1739–40), 1: 6.

34 Tilottama Rajan uses this phrase to explain how natural history became social history in the Enlightenment through a methodological transference; see Rajan, "Spirit's Psychoanalysis: Natural History, the History of Nature and Romantic Historiography," *European Romantic Review* 14.2 (2003): 187. Wimsatt made a similar claim in his study of Johnson's prose style: there was "a strain in the empirical writers whose books Johnson read, a character of the very tradition, which promoted the metaphor between matter and spirit." Wimsatt, *Philosophic Words*, pp. 42–43, 13.

35 John Locke, *An Essay concerning Human Understanding*, Roger Woolhouse (ed.) (New York: Penguin, 1997), p. 55.

36 Ibid., pp. 147, 109, 119, 147–48, 152, 154, 155, 157, 159.

37 Ibid., p. 157, my emphasis.

38 Samuel Johnson, "Preface to Pope," Vol. 7 of *Prefaces, Biographical and Critical, to the Works of the English Poets* (London: J. Nichols, 1781), p. 270.

39 Alexander Gerard, *An Essay on Genius* (London, 1774), pp. 71, 86, *Eighteenth Century Collections Online*, http://find.galegroup.com.proxy.library.vanderbilt.edu/ecco, 15 April 2011.

40 Joshua Reynolds, *Discourses on Art*, Robert R. Wark (ed.) (New Haven, CT: Yale University Press, 1997), pp. 44, 106.

41 Mary Wollstonecraft, *A Vindication of the Rights of Woman*, 1792, in *The Works of Mary Wollstonecraft*, Vol. 5, Janet Todd and Marilyn Butler (eds.) (New York: New York University Press, 1989), pp. 91–92; Hannah More, *Strictures on the Modern System of Female Education*, 1799, in *Selected Writings of Hannah More*, Robert Hole (ed.) (London: William Pickering, 1996), pp. 172–73. Subsequently cited in text.

42 Davy, *Collected Works*, 4: 2.

43 Ibid., 4: 4–10.

44 Ibid., 4: 11–31.

45 As critics have noted, Wordsworth's additions to the 1802 Preface to *Lyrical Ballads* are likely a response to Davy's "Introductory Discourse" to his 1801 lecture series. See Roger Sharrock, "The Chemist and the Poet: Sir Humphry Davy and the Preface to Lyrical Ballads," *Notes and Records of the Royal Society of London* 17.1 (May 1962): 57–76.

46 Coleridge and Wordsworth, *Lyrical Ballads* (1802), pp. xxxii–xxxvi.

47 Ibid., p. xxxvi.

48 Ibid., pp. xxxii, xxxiii, xxxvi–xxxvii.

49 For a discussion of Wordsworth's investment in professionalization, see Mark Schoenfield, *The Professional Wordsworth: Law, Labor, and the Poet's Contract* (Athens: University of Georgia Press, 1996). For a treatment of discipline formation in the eighteenth and early nineteenth century, see Robin Valenza, *Literature, Language, and the Rise of the Intellectual Disciplines in Britain, 1680–1820* (Cambridge: Cambridge University Press, 2009); for poetry as a discipline defined by its lack of a clearly defined subject of enquiry, see Valenza, pp. 139–72.

50 I would characterize this as "transdisciplinary" because it specifically refers to the transference of methods from one discipline to another, and seeks for a greater unity of knowledge than is provided by disciplinary approaches; as I discuss below, this second characteristic of transdisciplinarity aligns closely with the late-eighteenth-century changes in the goals of induction.

51 Klancher, *Transfiguring*, p. 139.

52 Ibid., p. 139.

53 Abrams, *Mirror*, p. 159.

54 Ibid., pp. 160–67.

55 Julie Ellison, "The Politics of Fancy in the Age of Sensibility," *Re-visioning Romanticism: British Women Writers, 1776–1837*, Carol Shiner Wilson and Joel Haefner (eds.) (Philadelphia: University of Pennsylvania Press, 1994), p. 228.

56 In his "Description of Natural and Experimental History," Bacon isolates natural history as a preparative to induction, the aim of which should be "to seek out and gather together such store and variety of things as may suffice for the formation of true axioms" (*NO*, 253–54).

57 Quoted in Frans De Bruyn, "The Classical Silva and the Generic Development of Scientific Writing in Seventeenth Century England," *New Literary History* 32.2 (2001): 369.

58 John Lyon and Phillip R. Sloan, *From Natural History to the History of Nature: Readings from Buffon and His Critics* (Notre Dame, IN and London: University of Notre Dame Press, 1981), p. 38.

59 Ibid., p. 38.

60 Georges-Louis Leclerc, Comte de Buffon, *L'Histoire Naturelle, générale et particulière* (1744–88), Buffon @ web: l'édition en ligne, dir. Pietro Corsi, 17 April 2011, www.buffon.cnrs.fr, pp. 20, 39. Translations are my own.

61 Ibid., p. 51. Poovey's discussion of the "modern fact" as both a deracinated particular separate from theory and a singular event that constitutes evidence for a theory speaks directly to this midcentury change. See Poovey, *Modern Fact*, pp. 94–97 and 214–63.

62 Ibid., p. 51.

63 William Smellie, Preface to *Natural History, General and Particular, by the Count de Buffon* (Edinburgh, 1780–85), p. xi. While the "Premier discours" was not translated into English sentence by sentence until the nineteenth century, the ideas it contained – particularly the critique of taxonomy and the importance of moving beyond fact collecting to the synthetic work of analogy – circulated widely in Britain through Smellie's translation, as well as Oliver Goldsmith's popular *History of the Earth and Animated Nature* (London, 1774). Goldsmith's popularization draws materials from Buffon and reiterates – with much reorganization and emendation – Buffon's critiques and commentary while also (ironically) chastising the French writer for his lack of method.

64 Siskin and Warner, "This Is Enlightenment," pp. 17–18.

65 James Llana argues that natural history and Diderot's discussions of the encyclopedia were influenced by his reading in natural history and specifically Buffon. See James Llana, "Natural History and the *Encyclopédie*," *Journal of the History of Biology* 33.1 (2000): 1–25.

66 Yeo, *Encyclopedic Visions*, pp. xiv–xv, 1–4, 22–32.

67 Jean Le Rond d'Alembert, *Preliminary Discourse to the Encyclopedia of Diderot*, Richard Schwab (trans.) (Chicago: University of Chicago Press, 1995), p. 47.

68 Jacques Roger, *Buffon: A Life in Natural History*, Sarah Lucille Bonnefoi (trans.) (Ithaca, NY: Cornell University Press, 1997), p. 198; for a discussion of the *Histoire Naturelle*'s reception more broadly, see pp. 184–200.

69 Mary Poovey labels this moment a "*belated* effect of Bacon's empiricism." Poovey, *Modern Fact*, 15. Poovey's characterization is somewhat anachronistic. In eighteenth- and early-nineteenth-century accounts, Bacon may have given a "splendid impulse to Empiricism," but he was not an empiricist himself (quoted in Hans Aarsleff, *From Locke to Saussure*; Minneapolis: University of Minnesota Press, 1982, p. 143). It was not until the mid-nineteenth century – amid claims that inductive method was detrimental to the advance of the physical sciences – that Bacon took on the derogatory title of empiricist. See Aarsleff, pp. 120–45, and Pérez-Ramos, pp. 25–26.

70 Hume, *Treatise*, 3: 303–4.

71 Dear, *Discipline and Experience*, pp. 11–31.

72 Thomas Reid, *An Inquiry into the Human Mind, on the Principles of Common Sense*, 2nd ed. (Edinburgh, 1765), p. 210.

73 Ibid., p. 203.

74 Ibid., pp. 210, 38–41.

75 Thomas Reid, *Essays on the Intellectual Powers of Man* (Edinburgh, 1785), pp. 560–62. The *Essays* address a number of sticky points raised by critics:

For example, in the same passage cited above, Reid admits that first principles might yield "only probable conclusions" as well as those of absolute certainty.

76 Yeo, *Encyclopedic Visions*, pp. 1–5.

77 Ernst Behler, *German Romantic Literary Theory* (Cambridge: Cambridge University Press, 1993), pp. 284. Wordsworth articulates a similar distinction in a canceled passage in the "Convention of Cintra" (1809), in which he sets Bacon's "comprehensive and sublime" mind against "the experimentalists who deem themselves his disciples." Quoted in Smith, *Fact and Feeling*, p. 52.

78 By the early nineteenth century, the idea that "indiscriminate collection of facts will lead eventually and inevitably to the formation of a theory" had acquired the label of "naïve" Baconianism. Smith, *Fact and Feeling*, p. 16.

79 Ibid., p. 336.

80 Tilottama Rajan, "The Encyclopedia and the University of Theory: idealism and the Organization of Knowledge," *Textual Practice* 21.2 (2007): 342–44. My emphasis.

81 Ibid., 345–47.

82 David Wood, Introduction, *Notes for a Romantic Encyclopedia*, by Novalis (Albany: State University of New York Press, 2007), p. xvii.

83 Novalis, *Notes for a Romantic Encyclopedia*, David Wood (trans. and ed.) (Albany: State University of New York Press, 2007), p. 32.

84 Chad Wellmon, "Touching Books: Diderot, Novalis, and the Encyclopedia of the Future," *Representations* 114 (Spring 2011): 67. Wellmon reads Novalis's pointedly anti-disciplinary position and obsession with form as a response to information overload and the proliferation of print in the second half of the eighteenth century. This reading suggests an important qualification to Siskin and Warner's argument that the response to the print saturation in the final decades of the eighteenth century was a new protocol for knowledge, "the enabling constraints of disciplinarity." Siskin and Warner, "This Is Enlightenment," pp. 19–20. The drawing of disciplinary boundaries was one response, but an insistent transdisciplinarity was another. As with the idealist encyclopedia, this resistance to specialization and separation of fields characterizes the composite order.

85 Hume, *Treatise*, I: 6, 10.

86 Ibid., p. 27.

87 David Hume, *An Enquiry concerning Human Understanding*, 1772, Tom L. Beauchamp (ed.) (Oxford: Oxford University Press, 1999), p. 102.

88 Ibid., p. 102.

89 Ibid., p. 104.

90 Jules David Law, *The Rhetoric of Empiricism: Languages and Perception from Locke to I. A. Richards* (Ithaca, NY: Cornell University Press, 1993), p. 7. Law's study of empiricism thus replaces the standard line – that empiricism is merely an observation-based epistemology – with attention to its rhetorical figures and particularly the "metaphorics of 'reflection'" that, he argues, are at the core of empiricist theories of perception.

91 Jacques Derrida, "White Mythology: Metaphor in the Text of Philosophy," *Margins of Philosophy*, Alan Bass (trans.) (Chicago: University of Chicago Press, 1982), pp. 207–71.

92 Hugh Blair, *Lectures on Rhetoric and Belles Lettres*, 2 vols. (Edinburgh, 1783), 1: 37.

93 Edmund Burke, *A Philosophical Enquiry into Our Ideas of the Sublime and Beautiful and Other Pre-revolutionary Writings*, David Womersley (ed.) (London and New York: Penguin, 1998), pp. 53–54.

94 Ibid., p. 54.

95 Ibid., pp. 51, 79. For Burke, the body and mind affect each other reciprocally, and his goal is to determine "what affections of the mind produce certain emotions of the body; and what distinct feelings or qualities of body shall produce determinate passions in the mind." Ibid., p. 159.

96 Ibid., p. 54.

97 Margreta de Grazia, "Shakespeare in Quotation Marks," *The Appropriation of Shakespeare: Post-Renaissance Reconstructions of the Works and the Myth*, Jean I. Marsden (ed.) (New York: St. Martin's Press, 1992), pp. 57–58.

98 Ibid., pp. 59, 61.

99 Fielding, *Tom Jones*, 1: vii.

100 Ibid., 1: 31.

101 Peter Cosgrove, "Undermining the Text: Edward Gibbon, Alexander Pope and the Anti-authenticating Footnote," *Annotation and Its Texts*, Stephen Barney (ed.) (New York: Oxford University Press, 1991), pp. 130–52.

102 Anthony Grafton, *The Footnote: A Curious History* (Cambridge, MA: Harvard University Press, 1997), pp. 34–55.

103 William Jones, *The Works of Sir William Jones*, 6 vols. (London: G. G. and J. Robinson, 1799). See especially "The Lunar Year of the Hindus," *Works*, 1: 375–411.

104 Thomas Percy, *Reliques of Ancient English Poetry*, 3 vols. (London: Dodsley, 1765). For a discussion of Percy's methods of compiling and arranging the materials for the press, see Nick Groom, The Making of Percy's *Reliques* (Oxford: Oxford University Press, 1999), pp. 145–235.

105 Horace, *Q. Horatius Flaccus, ex recensione & cum notis atque emendationibus Richardi Bentleii*, Richard Bentley (ed.) (Cambridge, 1711). Alexander Pope, *The Dunciad Variorum* (London: A. Dod, 1729). Nineteenth-century editions of Bentley's Horace sometimes reprint his emendations as footnotes, a practice that clearly shows what Pope's formatting choice was intended to mock. See *Q. Horatius Flaccus, Ex Recensione et cum Notis Atque Emendationibus Richardi Bentlii* (Leipzig, 1826).

106 James Grainger, *The Sugar Cane: A Poem in Four Books, with notes* (London: R. and J. Dodsley, 1764).

107 Thomas Gray, *Poems, a new edition* (London: J. Dodsley, 1768). For a discussion of Gray's notes as part of his reaction against the commodification of literature, see Linda Zionkowski, "Bridging the Gulf Between: The Poet and the Audience in the Work of Gray," *ELH* 58.2 (1991): 341–42.

108 This practice is an omnipresent characteristic of 1790s reviews of literary works, of which the reviews of Coleridge's *Poems* (1796) provide a clear example: Quotations are introduced as a "specimen[s]" of the poems' "characteristic excellencies and defects," or, in the case of narrative poems, as part of the reviewer's summary of the plot. J. R. de J. Jackson (ed.), *Coleridge: The Critical Heritage* (London: Routledge & K. Paul, 1970), pp. 32–38.

109 See Barbara Benedict, *Making the Modern Reader: Cultural Mediation in Early Modern Literary Anthologies* (Princeton, NJ: Princeton University Press, 1996); Leah Price, *The Anthology and the Rise of the Novel* (Cambridge: Cambridge University Press, 2000); and William St Clair, *The Reading Nation in the Romantic Period* (Cambridge: Cambridge University Press, 2007).

110 Vicesimus Knox, *Elegant Extracts in Prose, a new edition* (London, 1784), pp. iii–iv.

111 Edmund Burke, *Reflections on the Revolution in France* (London, 1790), p. 12. For an extended discussion of this material, see Duff, *Romanticism and the Uses of Genre*, pp. 187–91.

112 Mary Wollstonecraft, *A Vindication of the Rights of Men* (London, 1790), pp. 61–62. While noting that Burke "buttresses his arguments with literary allusions and citations," Duff argues for reading Burke's *Reflections* as a "paradigm for a type of miscellaneous writing which implements the aesthetic ideal of organic unity." Duff, *Romanticism and the Uses of Genre*, p. 189. I would argue for an alternative trajectory, in which the struggles over quotations in the 1790s generated the need for theories of organic unity in the early decades of the nineteenth century.

113 de Grazia, "Shakespeare," p. 66.

114 Piper, *Dreaming*, p. 15.

115 Anna Seward to William Hayley [29 Jan. 1789], in *Letters of Anna Seward: Written Between the Years 1784 and 1807*, 6 vols. (Edinburgh: Constable, 1811), 2: 223–24.

116 Charlotte Smith, *Elegiac Sonnets and other essays*, 2nd ed. (Chichester, 1784), p. iii.

117 Charlotte Smith, *Elegiac Sonnets*, 3rd ed., p. vi.

118 Ibid., pp. 2, 39.

119 Kirkley, *Biographer at Work*, p. 164. Kirkley is rejecting this assessment, which she sees in earlier studies such as Lawrence Lipking's *Ordering of the Arts in Eighteenth-Century England* (Princeton, NJ: Princeton University Press, 1970).

120 Reddick, *Johnson's Dictionary*, p. 9.

121 Ibid., p. 8.

PART I

Making Texts
The Annotated Poem

CHAPTER 2

Erasmus Darwin's Prose of the World
Induction and the Philosophical Poem

In his long scientific poem *The Loves of the Plants* (1789), Erasmus Darwin makes a definitive statement about the mode of presentation best suited to his subject: "Science is best delivered in Prose, as its mode of reasoning is from stricter analogies than metaphors or similes" (*LP*, p. 43).[1] Inserted after 430 lines of figurative verse on the topic of Linnaean botany, Darwin's statement encapsulates the odd tensions definitive of this text. The long allegorical poem carries an extensive armature of "philosophical notes," ostensibly explaining the scientific ideas presented by way of metaphor and simile in the verse. Between cantos of annotated verse, Darwin introduces three prose Interludes, cast as dialogues between the poet–botanist and his bookseller. The Interludes theorize what the reader has experienced on every page – the juxtaposition of verse and prose, allegorical poetry and experimental science. *The Loves of the Plants*, I argue here, reflects Darwin's self-conscious attempt to posit a relationship between the methods of "science" and literature through the *structure* of his text.

This chapter considers a perennial question in studies of Darwin: his science vis-à-vis his aesthetics. The earliest full-length treatment of Darwin by James Venable Logan in 1936 focused on Darwin's aesthetic theory, but modern studies – beginning with Desmond King-Hele's biography *Doctor of Revolution* (1977) – instead take up Darwin's scientific achievements. In these studies, Darwin appears as a forerunner of evolutionary science whose poetic diction looks backward, a throwback to the Augustan age on the eve of Romanticism.[2] Only in the past fifteen years have critics begun to reconsider the relationship between Darwin's scientific and literary projects. In *Romantic Rocks, Aesthetic Geology*, Noah Heringman proposes that Darwin's *The Botanic Garden* – comprised of *The Loves of the Plants* (Part II, 1789) and *The Economy of Vegetation* (Part I, 1791) – displays a "deep structural identity between scientific and aesthetic principles" and "presumes a confidence in the epistemological function of poetry, its ability to provide an *organon* of the modes of knowledge."[3] In an article tracing

Darwin's debt to Lucretius, Noel Jackson makes a similar argument: Darwin's approach to the genre of the philosophical poem "promotes poetry not as subordinate to philosophical ratiocination but as its unlikely ground."[4]

These astute critical assessments have landed on the most vexing aspect of Darwin's text – the uneasy relationship between the styles (prose and verse) and modes (science and poetry) of knowing that structure *The Botanic Garden*. Heringman and Jackson allow poetry a centrality in Darwin's work it has rarely been accorded, in part because Darwin himself everywhere announces its triviality. Alan Bewell summarizes this problem: "Believing that poetry amuses, while prose instructs, Darwin continually undercuts the importance of his 'Poetic Exhibition.'"[5] This should not, Bewell argues, distract us from the "serious philosophical and commercial vision" put forward more emphatically in *The Economy of Vegetation*.[6] Bewell is certainly right: in contrast to *Economy*, Darwin's verse in *Loves* is insistently playful, pitching through a panoply of genres from georgic to gothic, trading on sensibility one moment and sublimity the next. In the Proem, Darwin instantiates this play in a direct address to his reader, asking an implied female reader to enter his "Enchanted Garden" and contemplate the flowers exhibited "as diverse little pictures suspended over the chimney of a Lady's dressing room, *connected only by a slight festoon of ribbons*" (*LP*, p. vi, original emphasis).[7] While overtly courting a female readership, this passage also draws attention to the artistry and disjunction of his flowery verse, which, as the Advertisement indicates, is intended to "lead" the reader "from the looser analogies, which dress out the imagery of poetry, to the stricter ones, which form the ratiocination of philosophy" (*LP*, n.p.).

In this much cited statement, the central tension within Darwin's project comes to the fore. As a founding member of the Lunar Society, Darwin worked to promote the growing authority of experimental science in British culture, and the notes to *The Botanic Garden* are a clearinghouse for cutting-edge chemical and electrical experiments and descriptions of the latest technological advances, drawn from books, the *Philosophical Transactions of the Royal Society*, periodicals, his own observations, and letters from his friends (including Josiah Wedgwood, James Watt, and Matthew Boulton). Educated in Latin and Greek classics, Darwin valued literature for its powers of seduction – he wooed both of his wives with witty, sentimental verses – and for poetry's capacity to elicit mental and emotional responses by bringing imaginary scenes vividly before the eye.[8] While clearly differentiating between the work of poetry and that of philosophy – a term Darwin uses to refer to the inductive, experimental science of his notes – Darwin also suggests a likeness in their methods: both poetry and philosophy trade in analogies. Darwin builds *Loves* inductively from a storehouse of observations, experiments, reports, and excerpts drawn from various sources and threaded together with analogies. In this compositional strategy, he follows the broad shift in scientific enquiry away from compiling and arranging to the more "philosophical" activity of comparing, distinguishing, and linking by analogy described in Chapter 1. In his notes to *Loves*, Darwin employs this new goal to extend the seventeenth-century concept of "botanical analogy" into a comprehensive worldview underwritten by analogical reasoning. Darwin's choice to label the rhetorical figures of his verse – and particularly the omnipresent epic simile – as "loose analogies" indicates his commitment to a poetics methodologically parallel to, but functionally distinct from, the inductive method of experimental science.

Where authors in early decades of the century assumed that verse was an appropriate form for conveying philosophical and scientific ideas, Darwin's text materially divorces the work of poetry from that of experimental science.[9] In doing so, he sought to address a concern endemic to late eighteenth-century empiricist philosophy more broadly. I argue that the relationship between prose and verse in Darwin's text exhibits a complex and calculated response to the problem of induction. From its earliest formulations in the seventeenth century, experimental science had confronted the uncertain capacity of language to convey knowledge gleaned through the senses. Analogy, even as it held out the possibility of synthesizing an ever-growing heap of facts, simultaneously cast doubt on the epistemological ground of induction, the fundamental first step of observation. Lodged firmly in the mind's capacity to forge associations, analogy brought the truth claims of experimental science uncomfortably close to the rhetorical techniques – metaphor, simile, allegory, personification – by which art deceives the senses. In *Loves*, Darwin proposes a formal solution to this conceptual problem: He bifurcates science and literature structurally, setting them against each other in the composite form of the annotated poem and marking their difference on the printed page.

This chapter borrows its title from Maurice Merleau-Ponty, who begins *Prose of the World* with the claim that "we all secretly venerate the ideal of a language that in the last analysis would deliver us from language by delivering us to things."[10] What Merleau-Ponty sees as a universal desire I take as an Enlightenment legacy to Romanticism, one made palpable in Darwin's verse–prose composite. While striving to demarcate his strict, analogical prose from the figurative instabilities of verse, Darwin's text ultimately broadcasts the impossibility of sustaining this opposition. Built from the same materials, the "ratiocination of philosophy" inevitably leaps across the typographic boundary to become a metaphor in the verse. In embracing the rhetorical play of allegorical verse as an aesthetics parallel to analogical science, Darwin's work of containment ultimately undoes its own formally demarcated boundaries – the ideal of precise, unadorned prose delivers us, predictably, not to things but back into language itself. The result is a work that strives to uphold the synthetic capacity of analogy while continuously releasing the strict analogies of experimental science into the play of figurative verse. In *The Economy of Vegetation* – composed after he had completed *Loves* – Darwin begins to consider how to solve the destabilization of analogy he had produced formally in his first long poem. Drawing on Francis Bacon's treatment of classical mythology as allegories of scientific knowledge, Darwin proposes the hieroglyph as a conduit between truth and figure, science and art. This alternative approach – which reimagines allegory as an emblem of the lost knowledge of nature rather than a rhetorical art of illusion – came to guide Darwin's final poem, *The Temple of Nature*, a totalizing vision of life from generation and sexual reproduction to the development of the mind and civil society. *The Temple of Nature* is Darwin's final answer to the problem of induction, reasserting analogy's synthetic capacity by revealing fact masquerading as figure.

While I trace Darwin's thinking on induction through three major poems in this chapter, *Loves* was his first attempt to conceptualize the relationship between experimental science and aesthetics, and for me it remains his most important work. Aside from its incredible popularity in the 1790s – it was read, discussed, and quoted by all of the other authors I treat in this study – the text synthesized much of conventional eighteenth-century thought on the prose style and methods appropriate to experimental science. At the same time, it put forward a poetics based on existing aesthetic theory, but one that remakes eighteenth-century concepts of the way art works on the viewer to produce deceptive reverie, the centrality of visualization to poetry, and how poetry cultivates fanciful similitudes. Whatever Darwin's intensions, the text's composite form exposes the methodological and theoretical debates it is entering. Of equal importance for my succeeding chapters, Darwin's text opened the door to a slew of questions about the place of induction in moral philosophy, aesthetics, and literature: What are the implications of transferring a method of enquiry from one sphere of knowledge production to another? Can one methodology successfully, as Bacon suggested, be applied to *everything*? What kind of poetics would be conformable to the episteme of experimental science?

What happens – formally and conceptually – when an inductive process of composition becomes visible in the layout of the printed page? What are the epistemological and aesthetic consequences of the verse–prose composites that become so popular in succeeding decades? For the next generation of authors, Darwin's verse–prose composite supplied a model for how literature might negotiate – more or less successfully – the methodological legacy of experimental science and empiricist moral philosophy. It also raised questions about the inductive method of literary composition that would plague Darwin's successors.

Plain Style and the Annotated Poem

However odd it may appear at first glance, Darwin's *The Botanic Garden . . . A Poem with Philosophical Notes* is not unique in eighteenth-century poetry. The period saw a veritable explosion of long poems on "scientific" topics, ranging from the structure of the universe to animal husbandry to the cultivation of sugar cane in the West Indies.[11] These poems generally fit into one of two traditions. Many – including John Philips' *Cyder* (1708), James Thomson's *The Seasons* (1730), John Dyer's *The Fleece* (1757), and Grainger's *The Sugar Cane* (1764) – emulated Virgil's *Georgics*, which Darwin cites as a "much admired" piece of didactic poetry (*LP*, p. 43). Another set of "philosophical poems" take their impetus from Lucretius' *De Rerum Natura* and its seventeenth- and eighteenth-century imitations in Latin and English.[12] While brief annotations of place names or passages from classical authors were common in eighteenth-century georgics, only Grainger's West Indian poem includes annotations on the scale of Darwin's. Grainger's notes detail his first-hand observations of local geography, flora, fauna, soil, and climate, coupled with disquisitions on colonial history and medical treatments for common diseases.

While he may have known Grainger's work, Darwin's annotation practice (like his choice to write in heroic couplets) was more likely rooted in early eighteenth-century philosophical poems. The second edition of Henry Baker's *The Universe, A Philosophical Poem, intended to Restrain the Pride of Man* (1746), for example, likely borrowed its generic label from *Creation, a Philosophical Poem* (1708) by Sir Richard Blackmore (a work modeled on Lucretius but stridently opposed to his Epicurean philosophy), but the massive apparatus of footnotes in *The Universe* connects it to a more famous contemporary work, Pope's *An Essay on Man* (1734). If William Creech's heavily annotated translation of Lucretius (1682) initiated a vogue for philosophical poems in English, Pope authorized the

trend. The expanded 1745 edition of *An Essay on Man* included notes by
William Warburton based on an earlier impassioned defense of the poem.
Warburton's first note extends Pope's title to define the genre, labeling the
poem "a Philosophical Enquiry into [Man's] Nature and End, Passions and
Pursuits."[13]

In *The Loves of the Plants*, Darwin couples the georgic's stated didactic end with the heroic couplets and speculative notes of the philosophical poem.[14] But *Loves* diverges dramatically from both traditions. Unlike
earlier philosophical poems, Darwin's allegorical verse – in which nymphs
and swains stand in for the sexual organs of plants – does not overtly pro-
pound an ethical system or theological position. The poem's machinery
replicates that of Pope's *Rape of the Lock* and it is possible, as I discuss
below, to read Darwin's verse as social satire; however, his notes are not
of the *Dunciad Variorum* variety. Like those appended to Grainger's georgic, they eschew satirical jabs in favor of serious scientific and historical
content. While claiming a pedagogical end similar to that of the georgic,
Darwin's verse–note combination teaches its lessons in quite a different
way. Grainger offers advice and admonition directly to the reader: "Let sun
and rain mature thy deep-hoed land" and "Planter, improvement is the
child of time."[15] In contrast, Darwin's lines explaining the order and class
of vernal grass read, "*Two* gentle shepherds and their sister wives/With thee
ANTHOXA! lead ambrosial lives" (*LP*, I: 85–86). The name of the plant
is given in all caps, and the italicized *two* refers to the plant's class (Dian-
dria, two stamens) within the Linnaean binomial system of classification.
The characteristics of the order are further detailed in the accompanying
footnote. Any sequence of couplets is thus mediated by the overarching
allegorical structure of the text, in which the footnotes serve as a "key" to
images in the verse. If Darwin's poem has a didactic end, that end *requires*
the notes; the notes are an integral part of the text, not (as is the case with
Warburton's annotations to *An Essay on Man*) a paratext "dedicated to the
service of something other than itself that constitutes its raison d'être."[16]

The centrality of the notes to Darwin's poem has led many critics to take
his statement of its design at face value and flip the text–paratext relation:
the playful, amorous verse is merely a "vestibule," an entranceway to the
"ratiocination of philosophy" contained in the prose notes.[17] Darwin himself promoted this view explicitly in the Advertisement, which claims that
the work aims to lead *from* poetry *to* the ratiocination of philosophy. When
the text is read in this direction, the tonal and stylistic rift between verse
depiction and prose description becomes both striking and obvious, as we
move from "With charms despotic fair CHONDRILLA reigns, / O'er the

soft hearts of *five* fraternal swains" (*LP*, I: 97–98) to "[t]he numerous flo-
rets, which constitute the disk of the flowers of this class, contain in each
five males surrounding one female, which are connected at top, whence the
name of the class" (*LP*, p. 11). The prose conspicuously lacks the adjectival
modifiers – the poetic diction – so abundant in the verse, replacing them
with a string of prepositional clauses. If *Economy* achieves a greater continuity between image and explanation,[18] *Loves* appears calculated to focus
attention on a fundamental stylistic disparity between ornamented verse
and stripped-down prose. The question of primacy – does the verse exist
merely to introduce the prose, or does the prose explain the verse? – seems
less pressing than the question of why Darwin so emphatically differentiates poetry from prose. Further, contrary to the logic inherent to both
of his source genres, why does he use the form of the annotated poem to
amplify this disparity?[19]

We might begin to address this question by locating the source of Darwin's claim that "science is best delivered in prose." As Pope put it in *An
Essay on Man*, it is difficult to treat a philosophical subject too "*poetically*,
without sacrificing Perspicuity to Ornament, without wandering from the
Precision, and breaking the Chain of Reasoning."[20] Darwin takes this
observation a step further, arguing that a "superfluity of poetic ornament"
will "enervate" prose, making it "tedious and impertinent" particularly
"in graver works, where we expect to be instructed rather than amused"
(*LP*, p. 42). In these statements, Pope and Darwin voice a well-established
link between clear, concise, strong prose and the ideal presentation of scientific knowledge. The best-known statement of this position occurs in
Thomas Sprat's *History of the Royal Society* (1667): to combat the "mists
and uncertainties" that "specious *Tropes* and *Figures* have brought on our
Knowledge," the society has adopted

> a constant Resolution, to reject all the amplifications, digressions, and
> swellings of style: to return to the primitive purity, and shortness, when
> men deliver'd so many *things*, almost in equal number of *words*. They have
> exacted from all their members, a close, naked, natural way of speaking; pos-
> itive expressions; clearness; a native easiness: bringing all things as near the
> Mathematical plainness, as they can.[21]

Sprat drew this idealized portrait of the Royal Society's "manner of Discourse" from Bacon's pronouncements in the *Novum Organum*. The first
step of Bacon's method for the Interpretation of Nature involves collecting
particular observations into natural histories. As Bacon suggests, in order
to gather a store of things on which to perform induction, one must first

lay aside all "citations or testimonies of authors ... disputes and controversies and differing opinion; everything in short which is philological"
(*NO*, 254). Observations and experiments should be "set down briefly and
concisely" without recourse to "ornaments of speech, similitudes, trea-
sury of eloquence, and such like emptinesses" (*NO*, 254). Sprat turns
Bacon's suggestions into a mandate for the Royal Society, institutionalizing
the steady stream of prefatory exaltations of "plain style" in seventeenth-
century scientific and theological texts.[22] Darwin (like Pope before him)
was thus confronted with two seemingly contradictory traditions: the classical tradition of didactic poetry on scientific themes and seventeenth-
century disavowal of rhetorical ornament in the investigation of nature.

Barely below the surface of Sprat's pronouncement lies an abiding epistemological concern about language's capacity to capture and convey knowledge about physical reality. The divergence of *verba* and *res* is perhaps most
familiar from Locke's assessment that words "interpose themselves so much
between our understandings, and the truth" that an obscurity of definition
is likely to produce disorder in the mind.[23] The desire to bridge the gap
between words and things yielded various schemes in the seventeenth century, including the astronomer Seth Ward's proposition in the *Vindiciae
Academiarum* (1654) to reduce all language to a finite number of mathematical symbols. As Ward claimed, "Such a language as this (where every
word were a definition and contain'd the nature of the thing) might not
unjustly be termed a naturall Language."[24] Propositions of this ilk gave life
to Swift's parody of the Royal Society in *Gulliver's Travels*: one projector
in the school of languages proposes to reduce everything to nouns, while
another has devised a plan to abolish language entirely by requiring each
person to carry all the things necessary for conversation in packs on their
backs.[25]

Despite Swift's satiric jabs, the project of bringing words closer to things
recurred throughout the eighteenth century. Darwin's own proposal to
replace Latin words with English in his translation of Linnaeus's *Systema
Vegetabilium* fits within this lineage. As he suggested in a 1781 letter to
Joseph Banks in the initial stages of the project, "as the english language
bears compound words better than the latin, [the translators] hope to
express the meaning of Linnaeus ... with more precision in english, than
could be done latin."[26] In his Preface to the published translation, Darwin complains that William Withering's *Botanical Arrangement* of English
plants has not only left out (for the sake of propriety) the sexual distinctions
of Linnaeus's system, but has also "loaded the science with an addition of
new words."[27] Darwin then justifies his choice to retain Linnaeus's terms

(with English endings) with a familiar logic: since "new ideas require new words to represent them," the Latin is to be preferred because English words "would be liable to present to the mind the vulgar meaning, which is not sufficiently *precise* for the purposes of science."[28] The mandate for precise language – coupled with the consensus of forty prominent botanists Darwin consulted about his translation – forced him to argue for the clarity of introducing Latinisms into English.

Darwin's posthumously published composite text *The Temple of Nature* (1803) revisits this problem of linguistic precision. In the final footnote to the poem, Darwin meditates on the eventual expulsion of figurative language from daily life, suggesting that "as science improves and becomes more generally diffused, [modern languages] will gradually become more distinct and accurate than the ancient ones; as metaphors will cease to be necessary in conversation, and only be used as the ornaments of poetry."[29] Science would eventually purge prose of figures, allowing it to fully represent things themselves. The final words of Darwin's literary career constitute a dream of being delivered from metaphor – or at least containing it in its own sphere, that of poetry.

In this context, Darwin's choice of the annotated poem appears as an act of separation and containment: It allowed him to materialize these two distinct linguistic realms and keep them apart. On the upper half of the page, metaphor had free rein; on the lower half, the prose notes were accommodated to the precise representation of things by which scientific knowledge could be conveyed. The particular character of Darwin's science, however, made such a strict separation difficult, if not impossible, to sustain. In *The Botanic Garden*, Darwin seeks to legitimate a speculative, analogical science under the aegis of experimental philosophy – a goal commensurate with the reinvention of Baconian induction in eighteenth-century natural history.[30] As outlined in Chapter 1, the seventeenth-century project of an undirected accumulation of facts gave way to an eighteenth-century drive for synthesis by combining disparate observations and experimental results into a comprehensive totality. Running the gamut of contemporary scientific knowledge, Darwin's notes in *The Botanic Garden* mediate between a seemingly undirected accumulation of particulars that keeps science open to revision and the synthetic work of generating a complex web of analogical relations. Analogy, however, had its pitfalls, as contemporary philosophers were quick to point out. Grounded in the mind's propensity to forge associations, analogical reasoning could lead one to mistake rhetorical figures for relations of truth. By demarcating separate spaces for imaginative verse and analogical science, Darwin could, theoretically, contain the rhetorical play of figurative language. What happened in practice, however, was quite another matter.

"Knowledge Broken" and Strict Analogies

Seventeenth-century proponents of Bacon's method took his directives to heart, at least rhetorically.[31] To keep the Idols at bay, Bacon recommended collecting observations without discrimination, leaving nothing out that might contribute to the general heap of knowledge. The ordinary, familiar, filthy, trifling, things that have no use in themselves – all must be set forth, numbered, weighted, measured, and defined (*NO*, 258–59). This was, of course, the work exemplified in the *Philosophical Transactions*, a detailed record of observations and experiments contributed by many hands. In accordance with Bacon's prescription, the *Transactions* gathered up whatever came their way. Methodologically, the initial step of Baconian induction was, as Sprat suggested of Bacon's own natural history, "to take all that comes, then to choose; and to heap, rather, then to register."[32] Darwin had this directive in mind when he proposed forming a library of member's work in his presidential address to the newly formed Derby Philosophical Society in 1784. By publishing their own miscellaneous papers, the Society "may add something to the common Heap of knowledge; which I prophesy will never cease to accumulate, so long as human footstep is seen upon earth."[33]

For Bacon, the project of undifferentiated accumulation had a generic requirement. As he argued in *The Advancement of Learning* (1605), when knowledge "is delivered to be continued and spun upon by a succession of labors, [it] requireth a method whereby it may be transposed to another in the same manner as it was collected."[34] Bacon contrasts this communally produced knowledge to that which aimed "to teach and instruct for use and practice," which could be presented by a more "compendious" method. Pedagogy, in other words, requires the more expedient form of a summary, while the groundwork for induction must remain open for "re-examination and progression."[35] To preserve this openness, Bacon advocates writing in aphorisms, a form in which "the discourse of illustration is cut off; recitals of examples are cut off; discourse of connexion and order is cut off; descriptions of practice are cut off; ... Aphorisms, representing a knowledge broken, do invite men to enquire farther."[36] Unlike the closed system of knowledge presented in a treatise, aphorisms mirror the procedure of piecemeal accumulation. As a matter of course, Sprat celebrates the aphoristic form of the *Philosophical Transactions*. The "roving, and unsettled course" of their registers (where there is "seldom any reference of one matter to the next") proceeds from "a mature, and well grounded *premeditation*": by registering only histories and refusing to reduce the varied contents to a system, "they have left room for others, that shall succeed, to *change*, to *augment*, to *approve*, to *contradict* them, at their discretion."[37]

This ethos informs Darwin's presentation of science in *The Botanic Garden*. In the Apology to *Economy of Vegetation*, Darwin draws attention to the speculative nature of the science presented in his notes. While his conjectures are sometimes not "supported by accurate investigation or conclusive experiments," extravagant theories "are not without their use [where knowledge is imperfect]; as they encourage the execution of laborious experiments, or the investigation of ingenious deductions, to confirm or refute them" (*EV*, p. vii). Rather than a transgression of the methods of experimental science, Darwin imagines his conjectures as provocation to further observation and experiment. Presenting his speculations in disconnected footnotes and endnotes reinforces this agenda: like his epistolary exchanges with Wedgwood, James Watt, Boulton, and Richard Lovell Edgeworth, Darwin envisioned his notes as dialogic, engaged in a multi-sided conversation that would generate new experiments. To provoke readers to "enquire farther," Darwin poses direct questions: Very early in *Loves*, he queries, "perhaps all the products of nature are in their progress to greater perfection?" (*LP*, p. 7). The mimosa or sensitive plant raises a more specific question: If the situation of the leaves "after being exposed to external violence resembles their sleep ... may it not be owing to a numbness or paralysis consequent to too violent irritation, like the faintings of animals from pain or fatigue?" (*LP*, p. 25). Alongside such direct queries, Darwin's conditionals ("may," "seems," "perhaps," "might") continually remind his reader not to take the information presented in the notes at face value. More than a pedagogical device, the prose annotations cultivate a communal model of interaction and exchange grounded in the Baconian ideal of growing knowledge out of knowledge broken. Darwin's text is fundamentally invested in a model of scientific enquiry lodged in the steps of induction; the result is an open, incremental movement toward the formulation of the principles of organic life.

Working within this model, Darwin's notes compile the most up-to-date information on physics, galvanism, chemistry, geology, and mechanics along with botany and natural history – information drawn from current scientific dictionaries, the *Philosophical Transactions*, and his own correspondence. The notes to *Loves* and *Economy* cite, quote, and paraphrase works across a wide range of fields by a multinational cast of authors. In the first canto of *Loves*, for example, Darwin cites Colin Milne's *Botanical Dictionary* (1775); *A Discourse Concerning the Irritability of Some Flowers*, translated from the work of the Italian botanist Giovambatista dal Colvolo and published by Dodsley in 1767; and Michel Adanson's *Voyage to Senegal, the Isle of Goree, and the River Gambia* (London: J. Nourse, 1759), translated from the French (*LP*, pp. 9, 11, 16). In the first 20 pages of *Economy*, he cites Buffon's description of the Siam pig from volume 6 of *L'Histoire Naturelle* (1755); John Herschel's description of Mars in volume 74 of the *Philosophical Transactions of the Royal Society* (1784); Antoine Lavoisier's *Traité élémentaire de chimie* (1789) on the chemical composition of air; Darwin's own article on the mechanical expansion of air at high altitudes in volume 78 of the *Philosophical Transactions* (1778); and experiments on phosphorus by Jacopo Bartolomeo Beccari translated by Benjamin Wilson and published by Dodsley in 1775 (*EV*, pp. 8, 9, 11, 16, 17). Darwin also collected material from sources other than published works. While working on the notes, he often asked his friends, medical acquaintances, and other members of the Lunar Society to supply details on their current research and inventions. Darwin's letter to Watt in November 1789, for example, requests information on the steam engine for the note on p. 26 of *Economy*.[38] A letter to Boulton in December 1789 pleads for more information, specifically on Boulton's application of the steam engine to coining; Boulton's extended reply supplied material for lines 253–96 of Canto 1, the note on p. 29, and Additional Note XI in *Economy*.[39] Like his communal approach to knowledge production, Darwin's compositional method is inductive: he accumulates material from various sources and uses it to build the poem–note composite.

Darwin's notes strove to be cutting-edge and comprehensive, but his compositional method produced a piecemeal text: although he included many cross references, related information might appear hundreds of pages later in a note to something completely different, and issues raised in the footnotes were often continued or amplified in long endnotes. The overall effect of the annotations is certainly that of an unorganized heap of broken knowledge, but individual notes often adhere to a discernable progression modeled after the steps of induction. For example, a note in *Economy* on *Gymnotus* (a South American fish, as he designated it, that generates an electric field) first details facts about the characteristics of the fish from experience (Darwin's own and that of others) and then turns to the specific description of its organs provided by John Hunter in the *Philosophical Transactions* (*EV*, p. 20). Description gives way to an experiment detailing how electricity is accumulated on the surface of a Leyden jar, and, more particularly, the relation between the thinness of the glass and the amount of electricity condensable on the surface. Darwin then returns to the "real world" object – the fish – reasoning by analogy that "if an animal membrane, as thin as the silk-worm spins silk, could be so situated as to be charged like the Leyden bottle, without bursting, (as such thin glass would be liable to do), it would be difficult to calculate the immense quantity of electric fluid, which might be accumulated on its surface" (*EV*, p. 20). In its movement from observation to experiment to analogy, Darwin's note follows the trajectory definitive of inductive method in the period. As Humphry Davy succinctly put it in his *Elements of Chemical Philosophy* (1812), "by observation, facts are distinctly and minutely impressed on the mind. By analogy, similar facts are connected. By experiment, new facts are discovered; and, in the progression of knowledge, observation, guided by analogy, leads to experiment, and analogy confirmed by experiment, becomes scientific truth."[40]

While Darwin stops short of affirming truth – it would indeed be "difficult to calculate" without performing further experiments on the fish itself – the procedure mapped in his notes is rooted in the eighteenth-century desire to move beyond collection and arrangement to, as Buffon put it in 1748, "something grander and more dignified ... the combination of observations, the generalization of facts, linking them together by the power of analogies."[41] Reasoning by analogy, as critics have noted, is the foundation of Darwin's scientific and philosophical position across all of his works.[42] More specifically, Darwin adopts the long-standing "botanical analogy" – the analogy between animals and plants central to Linnaean taxonomy – in many of the notes to *Loves*.[43] To take one example, when describing the floating mechanism of the seaweed *Ulva*, Darwin suggests that "the air-bladders of fish seem to be similar organs, and serve to render them buoyant in the water" (*LP*, p. 34). This comparison yields a second, that of "seed vessels distended with air" that "seem to be analogous to the air-vessel at the broad end of the egg" (*LP*, p. 34). In both comparisons, the common feature is an enclosed space holding air, but Darwin differentiates them by use: The bladders of fish and seaweed allow them to float, while the air pockets in the seed vessel and egg likely serve to aid respiration. The connection in each set of instances is thus forged on the basis of function rather than external resemblance.

As Michel Foucault has argued, comparison underwent a transformation in the seventeenth century, shifting from the work of revealing a world of infinite resemblances to become a function of mental ordering and analysis.[44] As a result, analogy could be claimed as the "ground of philosophical reasoning" in eighteenth-century natural and moral philosophy. Compiling a litany of authorities, Dugald Stewart pinpoints the conventional definition: Analogy is properly "a resemblance between things *with regard to some circumstances or effects*"; quoting Adam Ferguson, Stewart continues, "things which have no resemblance to each other may nevertheless be analogous; analogy consisting in a resemblance of relations."[45] Stewart draws a well-established example from Ferguson, "the analogy between the fin of a fish and the wing of a bird; the fin bearing the same relation to water which the wing does to air."[46] Darwin's analogy between air vessels in plants and fish bladders is of the same ilk: they stand in the same relation to flotation, even though one is a leaf formation and the other an internal organ. This kind of analogical reasoning led Coleridge to celebrate Darwin's work as the first step in remaking botany into a science of relations. Rather than subscribing to an older "chain of being" model (in which the highest-order plant most closely resembles the lowest-order animal), Darwin had suggested a relation of "corresponding opposites" between plant and animal realms (*F*, 1: 470). With a mind formed by observation but unaided by "partial experiment," Darwin glimpsed what would later become clear to minds capable of "demonstrating its objective truth by induction of facts in an unbroken series of correspondences in nature" (*F*, 1: 470).[47] For Coleridge, Darwin's speculative linking in *The Botanic Garden* initiated, but could not bring to fruition, the renovation of botanical science.

In his partial recuperation of Darwin's speculative botany, Coleridge finds fault in how Darwin used experiment in his analogical science. In the above case of *Gymnotus*, for example, Darwin draws an analogy between the glass surface of the Leyden jar and the fish's skin, postulating that we can account for the high degree of electrical current condensed on the exterior membrane by analogy to the way increasingly thinner glass collects greater quantities of electricity. In place of the "botanical analogy" between plant and animal, Darwin puts forward a relation based on an experiment. While this may seem an appropriate use of analogy according to Davy's definition, his explanation of inductive method suggests otherwise. To show how observation, analogy, and experiment work in tandem to yield scientific truth, Davy begins by drawing the reader's attention to the air globules that form on submerged vegetable filaments when exposed to light – this is an observation. He then describes an experiment for collecting the air produced by the filaments and testing its "purity" (meaning oxygen content) with a candle. Finally, he suggests "the inquirer reasons by *analogy*" if "the question is put, whether all vegetables of this kind, in fresh and salt water, do not produce such air under like circumstances."[48] In this instance, we see Davy employing analogy in a very limited sense: analogies are connections made in the mind and thus are speculative, but they must be drawn between things of the *same* kind under *like* circumstances. The relation between the Leyden jar's glass surface and *Gymnotus*'s skin does not qualify as a legitimate analogy in this limited sense – neither object nor circumstance is preserved in the movement from external nature to experimental situation.

Darwin's notes are largely comprised of this more capacious and tenuous type of analogy, a variety of reasoning that drew admonition from his contemporaries. As Stewart commented on the resemblance of relations in the fin–wing analogy,

> This definition is more particularly luminous, when applied to the analogies which are the foundation of the rhetorical figures of metaphor and allusion; and it applies also very happily to those which the fancy delights to trace between the material and the intellectual worlds; and which (as I have repeatedly observed), are so apt to warp the judgment in [its speculations] concerning the phenomena of the human mind.[49]

As Catherine Packham has shown, Stewart was voicing a common objection to analogical reasoning. Citing George Campbell and Thomas Reid – also, like Stewart, part of the Scottish Enlightenment movement employing inductive method to study the mind – Packham argues that analogy was seen as eminently suited to poetry by being evocative of the pleasure the mind receives in perceiving correspondences. By the same token, analogy was patently dangerous when used in natural philosophy because of its propensity to present as true what might be merely metaphor.[50]

Darwin was clearly aware of this long-standing critique of analogy, and he makes a distinction very like Stewart's in the Preface to his medical treatise *Zoonomia* (1794–96):

> The great CREATOR of all things has infinitely diversified the works of his hands, but has at the same time stamped a certain similitude on the features of nature, that demonstrates to us, that *the whole is one family of one parent*. On this similitude is founded all rational analogy; which, so long as it is concerned in comparing the essential properties of bodies, leads us to many and important discoveries; but when with licentious activity it links together objects, otherwise discordant, by some fanciful similitude; it may indeed collect ornaments for wit and poetry, but philosophy and truth recoil from its combinations.[51]

The usefulness of analogy in scientific writing, Darwin insists, turns on the distinction between "essential properties" and "fanciful similitude." However, as his own rhetorical flourish demonstrates, this boundary was difficult to maintain: the passage begins with a fanciful figure, the "face of nature" revealing the family resemblance of its figurative offspring. In the act of enforcing distinction, Darwin has grounded rational analogy in a metaphor akin to the verse allegories of *The Loves of the Plants*.

This condition – in which the foundation of philosophical truth tips over into fanciful figure – constitutes a defining trait of Darwin's verse–note composite in *Loves*. I'll take as my example an extreme case, Darwin's description of "Polypodium Barometz," a fern native to China. The lines depicting the fern display a curious interplay of metaphors. The section begins as follows:

> E'en round the pole the flames of Love aspire,
> And icy bosoms feel the *secret* fire! –
> Cradled in snow and fan'd by arctic air
> Shines, gentle BAROMETZ! thy golden hair;
> Rooted in earth each cloven hoof descends,
> And round and round her flexible neck she bends;
> Crops the grey coral moss, and hoary thyme,
> Or laps with rosy tongue the melting rime;
> Eyes with mute tenderness her distant dam,
> Or seems to bleat, a *Vegetable Lamb*.
>
> (*LP*, I: 247–56)

The note follows suit, proceeding through a series of analogies: A fern with "some resemblance to a Lamb" is "everywhere cover'd with the most soft and dense wool, intensely yellow"; this "thick downy clothing ... seems designed to protect them from the injuries of the cold, like the wool of animals" (*LP*, p. 24). Already the analogy is working at three levels: that of visual resemblance between fern and lamb, that of a likeness of function between plant covering and sheep covering, and that of linguistic equivalence (plant "wool" is "like" animal "wool"). This conflation of botanical analogy with simile is reinforced by a reference to the name given the plant by Sir Hans Sloane – the "Tartarian Lamb" – and to the "curious print of it, much resembling a sheep" included in the 1786 edition of John Evelyn's *Terra* (*LP*, p. 24). A later edition of Darwin's works includes an illustration based on the plate in Alexander Hunter's edition of Evelyn (Fig. 5).

Darwin's rhetorical playfulness in the verse, it would seem, infiltrates the note, wreaking havoc on the relation of function between the fern's

Fig. 5 Illustration of Barometz, Erasmus Darwin, *The Works of Erasmus Darwin, containing The Botanic Garden in two parts, and The Temple of Nature*, 3 vols. (London, 1806), facing p. 37. Courtesy of Beinecke Rare Book and Manuscript Library, Yale University.

yellow covering and the sheep's wool. This condition was to a large degree inevitable because Darwin followed an inductive method of composition, building his imagery and notes from the same sources. Like his notes, the verse was a fabric of observations and experiments recorded in his Commonplace Book and correspondence, as well as excerpts from the *Philosophical Transactions*, scientific dictionaries, and other publications. Manufactured from the same stuff, the note's strict analogies have no choice but to leap the generic boundary – materialized in the typographic difference in font size and white space between the text blocks – to become rhetorical figures in the verse (Fig. 1). Darwin is aware of this condition – as the linguistic play on wool in the note suggests – but he is not, I would argue, purposefully undermining the foundation of his analogical science. While registering the figurative language of poetry, in the notes Darwin seeks to neutralize the effects of rhetorical play by embedding his analogies in a chain of observation and experiment that conform to inductive method.

Let me explain this strategy further. After the matrix of analogies quoted above, Darwin introduces a series of linked experimental results. Noting that the plants' "clothing" seems designed to protect them from the cold, he provides an explanation: "those bodies which are bad conductors of electricity, are also bad conductors of heat, as glass, wax, air" (*LP*, pp. 24–25). Reasoning from an experimentally confirmed fact – it was well known that glass, wax, and air did not conduct electricity – Darwin lends support to a new analogy. He then supplies the experimental evidence: Wax or glass can be "melted by the flame of a blow-pipe very near the fingers which hold it, without burning them," and thus air "being confined on the surface of animal bodies, in the interstices of their fur or wool, prevents the escape of their natural warmth" (*LP*, p. 25). Bad conductors are good insulators, so trapped air functions similarly to wax.[52] The playful conflations of the note's opening have been re-inscribed within a set of verifiable experimental results, raising them above mere rhetoric. Darwin has, in other words, used one type of analogy – one conformable to the procedures of experimental science – to give real substance to relations of function, resemblance, and naming.

This evidence has not, of course, proven that the fern's "wool" protects it from the cold. The reader must accept the "botanical analogy" between animal wool and plant covering for the above experiment to have meaning within the context of Darwin's discussion of *Barometz*. To substantiate this broader relation, Darwin extends the note's analogical reasoning even further. After mentioning that whale blubber seems designed to serve the same purpose as animal fur, Darwin suggests that snow protects vegetables from frost because "it is a bad conductor of heat itself and contains much air in its pores" (*LP*, p. 25). This observation is again confirmed by experiment:

> If a piece of camphor be immersed in a snow-ball except one extremity of it, on setting fire to this, as the snow melts the water becomes absorbed into the surrounding snow by capillary attraction; on this account when living animals are burry'd in snow, they are not moistened by it; but the cavity enlarges as the snow dissolves, affording them both a dry and warm habitation. (*LP*, p. 25)

In this second series of analogies, the experiment mediates between two observations, confirming that snow works to insulate both vegetables and animals. Experiment thus confirms the larger umbrella analogy between plants and animals, which in turn suggests that the fern's "wool" might express a more than figurative relation. By translating the initial linguistic punning of a plant that is called a lamb into relations supported by observation and experiment, Darwin deflects analogy's potential to "warp the judgment." He has, in effect, turned metaphor into a matter of fact. By structuring his notes to mirror the legitimate procedure of scientific enquiry Darwin would secure his analogical science from the licentious activity of poetry.

Returning now to the opening lines of the verse, we can see how the metaphor of burning passion in an icy bosom prefigures the note's conclusions. The poetic lines introduce the concept that being "cradled in snow" will insulate the fern and protect it from the cold, keeping its love-flame alive. The piling up of "strict" analogies in the note thus explains why "E'en round the pole the Flames of Love aspire," while the personification – Barometz with the golden locks – figures forth the experiment with camphor, an experiment that reclaims analogy from its devolution into fanciful associations. The result depends on the directionality of reading: When burning passion becomes burning camphor, the note's inductive method has exposed the truth hidden in language – words are as hieroglyphs of things (a possibility Darwin would later take quite seriously, as I suggest in this chapter's conclusion). When burning camphor becomes burning passion, ratiocination is again opened to the charge of taking superficial connections for philosophical truths. The very generic choice that allows Darwin to demarcate and differentiate between prose and verse also displays the impossibility of maintaining the separation between fact and figure.

In his attempt to manufacture the boundary between ratiocination and rhetoric – a boundary materially present on virtually every page of the book – Darwin produces the precise conflation of truth and figure that he set out to counteract. The notes follow an inductive process, plotting the movement from observation to experiment to analogy that should yield scientific truth. However, having remade this series into a loosely linked series of fanciful relations in the verse, the synthetic work of the prose note is undermined by the loose analogies of fancy, destabilizing the inductive chain of ratiocination. This back and forth between consolidation and undoing continues until the text concludes. Put bluntly, Darwin's attempt to contain the work of figuration is undermined by the way his compositional process inheres in the structure of his text.

The question of what should be given primacy – verse or note – appears to depend on the directionality of reading. Allowing Darwin's objective to be the growth and dissemination of scientific knowledge, verse appears as the supplement of prose, "adding only to replace," revealing what experimental philosophy would rhetorically maneuver to hide about itself – the impossibility of attaining a language perfectly reflective of things.[53] However, if verse retains its ostensible position as the primary text, we see something else. The notes substantiate the loose analogies of verse, uncovering their hidden meaning and legitimating each by relation to another, *ad infinitum*. It is by the heaping up of analogies in the note that we come to know that the fern's wool signifies beyond the metaphorical. How we judge the effect of Darwin's verse–prose composite depends on where we position him on Foucault's continuum: Is he a typical Enlightenment figure unwittingly undermining the ground of his own position, or a Renaissance throwback, engaged in "restoring the great unbroken plain of words and things"?[54]

It is too easy, I think, to stop here. Regardless of the instabilities resulting from the composite form, Darwin used this structure to put forward a specific relationship between science and aesthetics. Rather than casting verse as a medium, outgrowth, ground, or subversion of his analogical science, the Interludes in *Loves* suggest the philosophical notes will find their "corresponding antithesis" in the allegorical poem.[55] In the Interludes, Darwin presents poetry not as the handmaiden, nor as the supplement, to science, but as a science in its own right – a field of knowledge with its own style, methods, and goals. Constituting an aesthetic treatise in the empiricist tradition, the Interludes set forth parameters for artistic production that run parallel to those of experimental science, but are nonetheless distinct from it. Read through the Interludes and Advertisement, the text of *Loves* essentially bifurcates the work of analogy into two versions of induction: an analytical method of producing true, precise knowledge of the world, and an allegorical method of producing the pleasurable deceptions of art. Thus, even as the boundary Darwin draws between plain prose and figurative verse is continually – inevitably – transgressed, his aesthetic theory mollifies the epistemological threats figurative language posed to experimental philosophy by promoting allegory as the antithetical counterpart to an experimental, analogical science.

The Aesthetics of Allegory

Barometz's golden hair and fiery passion emblematize the structuring principle of *Loves*: Personification produces the larger framework of allegory between women and pistils, men and stamens. This simple equation is often complicated by what is being described. In the poem, Barometz begins as a woman, but, in tandem with the note, she becomes a "Vegetable lamb" (*LP*, I: 256). Even when the personification remains constant throughout a segment of verse, it is often entangled, as when the five stamens of Cinchona (Peruvian bark) hasten to "aid" the pistil-maid by chopping down the tree that they, together, comprise (*LP*, II: 388–90). In *Loves*, the personified pistils (and, to a lesser degree, the stamens) are both objects and agents; they represent a specific order of plant within the system of Linnaean taxonomy while also taking on the characters of a submissive wife, seductress, gothic heroine, teacher, nurse, sorceress, child murderer, and so on. The plant's characteristics – Papyrus was the first paper, Foxglove cures dropsy, the berries of *Menispermum* intoxicate fish – lend the maids their personalities, linking the processes of external nature to the workings of human psychology.

As such, the allegoric structure of *Loves* acts in concert with Darwin's later works, particularly the posthumously published *Temple of Nature*, which propounds "a single sustained theory of the material basis of the formation of the universe and, finally, of the human psyche and social organization."[56] As Martin Priestman suggests, Darwin's vision in *Temple* was closely linked to the theories of Scottish Enlightenment thinkers such as Joseph Black, Adam Smith, Hume, and Reid and their application of the method of experimental philosophy to the investigation of the mind, language development, and the progress of society.[57] As Hume put it in his *Treatise of Human Nature*, the "Science of Man" was grounded in the empiricist approach to moral subjects recommended by Bacon and initiated by Locke's *Essay concerning Human Understanding*.[58] According to Bacon, inductive method should embrace not only natural philosophy, but likewise

> the other sciences, logic, ethics, and politics, should be carried out by [inductive] method ... For I form a history and tables of discovery for anger, fear, shame, and the like; for matters political; and again for the mental operations of memory, composition and division, judgment and the rest; not less for heat and cold, or light, or vegetation, or the like. (*NO* 112)

If memory, politics, and vegetation could be investigated using the same method, then mind and matter implicitly arose from a common cause – from "*one parent*," as Darwin put it in *Zoonomia*, who stamped a similitude on the features of nature. The allegory of pistils and maids might, then, speak the truth of human nature.

A number of critics have argued (implicitly or explicitly) for understanding the structure of *Loves* in this way. As Bewell notes, Linnaean botany created a "wide analogical thoroughfare between plants and humans," which, Tim Fulford suggests, prompted Darwin to try "to explain human nature by analogy with plant reproduction."[59] This idea underwrites much of the criticism of the poem's gender politics: By personifying the sexual system of Linnaean taxonomy in his verse, Darwin amplified the sociosexual implications of botany, producing a commentary on gender norms and sexuality. For example, when the heterogeneity of plant sexuality is anthropomorphized in the poem, Fredrika Teute suggests, "the resulting plethora of alternative sexual liaisons smothered any normative heterosexual, monogamous model" of sexuality, implicitly calling into question "the artificiality and restrictiveness of monogamous marriage."[60] Other critics have come to quite different conclusions. Rather than sexual liberation for its female reader, Ann Shteir has argued that Darwin's poem "naturalizes conventional sexual politics" with images "polarized between the chaste, blushing virgin and the seductive, predatory woman."[61] In either case, sociosexual commentary begins when the poem's maids are imbued with the characteristics of plants, or, put another way, when the taxonomic system of Linnaean botany becomes a principle for understanding human sexuality. Reading *Loves* as a commentary on human sexuality thus relies on seamless transition from the science in the notes to the figures in the verse. The personifications embody the consonance of matter and mind that conjoins Darwin's science to a materialist psychology.

En route to Darwin's aesthetic theory, I want to pause for a moment to consider what kind of conclusions this model of reading yields. I'll focus on a typical two-line couplet from early in Canto I, which (along with the striking scene of Tahitian marriage that concludes Canto IV) supplies most of the examples in the above readings. Between Turmeric and Iris, we meet Alcea: "With vain desires the pensive ALCEA burns,/And, like sad ELOISA, loves and mourns" (*LP*, I: 69–70). By way of simile, Alcea is likened to the eponymous heroine of Pope's "Eloisa to Abelard," cloistered in her convent cell and burning with once illicit and now impossible passion (her lover, Abelard, having been castrated by her family). Within the analogy between woman and pistil, Darwin's note informs the reader of their shared problem: in the Double Hollyhock, "the petals become so numerous as totally to exclude the stamens, or males," leaving the pistil unpollinated (*LP*, p. 8). In the movement from verse to note, Darwin translates Alcea's burning desire into something about which botanical science can produce knowledge: there were just too many petals in the way.

Written in Eloisa's voice as an epistle to Abelard, Pope's poem is a study in emotional turmoil, tracing Eloisa's mental acrobatics as she denies, embraces, and attempts to understand her burning passion. As a literary figure for Alcea's situation, Eloisa introduces all the complexity and indeterminacy of feeling. While Pope's verse plays on this irresolution, Darwin invokes Eloisa's overheated mind while inscribing its frantic motions within an empiricist epistemology. As Darwin's note explains, the hollyhock's "double flower, so much admired by the florists are termed by the botanist vegetable monsters" (*LP*, p. 8). Moving from external nature to human nature, Alcea the double Hollyhock renders Eloisa's plight transparent and comprehensible by empiricist moral philosophy: she embodies the monstrosity of magnified femininity. Read in the other direction, however, the multiplication of petals preventing sexual reproduction might represent Eloisa's family and the couplet thus appears to advocate consummating desire against the wishes of one's restrictive parents – until we come back to the consequences of these actions (castration and the convent), which appear (in Darwin's long list of other vegetable monsters) as the naturalized outcome of socially illicit actions.

This brief analysis raises a question of intention and agenda. Did Darwin set out to naturalize the antiquated, gothic situation of Pope's "Eloisa to Abelard"? A kindred passage from *Economy* sheds light on this question. The section begins by describing the fire nymphs as agents of chemical processes: "Nymphs! you disjoin, unite, condense, expand / And give new wonders to the Chemist's hand" (*EV*, I: 223–24). A series of examples culminates when the Nymphs "mark with shining letters KUNKEL's name / In the pale Phosphor's self-consuming flame" (*EV*, I: 231–32). To illustrate the "slow combustion" of phosphorus (produced experimentally by Johann Kunckel in 1668 and described in a note), Darwin supplies a simile:

> So the chaste heart of some enchanted Maid
> Shines with insidious light, by Love betray'd;
> Round her pale bosom plays the young Desire,
> And slow she wastes by self-consuming fire.
> (*EV*, I: 233–36)

The conjunction "so" (a poetic technique I will return to momentarily) seems to substantiate an analogy between chemical process and feeling heart: just as phosphorus eventually burns itself out, the lovelorn maid will eventually be consumed by her secret desire. But can we really understand the flames of desire in the same way as the production of "light from putrid fish, as from the heads of haddocks" (*EV*, Additional Notes, p. 19)? There is something tongue-in-cheek in introducing the enchanted Maid into the chemical decomposition of matter. Rather than amplifying philosophical relations, the verse "links together objects, otherwise discordant" with a fanciful similitude: physically luminous fish heads conjoined to the metaphorically luminous desiring heart.[62] We are, Darwin reminds us, in poetry's domain of licentious activity.

Read via the phosphoric maid in *Economy*, Alcea illuminates a fundamental condition of Darwin's allegorical verse. As Theresa Kelley aptly puts it, in allegory "there is always an irreducible difference between allegorical representation and its referent."[63] Alcea figures forth the characteristics of the hollyhock – specifically, the production of eunuchs – while remaining within the realm of representation: "She" does not stand in for an actual woman but rather, as the simile to Eloisa indicates, is a poetic device borrowed from the genre of amorous epistle. As Bewell notes, Darwin "draws on the overt artificiality of pastoral convention" (among others) in *Loves*,[64] and the maids often appear in overdetermined scenes of gothic horror or sentimental pathos, insistently voicing their status as conventional poetic figures. And this, I am suggesting, is what Darwin would like them to remain. This is not to say that contemporary reviews and modern critics are wrong to read the poem as a commentary on sexuality, for its subject matter – Linnaean botany itself – certainly invites such an interpretation. The structural allegory of *Loves*, however, does not ask us to travel down the thoroughfare between mind and matter, but rather continually draws our attention the artificial, arbitrary nature of the verse's personifications – their status as "loose analogies."

These loose analogies appear through the proliferation of epic or Homeric similes, the most common device in Darwin's poetic repertoire. Simile posits a likeness, but as Darwin argues in Interlude II of *Loves*, its representation "should not very accurately resemble the subject" because it would then "become a philosophical analogy, it would be ratiocination instead of poetry" (*LP*, p. 84). Homer serves as Darwin's exemplary case: "any one resembling feature seems to be with him a sufficient excuse for the introduction of this kind of digression; he then proceeds to deliver some agreeable poetry on this new subject, and thus converts every simile into a kind of short episode" (*LP*, p. 84). This description perfectly captures Darwin's use of simile: On the most tenuous of connections, he launches into a new subject and expatiates on it, sometimes at great length.

For example, let us return for a moment to the wooly fern Barometz. After the ten lines personifying Barometz first as an icy-bosomed maid and then as a Vegetable Lamb, Darwin introduces an extended Homeric simile:

– So, warm and buoyant in his oily mail,
Gambols on seas of ice the unwieldly Whale;
Wide-waving fins round floating islands urge
His bulk gigantic through the troubled surge;
With hideous yawn the flying shoals He seeks,
Or clasps with fringe of horn his massy cheeks;
Lifts o'er the tossing wave his nostrils bare,
And spouts pellucid columns into air;
The silvery arches catch the setting beams,
And transient rainbows tremble o'er the streams.
                              (*LP*, I: 257–66)

This long description finds its impetus in the note. In the midst of his discussion of imperfect conductors, Darwin suggests that the fat of whales "seems design'd for the same purpose of preventing the too sudden escape of the heat of the body in cold climates" (*LP*, p. 25). This analogy appears as a speculative aside in the catalog of experiments on conductivity and heat – although, of course, the relation of whale oil to wax would have been obvious to any eighteenth-century reader. The striking difference, however, is that while the note works to create a chain of experimentally verified relations, the verse cultivates rupture and digression. When the bleating vegetable lamb suddenly and unexpectedly yields a detailed description of the whale's hideous yawn and pellucid spouting, the relation is clearly presented as a product of fancy, not ratiocination.

Darwin's practice in verse conforms to his poetic theory, which itself conforms to eighteenth-century distinctions between imagination and judgment. As Locke suggests in the *Essay*, wit lies mainly in "the assemblage of ideas, and putting those together with quickness and variety, wherein can be found any resemblance or congruity, thereby to make up pleasant pictures, and agreeable visions in the fancy," while judgment "lies quite on the other side, in separating carefully, one from another, ideas, wherein can be found the least difference."[65] Drawing explicitly on Locke's distinction, William Beckford (in a long letter to his guardian Lord Thurlow in 1778) describes the imagination as a faculty that "delights to disjoin, or jumble [ideas] together with the wildest caprice, and cares not for method, or arrangement, or any thing else provided she holds up a Pleasant picture to the mind," while the judgment works "to marshal them in Order to examine their relation or disagreement, and to chain down each to its proper place."[66] While Beckford's point is to convict himself of indulging too freely in the imaginative part of his education, his playful letter suggests how Locke's distinction had been transformed in the latter half of the century: judgment forms orderly chains of relations, while fancy jumbles and disjoins things with caprice.

In late-eighteenth-century empiricist aesthetics, the division between fancy (and its closely aligned sister, imagination) and judgment was adopted to differentiate scientific from poetic genius. Gerard's *Essay on Genius* (1774) provides the most explicit formulation. Like many of his contemporaries, Gerard believed "a just and regular induction" based on a substantial collection of "facts" about mental operations would yield the principles guiding these operations.[67] He therefore sought to generate general principles by way of an accretion of particular examples, prominently Homer and Newton, who illustrate genius in their respective productions. For Gerard, the poet and natural philosopher share the same process of invention – the route from collecting observations, to selecting and disposing them in a design, to the comparison and combination of parts – but there are specific limits to this correspondence. While Gerard repeatedly conjoins "varieties" of genius in Parts I and II of the *Essay*, he devotes Part III to distinguishing two ends of genius, truth and beauty, the provinces of the sciences and arts respectively. The most salient aspect of this division, Gerard argues, is that "a genius for science is formed by penetration, a genius for the arts, by brightness," where "penetration implies an aptness to be affected only by the closest and strongest relations of things; and that brightness implies a propensity to be influenced by such relations as are slighter and more remote."[68] The more obvious the relations perceived by the mind, the more its genius belongs to a scientific temperament; the more remote the relations, the more poetic its genius.

When Darwin differentiates Homeric simile from philosophical analogy in the second Interlude in *Loves*, he draws on the authority of empiricist aesthetics from Locke to Gerard. Poetry's loose analogies are related to, but distinct from, the strict analogies of science: both are inductive, the difference being a matter of degree rather than kind. Within the verse, simile produces the capricious jumble appropriate to the pleasure the mind takes in fanciful resemblances, while the analogies in the notes follow a logical chain of observation and experiment. In empiricist aesthetics, I am suggesting, Darwin found a way of reconciling the work of analogy in experimental science and imaginative literature – of plotting a relationship between these realms without conflating their functions or goals. *Loves*, in other words, theorizes and dramatizes a relation-based poetics running parallel to the analogical science of the notes.

If simile performs the fundamental work of poetic linking, allegory – and personification more specifically – is the conceptual key to Darwin's aesthetic theory. Homeric simile found favor with the Augustans, especially in satire. Darwin's embrace of allegory is more unusual, running against a steady stream of disparagements by critics from Addison to Johnson. As Darwin's verse–note composite makes palpable, allegories have the dangerous propensity to act as if the "barrier between reality or history and abstraction were a porous membrane instead of guarded wall that protects what is true from what is not."[69] Kelley illustrates why this conflation troubled Locke and his philosophical progeny: By putting the arbitrary relation between words and what they represent on display, "allegory dramatizes the potential risks and anomalies of representation by blowing them up into monstrous, and at times monstrously feminine, figures that look very much like all-too-concrete universals."[70] Alcea, then, is indeed monstrous, but as much for the representational instability she and her sisters introduce as for her sexual transgressiveness. An anathema to plain style and its smooth transition between words and things, allegories of her ilk, according to Lord Kames, ought to be "confined within their own sphere" and not allowed to mingle with the real.[71]

From within the allegorical poem, Darwin's Interludes invoke a range of eighteenth-century strategies for containing the troubling aspects of allegorical representation. In line with Addison and Joseph Spence, he identifies allegory with uncomplicated visual images: allegories and personifications, he says, are "arts of bringing objects before the eye, or of expressing sentiments in the language of vision" (*LP*, p. 43).[72] Following Kames, Darwin also objects to mixing allegorical and "natural" figures. An allegorical representation, he argues, must remain "indistinct" or abstract so that it "does not compel us to attend to its improbability" (*LP*, pp. 44–45). These positions may well seem at odds: How does an image remain indistinct while being brought before the eye? Darwin suggests that a "certain degree of probability" is necessary "to prevent us from revolting with distaste from unnatural images; unless we are otherwise so much interested in the contemplation of them as not to perceive their improbability" (*LP*, p. 45). The "unless" is crucial to Darwin's use of allegory. In comparison to dream reverie (drawn from Kames's theory of "ideal presence"), in which we cannot detect the difference between ideas derived from sensation and those produced by the imagination, Darwin casts the work of allegory as deception: If the poet or painter is skilled, we should be convinced that objects "suggested to our imaginations" actually exist before us (*LP*, p. 47–48). In bringing images before the eye, allegory has the opposite goal from philosophical analogy: to be successful, it must persuade us to take illusion for truth.

In making this argument, Darwin has deviated from his source. For Kames, introducing imaginary persons or improbable facts will cause the judgment to revolt and destroy the reverie, and he therefore bans allegory from epic poetry. However, Kames notes, such figures are acceptable in other genres, where they "amuse by their novelty and singularity"; in a poem "professedly ludicrous," the "strict imitation of nature is not required" because the intention is not to rouse our sympathy.[73] Such a poem may therefore "employ machinery to great advantage; and the more extravagant the better."[74] As Darwin puts it, as long as the images "so much interest the reader or spectator as to induce the reverie," "it is not of any consequence, whether the representation correspond with nature" (*LP*, p. 49). In fact, "the further the artist recedes from nature, the greater the novelty he is likely to produce," as is evident when "the daring pencil of Fusseli [sic] transports us beyond the boundaries of nature, and ravishes us with the charm of the most interesting novelty" (*LP*, p. 49). With these reflections, Darwin has, in effect, hijacked Kames's theory of reverie by transferring it from the highly valued mimetic genre of epic (or history painting) into genres in which allegory has free reign, such as Henry Fuseli's gothic fantasies. In Darwin's aesthetics, allegory can produce a reverie in which we believe and feel for allegorical figures, even as these figures insist on their own artificiality and improbability by actively transgressing the boundaries of nature (as the maid-cum-lamb Barometz does most extravagantly).

This aesthetic theory accounts for the animation of Darwin's personifications. Rather than the static, fixed allegorical figures common in earlier eighteenth-century verse, Darwin's metamorphosed plants sigh, cry, pant, and yearn with great vitality. They have not, however, truly put on the form of flesh and blood.[75] Rather, as Darwin suggests in the Proem to *Loves*, they are produced by the camera obscura, "lights and shades dancing on a whited canvas, and magnified into apparent life!" (*LP*, p. v). Their life-like quality, in other words, is an illusion produced by the technology of poetry and its animating arts of allegory and personification. The magic lantern might be a more fitting metaphor for Darwin's allegorical practice, as it does not present images "perfectly resembling their objects," but rather conjures up imaginary scenes so vivid that they deceive us into belief – even though these scenes are improbable if not impossible.[76] Darwin devotes an extended epic simile in Canto III to praising Henry Fuseli's allegorical painting *The Nightmare* on precisely these grounds. Leaping off a description of laurel leaves and their effect on the Pythian priestess – "She speaks in thunder from her golden throne / With words *unwill'd*, and wisdom not her own" – Darwin shifts the scene with a simile:

So on his NIGHTMARE through the evening fog
Flits the squab Fiend o'er fen, and lake, and bog;
Seeks some love-wilder'd Maid with sleep oppress'd,
Alights, and grinning sits upon her breast.
– Such as of late amid the murky sky
Was mark'd by FUSSELI'S poetic eye;
Whose daring tints, with SHAKESPEAR'S happiest grace,
Gave to the airy phantom form and place. –
Back o'er her pillow sinks her blushing head,
Her snow-white limbs hang helpless from the bed;
While with quick sighs, and suffocative breath,
Her interrupted heart-pulse swims in death.
– Then shrieks of captured towns, and widow's tears,
Pale lovers stretch'd upon their blood-stain'd biers,
The headlong precipice that thwarts her flight,
The trackless desert, the cold starless night,
And stern-eye'd Murder with his knife behind,
In dread succession agonize her mind.
O'er her fair limbs convulsive tremors fleet,
Start in her hands, and struggle in her feet;
In vain to scream with quivering lips she tries,
And strains in palsy'd lids her tremulous eyes;
In vain she *wills* to run, fly, swim, walk, leap;
The WILL presides not in the bower of SLEEP.
– On her fair bosom sits the Demon-Ape
Erect, and balances his bloated shape;
Rolls in their marble orbs his Gorgon-eyes,
And drinks with leathern ears her tender cries.

(*LP*, III: 49–78)

Like a magic lantern – conventionally used to produce terrifyingly real scenes of ghosts and apparitions – Darwin suggests that Fuseli has brought an indistinct abstraction before the eye, giving it "form and place." Like the exhibition catalogs of poetic excerpts to Fuseli's Milton Gallery that, as Luisa Calè shows, "encouraged readers to engage in an ekphrastic exercise," Darwin's re-presentation of Fuseli's painting turns image into narrative.[77] Darwin begins in abstraction ("some love-wilder'd Maid"), turning with each long dash to a new subject. A claim about Fuseli's artistic lineage is followed by two lines representing the scene in the painting, which Darwin then amplifies by describing – in vivid and gruesome detail – the sleeping woman's agonizing thoughts and physical sensations. Drawing on the dream theory he has borrowed and remade from Kames, Darwin interiorizes (and re-abstracts) the allegorical phantom, participating in what Terry

Castle has called the spectralization of mental space.[78] In this process, the verse animates the scene with a series of moving pictures that also read like instructions for writing a gothic novel. Darwin's lines, in other words, link Fuseli's ability to "transport us beyond the boundaries of nature" to his use of conventional gothic tropes, reinforcing the artifice of the allegorical representation while drawing us into sympathy with the helpless dreamer whose "WILL" has abandoned her in a very unpleasant "bower."[79]

While epic simile substantiates a relational poetics parallel to the philosophical analogies of Darwin's notes, the larger structure of allegory in *Loves* stands as the antithetical counterpart to his science. The notes plot scientific truth in the progression of observation, analogy, and experiment; the allegorical verse performs its status as rhetorical figure, actively cultivating the arts of deception and illusion. The foundation of art for Darwin is contained in its relation to dream and reverie. Successful art makes us *unable* "to compare [ideas] with our previous knowledge of things" – the precise opposite of the foundation of his analogical science (*LP*, p. 47). The composite form Darwin chose for his text reflects this relation between science and poetry. Running alongside each other on almost every page, the verse and prose are circumscribed within their individual spheres of representation, distinguished by font and delimited by a swath of typographic white space. While acknowledging the close affinity of scientific analogy and poetic figure – both are produced inductively – *Loves* differentiates their function and goals, propounding an aesthetic position antithetical but correspondent to that of experimental science.

As I suggested above, the work of containment and differentiation performed by Darwin's verse–note composite is continually unraveled by the composite form itself. The act of putting allegory into dialogue with philosophical analogy – of building metaphors with the observations and experiments – makes the theoretical concerns plaguing Locke and Kames into visible, palpable effects. In registering the divisions that would become the foundation of disciplinary separation in the structure of the text, Darwin allowed this boundary to be transgressed over and over, always reconstituting itself only to be dismantled. In this, Darwin's project is emblematic of what happens when authors import inductive method into moral philosophy and aesthetics; *Loves* merely exacerbates this condition by stacking corresponding aesthetic and scientific systems on top of each other.

The playful artificiality of the verse so prominent in *Loves*, however, is to a large degree missing from *Economy*. In his 1784 letter to Joseph Johnson offering *Loves* for publication, Darwin describes *Economy* as a short, 400-line preface to *Loves* with "3 or 4 times the quantity of notes, and those of more learned, and newer matter, but half which are not done."[80] Composed after *Loves* had been completed, *Economy* – as well as Darwin's final, posthumously published poem *The Temple of Nature* (1803) – cultivates a vision of allegorical verse that posits a very different relationship between poetry and science. As Heringman suggests, *Economy* brings the verse closer to the content of the notes, and "this continuity of image and explanation makes sense in light of Darwin's initial assertion [in the Apology to *Economy*] that myths are direct allegories of scientific observations."[81] While his analogical science remains conceptually unchanged, in these later poems we can see Darwin trying a different poetic system, one that replaces an aesthetics of illusion with an aesthetics that erases the gap between words and things. In reimagining allegories as hieroglyphs, Darwin embraces the enigmatic, mysterious character of linguistic representation while, as Foucault suggests of sixteenth-century writers, "forcing language to reside in the world, among the plants, the herbs, the stones and the animals."[82]

Real Figures: Darwin's Hieroglyphs

In *The Economy of Vegetation*, Darwin explores a conduit between the spheres of knowledge he had demarcated in *Loves* – a passageway that would become a regular thoroughfare in *The Temple of Nature*. Unlike *Loves*' personified maids and swains, personifications in *Economy* are abstract concepts, often acting as invisible agents behind the scenes. For example, fire nymphs lead Benjamin Franklin to seize lightning from the sky, and they awaken the "Vernal Hours" from "long repose" (*EV*, p. vii, I: 386, 428). These personified figures are drawn, as Darwin suggests in the Apology to *Economy*, from "the Rosicrucian doctrine of Gnomes, Sylphs, Nymphs, and Salamanders" because these were "originally the names of hieroglyphic figures representing the elements" (*EV*, p. vii). In place of the camera obscura and its dancing pictures, Darwin now puts forward a poetic system defined by its close tie to the "operations of Nature" (*EV*, p. vii).

Darwin develops his new aesthetic position in the first Canto of *Economy* through his treatment of a painting with content similar to that of Fuseli's *The Nightmare*, Francisco Goya's *Saint Francis Borgia at the Deathbed of an Impenitent* (1788). From the description of an electrical experiment in which a person standing on wax receives an electrical charge such that "O'er her fair brow the kindling lustres glare," Darwin introduces a short simile: "So round the virgin Saint in silvery streams / The holy Halo shoots it's [*sic*] arrowy beams" (*EV*, I: 353, 357–58). Darwin's note makes the specific referent of these lines clear:

I believe it is not known with certainty at what time the painters first introduced the luminous circle round the head to import a Saint or holy person.
It is now become part of the symbolic language of painting, and it is much to
be wished that this kind of hieroglyphic character was more frequent in that
art; as it is much wanted to render historic pictures both more intelligible,
and more sublime; and why should not painting as well as poetry express
itself in metaphor, or in indistinct allegory? A truly great modern painter
lately endeavored to enlarge the sphere of pictorial language, by putting a
demon behind the pillow of a wicked man on his death bed. Which unfortu-
nately for the scientific part of painting, the cold criticism of the present day
has depreciated; and thus barred perhaps the only road to further improvement in this science. (*EV*, p. 35)

In contrast to the position articulated in *Loves*, Darwin now advocates
introducing allegory alongside historical persons and events for the sake of
intelligibility – a claim fundamentally opposed to conventional eighteenth-
century wisdom about allegorical representation. This altered position is
underwritten by a new conception of allegory itself. Rather than a rhetorical device that advertises its illusory effects and irreducible distance from
the real, Darwin now associates allegory with the hieroglyph, an emblem
of an ideal transparency between sign and referent, word and thing. In his
combination of hieroglyphic characters – the halo and the demons – Goya
has advanced the "scientific" part of painting, its ability not just to bring
things before the eye but to convey a kind of truth.

While the camera obscura and Ovid's *Metamorphoses* introduce the allegorical figures of *Loves*, the hieroglyph obtains centrality in *Economy*. The
hieroglyph maps a direct corridor from scientific knowledge to poetry: As
Darwin argues in the Apology, the "Egyptians were possessed of many discoveries in philosophy and chemistry before the invention of letters; these
were then expressed in hieroglyphic paintings of men and animals; which
after the discovery of the alphabet were described and animated by poets"
(*EV*, p. viii). For this reason, Darwin conjectures, "many of the important
operations of Nature were shadowed or allegorized in heathen mythology,"
making myth the passageway between rhetorical figure and empirically
established facts about the natural world (*EV*, p. viii). The philosophical
analogies of science might be actuated in allegory and the bifurcated system
of *Loves* be brought into unity.

Darwin had the best of authorities for undertaking this project. The
father of inductive method, Bacon, had "ingeniously explained" many of
these myths in *Of the Wisdom of the Ancients*, originally published as *De
Sapientia Veterum* in 1609 (*EV*, p. vii). Admitting that "a little dexterity" of

wit can put meanings on allegories they were never intended to have, Bacon nonetheless decides to publish his interpretations of classical myths because "I find a conformity and connexion to the thing signified, so close and so evident, that one cannot help, but believing such a signification to have been designed and meditated from the first, and purposefully shadowed out."[83] On Bacon's authority, Darwin precedes to introduce and explain the signification of a series of myths in his notes to *Economy*, including the progressive formation of the earth contained in the "sublime allegory of Eros, or Divine Love, producing the world from the egg of Night," and the "allegorical story" of Hercules that countenances the theory that an ancient earthquake opened a passage between continents (*EV*, p. 8, 30). Darwin's assertion that scientific knowledge is embedded in the allegorical stories of myth finds its most ardent expression in Additional Note XXII on the Portland Vase, an eleven-page analysis of the vase as an artistic allegory for "scenical exhibitions" of the Eleusinian mysteries (*EV*, Additional Notes, p. 53). This transparent connection between scientific knowledge and allegorical representation in the Eleusinian mysteries in turn became the basis for the overarching structure of *The Temple of Nature*.[84]

In his later composite works, Darwin reinvents allegory, shifting it from a self-announcing rhetorical device to a conduit between scientific knowledge and the ancient origins of poetry as emblem. On Bacon's authority, in other words, Darwin seeks to reunite his bifurcated systems of science and aesthetics – to formulate an aesthetic position that would bind representation to reality. However, as Priestman notes, "the contrast between emblematic visual denotations, which is what [Darwin] took the hieroglyphics to be, and the misleadingly temporal and casually metaphorical connotations of ordinary written language" runs throughout Darwin's notes to *The Temple of Nature*. In his final poem, Darwin's faith in successfully bringing words closer to things was continually troubled by the very instabilities put on display in *Loves*. Darwin did not, to his own satisfaction, solve the dilemma of how to bring poetry into alignment with experimental science; as his final note to *The Temple of Nature* indicates, he could only imagine a future in which science had so permeated language and culture that conversation could be purged of figurative language, and metaphor could be entirely contained in the realm of poetry.

As I have argued, the disconnect between words and things which appears powerfully in empiricist philosophy after Locke appears in Darwin's poem as a manifestation of the problem of induction. In attempting to formulate parallel but antithetical scientific and aesthetic principles in *Loves*, Darwin had recourse to a specific form, the annotated poem, through which he attempted to demarcate fact from fancy, ratiocination from rhetorical flourish. Darwin's formal choice was underwritten by a distinction between the work of poetry and that of prose already in place in the early eighteenth century. What made Darwin's work important for authors of the succeeding generation, however, was how he mobilized this distinction. After Darwin's *Loves*, the push and pull of prose and verse on the page conveyed something about making knowledge and making texts that it had not signaled before. As an instantiation of inductive method in experimental science and empiricist aesthetics, the composite order both materialized compositional process and exposed its gaps and fissures.

NOTES

1 To avoid confusion, I will cite Darwin's verse by canto and line number and his prose notes and paratexts by page number.

2 King-Hele identifies Wordsworth and Coleridge's borrowings from Darwin while also voicing the conventional view that *Lyrical Ballads* constituted a radical formal break from Darwin's ornate verse. Desmond King-Hele, *Doctor of Revolution: The Life and Genius of Erasmus Darwin* (New York: Faber & Faber, 1977), pp. 266–70; see also Desmond King-Hele, *Erasmus Darwin and the Romantic Poets* (New York: St. Martin's Press, 1986), pp. 62–122.

3 Heringman, *Romantic Rocks*, pp. 199, 211.

4 Noel Jackson, "Rhyme and Reason: Erasmus Darwin's Romanticism," *Modern Language Quarterly* 70.2 (2009): 182.

5 Alan Bewell, "Erasmus Darwin's Cosmopolitan Nature," *ELH* 76.1 (2009): 29–30.

6 Ibid., 30.

7 In a letter of April 24, 1790, Darwin credits Richard Lovell Edgeworth with the "best part" of the "proem," the analogy between the poem and a "festoon of ribbon." Erasmus Darwin to Richard Lovell Edgeworth, 24 April 1790, in *Collected Letters of Erasmus Darwin*, Desmond King-Hele (ed.) (Cambridge: Cambridge University Press, 2007), p. 202.

8 For Darwin's poetic epistles to Mary Howard and Elizabeth Pole, see Darwin, *Collected Letters*, pp. 41, 138–39. Among the many letters on scientific subjects from Darwin to the manufacturer Matthew Boulton, there are a set of poetical directions for making an ormolu tea-vase for Mrs. Pole; see Darwin, *Collected Letters*, pp. 146–47. When the subject was love, Darwin's preferred genre was verse.

9 Heringman argues that Darwin's project was aimed at synthesizing literature and science, an object "possible only as the result of a perceived gap that must be bridged." Heringman, *Romantic Rocks*, p. 211.

10 Maurice Merleau-Ponty, *Prose of the World*, Claude Lefort (ed.), John O'Neill (trans.) (Evanston, IL: Northwestern University Press, 1973), p. 4. For similar reasons, Michel Foucault also borrowed Merleau-Ponty's title for his

discussion of the Renaissance episteme of resemblance in Chapter 2 of *The Order of Things*.

11 For a survey of precedents to Darwin's poem, see James Venable Logan, *The Poetry and Aesthetics of Erasmus Darwin* (Princeton, NJ: Princeton University Press, 1936), pp. 120–36.

12 Perhaps surprisingly, Lucretius was an important model for Jesuit authors, most famously Benedict Stay, who wrote a six-book poem on Cartesian physics (*Philosophiae libri vi*, 1744), followed by a ten-book poem on Newtonian physics (*Philosophia recentior*, 1755–1791) annotated by the Jesuit physicist Roger Boscovich. See Yasmin Haskell, "Religion and Enlightenment in the Neo-Latin Reception of Lucretius," *The Cambridge Companion to Lucretius*, Stuart Gillespie and Philip Hardie (eds.) (Cambridge: Cambridge University Press, 2007), pp. 199–200. Cambridge Collections Online. 31 July 2010.

13 Alexander Pope, *An Essay on Man, Enlarged and improved by the author. With notes by William Warburton, M.A.* (London, 1745), p. 29. *Eighteenth-Century Collections Online*, http://galenet.galegroup.com.proxy.library.vanderbilt.edu/servlet/ECCO, 31 July 2010. Pope had of course parodied overly erudite scholarly notes in *The Dunciad Variorum* (1729); Warburton is thus also attempting to differentiate his explanatory, philosophical notes from the pedantic annotations of contemporary textual critics like Richard Bentley.

14 All of these georgics were composed in blank verse. As Noel Jackson has argued, resonances with *De Rerum Natura* appear throughout Darwin's verse. Less has been made of Pope's influence, but Darwin was certainly familiar with *An Essay on Man*: he quoted from it in an early letter to his brother William, along with *An Essay on Criticism* – see Darwin, *Collected Letters*, pp. 7–8; the Rosicrucian machinery of *Economy* is borrowed directly from Pope's *The Rape of the Lock*; and Darwin corrects a line from "Windsor Forest" in Interlude I to exemplify how poetry should bring the idea of a visible object to the mind (*LP*, p. 42).

15 James Grainger, *The Sugar-Cane: A Poem* (London, 1764), in *The Poetics of Empire: A Study of James Grainger's* The Sugar-Cane *(1764)*, John Gilmore (ed.) (London: Athlone Press, 2000), ll. 199, 278.

16 Genette, *Paratexts*, p. 12. One might make a similar claim about Grainger's extensive annotations, which do at least as much to familiarize the reader with the West Indian geographical and sociopolitical context as the poem itself. However, as John Gilmore notes, Grainger's conscious adoption of the Virgilian georgic and his use of Miltonic blank verse were calculated to "establish the dignity and importance of his subject, and this would have been understood by his contemporary readers." John Gilmore, Introduction, *The Poetics of Empire: A Study of James Grainger's* The Sugar-Cane *(1764)* (London: Athlone Press, 2000), p. 30. The same cannot be said of Darwin's playful, amorous couplets in *Loves*, although the notes and verse are more tonally consonant in *Economy*.

17 Erasmus Darwin, *The Botanic Garden; A Poem, in two parts. Part I. Containing The Economy of Vegetation . . . with Philosophical Notes* (London: J. Johnson, 1791), p. v. Subsequently cited in text as *EV*; the verse is cited by canto and line

number, the prose by page number. Noel Jackson summarizes this critical tendency at length; see Jackson, "Rhyme and Reason," 172–75.

18 Heringman suggests that this continuity establishes the "plausibility" of the
images in the verse, and therefore acts as "a defense of poetry as a medium for
knowledge." Heringman, *Romantic Rocks*, p. 200. In contrast, I argue below
that Darwin's verse is not designed as a medium for conveying scientific knowledge but rather to embody an aesthetic position that parallels the methods of
experimental science.

19 Stuart Curran discusses the assumptions (or logic) of any form or genre as "a
structuring principle that in a large part predetermines ideological orientation."
Curran, *Poetic Form*, p. 10.

20 Pope, *An Essay on Man*, p. 20, original emphasis.

21 Sprat, *History*, pp. 112–13.

22 For a series of examples, see Richard Foster Jones, "Science and English Prose
Style," pp. 75–110. On the basis of this evidence, Jones argues that New Science
provoked a radical change in prose style in the seventeenth century. Numerous
critics have pointed to the oversimplifications in Jones's thesis, and particularly to his lack of attention to the political and theological underpinnings
of these statements; see especially Brian Vickers, "Royal Society," pp. 3–76,
and Markley, *Fallen Languages*, pp. 1–33. Jones wrote in response to Morris
Croll's argument that changes in prose style derived from an anti-Ciceronian
disavowal of humanist eloquence, a view qualified by Robert Adolph and John
Steadman, both of whom treat the Jones–Croll controversy at length. See
Robert Adolph, *The Rise of Modern Prose Style* (Cambridge, MA: MIT Press,
1968); and John Steadman, *The Hill and the Labyrinth: Discourse and Certitude in Milton and His Near-Contemporaries* (Berkley: University of California
Press, 1984). How prose style changed in the seventeenth century, or what conjunction of forces precipitated this change, concerns me less here than how
the massive outpouring of statements conjoining plain style and experimental
science inflected eighteenth-century philosophical verse.

23 Locke, *Essay*, p. 435.

24 Quoted in Adolph, *Prose Style*, p. 185.

25 Jonathan Swift, *Travels into several remote nations of the world. In four parts. By
Lemuel Gulliver, first a surgeon, and then a captain of several ships*, 2 vols. (London, 1726), 2: 75–76. Eighteenth Century Collections Online, http://galenet.
galegroup.com.proxy.library.vanderbilt.edu/servlet/ECCO, 15 August 2010.

26 Darwin, *Collected Letters*, p. 190. Darwin's translations of Linnaeus's works were
issued as *A System of Vegetables* (1783) and *The Families of Plants* (1787), with
"A Botanical Society at Lichfield" listed as the translator, although the other
members – Brooke Boothby and Joseph Jackson – had only minor roles in the
project. See King-Hele, *Doctor of Revolution*, pp. 144–47 and 174–75.

27 Carl von Linné, *A System of Vegetables, according to their classes genera orders
species with their characters and differences*, 2 vols., A Botanical Society at Lichfield (trans.) (Lichfield, 1783), p. ii. Eighteenth Century Collections Online,
http://galenet.galegroup.com.proxy.library.vanderbilt.edu/servlet/ECCO,
5 Aug. 2010.

28 Ibid., p. ii, emphasis mine.

29 Erasmus Darwin, *The Temple of Nature; or The Origin of Society, a Poem with Philosophical Notes* (London, 1803), Martin Priestman (ed.), Romantic Circles Electronic Editions, 2006, 15 August 2010, http://www.rc.umd.edu/editions/darwin_temple/addnotes/addnote15.html.

30 For the transformation of Baconian method from an emphasis on accumulation to a more speculative approach, see Jonathan Smith, *Fact and Feeling*, pp. 11–44.

31 For a discussion of the ceremonial adherence to Bacon's inductive method in the nineteenth century, see Chapter 1.

32 Sprat, *History*, p. 36.

33 Quoted in King-Hele, *Doctor of Revolution*, p. 160.

34 Bacon, *The Advancement of Learning*, p. 248.

35 Ibid., p. 248.

36 Ibid., p. 404.

37 Sprat, *History*, pp. 115–16; italics in the original. This position was also a target of Swift's satire: A professor of "speculative learning" in Lagado shows Gulliver several folio volumes "collected of broken sentences," which he has produced by spinning words strung on wires and from which he will (eventually) compose a "complete body of all arts and sciences." Swift, *Travels*, 2: 72–74.

38 Darwin, *Collected Letters*, p. 353. I am grateful to Emily August for bringing this letter to my attention.

39 Ibid., pp. 197–99.

40 Davy, *Collected Works*, 4: 2.

41 Buffon, *L'Histoire Naturelle*, p. 50.

42 See especially Philip Ritterbush, *Overtures to Biology: The Speculations of Eighteenth-Century Naturalists* (New Haven, CT: Yale University Press, 1964), pp. 159–68, and Catherine Packham, "The Science and Poetry of Animation: Personification, Analogy, and Erasmus Darwin's *Loves of the Plants*," *Romanticism* 10 (2004): 191–208.

43 Ritterbush cites the "Additional Notes" to *Economy* as "one of the most extensive series of analogies ever entertained between plants and animals." Ritterbush, *Overtures*, p. 163. As both Ritterbush and Bewell note, Linnaeus's taxonomic system drew much of its persuasiveness from the existing botanical analogy between animals and plants. Ritterbush, p. 110, and Alan Bewell, "'Jacobin Plants': Botany as Social Theory in the 1790s," *Wordsworth Circle* 20.3 (1989): 133.

44 Michel Foucault, *The Order of Things: An Archaeology of the Human Sciences* (New York: Routledge, 1994), pp. 54–55.

45 Dugald Stewart, *Elements of the Philosophy of the Human Mind*, vol. 2 (Edinburgh: Constable, 1814), p. 385. Eighteenth Century Collections Online, http://galenet.galegroup.com.proxy.library.vanderbilt.edu/servlet/ECCO, 27 August 2010. Italics in the original.

46 Ibid., p. 385. This type of analogy was also an important component of Bacon's inductive method: As he suggests in the *Novum Organum*, "the investigation and observation of the resemblances and analogies of things ... [can]

detect the unity of nature, and lay a foundation for the constitution of sciences" (*NO*, 166–67). He adds a "strict and earnest caution" that one must
only use "conformable and analogous instances which indicate ... real and
substantial resemblances; resemblances grounded in nature, not accidental or
merely apparent" (ibid.). Bacon gives the fin–wing analogy as an example of a
true "conformable instance," while labeling the analogy between man and an
inverted plant "an absurd similitude" (ibid.).

47 In this passage, Coleridge casts Darwin as an example of the "leading thought"
    or mental "Initiative" that must precede the use of induction in the sciences;
    for Coleridge, Baconian induction could not produce theory by building up
    from particular facts to generalizations without a pre-existing idea. In his ana-
    logical notes, Darwin supplied such an idea, even if he (according to Coleridge)
    lacked the capacity to formulate the laws of organic nature through "decisive
    experiment" (*F* 1: 476–8: 470).

48 Davy, *Collected Works*, 4: 2.

49 Stewart, *Elements*, pp. 385–86.

50 Packham, "Science and Poetry," 198–99.

51 Erasmus Darwin, *Zoonomia; or, the Laws of Organic Life*, 2 vols. (London, 1794–
    96), 1:1. Italics in the original.

52 Darwin had formulated this concept in a letter to Wedgwood in 1784, where he
    suggests "there is a great analogy between the laws of the propagation of heat,
    and those of electricity, such as the same bodies communicate them easily, as
    metals, and the same bodies more difficultly, as glass, wax and air." Darwin,
    Collected Letters, p. 227.

53 Here, I am appropriating Jacques Derrida's concept of the supplement, as he
    develops it in his analysis of Rousseau's vexed opposition between speech and
    writing. See Jacques Derrida, *Of Grammatology*, Gayatri Chakravorty-Spivak
    (trans.) (Baltimore: Johns Hopkins University Press, 1976), pp. 144–45.

54 Foucault, *The Order of Things*, p. 40.

55 From the external evidence of his correspondence, it appears that *Loves* began
    to come into being as early as 1781, when Darwin sent Joseph Banks "a poem"
    partly written by Anna Seward and partly by William Sayle, but "corrected"
    and annotated by Darwin. Darwin, *Collected Letters*, p. 195. While there is
    no empirical evidence for this claim, I suspect the Interludes and Advertise-
    ment were written after the poem–note combination was well under way or
    complete, since these prose interjections comment on and attempt to explain
    the relationship between verse and prose as it appears in the text. There-
    fore, it is unlikely that Darwin created the poem–note combination with the
    explicit intention of positing parallel scientific and aesthetic systems; rather, I
    believe he grafted the aesthetic theory onto the already existing work, much as
    Wordsworth did with the Preface to the 1800 edition of *Lyrical Ballads*.

56 Martin Priestman, Introduction to *The Temple of Nature; or the Origin of Soci-
    ety*, by Erasmus Darwin, Romantic Circles Electronic Editions, 2006, Sec-
    tion 8, http://www.rc.umd.edu/editions/darwin_temple/intro.html, 15 August
    2010. Maureen McNeil draws on *Temple* to support her claim that for Darwin,

"the only method whereby human claims to knowledge of nature and natural laws could be validated involved a monistic account of a common origin for nature and mind," and therefore "Darwin sought to provide a framework which would incorporate all social, intellectual and moral developments into the operation of nature." Maureen McNeil, *Under the Banner of Science: Erasmus Darwin and His Age* (Manchester, UK: Manchester University Press, 1987), p. 55. While I agree with these conclusions, I find their application to the allegorical structure of *Loves* untenable, as I detail below.

57 Priestman, Introduction to *Temple*, Section 11.
58 Hume, *Treatise*, p. 6.
59 Bewell, "Jacobin Plants," 134; Tim Fulford, "Coleridge, Darwin, Linnaeus: The Sexual Politics of Botany," *Wordsworth Circle* 28 (1997): 128.
60 Fredrika Teute, "The Loves of the Plants; or, The Cross-Fertilization of Science and Desire at the End of the Eighteenth Century," *Huntington Library Quarterly* 63.3 (2000): 323; Bewell, "Jacobin Plants," 135. While Darwin's poem did in fact have a liberating influence on women authors, I would suggest this had more to do with its combination of literary and scientific authority than with a change in sexual mores.
61 Ann Shteir, *Cultivating Women, Cultivating Science: Flora's Daughters and Botany in England 1760–1860* (Baltimore: Johns Hopkins University Press, 1996), p. 27.
62 Darwin, *Zoonomia*, 1: 1.
63 Theresa Kelley, *Reinventing Allegory* (Cambridge: Cambridge University Press, 1997), p. 5.
64 Bewell, "Jacobin Plants," 134.
65 Locke, *Essay*, p. 153.
66 William Beckford, "A Letter from Geneva, May 22, 1778," MS Beckford d. 9, fols. 34–43, Bodleian Library, Oxford. Beckfordiana: The William Beckford website, http://www.beckford.c18.net/wbgenevaletter.html, 15 August 2010.
67 Gerard, *Essay on Genius*, p. 5. This position also informs the work of Gerard's more famous contemporary, Edmund Burke, whose *Philosophical Enquiry* opens with the claim that an accurate understanding of the sublime and beautiful can only result from a "diligent examination of our passions," "a careful survey of the properties of things," and "a sober and attentive investigation of the laws of nature." Once this empirical process of observation, collection, and investigation has been completed, "the rules deducible from such an enquiry might be applied to the imitative arts." Burke, *Philosophical Enquiry*, p. vii.
68 Gerard, *Essay on Genius*, pp. 322, 325–26.
69 Kelley, *Reinventing Allegory*, p. 75.
70 Ibid., p. 75.
71 Henry Home, Lord Kames, *Elements of Criticism*, 3rd ed., 2 vols. (Edinburgh, 1765), 2: 388. Darwin's discussion of allegory in Interlude I draws on Kames, particularly in the concept of an ideal presence of an imagined object as a "waking dream" or reverie, and the destruction of this reverie by the introduction of "improbable" incidents and imaginary beings; see Kames, 1: 82–85, 94.

72 For a discussion of Spence's requirement that allegory "speak to the eyes," see Kelley, *Reinventing Allegory*, pp. 76–77.

73 Kames, I: 94–95.

74 Ibid.

75 Here I'm drawing on Kelley's suggestion that "Romantic allegory welds its abstractions to 'flesh and blood', the world of lived particulars and feeling." Kelley, *Reinventing Allegory*, p. 94.

76 Jonathan Crary, *Techniques of the Observer: On Vision and Modernity in the Nineteenth Century* (Cambridge, MA: MIT Press, 1990), p. 33. Crary notes that the perfect coincidence of image and object offered by the camera obscura was "haunted by its proximity to techniques of conjuration and illusion"; this did not, however, effectively challenge the dominant model of the camera obscura as an emblem for a new objective and comparative mode of empiricist observation. Ibid., p. 33.

77 Luisa Calè, *Fuseli's Milton Gallery: "Turning Readers into Spectators"* (Oxford: Oxford University Press, 2006), p. 71.

78 Terry Castle, *The Female Thermometer: Eighteenth-Century Culture and the Invention of the Uncanny* (New York and Oxford: Oxford University Press, 1995), pp. 141–42.

79 As in Swift's designation of the prostitute's fourth-story garret as a bower in "A Beautiful Young Nymph going to Bed," there is more than a touch of irony in Darwin's word choice here.

80 Darwin, *Collected Letters*, p. 235.

81 Heringman, *Romantic Rocks*, p. 200.

82 Foucault, *The Order of Things*, p. 35.

83 Francis Bacon, *Of the Wisdom of the Ancients,* in vol. VI of *The Works of Francis Bacon*, James Spedding, Robert Leslie Ellis, and Douglas Denon Heath (eds.) (London: Longman et al., 1857–1874; Facsimile. Stuttgart–Bad Cannstatt: F. Frommann Verlag G. Holzboog, 1961–63), p. 697.

84 A full treatment of Darwin's conjunction of science and art through myth in *The Temple of Nature* is beyond the scope of this chapter. For an insightful if brief analysis, see Priestman, Introduction to *Temple*, Section 5, as well as the editorial note to line 137 of Canto I. See also Irwin Primer, "Erasmus Darwin's *Temple of Nature*: Progress, Evolution, and the Eleusinian Mysteries," *Journal of the History of Ideas* 25.1 (1964): 58–76, and Elizabeth Sewell, *The Orphic Voice: Poetry and Natural History* (New Haven, CT: Yale University Press, 1960).

CHAPTER 3

Poetics of the Commonplace
Robert Southey's Analogical Romance

[S]uch a collection of "choice passages" we have never previously met
with. They are drawn from works of all classes, and from every age of
our literature, and bespeak an acquaintance, at once minute, unique
and comprehensive . . . An ample index is happily supplied, which
serves the purpose of a skillful guide in what would otherwise be a
trackless though rich wilderness.

Review of *Southey's Common-place Book*,
First Series, in the *Eclectic Review*, 1850

As reviews of his posthumously published *Common-place Book* indicate,
Robert Southey's indefatigable drive to compile curious facts from obscure
sources and employ them in his literary works determined his contemporary reception, the posthumous construction of his character, and his critical fate as the oft-forgotten member of the Lake School. Until the recent
surge of interest in Southey's poetry and prose, he most often entered scholarly discussions by way of Francis Jeffrey's seminal review of *Thalaba the
Destroyer* (1801) in the first number of the *Edinburgh Review* – a review that
appends a damning portrait of the new school of poets to an explicit critique of Southey's piecemeal method of making epic poems. Like Darwin's
Botanic Garden, Southey's "metrical romance" was composed of materials
from various sources compiled in a commonplace book and later trans-
mogrified into a verse–note composite. Jeffrey's review took direct aim
at the resulting form and structure: because it was "entirely composed
of scraps," *Thalaba* was a "jumble of all the measures that are known in
English poetry, (and a few more)" and the "conduct of the fable [is] as disorderly as the versification" (*RS*, 78, 80).[1] Southey's correspondence and
manuscripts suggest that Jeffrey was merely stating the obvious – Southey
made no secret of his inductive compositional methods, and he was, by and
large, pleased with Jeffrey's review despite its tangential opening and satiric
bite.[2]

113

Between 1793, when he began *Joan of Arc* with Coleridge, and 1814, when he completed *Roderick, The Last of the Goths*, Southey composed five long poems in this manner, comprising more than 30,000 lines of verse bolstered by hundreds of pages of notes. If the sheer quantity staggers the imagination, we should recall that Southey worked on these poems in the time left over once more lucrative tasks, such as reviewing, had been completed. As he suggested in 1814, "something of magnitude I must always have before me to occupy me in the intervals of other pursuits, and to think of when nothing else requires attention" (*LC*, 305). While individually "of magnitude," Southey envisioned these long poems as parts of an even larger project, the plan he formulated at age fifteen to write a series of narrative poems "exhibiting all the more prominent and poetical forms of mythology which have at any time obtained among mankind."[3] Inspired by his reading of Bernard Picart's comparative account of the *Cérémonies et coutumes religieuses des tous les peuples du monde* (1723; translated as *Ceremonies and Religious Customs of the Various Nations of the Known World* in 1741), Southey's comprehensive poetic project would encompass all aspects of Man, Nature, and Society, focalized through a historical and anthropological lens.

Southey's poetic instantiation of his comprehensive vision does for Hume's "Science of Man" what Darwin's *Botanic Garden* did for Enlightenment experimental science. Much like Wordsworth's *Recluse*, however, Southey's vision never fully materialized, but he continued to accumulate materials and plan new poems in the series throughout his life. From the 1790s to the 1830s, his notebooks abound with excerpts from various genres (travel narrative, natural history, church history, economic treatises, periodical reviews, etc.), and his letters continue to outline new poems, outgrowths of these materials.[4] In the final stages of composing *Roderick* in November 1814 he dismally reflected, "perhaps I shall never venture upon another poem of equal extent, and in so deep a strain," but at the same time he was casting about for his next subject, telling Walter Scott, "I shall either go far north or far east for scenery and superstitions, and pursue my old scheme of my mythological delineations" (*LC*, 310, 305). This global vision of comparative mythology – along with the explicitly Orientalist and imperialist content of his long poems – has generated much of the recent critical interest in Southey. Variously labeled by critics as anti-imperialist or as defenses of the empire, Southey's works have by and large been seen to manifest ambivalence, neither fully subsuming other cultural perspectives into a Western vision nor sitting comfortably within the mindset of radical otherness, particularly one defined by superstition and blind faith.[5] In this chapter, I demonstrate that the ideological ambivalence characteristic of Southey's long poems is a product of his compositional methods, and that the composite form of his poems replicates a tension within turn-of-the-century history writing. What critics have marked as Southey's "inability" to formulate a coherent poetic or political stance arose directly, I argue, from the inductive procedure he followed to collect, arrange, compare, and compound materials for these annotated poems.[6] The procedure he follows to build his verse–prose composites partakes of the procedures of antiquarianism, a field defined by its omnivorous pursuit of the curious facts of history. His project of rendering comparative mythology in a series of epics, in contrast, takes its impetus from the totalizing narrative of uneven social development propounded in Enlightenment conjectural or philosophical history. Antiquarianism's inductive method – and particularly the undifferentiated accumulation of objects and texts without distinction or exclusion – stood at odds with the comprehensive and synthesizing project of eighteenth-century conjectural history. Southey's annotated long poems put this tension on display, illuminating the emergence of history as a modern discipline out of the collision between a fragmented and contradictory evidentiary base and the perceived necessity of forging these materials into a coherent narrative of the past's relation to the present and future. Southey's composite orders thus participate in the Enlightenment striving toward an encyclopedic totality of knowledge, while materially enacting – in the tension between the totalizing romance narrative of the verse and the fragmented heap of dubious facts in his annotations – the impossibility of a synthetic whole arising from the inductive method of empiricist moral philosophy.

Even as Southey's annotated epic poems materially encode the tensions within historical writing at the turn of the century, his project was a fundamentally literary one. The storehouse of history provided the materials, but Southey's goal was to generate a new species of epic romance. As with Darwin's *The Loves of the Plants* or Charlotte Smith's "Beachy Head" (discussed in the Interlude following this chapter), Southey's long poems were woven from fragments, bits and pieces of other works rewritten and strung together to make a tenuous whole.[7] Creating a tapestry of history whose elements refused to cohere, Southey continually faced charges of unoriginality or – more damningly from the perspective of Coleridgean aesthetics – of not seeing the forest for the trees. Even though he sought to attain a degree of formal coherence in his long poems, Southey remained a staunch devotee of miscellany as a literary principle. While working on his epic–romances, Southey compiled two volumes of *The Annual Anthology*

(1799, 1800), which mix his (sometimes unattributed) poems with those of his friends and other *Morning Post* contributors, including Coleridge, Wordsworth, Charles Lamb, Charles Lloyd, Humphry Davy, Joseph Cottle, Amelia Opie, and Mary Robinson. In 1805, Southey compiled a collection of his "minor" verse in *Metrical Tales and other poems*, and in 1807 he published *Specimens of the Later English Poets*, which he labeled a *hortus siccus* of poetry – an exhibition of "the reprobate, as well as the elect," specimens of all types of verse that might "find their place upon the shelves of the collector."[8] In these works, Southey creates an antiquary's mishmash of verse forms, and these disorderly collections mirror the formal jumble of his epics. As I argue in the final section of this chapter, more than the inevitable outcome of his compositional procedures, the formal discontinuity of the collection became for Southey a sustaining aesthetic principle, one that he brought to fruition in his unfinished, satirical prose–verse composite *The Doctor*.

The previous chapter was concerned with showing the result of importing inductive method into aesthetics; Darwin's *Loves* recognizes a fundamental parity between the inductive method of experimental science and fancy's "method" of making verse. Darwin's understanding of this analogical relation took its cue from the adaptation of inductive method into moral philosophy charted in the first chapter of this study, which indicated that empiricist aesthetics and its derivation from the inductive method of experimental science was well established by the end of the eighteenth century. This chapter goes into greater detail about the compositional process that Darwin and Southey shared with many of their contemporaries. My concern here is what happens when an author uses inductive method to make poems and how the verse–prose composite puts this compositional process on display. This difference in focus derives in part from the greater availability of archival material in Southey's case, but it is also conditioned by the ten-year span between their works. As Jeffrey's criticism suggests, the form Darwin pioneered had become widely recognized and even more widely practiced by the turn of the century. As a consequence, the inductive method of making poems and its material manifestation on the printed page were wielded in ongoing skirmishes over the cultural work of poetry and the status of authorship.

Poetics of the Commonplace

In the *Life and Correspondence of Robert Southey*, Southey's son Charles Cuthbert Southey outlines his father's process of "acquiring and arranging the contents of a book": As he scanned the pages, he would mark anything useful with a slip of paper, noting the subject, and "in the course of a few hours he had classified and arranged everything in the work" (*LC*, 469). Having completed this taxonomy of topics, Southey then transcribed the "choicest passages" into separate notebooks for later use. In an 1809 letter to his brother Harry, Southey describes the second step in the "art of historical book-keeping": "Make your writing books in foolscap quarto & write on only one side of a leaf; draw a line down the margin, marking off space enough for your references, which should be given at the end of every paragraph, – noting page, book or chapter of the author referred to."[9] Once passages had been entered on the recto, the facing page should be used to correct and amplify this account, as a loosely bound manuscript labeled "El Dorado" in the Saffron Walden Museum collection of Southey's papers shows.[10] Southey goes on to tell Harry that the notebook as a whole should organize extracts by topic, and each quotation should be indexed under the appropriate topic. "In this manner," Southey boasts, "the information which is only to be got at piecemeal, and oftentimes incidentally when you are looking for something else, is brought together with the least trouble, and almost imperceptibly" (*SL*, 2: 156–57).

While Southey's model reflects an envisioned ideal that exceeds his actual practice, the description fits securely within the commonplace tradition. Southey's directions mimic *Bell's Common-place Book*, a preformatted, printed commonplace book, a copy of which was used by Erasmus Darwin. This mainly blank book opens with instructions for establishing an index of heads with cross references and entering extracts followed by author, title, and page numbers, with the margins reserved for headings.[11] (Darwin did not follow the directions and instead covered his pages with notes on medical cases and doodles of machines.[12]) The anonymous editor of *The New Commonplace Book* (1799) further suggests making entries on the verso, leaving the facing page blank "for the insertion of any subsequent matter, that may occur on the same subject," and leaving several pages blank at the beginning to extend the index.[13] Southey's notebooks rarely replicate this format precisely, but he does often group extracts together, use the margin of each page to cite his sources, and provide a detailed index at the beginning of each book.[14] After his death, these notebooks became the basis for the four-volume series *Southey's Common-place Book*, edited by his son-in-law John Wood Warter.[15] In his Prefaces, Warter isolates Southey's defining characteristic, the "methodic virtue" (as Carlyle put it in 1867) of a "devout, and gifted collector" (*RS*, 463). For Warter, Southey's notebooks reveal not only the extent of his knowledge but also "the comprehensive grasp of that gigantic intellect."[16] The massive, well-ordered collection, in other words, stands in for an all-encompassing mind – a mind able to marshal and digest a vast diversity of matter.

Warter's claims about the mental benefits of organizing materials derived from the commonplace tradition as it developed after Bacon. Rooted in the fifteenth-century rise of London's merchant class, Renaissance collections of sententious passages took their cue from Erasmus's *De copia verborum*, which describes a method of arranging passages in a notebook.[17] In the early seventeenth century, Bacon appropriates this tradition and blends it with inductive method: in his advice to Fulke Greville on research, Bacon praises "Collections under Heads & Common Places" because they "have in them a kind of Observacion" that "breeds Experience."[18] Here, Bacon casts existing commonplace practices as akin to the process of collecting "a store of particular observations," subsequently "well arranged" and "digested" in order to arrive, via induction, at "the unity of nature in substances most unlike" (*NO*, 94, 96, 120). By the mid-eighteenth century – concomitant with the turn in natural philosophy from accumulation and arrangement to synthesis and linking by analogy discussed in the previous two chapters – the inductive method of the commonplace book became available for resolving the cognitive dissonance produced by a life of reading.[19] As the logistician William Duncan argued, because discoveries often arise haphazardly or by chance, the knowledge a person accumulates over time is often "dispersed and scattered, without Subordination, or any just and regular Coherence."[20] Carefully digesting the materials enables one "to discern their several Connections and Relations," and thereby "to ascertain the various Divisions of Human Knowledge, and so to adjust and connect the Parts in every Branch, that they may seem to grow one out of another, and form a regular Body of Science."[21] In this view, Southey's "art of historical bookmaking" would, theoretically, produce an encyclopedic vista – a vantage point above the vast labyrinth of knowledge from which the philosopher, as d'Alembert suggested in the Preliminary Discourse to the *Encyclopédie*, "can discern the general branches of human knowledge, the points that separate or unite them; and sometimes he can even glimpse the secrets that relate them to one another."[22] The process of amassing, arranging, and connecting extracts, in other words, provided the foundation on which a system of world mythology could be built.

In keeping with this tradition, Southey envisioned his collections as raw materials, valuable only after they had undergone a metamorphosis. As he wryly reflected in 1822, delays in his current project were the result of "my besetting sin – a sort of miser-like love of accumulation":

> Like those persons who frequent sales, and fill their houses with useless pur-
> chases, because they may want them sometime or other; so am I forever
> making collections and storing up materials which may not come into use
> till the Greek Calends. And this I have been doing for five and twenty years!
> It is true that I draw daily upon my hoards, and should be poor without
> them; but in prudence I ought now to be working up those materials rather
> than adding to so much dead stock. (*LC*, 413)

Southey imagines his collections as reserve capital on which he can draw at
any time (much like the life insurance he purchased with the Laureateship
salary),[23] but recognizes that paying in without withdrawing creates "dead
stock" or inventory gathering dust in the warehouse. Materials diligently
collected must be transformed to yield an adequate return on his twenty-
five-year investment.

Southey's letters describe, repeatedly and in detail, the process by which
his stock of materials became a saleable commodity. Turning to his proposed history of Portugal after the completion of *Thalaba* on 1 May 1800,
he writes to Coleridge, "my plan is this: immediately go through the chronicles in order, and then make a sketch of the narrative; the timbers put
together, the house may be finished at leisure"; several months later, he
adds: "my work in England will be chiefly to arrange and tack together;
here I have been gutting, and go home to digest" (*LC*, 123, 142). Extensive reading allows him to produce the "skeleton" of a work, which he then
makes into "flesh, blood and beauty" by arranging and digesting the materials he has transcribed in his notebooks (*LC*, 146). A loosely bound, undated
manuscript describing the story of Pelayo (later to become *Roderick, The
Last of the Goths*) shows the next step in the process.[24] The manuscript
opens with a list of principal characters, followed by the skeleton of the
poem: "a fine opening would be Pelayo keeping a vigil for his Father's
soul," and so on, outlining the poem's major events by character, action,
and purpose. The outline is followed by several pages of extracts from the
earliest Spanish novel, *Crónica Sarracina* by Pedro del Corral, eventually
giving way to a series of more scattered references: "Pyramid at Gyon with
its steps D D p. 41. The Anas Sestanas – erected by I Sestius in honor of
Augustus. They stood on the sea shore at the mouth of the river Abono
D. D. p. 43. The wild ass. Beasts. Wolves. Wild Boars. Eagles Mad wolves.
Mariaca 212. Fire-flies – grillo – flying grasshopper."[25] With the skeleton
in place, Southey begins the work of digesting the details that will become
the poem's imagery, the flesh on the bare bones of plot.

Southey's metaphor raises the specter of *Frankenstein*, and his critics did cast the long poems – particularly those based on Eastern

mythologies – as monstrous. In reviews of his epics, Southey's erudition and its textual manifestations were targets of critics' ire as much as the poems' mythological content. Reviews of *The Curse of Kehama* note the "unwearied industry," "the perseverance, and the extensive research of the learned author," which produced a poem "fed and supported by vast sources of knowledge and observation" but abounding in "incongruities" (*RS*, 132–33, 147). Like *Thalaba*, it was "a gallery of successive pictures" painted in "colours of superlative brilliancy [on] a canvas of endless extent" (*RS*, 91, 146). As Southey's friend William Taylor gently chided, while overflowing with beautiful metaphors, *Thalaba* showed a "want of concatenation, of mutual dependence, of natural arrangement" in the sequence of events (*RS*, 92). *Madoc*, too, was taken to task for its incongruities and wild improbabilities, while also being so "ponderous" as to "fatigue the patience of the reader" (*RS*, 104). *Roderick*, the most successful of Southey's long poems, was deemed "too long by half," injured "by a too great minuteness of detail," and overburdened by "a voluminous collection of notes" (*RS*, 176, 188). According to critics, the poems contained a superfluity of information that refused to cohere: the multitude of beautiful descriptions, rapid succession of incidents, and armature of annotation replicated the piecemeal method of composition, where pillars, pyramids, mad wolves, and fireflies were grafted onto a wild and rambling "march of events" (*RS*, 92).

While other reviews hinted at the connection between Southey's research methods and the structure of his poems, Jeffrey's review of *Thalaba* in the first issue of the *Edinburgh Review* maps a causal relation. Jeffrey plots how, having decided to write an Oriental poem, Southey undertook a purposeful course of reading to ferret out fit materials. Having copied out all manner of incidents "susceptible of poetical embellishment, or capable of picturesque representation," Southey then adopts a fable that will allow him to "work up all his materials, and interweave every one of his quotations, without any *extraordinary* violation of unity or order" (*RS*, 83, original emphasis). With a plan in place, "he began to write; and his poem is little else than his commonplace book versified"; the result, Jeffrey scoffs, is that the "composition and harmony of the work" resembles the pattern of a "patchwork drapery" (*RS*, 83–84). For Jeffrey, Southey merely performs the work of the editor, stitching together scraps of other books "in judicious combinations."[26]

This apparently damning assessment disturbed Southey less than the review's distracting critique of Wordsworth's Preface to *Lyrical Ballads*. The reason: For the most part, he concurred with the literary tenets Jeffrey put forward. Responding to the review in his letter to Wynn, Southey affirmed that "a narrative poem must have its connecting parts: it can not be all interest and incident, no more than a picture all light" (*LC*, 157). To meet this requirement, Southey undertook major pre-publication revisions of both *Madoc* and *Thalaba*. Of the latter, he wrote to Wynn from Lisbon in 1801,

> Thalaba is now a whole and unembarrassed story: the introduction of Laila is not an episode, it is so connected with the murder of Hodeirah and the after actions of Thalaba, as to be essentially part of the tale. Thalaba has certainly and inevitably the fault of Samson Agonistes – its parts might change place; but, in a romance, epic laws may be dispensed with. (*LC*, 141–42)

In rewriting Books XI and XII, Southey meshed the episodes into the larger framework, making them essential parts of a whole.[27] However, there remained the niggling issue of concatenation: As Samuel Johnson had observed of Milton's *Samson Agonistes*, "the intermediate parts have neither cause nor consequence, neither hasten nor retard the catastrophe."[28] With everything stitched into place, Southey recognizes an *inevitable* flaw, which he chalks up to genre. As Joseph Addison argued in his defense of *Paradise Lost*, in the epic "no single Step should be omitted in that just and regular Progress which it must be supposed to take from its Original to its Consummation."[29] As Southey would have it, a "metrical romance" – *Thalaba's* subtitle, alluding to the mid-eighteenth-century recovery of medieval romances – was a much looser affair.

In drawing this distinction, Southey was being more than a little disingenuous. Even as he claimed to embrace the episodic narrative structure of romance, his revisions aimed to remake a series of episodes into an "unembarrassed" whole. As Stuart Curran notes, this tension between practical aims and generic designation stems, at least in part, from the very blurry line separating epic and romance in the period.[30] If Aristotelian poetics demanded that all events in an epic must "grow out of one another in the most natural order," Addison had already pointed out that Milton excelled his classical predecessors in this requirement. *The Aeneid*, in particular, included "episodes which may be looked upon as Excrescencies rather than as Parts of the Action."[31] As Philip Hardie has argued, this aspect of Virgil's poem left a legacy of generic conflation: While striving for totality and closure, Virgil's literary successors continually thwart epic progression, instead wandering after the partial gains and always-deferred goal of romance.[32] Peripatetic and totalizing, all of Southey's annotated poems straddle epic and romance, driving forward – in a series of loosely connected

episodes – toward an inevitable conclusion, in this case Thalaba's unal-
terable destiny as the destroyer of Domdaniel.

As Jeffrey's criticism indicates, accounting for *Thalaba*'s disorderly progression generically merely covers over a fault line inherent in Southey's
compositional method. As early as the seventeenth century, it was feared
that readers "make too much ado about collections" such that "all their
learning amounts to but a deal of injudicious scribble, and raking together
scraps of authors."[33] By the end of the eighteenth century, Hannah More
assessed collections of "Beauties" in by then familiar terms: Collections of
"scanty and penurious sources of short writings of the easy kind . . . form
no concatenation of ideas, nor any dependent series of deduction" (*SFE*,
192). For More – and many of her contemporaries who subscribed to Lockean educational theory (discussed in Chapter 4) – collections of extracts
produced desultory minds incapable of "that power of arrangement which
knows how to link a thousand consecutive ideas in one dependent train,
without losing sight of the original idea out of which the rest grow, and
on which they all hang" (*SFE*, 182). Coleridge's view was equally disparaging: In the *Biographia Literaria*, he satirizes "the reading of the reading
public," nine-tenths of which was drawn from magazines and "a shelf or
two of BEAUTIES, ELEGANT EXTRACTS and ANAS" (*BL*, I: 48). By
browsing collections housed in circulating libraries, Coleridge complained,
the contemporary reader was engaged in "a sort of beggarly daydreaming,
during which the mind of the dreamer furnishes for itself nothing but lazi-
ness and a little mawkish sensibility" (*BL*, I: 48). Under the sway of such
assessments, rather than the ultimate synthesis promised by proponents
of inductive method from Bacon to William Duncan, Southey's methods
were liable to end in disorder and distraction.

Southey's compositional procedures underwrote his contemporary critical reception, and the aesthetic assessment proffered in reviews has clung
to him and defined to a large degree his place in (or displacement from)
the Romantic canon. Jeffrey's ironic jab at *Thalaba*'s "judicious combinations" isolates precisely where Southey's procedures translate into aesthetic
evaluation. As *The Critical Review* contended, Southey might have had the
potential for high poetical genius, but he could not be classed with the
first of modern poets because he was "entirely deficient in that corrective
quality of mind, without which it is impossible for the most astonishing
talents to produce real greatness in any one department of art or science; we
mean a cool, steady, and comprehensive judgment" (*RS*, 137). This assessment derives from late-eighteenth-century empiricist theories of genius discussed in the previous chapter. The imagination's "methodizing power,"

as Gerard argued, allows the poet or scientist to take "a comprehensive view of every subject to which his genius is adapted," while the judgment induces the "habit of correctness in thinking, and ensures the mind to move straight forward to the end proposed, without declining into the byepaths which run off on both sides."[34] Without judgment, the most comprehensive mind is likely to produce a "huge collection of conceptions" piled up in a "confused heap" rather than a "regular work" united by a "proper disposition" of elements.[35] If he lacked this faculty, comprehensiveness would not enable Southey to grasp the multitude of connections – standing above the labyrinth of knowledge he had amassed, he may have glimpsed the secret relations but could not transmute them into a cohesive whole.

As part of a literary movement that – practically from its inception – valued coherence and resolution as aesthetic ideals, Southey's piecemeal method could only do him harm, particularly under the sway of evolving definitions of fancy and imagination. As early as 1796, Coleridge had already concluded that, while exhibiting great powers of language, Southey "does not possess opulence of Imagination, lofty-paced Harmony, or that *toil* of thinking, which is necessary in order to plan a *Whole*" (*RS*, 49).[36] For Coleridge, Southey was and would always be a poet of fancy, not – like Shakespeare or Wordsworth – of the imagination: Southey was adept at the work of collecting, arranging, aggregating, associating, disposing, embellishing, and mixing, but lacked the predominant attribute of masculine genius, the ability to synthesize and transform materials into something new.[37] Despite his systematic approach to composition, Southey lacked the "habit of method" by which "things the most remote and diverse in time, place, and outward circumstance, are brought into mental congruity and succession" (*F*, 1: 455). The patient, industrious, erudite Robert Southey of the *Biographia Literaria* (1817) – Coleridge praises Southey's "matchless industry and perseverance" and his ability to combine "so much truth and knowledge with so much life and *fancy*" (*BL*, I: 63–64, my emphasis) – stands as a foil for Coleridge's co-dependent concepts of method and imagination. This portrait of Southey in turn provoked Coleridge's characterization of the "man of education" in the "Essays of Method" (1818) as someone with the "habit of foreseeing, in each integral part . . . the whole that he then intends to communicate" (*F*, I: 449).[38]

Coleridge's assessment of his fellow Lake poet picks up on Southey's own vexed relationship to his compositional procedures. A striking instance of self-reflection occurs in a draft manuscript of *Madoc*, composed in 1801–04, which registers the tension between promised synthesis and perceived incoherence. The manuscript opens with a skeleton plan for a wholesale revision of the long poem, mapping out incidents and imagery section by section. Before beginning the sketch of Part II ("Madoc in Aztlan"), Southey interrupts the neat trajectory with a reflection on the process he is engaged in:

> It is remarkable that tho incidents & single thoughts flash into my mind at all times unsought & unexpected, the wind blowing when where it listeth. I have yet no power of combining them when the pen be in my hand. If my attention be at all concentrated when walking it is then [fast?] scenes & imaginary events [begin] arising out of them. But most certainly I go on with so desultory & unoccupied a mind that my eye is awake to every animated object. The pen is my wand without which I can work no wonders.[39]

If only for a moment, Southey meditates on what it feels like to bring order to nearly 9000 lines of verse and their accompanying notes. To escape the flashing series of disconnected pictures in his mind, he perambulates through landscape, letting scenes and events wash over him in rapid succession; he is awake to the minutiae of nature but unable to combine event, incident, and imagery into the fabric of the poem. It is the pen, not the man, which contains the magic power of synthesis, and its absence frustrates and discomfits him.

By its very location – embedded within a "skeleton" in the process of being fleshed out with details – Southey's reflection redefines as a methodological impasse what Coleridge might call a failure of the imagination. Having amassed a considerable stock of carefully arranged and digested materials, Southey has arrived at the crucial step of combination and synthesis, only to find himself beset by a swarm of particulars. Southey had contracted, much to his dismay, a condition endemic to seventeenth- and eighteenth-century experimental philosophy: The process of collecting, arranging, comparing, and distinguishing might yield conglomerates instead of wholes, single thoughts rather than synthetic truths. In designating Southey a poet of fancy, Coleridge registers the methodological problem of induction in empiricist aesthetics, but this "problem" was endemic in eighteenth-century moral philosophy more broadly. As Julie Ellison has suggested, "Fancy treats experience as matter that can be manipulated but not transformed. It conforms to the process of intellectual sorting – arrangement, classification, and comparison – that constituted the methodological core of the human sciences."[40] As I detail below, the products of Southey's fancy – his long annotated poems – constitute a textual space where the rifts within the newly developing disciplines of anthropology and history become materially palpable and open to negotiation. To draw out these tensions, I now turn to the target of Jeffrey's attack, *Thalaba the Destroyer*, and examine the composite form Southey's method generated in practice.

Annotation, Antiquarianism, and the Disciplines of History

The 1801 first edition of *Thalaba the Destroyer* put Southey's method on display. After some back and forth with the publisher, a massive armature of notes appeared on the bottom of each page.[41] As a consequence, Southey's practice of borrowing and compiling scraps of other texts is immediately obvious and continually visible: Jeffrey complained that Southey "generally lays before his readers the whole original passage from which his imitation has been taken" (*RS*, 83). While Jeffrey meant to divest Southey of any claim to originality, he also drew attention to the outcome of Southey's compositional procedure. Southey's letters show that as he was outlining *Thalaba*'s narrative, he was also "gutting" libraries in Exeter, "laying in a good stock of notes and materials" (*LC*, 114). Explaining his process to Coleridge in 1799, he admitted, "some progress is made in the sixth book of Thalaba [but] my notes are ready for the whole – at least there is only the trouble of arranging and seasoning them" (*LC*, 116).[42] The notes, in other words, were written up in accordance with the skeleton plan and organized as the poem was composed. Nicola Trott suggests that Southey made very little distinction between annotation and versification,[43] but it is perhaps more precise to say one process generated the other: Southey's notes are the materials from which the poem has been made masquerading as authorizing paratext.

As Jeffrey claimed and Southey affirmed, the notes served to counter charges of plagiarism by documenting sources, but they also make visible the work of versifying.[44] In Book 1, for example, Southey describes the actual palace at Hirah as a point of comparison to the fictional palace Thalaba and his mother encounter in the Paradise of Irem (Fig. 6). The lines read as follows:

> Less wonderous pile and less magnificent
> Sennama built at Hirah, tho' his art
> Sealed with one stone the ample edifice
> And made its colors, like the serpents skin
> Play with changeful beauty: him, its Lord
> Jealous lest after-effort might surpass
> The now unequalled palace, from its height
> Dashed on the pavement down.[45]

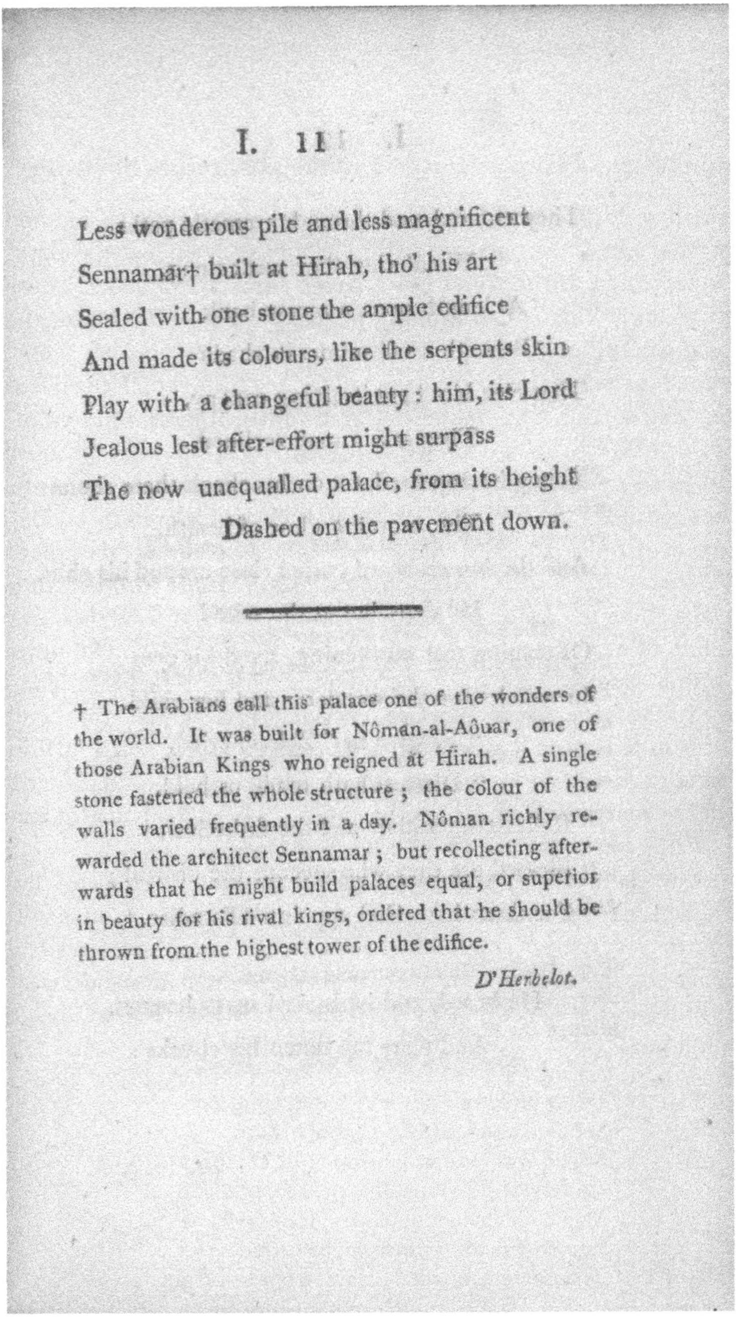

I. 11

Less wonderous pile and less magnificent
Sennamar† built at Hirah, tho' his art
Sealed with one stone the ample edifice
And made its colours, like the serpents skin
Play with a changeful beauty : him, its Lord
Jealous lest after-effort might surpass
The now unequalled palace, from its height
　　　　　Dashed on the pavement down.

————————

† The Arabians call this palace one of the wonders of
the world. It was built for Nôman-al-Aôuar, one of
those Arabian Kings who reigned at Hirah. A single
stone fastened the whole structure ; the colour of the
walls varied frequently in a day. Nôman richly rewarded the architect Sennamar ; but recollecting afterwards that he might build palaces equal, or superior
in beauty for his rival kings, ordered that he should be
thrown from the highest tower of the edifice.

D'Herbelot.

Fig. 6 Robert Southey, *Thalaba the Destroyer* (London, 1801), p. 11. Courtesy of the Albert
and Shirley Small Special Collections Library, University of Virginia.

The note, cued by a mark after the architect's name, appears directly below the lines in the 1801 edition.

> The Arabians call this palace one of the wonders of the world. It was built for Nôman-al-Aôuar, one of those Arabian kings who reigned at Hirah. A single stone fastened the whole structure; the colour of the walls varied frequently in a day. Nôman richly rewarded the architect Sennamar; but recollecting afterwards that he might build palaces equal, or superior in beauty for his rival kings, ordered that he should be thrown from the highest tower of the edifice. – D'Herbelot (*T*, p. 194)

If the reader dutifully followed the cue,[46] he or she would read the note and then return to the verse, presumably noticing how neatly Southey's ten syllable lines follow the progression of clauses in the note, reordering and embellishing the prose with anastrophe, simile, and alliteration. Versifying, as it appears here, entailed the work of ornamentation – a striking observation when taken alongside the previous note in *Thalaba*, a critique of "waste of ornament and labour" characteristic of Orientalist manuscripts and Eastern literature more generally (*T*, p. 194). The note–verse composite thus puts on display the "*Arabesque* ornament" of Southey's chosen irregular verse form, raising questions about what it means, poetically, to take up an Oriental subject (*T*, p. 3). At the same time, by documenting the source of Southey's description in Barthélemy D'Herbelot's 1697 *Bibliothèque orientale*, the note situates the poem in an intermediary space – Southey is in fact versifying his own translation of a French text – that allows the poet to maintain a certain distance between the verse and its Oriental subject.

Beyond opening his poetics to charges of base unoriginality or Eastern ornamental waste, as with Darwin's *Botanic Garden*, Southey's verse–note combinations in *Thalaba* obviously violate the conventional distinction between text and paratext. This is likely part of the reason that Jeffrey threads a critique of the Lake School through *Thalaba* – Southey's poem illustrates Wordsworth's claim in the Preface to *Lyrical Ballads* that there is "no essential difference between the language of prose and metrical composition."[47] Even so, the notes still perform conventional paratextual functions in relation to the verse narrative, often acting as a threshold or zone of transaction between author and reader, giving subtle guidance on how to read the poem.[48]

Take, for example, the introduction of Abdaldar's crystal ring, the central object in Thalaba's detection by and preservation from the sorcerers of Domdaniel. The ring is initially described as a "powerful gem" that

condensed
Primeval dews that upon Caucasus
Felt the first winter's frost.
Ripening there it lay beneath
Rock above rock, and mountain ice up-piled
On mountain, till the incumbent mass assumed,
So huge its bulk, the Ocean's azure hue.

(*T*, 2: 237–43)

The appended note explains this geological reference by way of two signi-fications of the verb "condensed." Quoting a 1750 compilation of ancient authors, *The Mirror of Stones*, the note suggests, "some imagine that the crystal is snow turned to ice which has been hardening thirty years, and is turned to rock by age" (*T*, p. 208). Southey then cites a report from Jean Baptiste Tavernier's seventeenth-century travel narrative of a crystal, belonging to the Prince of Monaco, formed with water trapped inside of it. The ring belongs to antiquity, compressed to solidity by long stretches of geologic time while also containing condensed liquid from the earliest history of the earth. The third part of the note, however, renders these descriptions suspect. Southey quotes Buffon's *L'Histoire Naturelle*, which gives a quite different assessment: "Crystal, precious stones, every stone that has a regular figure . . . are only exudations, or the concreting juices of flint in large masses; they are, therefore, new and spurious productions" (*T*, p. 208). In the third part of the note, the primeval ring has been exposed as a fake, a revaluation that foreshadows Thalaba's dangerous reliance on it for protection and his eventual exchange of the ring for the more power-ful and purer talisman of faith. Through the conflict of sources, the note's documentary function has become pedagogic, supplying the reader with a way of grasping the ring's evolving significance to the poem's plot.

In the printed book, Southey's notes thus work in tandem with the verse, lending authority to its imagery and providing a guide to its narrative development. At the same time, the notes might also undermine the verse's representations, as the quotation from Buffon invalidates the depiction of the ring in the verse by eroding the legitimacy of its sources. Southey's reading cue, in other words, has the byproduct of casting the verse itself as spurious, a deceptive fiction manufactured with sham materials. Again like Darwin's *Loves*, this tension between note and verse recurs innumer-able times in Southey's long poems, producing an effect already familiar to Romantic-era readers through Edward Gibbon's monumental work of historical scholarship, *The Decline and Fall of the Roman Empire*. Gibbon employs a system of annotation "that not only incorporates authorities, facts, and details that would impede the narrative process [of the text], but that also contradicts and counteracts aspects of the narrative."[49] By piling up "facts" from sources that stand at odds with, qualify, or otherwise invalidate each other, Southey, like Gibbon, introduces ripples into the narrative fabric of his primary text. Southey's authenticating apparatus thus preserves the contradictions that surfaced in his extensive reading. The procedure he recommended to Harry – entering quotations from the best authors on the verso of his commonplace book, and "correcting" this account with additions from other sources on the recto – undergirds the poetic text. Far more than their mere presence on the bottom of the page, it is the *kind* of note Southey writes that fractures the poem's sequential narrative.

In their propensity to pile up historical sources, Southey's notes sit between the Enlightenment histories of Gibbon and David Hume and the "scientific history" developed by Leopold von Ranke in the 1820s. As Anthony Grafton details in his wide-ranging study *The Footnote*, Ranke followed a commonplace procedure very much resembling Southey's: he divided the pages of his notebook into columns, one devoted to his main source and the other to "complementary or divergent accounts," which allowed him to make a "systematic comparison" of his sources.[50] Southey employed the same procedure as later systematic historians, but his product more closely resembles those of Ranke's Enlightenment precursors. As critics of Gibbon pointed out, his great sin was "heaping up without distinction citations to authorities who actually disagreed."[51] This condition at least partly derives from Gibbon's fusion of two kinds of history, the "broad viewpoint of the *philosophes* with the minute erudition of the antiquaries."[52] This tension within historical scholarship at the end of the eighteenth century accounts for Southey's uneasy combination of large-scale analogies between cultures with the particular facts of antiquarian research.

Even as Gibbon borrowed models of criticism and source citation from antiquarian scholars, he (like many of his generation) mocked the antiquarian enterprise for its unswerving devotion to details. Following the same mandates as the Royal Society for the undirected pursuit of natural knowledge, seventeenth- and eighteenth-century antiquarians gathered up the stuff of history, indiscriminately collecting everything curious or remarkable, regardless of its perceived value.[53] Robert Burns's gentle satire of his friend, the antiquarian Francis Grose, draws a typical portrait of the omnivorous antiquarian collector: "He has a fouth o' auld nick-nackets: / Rusty airn caps and jinglin jackets, ... And parritch-pats and auld saut-backets, / [from] Before the Flood."[54] Grose himself admits that antiquaries had long been seen as "plodding fellows, who, wanting genius for nobler studies, busied themselves in heaping up illegible Manuscripts, mutilated Statues, obliterated Coins, and broken Pipkins!"[55] Antiquaries collected physical remains to confirm or counter textual authorities, but the focus on objects coexisted with the equally strong strain of bookish antiquarianism, emblematized by Isaac D'Israeli's *Curiosities of Literature* (1791).[56] D'Israeli's collection of heterogeneous curiosities emerged out of a long-standing scholarly tradition. As Grafton notes of the German Jesuit Athanasius Kircher, the seventeenth-century antiquarian was characterized by "an encyclopedic willingness to accommodate the incongruous and the alien, one that allowed many voices to speak" on the same page.[57] Like his object-centered counterpart, the bookish antiquarian was defined by his attachment to curious facts heaped together without the additive of continuous narrative.

Metaphorically equating these forms of antiquarian collecting, Thomas Love Peacock would later characterize all of Romantic poetry in this mold. In contrast to philosophers and historians who were "accelerating the progress of knowledge," contemporary poets were "wallowing in the rubbish of departed ignorance."[58] Their reliance on antiquarian research and traveler's accounts gave rise to their compositional practices – Scott "digs up," Byron "cruizes," Wordsworth "picks up" – but Southey was the worst offender: he "wades through ponderous volumes of travels and old chronicles, from which he carefully selects all that is false, useless, and absurd as being essentially poetical."[59] For Peacock, the problem was procedural. By using "disjointed relics of tradition and fragments of second-hand observation," poets had rejected the very essence of poetry, that

> philosophic mental tranquility which looks round with an equal eye on all external things, collects a store of ideas, discriminates their relative value, assigns to all their proper place, and from the materials of useful knowledge thus collected, appreciated, and arranged, forms new combinations that impress the stamp of their power and utility on the real business of life.[60]

Peacock's ideal describes Southey's inductive compositional method – following the steps of observation, collection, distinction, arrangement, recombination – but places its emphasis on the outcomes of progress, use, and utility, qualities at odds with the antiquary's haphazard accumulation of historical minutiae.[61]

Peacock drew his metaphor – the philosophic prospect set against antiquarian collecting – from an existing split in eighteenth-century historical inquiry. Alongside the antiquarian enterprise (and partly in response to the masses of data it had produced), moral philosophers from Hume and Adam Ferguson to Adam Smith and Dugald Stewart propounded a totalizing narrative of the progress of society. As Hume suggested in *A Treatise of Human Nature*, the "Science of Man" sought to apply the inductive method experimental science to study the development of the mind, language, and society.[62] Lacking the observable facts and phenomena of chemical philosophy or natural history, travel narratives and ethnographic accounts became the fodder for the laboratory of moral science.[63] This evidentiary base allowed authors to draw large-scale analogies across cultures, based on the premise that civilizations progress in a uniform pattern but at an unequal pace. As Ferguson puts it in *An Essay on the History of Civil Society* (1767), "it is in [the] present condition [of Arab clans or American tribes], that we are to behold, as in a mirrour, the features of our own progenitors."[64] The antiquarian project of collecting and categorizing historical objects and texts supplied empirical groundwork for this conjectural or philosophical history,[65] but as Susan Manning has argued, antiquarians also resisted the sweeping narrative through which the Science of Man united the branches of human history and mapped the analogical relations between cultures.[66] While conjectural history strove to give the past a "compelling and convincing narrative shape," for the omnivorous collector the allure of curious facts outweighed the need to fill the gaps in historical narrative.[67]

As his manuscript notebooks and published *Common-place Book* make manifest, Southey was a collector of the antiquarian ilk, taking pleasure in out-of-the-way books and odd facts, the curious bric-a-brac of history. What he wrote to John Rickman in 1804 serves as a typical example: Southey proclaims, "I have more in hand than Bonaparte or Marquis Wellesley – digesting Gothic law, gleaning moral history from monkish legends, and conquering India, or rather Asia, with Albuquerque; filling up the chinks of the day by hunting in Jesuit chronicles, and compiling Collectanea Hispanica et Gothica" (*LC*, 178). Southey's empire, like that of other bookish antiquarians, consisted of the broken bits of obscure texts, brought together under headings in his well-arranged notebooks.[68] To empty his storehouse, Southey reworks this mass of sources, extending his antiquarian empire along the bottom of *Thalaba*'s pages.

While literally underwritten by antiquarianism, Southey's mythological poems depend equally on the analogical reasoning of the Science of Man. As Javed Majeed has shown, Southey viewed cultures comparatively, often drawing parallels between customs, beliefs, landscapes, and literary productions across geographical and national boundaries. The Preface to *The Byrth, Lyf, and Actes of King Arthur* (1817) articulates the position most explicitly: Southey writes, "in similar stages of civilization, or states of society, the fictions of different people will bear a corresponding resemblance, notwithstanding the differences of time and space."[69] Southey's choice to model *Thalaba*'s verse form on Frank Sayers' *Dramatic Sketches of the Ancient Northern Mythology* (1790) posits a relation between ancient Britons and the poem's "modern Arab" characters, an analogy asserted repeatedly in the footnotes (*T*, p. 193). Even more than the poems themselves, Southey's annotations are a "laboratory of cultures," one in which he experimented with a power of analogy to juxtapose and bind together the religious practices and beliefs of various nations.[70] The result exemplifies Manning's astute observation about why the Science of Man eschewed annotation: just as excessive annotation distracted the reader from a text's narrative progression, the antiquarian accumulation of detail "dismembered continuous, synthetic thought" – the very essence of conjectural history.

Southey's notes stage the conflict between the synthetic mode of conjectural history and the heaping-up of antiquarianism. Take, for example, a passage in Book III of *Thalaba*, when the sorcerer Abdaldar has been killed by a providential Simoom and buried in the desert, but is found expelled from his grave in the morning. In the note appended to Moath's question – "is the man / So foul with magic and all blasphemy, / That Earth like Heaven rejects him?" (*T*, 3: 90–2) – Southey catalogs reports of persons who refused to lie quiet in their graves. The first passage in the note cites three instances: first, the Old Woman of Berkeley (the subject of one of Southey's ballads), translated from Matthew of Westminster's 1570 publication in Latin and recording an event supposed to have taken place in the ninth century; second, the example of a young boy reported in St. Gregory's *Dialogues*, composed in the sixth century; and third, the case of Charles Martel, an eighth-century Frankish leader whose forces defeated the Muslim army at the Battle of Tours in 732 (*T*, pp. 213–14, 336). The second section of the note quotes a story from Morgan's 1728 *History of Algiers* about the corpse of Heyradin Barbarossa, an Ottoman Admiral who lived from 1478–1576 and ousted the Spanish from Algiers; according to Morgan, he was renowned for his cruelty to Christians.[71] In drawing an analogy between these instances, Southey outlines a typical Science of Man model of the progressive stages of society. What is reported by the Turks "as a certain truth" in the sixteenth century finds its Christian European counterparts 700 to 1000 years earlier (*T*, p. 214). Deploying the fundamental disparity on the timeline of cultural development, Southey casts Moath as both modern and ancient, Christian and Muslim, a man whose question encodes a long history of cultural and religious strife.

The third part of the note, however, shakes this seemingly stable analogical framework. The story about Barbarossa ends with the trick they used to make him stay in his grave: "a Greek wizard counselled them to bury a black dog together with the body" (*T*, p. 214). This provokes Southey to interject a brief comment: "In supernatural affairs dogs seem to possess a sedative effect" (*T*, p. 214). A long quote from Grimstone's 1608 *Historie of the Netherlands* follows, describing how, in 1170, a "bottomless hole" in a sluice in Flanders was finally stopped up by throwing a sea-dog in it, which occasioned the name of the town on the spot, Hondtsdam (*T*, p. 214). This conclusion to the note carries the reader very far from the verse, both geographically and topically. This part of the note has no bearing on the issue of evil persons being shaken out of their graves, there are no dogs in the verse (nor is a sea dog actually a dog), and the note's focus on Muslim–Christian conflict has vanished into the sluice along with the seal. This final section of the note is also four times longer than the other two sections combined; in following it to the end, the reader ends up several pages past the point in the verse where he or she left off, mid-line, with Moath's question. Had the note ended after quoting Morgan, the dog would have been merely another facet of Turkish supernatural beliefs, and the note just another analogy between cultures. With this long addition about Hondtsdam, however, it is no longer clear what exactly we are to say in response to Moath's question about blasphemy, or to think about the cultural comparison scripted in the first part of the note. Southey begins by replicating the hierarchy of cultures supported by conjectural history, but ends by destabilizing its analogical framework and thereby denying its comprehensive system of cultural relations. One more curious fact, running off at an angle, has toppled the structure that it was, perhaps, intended to support.

From this example, we might be tempted to read a political purpose into Southey's destabilizing notes, the antiquarian impulse driving a wedge into the project of Enlightenment conjectural history. Such a reading, however, fails to account for Southey's seemingly ambivalent position vis-à-vis the ideological assumptions that underwrite this project. If the seal in the sluice distracts readers from the focus on Muslim–Christian conflict, other notes appear to simultaneously uphold and dismantle the poem's depiction of Muslim culture and faith as barbaric and backward.[72] The most obvious example, the scene of the Christian captive's death by beating in Book IX, may be the most telling. Prefaced by a long description punctuated by rhetorical questions – "Why does the City pour her thousands forth?" – the verse narrative finally arrives at the "object of this day's festival, / . . . The Christian captive" (*T*, 9: 567, 618–20). In a gruesome portrait of unthinking idolatry, the executioners "beat his belly with alternate blows" while Muslim Priests sing a "hymn of glory to their Devil God" and the women spectators "clap their hands for joy / And lift their children up / To see the Christian die" (*T*, 9: 639, 626, 644–46). This scene appears to have little connection to the preceding narrative, until we learn that it is yet another of the witch Khawla's attempts to destroy Thalaba. Having failed to kill him by burning a wax effigy on a pyre of mandrake and manchineel, Khawla plans to collect the poisonous foam that will drip from the mouth of the red-haired captive as he dies and use it to poison Thalaba.

Southey appends a note to these lines, first quoting a 1643 account of a Mohammedan physician who beat a red-haired Italian boy to death to extract poison. This account is drawn from a French collection of tragic declamations, Tristan L'Hermite's *Plaidoyers Historique*, placing the action in the field of dramatic representation, not historical fact. After the long quote, Southey adds two comments that modify the story's exclusive application to Muslim culture. He first describes how the source for the note includes a charge (by the mother of the boy) that the Italian (presumably Catholic) physician to whom the boy was apprenticed would have done the same thing if he hadn't been afraid of the law. Southey then adds a barbed comment in his own voice: "As the Moslem [*sic*] employed a red-haired Christian in this manufactory, it should seem that a Turk ought to be used in Christendom. But as Turks are not easily caught, a Jew might do" (*T*, p. 281). Having raised the specter of the long history of gross mistreatment of persons of other faiths by Christians, Southey again shifts perspective by linking the supposedly Muslim practice with that of Brazilian Indians, who poison their arrowheads with the rotten flesh of their enemies. Southey's source, a seventeenth-century government document, states that "[a]fter the Spaniards came into that country and waged war on the Indians," they particularly sought after red-haired Spaniards for this purpose, whose flesh was supposed (by the report of the Spanish themselves) to produce a more virulent poison (*T*, p. 281). What was in the verse a simple indictment of Muslim cruelty and occult medicine has been transformed into an outcome of colonial conquest, a defense mechanism of the oppressed borrowed from the conqueror's self-image.

At this point, the note has conflated Muslim and Catholic cruelties, but (as with many of his notes) Southey pushes the point still farther. The next section of the note begins with a reference to Macbeth, bringing the stereotype and its gory legacy home to England, albeit in an earlier historical moment. The next comment – on the association of red hair and leprosy – leads Southey to mull over a historical conundrum: "It is singular that at the time when these opinions [about red hair] prevailed universally, golden locks should enter into almost every description of female beauty" (*T*, p. 281). If cross-cultural comparisons have revealed the stereotype as the product of imperial ambition, this aside (supported by a quotation, in Spanish, from a poetic description of Absalom's long red tresses) suggests the function of desire in the inhumane treatment of the Other. The final part of the note abstracts the problem even further by drawing an analogy between the "Turkish receipt" represented in the verse and the Javanese "method of procuring poison" by hanging a gecko by its tail, agitating it, and capturing the foam that drips from its mouth (*T*, pp. 281–82). Ranging through centuries and across the globe, the note ends by conflating people with animals in a larger continuum of human cruelty (the gecko sustains this torture for several months instead of the Christian captive's six hours). After this long detour, it comes as no surprise that Khawla's attempts to capture the foam from the dying captive in the verse are thwarted by Heaven in the verse: She has become, by way of the note, an emblem of a wanton disregard for life that transcends time, geography, and faith, and is thus rewarded (in the final line of Book IX) with a present from Darwin's *Botanic Garden*, the "Upas Tree of Death" (*T*, 9: 662). In the poem–note composite, nature supports the will of heaven to condemn any and all cultures – including the eleventh-century English ancestors of Southey's readers – whose faith negates their ability to recognize suffering.

This note thus preserves a temporal distance between the Muslim actors in this gruesome scene and Southey's modern British readers, while at the same time challenging the latter to consider the potential effects of their own phenotypical, cultural, or religious biases – most obviously in this example, those directed at red-haired Irish Catholics recently incorporated into Britain by the 1800 Act of Union. An 1801 trip to Dublin confirmed Southey's view: "like a true savage," the Irishman would be "difficult to civilize" (*LC*, 151). Here, Southey stands firmly on the ground of progressive history, and it would be a mistake to argue that his notes negate the cultural hierarchies that surface repeatedly in his letters and that undergird his mythological poems. Moreover, materialized in the poem's extensive annotations, Southey's inductive methods of collecting and arrangement carry the mark of legitimate science, one in which the poet–observer stands (in something akin to a position of colonial authority) above the backward cultures he depicts, whether ancient Britons, seventeenth-century Brazilian Indians, or modern Arabs. Even so, the notes' tendency to transgress their comparativist mode – particularly when they move beyond strict analogies to much looser associations – pushes against the ideological framework of

conjectural history. The product of antiquarian collecting, Southey's heap
of minutiae, both reinforces and disintegrates the comparative hierarchy
of cultures, advancing a universal ethics alongside damning portraits of
Christian and Muslim fanaticism.

Rather than political intervention or poetic failure, then, Southey's notes
make visible the strained relationship between the analogical project of
conjectural history and its evidentiary base – disparate facts and fictions
methodically collected from travel narrative, natural history, ethnographic
accounts, and literary works that are bound together despite obvious contradictions. On a macro level, the tension between antiquarianism and
conjectural history in *Thalaba* replicates the relation of the commonplace
book and the skeleton poem: The details that generate, fill in, and subsequently authorize the larger narrative framework always, *invariably*, exceed
its capacity for syncretism. Southey's poem exposes a tear in the very fabric of late eighteenth-century moral philosophy: the evidentiary base – the
particular instances upon which induction performs its magical work of
linking and combination – is defined by its refusal to congeal into a "natural" arrangement. The notes to *Thalaba* thus constitute a textual space
where the tensions within moral philosophy become materially palpable
and open to negotiation – a space in which competing versions of history
clash on a structural level.

Grafton has argued that in the modern era, the footnote "is bound up
with the ideology and technical practice of a profession."[73] As he demonstrates, notes demarcate the process by which the study of history was transformed into a critical discipline; they reveal how totalizing narrative and
evidentiary base were brought into collusion by way of conflict. Southey's
literary text stands at the crossroads of this development, bringing into
focus the subversive potential of the device by which we now measure
the integrity of historical narrative. However, even though Southey turned
much of his energy to writing history later in his career, he understood his
long poems as interventions in literary as much as historical debates. By
way of conclusion, I detail the poetic and aesthetic theory Southey formulated through his inductive methods of composition.

Aesthetics on the Verge of Parody

Critics of Southey's long poems have inevitably bumped up against ideological uncertainties like those I detail above: Southey appears to be a
hard line supporter of British imperialism and colonialism – until one
starts unpacking the twists and turns of his verse–note composites.[74] While

contemporary reviewers were quick to assert the (unintentional) failure of Southey's experiments, modern critics seek to discover, as Carol Bolton puts it, "Southey's motives."[75] For Fulford, the puzzling effect of *Thalaba*'s annotations is "a genuine tension, an ambivalence stemming from Southey's own uneasy mixture of admiration and distaste for the supernatural narratives he assiduously incorporated."[76] As Fulford suggests, ideological ambivalence is mirrored on a formal level: In *Thalaba*, Southey produced an "odd, and often uneasy, hybrid, a moralizing epic in the dress of a romantic entertainment."[77] Lynda Pratt assesses the 1797–1799 draft of *Madoc* in similar terms. In his attempt to craft a new kind of epic reflective of Pantisocratic ideals, Pratt suggests, Southey produces "a poem which is ideologically and generically confused and confusing."[78]

The ever-prescient Jeffrey also bundled the question of generic confusion with the issue of *Thalaba*'s "wild and extravagant" Oriental fictions (*RS*, 81). The poem's incoherent narrative – produced by stringing together scraps of other texts – is replicated in its experimental combination of measures "multiplied through the whole composition, with an unbounded license of variation" (*RS*, 78).[79] Nicola Trott astutely pinpoints the source of Jeffrey's reaction: "Southey's indefatigable sourcing is of a piece with the episodic detachability which characterizes the works themselves," such that his "epic writing was seen as having been vitiated by lesser genres."[80] Put another way, Southey's compositional method generated annotations at odds with themselves and with the narrative trajectory of the verse, but the long poems are also mixtures of genres spliced together and thus already prone to disaggregation. Southey's epic romances are doubly scripted to violate conventions of orderly narrative progression.[81]

While it takes some digging to uncover the tension between antiquarianism and conjectural history in the notes, Southey explicitly draws attention to moments when other genres – particularly the ballad – intrude into *Thalaba*'s quest narrative. At the end of Book VIII, for example, Khawla decides to transport the captive Thalaba to Mohareb's island. The description of their journey follows: "And away! away! away! / They were no steeds of mortal race / That drew the magic car . . . Away! away! away! / The Demons of the air / Shout their joy as the Sisters pass" (*T*, 8: 416–18, 425–27). Even before the first hint of repetition, the note intercedes to affirm, "My readers will recollect the Lenora," but immediately undercuts the charge of willful imitation: "the unwilling resemblance has been forced upon me by the subject. I could not turn aside from the road because Burger had traveled it before" (*T*, p. 270). Particular subjects belong, Southey implies, to certain genres; any attempt to disengage a demon-decked gallop from the formal elements of Gottfried August Bürger's infamous gothic ballad simply wouldn't work.[82] This idea constituted something of a poetic theory for Southey. He often categorized topics for poems by genre, of which the *Common-place Book* has many examples: "The story of Pausanias needs no alteration for a ballad"; "Sophonisba drinking the poison. A Monodrama"; "Eclogue. A winter evening. Children with their grandmother. They beg for a story. A ghost story. My mother's account of Moll Bee's murder, and the remorse of the murderer, that lead him to accuse himself."[83] In each instance, the story supplies the genre, which in turn generates the formal attributes of the poem.[84]

Within Southey's long poems, this poetic theory is a recipe for formal mixtures that refuse to gel into hybrids. Southey's introduction of the ballad of "Poulter's Mare" in Book I of *Thalaba* is an obvious instance of this, one Jeffrey found vexing enough to quote at length in his review. In the poem proper, Aswad, sole survivor of the idolatrous people of Ad, describes the act that saved his life. Passing by the starving camel bound to his father's grave, he is prompted his to set her free:

> Her limbs were lean with famine, and her eyes
> Looked ghastly with want.
> She knew me when I past,
> She stared me in the face,
> My heart was touched, had it been human else?
> I thought no eye was near, and broke her bonds
> And drove her forth to liberty and life.
>
> (*T*, 1: 344–50)

The lines alternate iambic pentameter with an irregular six-syllable line reminiscent of ballad meter. Southey's note confirms the interpolation of poetic forms. Line 347, he claims, was taken from "one of the most beautiful passages of our old Ballads," of which, although he had never seen it in print, he was able to recreate "an imperfect copy from memory" (*T*, p. 197). He then introduces a *40-line* excerpt from "Old Poulter's Mare" *in the footnote*, describing Poulter's unkind words to the old Mare and his subsequent regret at sending her away (Fig. 7).Poulter sends his kinsman Will to find the Mare, and after much searching (reminiscent of Betty Foy's peregrinations in Wordsworth's "The Idiot Boy"), Will finds her:

> He asked her how she did,
> She stared him in the face,
> Then down she laid her head again, –
> *She was in a wretched case.*
>
> (*T*, p. 198, original italics)

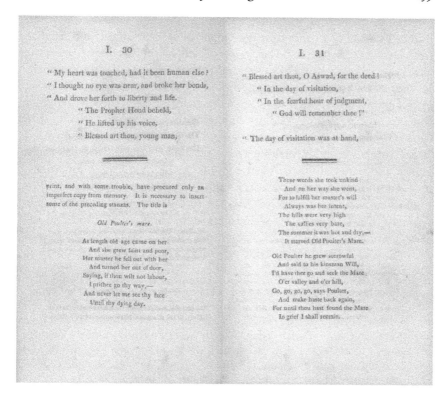

Fig. 7 Robert Southey, *Thalaba the Destroyer* (London, 1801), p. 30. Courtesy of the Albert and Shirley Small Special Collections Library, University of Virginia.

This faux ballad was likely penned by Southey himself, either (as Fulford suggests) as a spoof on Wordsworth or, I would suggest, on Coleridge's much maligned "To a Young Ass." In the note, contemporary poetic satire is caught masquerading as an old English ballad, and the metrical conformity between Prophet's proclamation in the poem proper and the ballad in the note pushes readers to question the significance of Aswad's life-saving act. On the printed page, the sympathy and fraternity emblematized in Aswad's freeing of the camel find their counterpart in Coleridge's Jacobin poem, but introducing "Poulter's Mare" also marks Aswad as a lackadaisical man of feeling, making him poetically outdated by 10 years rather than 400. The formal and material disjunctiveness only heighten the ballad's status as a "new antique," effectively undermining the analogy between Ancient Britons and modern Arabs along with the moral high ground – Aswad's humanity – that the passage seeks to establish.[85]

Jeffrey saw none of this, instead taking Southey at his word: "Mr. Southey's partiality to the drawling vulgarity of some of our old English ditties" is at its worst when he "seriously considers [the last three lines of the ballad] as the *ne plus ultra* of purity and pathos" (*RS*, 84–85). In the opening lines of his parody of Southey, *Sir Proteus* (complete with its own set of explanatory notes, often in Greek), Peacock also homes in on "Poulter's Mare" to ridicule Southey's commingling of antiquated and Orientalist in *Thalaba*. Neither Jeffrey nor Peacock seem to have considered the possibility that Southey could be making a joke, probably because *Thalaba*'s form, diction, and meter all insist "on the moral gravity of the tale's supernatural events and on its seriousness as a high cultural form."[86] However, this brand of note led a reviewer of *Roderick* to take Southey to task: While the poem shows "remarkable seriousness and simplicity of mind," in the notes "there is something hard, something sarcastic, something scoffing" (*RS*, 189). Coleridge seems to have agreed: in a letter to Charles Wynn in 1805, Southey muses:

> My notes when they are not of sober complection, are made in the quaintness of my heart & what I call quaint may doubtless by others be called pert or impertinent. The only question is whether they offend more persons than they please – for certain it is that what pleases one offends another. Coleridge used to beseech me not to put them at the bottom of the page, for he said he could not help laughing. But to say this was to praise the notes, & by putting them at the end I thought all objection obviated.[87]

Quaintness often seems to have been inclined toward satire, and like Coleridge, encountering "Poulter's Mare," I am tempted to laugh. "Poulter's Mare" is certainly not an isolated instance; there is a similarly satiric edge to many of Southey's brief interjections between quotations in *Thalaba*. Quips such as "in supernatural affairs, dogs seem to possess a sedative effect" are sprinkled throughout, often with unsettling implications for the poem's moral code of purity, faith, humanity, and Christian forgiveness (*T*, p. 214). To take only one example, in the midst of a note explaining that Khawla's ability to light a fire with her finger, Southey interjects, "Dead Saints have frequently possessed this phosphoric quality like rotten wood or dead fish" (*T*, pp. 273–74). As with Darwin's love-lorn maid who burns herself out like phosphorus, even if every source Southey quotes upholds the existence of "phosphoric miracles" the lingering stench of rotting fish makes it difficult to take either the saints or Khawla's witchcraft seriously. In one slight stroke of the pen, Southey has turned a lurid gothic scene fit for *The Monk* into something closer to Tam o'Shanter's dance of the witches.

Moments such as these find Southey sitting, as Geoffrey Grigson described it, "deliberately on the verge of self parody."[88] More than the structural condition endemic to his inductive compositional method or the field of historical research, the tension in these passages emanates from the poetic equivalent of a snarky gibe, directed at the seriousness of his generation of poets, himself included. If Southey's mythological poems tackle large-scale political, historical, and social issues – the progress of society, centuries of religious conflict, the power of faith, the effects of colonialism, the moral rectitude of Britain's imperial ambitions – moments of generic mixture reveal his propensity to poke fun at these lofty poetic ambitions. As the examples above suggest, when incommensurate genres mingle, this generates suspect analogies – between saints and putrid fish, camels and horses, dogs and seals – comparisons that raise questions about the core of Southey's poetic project: Can analogy generate knowledge about the natural or social world? Can splicing bits of texts into a composite form produce a coherent view of anything? The result is similar to what Trott finds in Southey's "minor" burlesque poem, "Gooseberry-Pie. A Pindaric Ode." Rather than striving for seamless coherence, the "striking formal effect is of a complete poem that has drawn attention to the separateness of its component parts."[89] Edging the boundary between gravity and farce, Southey foregrounds the very aspect of his poems that designated him a poet of fancy.

Casting a wide net over Southey's extensive and varied oeuvre, it becomes clear that – unlike Darwin, who strove to mollify the disjunctive potential of his chosen form in his successive works – Southey actively cultivated the comic and satiric potential of disunity and disjunction, especially later in his career. This becomes especially pronounced in his unfinished work *The Doctor*, which plays with and on the conundrum raised by his compositional methods and experiments with formal mixture. Perched somewhere between Sterne's ribald *Tristram Shandy* and Thelwall's earnest *The Peripatetic*, this novelistic miscellany takes the legacy of Southey's inductive method as its central theme and opening gambit. Having bantered through the work's conception, mulled over the typeface of its dedication, and composed an ante-preface on the function of prefaces, the unnamed author–character lays down a theory of composition:

> Order is the sanity of the mind, the health of the body, the peace of the city, the security of the state. As the beams to a house, as the bones to the microcosm of man, so is order to all things. Abstract it from the dictionary, and thou mayst imagine the inextricable confusion which would ensue. Reject

it from the alphabet, and Zerah Colburne himself could not go through the christcross-row. How then should I do without it in this history?[90]

Invoking the most arbitrary and naturalized of ordering schemas – the dictionary and alphabet – in conjunction with a mathematical prodigy's vain attempts to find his way into a schoolboy's hornbook, Southey makes it clear he will indeed do without order. In fact, his reflections on constructing the disorderly narrative are practically the only topic that brings coherence to the work. The skeleton and the house, Southey's favorite metaphors for his compositional procedures, resurface here as parodies of themselves, analogies for a de-composed world and its textual counterparts – treatises, sermons, poems, and whole volumes in which "the head might serve for the tail, and the tail for the body, and the body for the head – either end for the middle, and the middle for either end – nay, if you could turn them inside out like a polypus, or a glove, they would be no worse for the operation."[91] In this passage we can see why Southey remained untroubled by Jeffrey's charges and Coleridge's criticism: A striving for order that ultimately and inevitably produces a "want of concatenation" is here – and had long been – Southey's guiding aesthetic paradigm. In the structure of his long poems, Southey thus proposes a far more pragmatic Romantic aesthetic than its Coleridgean counterpart, one that acknowledges the simultaneous necessity and impossibility of grasping the secret relations between things and forming them into a regular body of knowledge.

NOTES

1 Southey wrote to Charles Wynn in 1802 that "the first part [of Jeffrey's review] is designed evidently as an answer to Wordsworth's Preface to the second edition of the Lyrical Ballads; and, however relevant to me, *quoad* Robert Southey, is certainly utterly irrelevant to Thalaba." *Life and Correspondence of Robert Southey*, Charles Cuthbert Southey (ed.) (New York: Harper & Brothers, 1855), p. 157. Subsequently cited in text as *LC*.

2 While he notes several "blunders" made by the reviewer and rejects the idea that the *entire* poem is borrowed from other sources, Southey concludes "the review altogether is a good one" (*LC*, 157).

3 Robert Southey, *Vindiciæ Ecclesiæ Anglicanæ* (London, 1826), p. 7, quoted in Daniel Sanjiv Roberts, Introduction, *The Curse of Kehama* by Robert Southey, vol. 4 of *The Poetical Works of Robert Southey* (London: Pickering & Chatto, 2004), p. ix.

4 Like many of his contemporaries, Southey often used a commonplace method (described below) to structure his notebooks. This led John Wood Warter to title the posthumously published notebooks *Southey's Common-place Book*. Modern editors (of Coleridge's *Notebooks*, for example) have preferred "notebook" over "common-place book," thus obscuring the connection between

Romantic authors' note-taking and compositional practices. To avoid confusion, I use "notebook" as a general category to refer to any book in which notes of any kind are entered, with the caveat that most of the notebooks discussed here and throughout this book, including those kept by Darwin, Southey, Honora Edgeworth, and Coleridge, have obvious connections to the commonplace tradition.

5 Recent critical treatments of *Thalaba* indicate the tenor of debates surrounding Southey's epics. Javed Majeed, for example, sets Southey's epics in the context of the oriental renaissance and its work of cultural comparison; for Majeed, Southey's epics "break isolated cultural idioms" and seek to "reunify cultures." Javed Majeed, *Ungoverned Imaginings: James Mill's* The History of British India *and Orientalism* (Oxford: Clarendon, 1992), pp. 57, 75. Mohammed Sharafuddin gives a similarly positive spin to Southey's work, focusing on the anti-imperialist, pro-Islamic aspects of the epic poems. Mohammed Sharafuddin, *Islam and Romantic Orientalism: Literary Encounters with the Orient* (London: I. B. Tauris, 1994). Taking a more skeptical view, Carol Bolton draws these assessments together, locating the poem as part of Southey's project of "nation and empire building" in which he simultaneously "othered" and domesticated foreign cultures. Carol Bolton, *Writing the Empire: Robert Southey and Romantic Colonialism* (London: Pickering & Chatto, 2007), pp. 2, 4. In tandem with discussions of empire, critics have demonstrated *Thalaba*'s stake in turn of the century religious controversies. Tim Fulford suggests that the witch Khawla stands in for the attraction and dangers of religious fanaticism and Jacobinism in Britain proper. Tim Fulford, "Pagodas and Pregnant Throes: Orientalism, Millenarianism and Robert Southey," *Romanticism and Millenarianism*, Tim Fulford (ed.) (New York: Palgrave, 2002), pp. 129–30. Daniel White extends these arguments to locate in *Thalaba* Southey's response to sectarian fragmentation in a "totalizing vision of history and morality" that expressed, through Islam, his "heterodox and Jacobin opposition to established authorities." Daniel White, *Early Romanticism and Religious Dissent* (Cambridge: Cambridge University Press, 2006), pp. 155, 170.

6 Carol Bolton and Lynda Pratt have separately cast Southey's ambivalence as an "inability" to put forward a coherent ideological position. See Bolton, *Writing the Empire*, p. 4; Lynda Pratt, "Revising the National Epic: Coleridge, Southey and Madoc," *Romanticism: The Journal of Romantic Culture and Criticism* 2.2 (1996): 155.

7 For a discussion of Smith's "Beachy Head" as a compilation produced from other works, see John M. Anderson, "'Beachy Head': The Romantic Fragment Poem as Mosaic," *The Huntington Library Quarterly* 63.4 (2000): 547–74.

8 Robert Southey, Preface, *Specimens of the Later English Poets, with preliminary notices* (London: Longman, Hurst, Rees and Orme, 1807), p. iv.

9 *Selections from the Letters of Robert Southey*, 4 vols., John Wood Warter (ed.) (London, 1856), 2: 156. Subsequently cited in text as *SL*. The notebooks I've examined are not quite this large (often 7″ × 5½″ rather than 8½″ × 6¾″), and they deviate from Southey's prescribed layout, as he seldom leaves the margins clear.

10 Robert Southey, Commonplace Book, MS 1910.39, Saffron Walden Museum, UK.

11 *Bell's Common-Place Book, Form'd generally upon the Principles Recommended and Practised by Mr. Locke* (London, 1770).

12 Erasmus Darwin's *Common-place Book*, Darwin House and Museum, Lichfield, UK.

13 *A New Commonplace Book* (London, 1799), pp. 2–3.

14 A set of three notebooks in the Keswick Museum indicate a well-established procedure: KES MG 218 (labeled "Collections for the History of Manners & Literature in England"), KES MG 415 (labeled "Notebook 3"), and KES MG 420 (labeled "Notebook 17") are approximately the same size, bound in red leather, and each contains an index of topical or textual headings referring to hand-numbered pages.

15 Warter retained Southey's order for bound collections on designated topics – for example, the material on pp. 439–558 of the *Common-place Book, First Series*, preserves the headings and order of KES MG218 – but rearranged materials from more miscellaneous notebooks. For example, Warter reorganizes the skeleton plan of *Thalaba the Destroyer* on pp. 137–46 and 231–40 of Saffron Walden MS41584 so that it appears continuously in the *Common-place Book, Fourth Series. Southey's Common-place Book*, 4 vols., John Wood Warter (ed.) (London: Longman, Brown, Green, and Longmans, 1850), 1: 439–558, 4: 181–89. In making these changes, Warter amplifies and sometimes creates the method and order he praises in his preface.

16 Ibid., 1: iii, 4: ii.

17 David Reed Parker, *The Commonplace Book in Tudor England* (Lannam, MD: University Press of America, 1998), pp. 4–5, and Peter Beal, "Notions in Garrison: The Seventeenth-Century Commonplace Book," *New Ways of Looking at Old Texts: Papers of the Renaissance English Text Society, 1985–1991*, W. Speed Hill (ed.) (Binghamton, NY: Renaissance English Texts Society, 1993), pp. 135–37.

18 Beal, "Notions," p. 138.

19 For a discussion of the development of commonplace practices in tandem with Enlightenment experimental philosophy, see Allan, *Commonplace Books*, esp. pp. 46–57.

20 William Duncan, *The Elements of Logick* (London, 1748), p. 270, Eighteenth Century Collections Online, http://galenet.galegroup.com.proxy.library.vanderbilt.edu/servlet/ECCO, 20 Sept. 2010.

21 Ibid., p. 271.

22 d'Alembert, *Preliminary Discourse*, p. 47.

23 See Michael Gamer, "Laureate Policy," *Wordsworth Circle* 42.1 (2011): 42–47 for a detailed discussion of Southey's obsession with life insurance.

24 Robert Southey, KES MG 224, Keswick Museum, Keswick, UK, pages unnumbered. In November 1808, Southey was still working on arrangement, "the materials not having quite settled into satisfactory order" (*LC*, 248); he began composing the poem on 21 January 1810 (*LC*, 256, 267). This manuscript was likely produced shortly after 25 November 1809, when Southey wrote to

inform his brother Tom that he planned to rise the next morning and work on plans for Pelayo, having finished *The Curse of Kehama* that day (*LC*, 256).

25 KES MG 224, Keswick Museum, Keswick, UK, pages unnumbered.

26 Jeffrey means "judicious" ironically; Southey's poetic stitching resembles that "met with in the mansions of the industrious, where a blue tree overshadows a shell-fish, and a gigantic butterfly seems ready to swallow up Palemon and Lavinia" (*RS*, 83). The more obvious bite of Jeffrey's satire is heightened by the reference to a 1788 poem by David Mountfort, "Palemon and Lavinia," which "enlarged" a scene in Thomson's *The Seasons* – a scene that in turn rewrites the Biblical story Ruth and Boaz. Jeffrey implies that Southey's stitchery is not only incongruous but also unoriginal.

27 This process is visible in the 1799–1800 manuscript of *Thalaba* in the British Library, BL Add. MSS 47884, which shows extensive revisions on the verso pages to the fair copy of the poem on the recto.

28 Samuel Johnson, *The Lives of the Most Eminent English Poets; with Critical Observations on their Works*. Vol. 1 of 4 (London, 1781), p. 262, Eighteenth Century Collections Online, http://galenet.galegroup.com.proxy .library.vanderbilt.edu/servlet/ECCO, 11 May 2011. I thank Ann Kibbie for insight into Southey's reference to Johnson.

29 Joseph Addison, *Notes upon the twelve books of Paradise lost. Collected from the Spectator* (London, 1719), p. 6, Eighteenth Century Collections Online, http://galenet.galegroup.com.proxy.library.vanderbilt.edu/servlet/ECCO, 12 Sept. 2010.

30 Curran, *Poetic Form*, p. 158. While acknowledging this, Curran devotes separate chapters to each form, on the basis that epic embellishes historical truth while romance deals in improbabilities. Ibid., pp. 131–32. This distinction was itself a matter of dispute in the period: In his "Essay on Ancient Metrical Romances," Thomas Percy argues that chivalric romance descended directly from the ancient historical songs of the Scalds or bards, and thus many of the romantic tales preserved in Northern libraries have their foundation in truth. Thomas Percy, *Reliques of Ancient English Poetry*, 3 vols. (London, 1765), 3: iii–v.

31 Addison, *Notes*, p. 5.

32 Philip R. Hardie, *The Epic Successors of Virgil: A Study in the Dynamics of a Tradition* (Cambridge: Cambridge University Press, 1993), pp. 1–3.

33 "Of Common Places, or Memorial Books: A Seventeenth-Century Manuscript from the James Marshall and Marie-Louise Osborn Collection," Earle Havens (ed.) (New Haven, CT: Yale University Press, 2001), p. 1.

34 Gerard, *Essay on Genius*, pp. 43, 81.

35 Ibid., p. 60.

36 Coleridge's assessment of Southey's faculties was itself preceded by a set of physiognomic descriptions penned in 1793 while Southey was visiting Charles Collins in Oxford. As one friend suggests, "were not the obliquity of the forehead much less arched than intense, the judgment expressed in the countenance might be equal to its imagination . . . His mind is capable of being filed

in an instant with the most extensive subject which he is more adapted to embrace or improve, than to analyze or divide his ideas. The man who can give a definition of genius can write a character of Southey but he who can write the character of Southey may not be able to define a genius." Southey Papers, Add MS 47887, British Library, London, UK.

37 For a discussion of the bifurcation of fancy and imagination in the late eighteenth century, see James Engell, *The Creative Imagination: Enlightenment to Romanticism* (Cambridge, MA: Harvard University Press, 1981), pp. 172–75.

38 See Chapter 5 for an extended reading of Coleridge's use of inductive method to formulate principles of literary criticism.

39 Robert Southey, KES MG 2680a and 2680b, draft MSS of *Madoc*, 1801–04, Keswick Museum, Keswick, UK.

40 Ellison, "Politics of Fancy," p. 228.

41 In June 1800, Southey proclaimed that the "notes will be too numerous and too entertaining to print at the bottom of the page." *Journals of a Residence in Portugal, 1800–1801 and a Visit to France, 1838: Supplemented by Extracts from his Correspondence*, Adolfo Cabral (ed.) (Oxford: Clarendon, 1960), p. 98. By January 20, 1801 Southey had changed his mind, writing to Charles Danvers, "as for the notes being printed at the bottom of the page, you know I think it far the best place for them and only gave it up on account of the great length of a few. This however is well altered and I am pleased." *New Letters of Robert Southey, Vol. 1: 1792–1810*, Kenneth Curry (ed.) (New York and London: Columbia, 1965), p. 236. At this point, Southey was pushed into accepting endnotes by the publisher Thomas Longman, but this decision was later altered (by Southey or Longman) and the poem appeared with notes at the bottom of the page. It is thus unclear where Southey wanted his notes to appear – he repeatedly changed his mind – but the placement of the notes was both an aesthetic and a technical issue. In subsequent editions and all his later poems, the notes were relegated to the end of each volume.

42 As he details to Harry in 1809, "much trouble is saved by writing [the notes] on separate bits of paper, each the half of a quarter of a foolscap sheet, numbering them, & making an index of them" so they are ready to send to the printer with the manuscript of the poem (*SL*, 4: 157). Since there are no extant manuscript copies of the notes to *Thalaba* (or any of the other long poems), it appears that Southey meant that these bits of paper would become the copy of the notes supplied to the printer and later destroyed. I thank Tim Fulford for this insight.

43 Nicola Trott, "Poemets and Poemlings: Robert Southey's Minority Interest," *Robert Southey and the Contexts of English Romanticism*, Lynda Pratt (ed.) (Aldershot: Ashgate, 2006), p. 77.

44 Jeffrey quipped that the notes were Southey's "vouchers" to keep his reputation from getting "ruined by the imputation of a single fiction" (*RS*, 83). In response, Southey protested that the reviewers "would have accused me of plagiarism where they could have remembered the original hint" (*LC*, 157).

45 Robert Southey, *Thalaba the Destroyer*, Tim Fulford (ed.), Vol. 3 of *Robert Southey: Poetical Works, 1793–1810* (London: Pickering & Chatto, 2004), Book 1, ll. 120–27. Subsequently cited in text as *T* (verse by book and line number, notes by page number).

46 Patricia White suggests that readers' evaluation of "text shapes" on a page quickly develops into a strategy "that can either integrate or ignore competing blocks," depending on the relative importance assigned to each. White, "Black and White," 82–84. As this suggests, a reader might have followed Southey's cue or not, depending on his or her previous experience with footnotes and their perceived function and value. To date, there is no comprehensive study of how readers in the Romantic period understood the function of footnotes in literary texts.

47 Coleridge and Wordsworth, *Lyrical Ballads* (1800), 1: 179.

48 Genette, *Paratexts*, p. 2. Southey regularly circulated manuscripts of his poems without the notes, but the long poems never appeared in print without annotations. This suggests that he saw the verse as capable of standing on its own, but only for a select group of familiar, trusted readers.

49 Cosgrove, "Undermining the Text," 146.

50 Grafton, *The Footnote*, p. 45.

51 Ibid., p. 100.

52 Ibid., p. 97; Grafton is summarizing Arnaldo Momigliano's argument in "Gibbon's Contribution to Historical Method," *Contributo alla storia degli studi classici* (Rome, 1955).

53 Stuart Piggott, *Ancient Britons and the Antiquarian Imagination* (New York: Thames and Hudson, 1989), p. 24. As Ruth Mack argues, antiquarians' "fascination with the past [was] permitted by science but without a theory of historiography," making them easy targets for satire. Ruth Mack, "Horace Walpole and the Objects of Literary History," *ELH* 75.2 (2008): 369. See Chapter 1 for a discussion of the procedures of the early Royal Society and its critics.

54 Robert Burns, "On the late Captain Grose's Perigrinations thro' Scotland, Collecting the Antiquities of that Kingdom," *Poems, chiefly in the Scottish Dialect*, 2 vols. Edinburgh, 1793. 2: 221.

55 Quoted in Mack, "Walpole," 369.

56 Rosemary Sweet, "Antiquaries and Antiquities in Eighteenth-Century England," *Eighteenth-Century Studies* 34.2 (2001): 189.

57 Grafton, *Footnote*, p. 153.

58 Thomas Peacock, "The Four Ages of Poetry," in *Peacock's Four Ages of Poetry, Shelley's Defense of Poetry, Browning's Essay on Shelley*, H. F. B. Brett-Smith (ed.) (Boston: Houghton Mifflin, 1921), p. 15.

59 Ibid., p. 15. Peacock echoes Jeffrey's review in concluding that "when [Southey] has a commonplace book full of monstrosities, [he] strings them into an epic."

60 Ibid., pp. 16–17.

61 Ina Ferris notes a similar utilitarian distinction between the pedagogical and antiquarian miscellany; see Ina Ferris, "Antiquarian Authorship: D'Israeli's

Miscellany of Literary Curiosity and the Question of Secondary Genres," *Studies in Romanticism* 45.4 (2006): 525. Peacock's emphasis on utility and progress would become the point of contention for Percy Shelley in *A Defense of Poetry*.

62 Hume, *Treatise*, 1:4.

63 Alan Bewell makes a similar claim in his discussion of Wordsworth's experimentalism; see Bewell, *Wordsworth and the Enlightenment*, pp. 3–16.

64 Adam Ferguson, *An Essay on the History of Civil Society* (Edinburgh, 1767), pp. 121–22, Eighteenth Century Collections Online, http://galenet.galegroup.com.proxy.library.vanderbilt.edu/servlet/ECCO, 10 October 2010.

65 By the late eighteenth century, as Rosemary Sweet shows, antiquaries began to consider their work as "providing the factual ballast to the conjectural vessel of historical narrative." Sweet, "Antiquaries," 188.

66 Susan Manning, "Antiquarianism, the Scottish Science of Man, and the Emergence of Modern Disciplinarity," *Scotland and the Borders of Romanticism*, Leith Davis, Ian Duncan, and Janet Sorensen (eds.) (Cambridge: Cambridge University Press, 2004), pp. 60–63.

67 Leo Braudy, *Narrative Form in History and Fiction* (Princeton, NJ: Princeton University Press, 1970), p. 1.

68 As my phrasing suggests, Southey often thought about his books and the materials he collected from them quite materially. Along these lines, Diego Saglia has argued that the East of Southey's Orientalist poems is "a treasure-house of discursive fragments on the material Orient." Diego Saglia, "Words and Things: Southey's East and the Materiality of Oriental Discourse," *Robert Southey and the Contexts of English Romanticism*, Lynda Pratt (ed.) (Aldershot: Ashgate, 2006), p. 176.

69 Quoted in Majeed, *Ungoverned Imaginings*, p. 53.

70 Ibid., p. 53.

71 J. Morgan, *A Complete History of Algiers*, 2 vols. (London, 1728), 1: 308, 340–41.

72 Conjectural history posited four stages of societal development based on modes of subsistence (hunter, shepherd, farmer, manufacturer), which in turn translated into stages of cognitive development and manners (savagery, barbarism, industrious cultivation of land, and civilized society). See Christopher Berry, *Social Theory of the Scottish Enlightenment* (Edinburgh: Edinburgh University Press, 1997), pp. 91–98.

73 Grafton, *Footnote*, p. 5.

74 Balachandra Rajan traces this pattern from Southey's correspondence to *The Curse of Kehama*, arguing that while Southey subscribed to a typical missionary view of Hinduism's monstrosity, many episodes and their notes "resist rather than assist imperialist devaluations of India." Balachandra Rajan, "Monstrous Mythologies: Southey and *The Curse of Kehama*," *ERR* 9.2 (1998): 208.

75 Carol Bolton, "*Thalaba the Destroyer*: Southey's Nationalist 'Romance,'" *Romanticism on the Net* 32–33 (Nov. 2003–Feb. 2004): n.p., http://www.erudit.org/revue/ron/2003/v/n32-33/009260ar.html, 19 Sept. 2010. Reviews of *Madoc* in particular cite the (seemingly unintentional) ludicrous effects of Southey's generic and stylistic choices; see the notices in *The Monthly Review*

and *The Literary Journal* rpt. in *RS*, pp. 102–04 and 108–10. The question
of intentionality has not disappeared: Fulford has argued that Madoc is "less
straightforwardly and successfully ideological than his prose" because it "often
unintentionally calls into question that superiority of British character and
beliefs which it seeks to endorse." Tim Fulford, "Heroic Voyages and Superstitious Natives: Southey's Imperialist Ideology," *Studies in Travel Writing* 2.1
(1998): 51.

76 Fulford, Introduction, *Thalaba the Destroyer*, pp. x–xi.

77 Ibid., p. viii.

78 Pratt, "Revising the National Epic," 155.

79 Ibid., 78.

80 Trott, "Poemets and Poemlings," p. 78.

81 As Darnton's discussion of commonplace method suggests, this opposition is
a modern invention: "unlike modern readers, who follow the flow of narrative
from beginning to end . . . early modern Englishmen read in fits and starts and
jumped from book to book," breaking "texts into fragments and assembl[ing]
them into new patterns" in their commonplace books. Robert Darnton, *A Case
for Books* (New York: PublicAffairs, 2009), p. 149. For the production of this
division in the Romantic period, see Chapter 5.

82 Southey does, however, put limits on what can be productively compared: In
the same note, he complains, "The 'Old Woman of Berkeley' has been fool-
ishly called an imitation of the inimitable Ballad [of Burger]: the likeness is
one of the same kind as between Macedon and Monmouth. Both are ballads,
and there is a Horse in both" (*T*, p. 270). Here Southey compares the superficial analogy between the two poems to the analogy between Alexander the
Great and Harry of Monmouth (drawn by Fluellen in Shakespeare's *Henry V*)
on the ridiculous coincidence that there were salmon in the rivers near their
birthplaces.

83 *Southey's Common-place Book*, 4: 192–5.

84 Trott also notes how Southey's punctuation (in both his titles and these descriptions) demonstrates the ease of detaching subject from meter, allowing incommensurate subjects and genres to challenge each other but also remain separate.
Trott, "Poemets and Poemlings," p. 80.

85 Susan Stewart uses "new antique" to describe the process of "distressing" by
which seventeenth- and eighteenth-century authors appropriated oral forms,
like the ballad, into print. Stewart concludes, "as soon as we hear the distressed
genre, its high seriousness, its inflexible form, its reverent tone, and its ven-
erable language, we also hear the works that undermine it." Susan Stewart,
"Notes on Distressed Genres," *Journal of American Folklore* 104.411 (1991): 6,
22. While Stewart positions Southey as a "polisher" of this tradition, many of
his notes – including this one – suggest a tongue-in-cheek stance on claims to
seriousness and authenticity. See also Susan Stewart, *Crimes of Writing: Problems in the Containment of Representation* (Oxford: Oxford University Press,
1991).

86 Fulford, Introduction to *Thalaba*, p. viii.

87 Letter 1134. Robert Southey to Charles Watkin Williams Wynn [18 December 1805], *The Collected Letters of Robert Southey, Part III: 1804–1809*, Carol Bolton and Tim Fulford (eds.), Romantic Circles Electronic edition, 2009. http://www.rc.umd.edu/editions/southey_letters/Part_Three/HTML/letterEEd.26.1134.html, 10 June 2014. I thank Tim Fulford for bringing this letter to my attention.
88 Quoted in Trott, "Poemets and Poemlings," p. 84.
89 Ibid., p. 77.
90 Robert Southey, *The Doctor*, 2 vols. (New York: Harper, 1872), 1: 47.
91 Ibid., 1:47.

The First Landing-Place
Prose Notes and Embedded Verse

In Chapters 2 and 3, I provided detailed case studies – of Erasmus Darwin and Robert Southey, respectively – that expose the epistemological, philosophical, formal, and material consequences of using inductive method to compose literary texts. These detailed examinations reveal the problem of induction was indeed a compositional conundrum that authors wrangled with in the Romantic period. This problem, however, may not have been intractable. It is possible to read the development of Romanticism's mixed forms as a "gradual overcoming of the technical problem of combining" discourses, as David Duff suggests of Walter Scott's historical novels.[1] Inductive method continued to be the dominant compositional practice into the first decades of the nineteenth century, and the verse–prose composites continued to pile up without abatement. That said, the visible, material aspect of mixture on the printed page became less pronounced in the first decades of the nineteenth century. In this brief Interlude,[2] I'll examine how and why the annotated poem was transformed in the decades after 1800 by the techne of printing before turning to a related composite form, prose with embedded verse, which I investigate in the second half of this study.

First, prominence and persistence. Consider how many Romantic "poems" are actually composites of verse and prose. Not only genre-bending works such as Darwin's *The Botanic Garden* or Blake's *The Marriage of Heaven and Hell* fall into this category, but those considered genre-defining, such as Coleridge's Conversation poems ("The Nightingale," "This Lime-Tree Bower My Prison") and Wordsworth's lyrics (the revised, four-stanza version of "I wandered lonely as a cloud" appears with a convoluted footnote in the 1815 *Poems*). Southey's five epic romances appeared amidst a host of other annotated epics, including Thomas Beddoes's *Alexander's Expedition* (1792), Amos Cottle's *Icelandic Poetry, or The Edda of Saemund* (1797), and Joseph Cottle's *Alfred* (1801) – all produced by members of Southey and Coleridge's Bristol circle. But mixing verse and prose was not simply the predilection of a geographically isolated coterie. After the second edition, Charlotte Smith's *Elegiac Sonnets* appeared regularly with notes, as did her long poems *The Emigrants* (1793) and "Beachy Head" (1807). Smith's antagonist and accuser Anna Seward likewise published a volume of heavily annotated topographical and antiquarian verse, *Llangollen Vale, with Other Poems* (1796). Recall, too, that annotated poems became wildly popular in the first decades of the nineteenth century: headnotes, marginal glosses, and notes bookend Scott's *The Lay of the Last Minstrel* (1805), *Marmion* (1808), and *The Lady of the Lake* (1810); Lucy Aikin's *Epistles on Women* (1810); Percy Shelley's *Queen Mab* (1813); all four cantos of Byron's *Childe Harold's Pilgrimage* (1812–18); and Felicia Hemans's popular volume *Records of Woman* (1825).

These are only the best-known, most obvious examples; hundreds more annotated volumes and individual poems populate the Romantic literary landscape. Critics have perhaps willfully forgotten this teaming multitude. Notes often disappear in anthologies and online editions, the cacophony of the composite swept under the carpet like a dirty secret. Looking closely at books printed in this period makes it obvious that the vast majority of Romantic-era literary texts show some degree of rough-mixing, which Duff defines as a "type of generic combination in which the formal surfaces of the constituent genres are left intact: heterogeneous elements are juxtaposed rather than integrated, thus creating the aesthetic effect of discontinuity."[3] While taking up a wide variety of topics, staking claim to various generic precedents, and experimenting with an array of meters and forms, Romantic poems are by and large composite orders. Some of the authors mentioned above strove for an aesthetic ideal of organic unity, but some Romantic-era authors purposefully cultivated the heterogeneous mixture and the polyvocal discontinuities of the verse–prose composite. If Southey's *The Doctor* looks more like *Tristram Shandy* or a postmodern novel than Victorian sensation fiction or Dickensian realism, it is for this reason.

Most authors, however, neither rejected nor embraced the composite, rather approaching the outcome of their labors with an ambivalence that might tip over into a reluctant acceptance. Charlotte Smith's posthumously published long poem "Beachy Head" is one of the period's most striking examples of this. The poem opens with an invocation to the "stupendous summit" of Beachy Head, from which the poet's "Fancy should go forth / And represent the strange and awful hour / Of vast concussion" that rifted England from France.[4] The sublime imagery of the cliff's history is immediately undermined by Smith's note, which confesses, "I never could trace the resemblance between the two countries."[5] This observation refers to the coastline, but broader divisions of culture and temperament are implied, belying the history of Norman and Roman conquest rehearsed later in the notes. Further, by undercutting the sublime scene presented in the verse, the note also undercuts its ostensible function. Rather than providing evidence for the poet's assertion of a vast concussion, the note confesses skepticism about this claim. This is not an isolated instance. Like Southey's epics, Smith's topographic poem is accompanied by a ream of notes that simultaneously invoke and contradict her legitimizing sources. However, unlike Darwin's or Southey's footnotes, Smith's gloss to the opening lines of "Beachy Head" appears 144 pages later *as an endnote*, and its existence is not signaled typographically in the poem proper. Smith's reader could quite easily gloss over the gloss, never realizing that it was there. It would seem, then, that Smith buried her notes at the end of the volume – as Southey did with *Madoc* in 1805, *The Curse of Kehama* in 1810, and *Roderick, The Last of the Goths* in 1814 – to mollify the disruptive effects of the verse–prose composite.

Several qualifications to this conclusion can, and should, be made. First and very simply, *Beachy Head: With Other Poems* was published posthumously, and we should be wary of making claims about Smith's intentions based on the structure of this volume. That said, Smith did write to her publisher Joseph Johnson in 1806 that "it seems to be the fashion of the day to print the notes at the end," and single-author volumes of poetry published after the turn of the century bear out her assertion.[6] After 1800, there is a marked shift away from footnotes toward headnotes and endnotes.[7] This fashion can be ascribed, in part if not fully, to printers and publishers. At the tail end of the hand press period, it was less laborious and thus less expensive to cast off the pages (a technique for estimating how much paper would be required) and to physically set the type if prose notes were printed separately from verse lines. Separating prose and verse also made it possible to typeset the poem and notes at different times, potentially using the same set of types and obviating the author's need to have notes and poem ready at the same time. This technical impetus may not have immediately changed authors' compositional processes – Southey, Smith, Scott, Shelley, and many others continued to draft poems and notes simultaneously – but it did change the visual aspect of the page. With surprisingly few exceptions, titles published after 1800 relegate notes to the end of the volume.

Authors may, then, have been following a fashion for endnotes introduced by publishers, in effect diminishing the visual effect of jostling forms. This technological and economic shift had a discernable effect on how authors *thought* about notes (and not, I am arguing, vice versa). Two examples from authors who exercised control over the production and appearance of their books will make this clear. Scott worked closely with the printer James Ballantyne on his collection of border ballads, *Minstrelsy of the Scottish Border* (1802–1803), and his first long poem, *The Lay of the Last Minstrel* (1805). This relationship with Ballantyne allowed Scott to exercise "remarkable control ... over not only over its poetic and editorial content but over every detail of the work's physical production."[8] In both books, Scott includes very brief footnotes identifying people and places or explaining Scottish words, but the long antiquarian notes – which are often themselves annotated and include embedded excerpts from other poems – appear elsewhere. In *Minstrelsy*, these longer notes follow (and sometimes precede) each individual poem; in *Lay*, the notes appear as a block of endnotes at the end of the volume. As with Smith's notes to "Beachy Head," Scott's endnotes are not signaled typographically in the poem. This choice allows the narrative poem to carry on uninterrupted, but perhaps more importantly, it configures the endnotes as a series of connected essays on topics of antiquarian and national interest only occasionally interrupted by italicized lines of verse they ostensibly comment on. Like Darwin's extensive endnotes on ancient mythology in *The Economy of Vegetation*, Scott's endnotes to *Lay* stitch together a series of excerpts to make a claim about history, in this case a genealogical history of his family that stands in for the political and literary history of the Scottish borders. The result is a more ideologically coherent – and at the same time more personal – statement of Scottish border identity than that put forward in *Minstrelsy*.

Shelley's notes to *Queen Mab* also drive toward the ideological and personal. As Neil Fraistat points out, Shelley "appears to intervene directly and minutely in the typesetting and distribution of his work" and "new evidence suggests that he may even have set type for some of his most radical early work."[9] Further, Shelley's

> Notes [to *Queen Mab*] constitute a compendium of eighteenth-century radical thought, along with some of its most prominent sources in the Renaissance and Classical antiquity. Printed in the same size typeface as the poem and filling almost half the volume, these Notes were more incendiary than the poem they further radicalized.[10]

Shelley's notes appear in block at the end of the volume, and as in Smith's "Beachy Head" and Scott's *Lay*, their existence is not indicated in the poem. According to Shelley, this made the notes "a safe [way] of propagating my principles, which I decline to do syllogistically in a poem" because their "philosophical, & Anti Christian" content would go "unnoticed in a Note."[11] It is only by assuming that his notes will appear as endnotes rather than footnotes – and that endnotes were so commonplace in volume of poetry as to be practically invisible – that Shelley can imagine readers missing their radical content. In both examples, moving the notes to the end of the volume prods authors to treat the poem as a medium or cover for an agenda put forward more explicitly in the notes than in the poem proper. On the most basic level, Shelley and Scott belie Darwin's assertion that prose and verse are fitted for different work – but unlike Darwin's *Loves*, their texts don't assert parallel aesthetic and epistemological positions on every printed page. Rather than staging a perpetual negotiation between them, restructuring the printed book after 1800 promoted a conceptual and functional distance between verse and prose.

Authors may not have overcome the problem of induction, but the change in where notes were printed provoked a change in attitude toward the compositional procedure that generated composites in the first place. Here, I'll turn to a poet who made little use of notes but commented extensively on the relationship between his sources and his poetry. When John Keats reflected on "How many bards gild the lapses of time" in 1816, he figured his source texts as food for his fancy: they sustained his work without getting in his way. Using the conventional term for excerpted passages in anthologies, Keats notes that even though "throngs" of "beauties" from other poems "intrude" on his mind when he sits down to write, they make "no confusion, no disturbance rude." The reason for this appears in the sestet: like the innumerable sounds of evening – birds, leaves, waters, bell – the poems he has read blur together into a "pleasing chime."[12] Not being able to distinguish one from another at a distance, Keats has turned a heap of little things into a kind of ambient music, something we hardly recognize or register consciously but that produces a mood or feeling. Coleridge's desperate list of rocks and waterfalls and mountains in his letter to Thelwall (quoted in the Introduction) has become those "unnumbered sounds that evening store" – and this, I would argue, exemplifies a new outlook, one that registers "pleasing music" where Coleridge saw only a "wild uproar."[13] Oversaturation hasn't gone away – Keats's list and its long dashes still signal textual excess – but his sonnet's Petrarchan conventions work to contain and control the influx of information, freeing the poet by making him unable to distinguish anything in particular. Moving or removing prose notes from the page allows the cacophony to blur into a murmur, bringing the verse back to its sole self.

Romantic poetry did not become less reflexive about the conditions of its production in the early decades of the nineteenth century, but those conditions were manifested differently both in the material aspect of the page and in the texts themselves. Keats's sonnet exemplifies a new attitude toward the poet's sources: as endnotes replaced footnotes, the evidentiary work of quotation and source citation seemed less important than what the verse had to say about itself and for the poet. This was partly underwritten by theories of organicism and the poet's synthetic imagination hatched in the first decades of the nineteenth century, most famously by Coleridge. As I discuss in the final chapter of this study, this theoretical position was itself a response to the problem of induction in practical criticism and cognitive theory.

The material aspect of the annotated poem changed around 1800 (and with it the anxious response to information overload), but the traces of authors' inductive method of composition remained. To return to "Beachy Head," notice that the poem is composed from snippets of Smith's published poetry, novels, and children's books, as well as prose and verse by other authors, some of which she had quoted or paraphrased in her earlier works.[14] These borrowed materials are reworked into the form of the prospect poem, organized and synthesized by the poetic consciousness whose Fancy surveys the sublime scene. The endnotes, as Jacqueline Labbe has argued, contain a persona often actively opposed to the poem's unifying lyric voice, but even if we set the notes aside, Smith's formal choices gradually undo the logic and coherence of her chosen genre.[15] By the poem's final 200 lines, the first-person speaker disappears entirely. In its place, Smith inserts two poems she originally listed separately in her proposed table of contents, "Shepherd of the hill" and "The wood walk" (the latter titled "Let us to woodland wilds repair").[16] Typographically offset and formally distinct from the rest of the poem, these inset poems appear as found pieces: in the poem, the author of these inset poems has vanished "in silence, gliding like a ghost ... Lost in the deepening gloom," but people still sometimes find "love-songs and scatter'd rhymes, / Unfinished sentences, or half erased, / And rhapsodies like this."[17] These lines introducing the second inset poem allegorize to the scattered and unfinished character of "Beachy Head" itself, drawing attention to the result of Smith's compositional practice of stitching together bits and pieces of other texts to make a tenuous whole. The conclusion to "Beachy Head" cultivates precisely the opposite of Wordsworth's accomplishment in *The Prelude*, the use of blank verse to subsume and integrate multiple genres into "psychic equilibrium."[18]

As I have argued elsewhere, Smith was acutely aware of her compositional process and its product.[19] By embedding these formally distinct poems, she draws attention to her compositional methods as clearly as Darwin and Southey do in their footnotes. And again, Smith was not unique in this respect; the practice of embedding short, formally distinct poems was as common as the annotated poem in the first decades of the nineteenth century.

I have space for only a few examples. In the sixth canto of *The Lay of the Last Minstrel*, Scott stages a competition between bards, one he materializes by embedding three formally distinct and separately titled poems, two in four-line stanzas of conventional ballad meter and one in Spenserian stanzas. Ten pages into Byron's *Childe Harold's Pilgrimage*, Harold seizes the harp and interrupts the progression of Spenserian stanzas by pouring out lines of alternating iambic tetrameter and trimeter; the inset poem is separately numbered in Arabic rather than Roman numerals. In the middle of Felicia Hemans's "Bride of the Greek Isle," rhymed couplets of nine or ten syllables give way to the ballad meter of an inset poem, "The Bride's Farewell." The list might go on and on, but I've chosen these specific examples for their resonance with each other. What Smith takes up at the end of her poetic career and life as a symbol for the poet's uncertain posthumous fate stands as an emblem for the Scottish bard's lost power in Scott's poem, and for the loss of nation, home, and family in Byron and Hemans – a loss that is marked formally by the shift to ballad meter. These poems look backward and forward; they recall the poet's cultural sway even as they trade on the recovered ballad's current popularity. Poems embedded in other poems thus materialize the Romantic self-consciousness about the cultural status of poetry in the early nineteenth century. The poet's compositional practice of stitchery is on display, but just as plainly, these poems reflect on the uncertain conditions of poetry's production and dissemination in Britain's increasingly commercialist literary marketplace – a marketplace where poetry vied with many other genres, including the novel, for sales and status.

This insight tips into another crucial point: Embedding poems was bound up with the conventions of prose as much as those of the annotated poem. Verse, both original and borrowed, appears in prose writing of all sorts in this period: in Smith's own novels and children's books; in prose fiction by Anne Radcliffe, Matthew Lewis, Sydney Owenson, John Thelwall, Maria Edgeworth, Scott (and his acolytes Washington Irving and James Fenimore Cooper in the United States), Mary Shelley, and even Jane Austen; and in essays by Wordsworth, Coleridge, William Hazlitt,

Charles Lamb, Thomas De Quincey, and many others. Reviews of literature are littered with excerpted verse – and while this is expected for
books of poetry, reviews of novels often excerpted and reprinted the poems
embedded in the fiction, often to the exclusion of the prose itself, leading savvy authors like Radcliffe and Smith to insert poems into their novels specifically for this purpose.[20] (Fig. 3) In the 1790s, embedded poems
were explicitly understood as marketing tools, but the practice had deeper
roots. As discussed in Chapter 1, quoting literature, and especially poetry,
was an essential component of moral philosophy and literary criticism in
the empiricist tradition from Hume forward. As I detail in Chapter 5,
Coleridge's literary critical practice (when he quotes Wordsworth or Shakespeare in the *Biographia Literaria* or *The Friend* [Fig. 4]) emerged as part
of a corpus of British Shakespeare criticism dedicated to quoting the bard.
Poetic excerpts litter aesthetic treatises from Burke's *Philosophical Enquiry*
(1757) on the sublime and beautiful to Gerard's *Essay on Genius* (1774) to
Gilpin's *Three Essays: On Picturesque Beauty; On Picturesque Travel; and On
Sketching Landscape* (1792), which concludes with a long, annotated poem
"On Landscape Painting." Flip or scroll through enough pages in natural
histories, topographical and antiquarian works, tours and voyage narratives, sermons, indeed all manner of printed prose in the final decades of
the eighteenth century, and you will encounter innumerable snippets of
verse, often indented and set off on the page. Consider: Amidst the charts
and tables of Gilbert White's *Natural History and Antiquities of Selborne*,
you will find quotations from James Thomson's *The Seasons* and White's
own (annotated) poem, "The Naturalist's Summer Evening Walk."[21] (John
Aikin's *An Essay on the Application of Natural History to Poetry* (1777) offers
instruction on how to compose such verse, in a prose essay riven with poetic
quotations.) So too in political and reform-oriented works: In *A Vindication of the Right of Woman* (1792), Wollstonecraft's case for reforming female
education is built in and on quotations, her excerpts from Milton's *Paradise
Lost* and Rousseau's *Emile* providing the blocks that her argument disman-
tles. And so on.

   As before, the litany of examples could continue – which underscores
how invisible embedded verse has become in modern critical treatments of
Romantic-era literature. Standing apart on the printed page, these snippets
of poetry were not invisible to contemporary readers, and they served
various functions for authors and their audiences. As I discuss in Chapter
1, the practice of embedding poetic quotations in prose fiction was not new
at the end of the century, but quotations did begin to function differently,
gradually shifting from containers of universal truths or *sententiae* to the

property of individual authors. Material from familiar sources might tap into a shared cultural lexicon to legitimate an author's argument or divert criticism, or authorize a character's political position or opinion, as quoting Thomson, Shakespeare, and Cowper does for the eponymous hero in Smith's *Desmond*.[22] Embedded poems might prod the reader into sympathy with the character who utters, reads, or composes it, especially when poetry provides solace in moments of emotional or physical turmoil – think of Austen's Anne Elliot frantically recalling verses as she watches Wentworth flirt with Luisa in *Persuasion*, or of Radcliffe's Emily St. Aubert reflectively composing a poem before the next onslaught of gothic terror in *The Mysteries of Udolpho*.[23] Alternatively, excerpted verse might express awe and wonder, stand in for the sublime, or become a conduit for horror or an organ of satire, as with "Alonzo the Brave and the Fair Imogene" in Matthew Lewis's *The Monk*. In all these cases, it became increasingly important to cite one's sources for borrowed quotations, or to represent the embedded verse as original poetry, practices Smith, Radcliffe, Owenson, Lewis, and Thelwall all follow.

Like the prose notes to long poems, embedded verse quotations from other works – even the author's own works – point to the procedure of building a text inductively from an extant textual archive. As a result, these verse snippets introduce formal discontinuity and cognitive dissonance, sometimes beyond that of prose footnotes to verse. While Smith's poems are (for the most part) carefully woven into the plots of her novels, Radcliffe's embedded verses often stand at odds, tonally and topically, with the gothic narratives that surround them. Thelwall's *The Peripatetic; or Sketches of the Heart, of Nature and Society; in a series of Politico-Sentimental Journals, in Verse and Prose, of the Eccentric Excursions of Sylvanus Theophrastus* (1793) presents a more extreme case of the jarring effects of embedded verse. Unlike the predominantly prose texts of his contemporaries, Thelwall's book may qualify as "prosimetrical," a term now used to describe the mixed forms of classical antiquity.[24] *The Peripatetic* stands apart in its own time because it includes as much verse as prose – and the pervasiveness of formal mixture invites Thelwall's explicit commentary on the composition and effects of his verse–prose composite. In its meta-critical stance, *The Peripatetic* excavates the philosophical roots and hoped-for outcomes of prose works saturated with poetry.

Like Southey's *The Doctor*, *The Peripatetic* combines digressive narrative techniques introduced by Sterne with Fielding's reflexive commentary on composing the work we are reading. Thelwall's Preface, which opens by invoking Fielding and Sterne in all caps, confirms his cultivation of formal discontinuity: his design was to unite "the different advantages of the novel, the sentimental journal, and the miscellaneous collection of essays and poetical effusions."[25] In his "Apology to the Critics" partway through the first volume, the narrator admits "rambling somewhat too long amoung the fields and green allies of poetical digression," but excuses himself by noting that in an excursive, miscellaneous work, it is better to "deal out" a narrator's character in "detached portions" rather than in a series of biographical memoirs.[26] As this suggests, the peripatetic narrator is the book's central character, and his looping, erratic journey iterates the text's composite form. Bearing the surname of the ancient peripatetic philosopher Theophrastus, the narrator travels on foot through bye ways, fields, and woods – he, like his observations, companions, and politics, departs from the turnpike road. Further, because the narrator's "sympathetic feeling for every sentient tenant of this many-peopled sphere" (discussed in the prose) is enabled by the movement between "*external* scenes" and "searching glances, inward thrown" (described in the verse), narrative progression is constantly interrupted by moments of self-reflection, which take the form of embedded poems.[27] (Fig. 8) The import of each episode and the book as a whole becomes apparent only by reading across prose and verse and connecting the ideas expressed in each to the other. Formal mixture enacts the narrator's cultivation of universal sympathy, simultaneously impressing it on the reader by way of the text's structure and the layout of the printed page.

Thelwall's book is a covert pedagogical tool, one that uses the composite's formal discontinuities to cultivate sympathy for anyone or anything suffering at the hand of injustice, malice, or prejudice. This agenda, the narrator makes clear, derives its force from "fair Reason's golden ray" – that is, from linked acts of observation, examination, contemplation, investigation, compilation, comparison, reflection, and reasoning by analogy. As the narrator relates, "the contemplation of natural phenomena" coupled with "the searching rays of investigation" helped him banish doubt and dogma, leaving in their place "universal benevolence."[28] Thelwall's text is patently inductive, molded on Bacon's method for the investigation of nature as applied by moral philosophy to the human mind and breast. Thelwall celebrated Bacon in his *Political Lectures* of 1794, calling him one of the "few favored sons of science and philosophy" who "adopted the principles of liberty" yet unknown to the generality of people.[29] The open, collaborative form of Bacon's inductive method appeared to promote a democratic ideology that appealed to Thelwall in the early 1790s, and he announces his embrace of both the process of inquiry and the

100   PERIPATETIC.

Thee, from thy throne, on Richmond's beauteous height,
  Where streams, groves, villas, at thy footstool lay,
Will I invoke, to say with what delight
  Among thy smiling scenes I wont to stray.

For thou hast seen me oft, at Evening hour,
  Thy wild-wood flowrets twining round my head,
With fixt regard each glowing tint devour
  By waining Phœbus o'er the welkin spread :—

And thou hast mark'd me, in the woodland scene,
  With infant fingers cull the mossy store,
And still, with meditative smile serene,
  Each various product's various hues explore :—

But chief where'er the silver-fretted brook
  Pour'd its low cadence, hast thou seen me stray,
To mark its eddies oft, with pensive look,
  While glanc'd the noon-tide, or the Lunar ray.

PAINFUL RECOLLECTIONS.

THERE was, however, one particular, in which, from a better motive than ambition, I could not but blush at the recollec-
        tion

PERIPATETIC.   101

tion of a temporary dissimilarity in the infant character of Edwin and myself. For so far was the generous sentiment, " His heart from cruel sport estranged, would bleed to work the woe of any living thing," from being strictly applicable to some few of my earliest years, that I often shudder to reflect on the cruel and selfish dispositions which nature seemed at one time to have implanted in my bosom. Nor was it 'till frequent opportunities of contemplating, with enamoured eye, the varied beauties of creation, in my eccentric rambles, and indulging the poetical studies to which they conducted, had soothed and meliorated my heart, that the blossoms of sensibility began to unfold themselves, and I awakened to a sympathetic feeling for every sentient tennant of this many-peopled sphere

Hail, Meditation ! modest maid !
  Who rov'st full oft, in thoughtful mood,
By haunted brook, or shadowy glade,
  Or o'er the heath-clad mountain rude
To meet the Muse, wild Fancy's child !
  Companion of thy pensive hours ;
Who glads the dark-hued forest wild,
  And decks the barren wold with flow'rs,

F 3   And

Fig. 8 John Thelwall, *The Peripatetic, or Sketches of the Heart, of Nature and Society, in a Series of Politico-Sentimental Journals in Verse and Prose*, 3 vols. (Southwark, 1793), 2: 100–101. By permission of the British Library, General Reference Collection 12355.aaa.17.

broken form recommended by Bacon on the title page of *The Peripatetic*: While Theophrastus legitimates the text's excursive roaming, "Sylvanus" describes its genre.[30] Classical literary miscellanies, sylvae were "collections of poetical pieces, of various kinds, and on various subjects."[31] At the end of the eighteenth century, the form had two seemingly distinct incarnations, one represented by a new edition of John Evelyn's *Silva: or, a Discourse of Forest-Trees* (1786) – a seventeenth-century agricultural treatise concerned with the maintenance of Britain's woodlands – and the other materialized in Ralph Heathcot's *Sylva: or, the Wood. Being a Collection of Anecdotes, Dissertations, Characters, Apophthegms, Original Letters, Bon Mots, and Other Little Things* (1788). Despite the difference in topic, these texts, like Thelwall's mixed-form "novel," draw authority from Francis Bacon's *Sylva Sylvarum, A Natural History in Ten Centuries* (1627), a posthumously published collection of observations intended as a foundation for a new science, the archive on which induction could be performed.

Bacon adopted the *Sylva* from classical literature to model the open presentation of knowledge in which "the discourse of connection and order is cut off," leading men to "enquire farther."[32] In *Timber: or Discoveries Made upon Men and Matter* (1640), Ben Jonson pinpoints the appeal of the sylva: "the Ancients called that kind of body *Sylva* or [Hylé] in which there were works of divers nature, and matter, congested; as the multitude call Timber-trees, promiscuously growing, a *Wood*, or *Forrest*."[33] As Frans De Bruyn points out, this form was useful to seventeenth- and eighteenth-century natural philosophy because it "could encompass provisionally a variety of parts without the whole as yet being known or fixed, but in the belief that the whole is ultimately knowable and determinate."[34] Like the aphorism at the level of the sentence or paragraph, the formal conventions of the sylva offered a generic precedent for miscellany and discontinuity that authorized the "collaborative, incremental, and open" process characteristic of inductive method.[35] The sylva was not, however, a completely random jumble of material; compilers and readers alike understood that the sylva's "disorderedness is premeditated and arises, in fact, from a provisional hypothesis of order," one that is never fully articulated but remains "to be discovered and discerned."[36] William Rawley, the editor of Bacon's *Sylva*, underscores this point: Although Bacon refused to "put these particulars into any exact Method ... he that looketh attentively into them shall find that they have a secret order."[37]

Labeling a work "sylva" at the end of the eighteenth century thus denoted order and disorder, connection and disjunction, confused heaping and careful arrangement – precisely the condition of Thelwall's *Peripatetic*. As Judith Thompson argues, "*The Peripatetic* at first glance appears utterly chaotic and disjunctive," but when read carefully, "its apparent formlessness resolves itself into a complex yet coherent intellectual pattern in which key ideas ... are highlighted and repeated with variation in intertwined clusters of episodes."[38] Thompson suggests this formal condition derives from Menippean satire, but the sylva is an equally compelling source. Like Heathcot's playful literary *Sylva*, Thelwall moves between generic modes and distinct forms, following a chain of associations that folds back on and illuminates the book's larger agenda. The formlessness of the text is purposefully cultivated, and it relies on the reader to synthesize ideas put forward in distinct forms to arrive at the text's moral message. Thelwall arranged the episodes, but the work of comparing "man in his varied conditions" and combining the results with "Nature's kind lesson" is placed on the reader.[39] The composite form of *The Peripatetic* – and the sylva's "secret order" waiting to be discovered – demands that the reader become an active participant in her own reeducation. The reader's task is rendered all the more difficult and imperative by the narrator's excursive wanderings: while undertaking this work of connection and linking by analogy, the reader is apt to get lost in those very byways and forest paths that promote Thelwall's ideal of universal benevolence.

As I discuss in the next chapter, Thelwall's embrace of formal discontinuity as a provocation to reeducation, a spur for readers to "enquire farther," was at the center of a debate over educational theory and practice in the final decades of the eighteenth century. Reformers from Hannah More and Maria Edgeworth to Mary Wollstonecraft and Charlotte Smith were split on the question of whether the discontinuous form of the miscellany would cultivate or derail a pupil's capacity for rational thought and ethical behavior. More and Coleridge commented on the dangers of miscellaneous collections of "beauties," which encouraged readers to skim and dip rather than reading deeply, thus creating "smatters" (*SFE*, 192–93). (This is, of course, the late eighteenth-century corollary to Google making us stupid.) The debate expressly turned on the perceived cognitive effects of excerpted poetry, which (its critics claimed) was apt to skew the mind and ruin the judgement by encouraging imaginative leaps, fanciful associations, and vacuous daydreaming. This characterization of the verse snippet in turn harkens back to the seventeenth-century elevation of "plain" or unornamented prose style in natural philosophy and experimental science, discussed in Chapter 2. At its core, the turn-of-the-century educational debate stages the conflict between two versions of Baconian induction: the drive for the clarity, concision, and logical progression of unornamented prose on the one hand, and the cultivation of an open, discontinuous, formally mixed presentation of knowledge on the other. Thelwall falls into the latter camp alongside Wollstonecraft and Smith; Hannah More and Richard Lovell Edgeworth, the foremost proponent of turning education into an experimental science, occupy the former. In the next chapter, I outline these debates before turning to the pages of books that self-consciously and materially dramatize the relation between a text's formal properties and its cognitive effects: pedagogical fictions for children. Through works by Anna Barbauld, Maria Edgeworth, and Charlotte Smith, the chapter pinpoints how debates over the pedagogical role of poetry and miscellaneous collections spurred authors to adapt or meld existing educational genres to mollify – or promote – the cognitive effects of the composite.

NOTES

1 Duff, *Romanticism and the Uses of Genre*, p. 181. While I agree in principle with Duff's conclusions, labeling this process an "overcoming" suggests a triumph of authorial will over textual matter that my case studies do not uphold.

2 Darwin uses the term "Interlude" to describe the prose essays between cantos of *The Loves of the Plants*; in *The Friend*, Coleridge describes the "Essays inserted for Amusement, Retrospect, and Preparation" as "The Landing-Place" (*F*, 1: 127).

3 Duff, *Romanticism and the Uses of Genre*, p. 178.

4 Charlotte Smith, *Beachy Head and Other Poems* (London: 1807), p. 1.

5 Ibid., p. 144.

6 Charlotte Smith, *Collected Letters*, p. 741.

7 Byron's *English Bards and Scotch Reviewers* is an exception to this rule, an anomaly provoked by an homage to the previous century's most famous satirist: Byron quotes Pope on the title page and his use of footnotes mimics that of Pope's *The Dunciad Variorum*. George Gordon, Lord Byron, *English Bards and Scotch Reviewers; A Satire* (London: James Cawthorn, 1810).

8 Millgate, "Scott's *Lay of the Last Minstrel*," 226.

9 Neil Fraistat, "The Material Shelley: Who Gets the Finger in Queen Mab?" *Wordsworth Circle* 33.1 (2002): 33.

10 Ibid., 34.

11 Percy Shelley, *The Collected Letters of Percy Shelley*, 2 vols., Frederick L. Jones (ed.) (Oxford: Clarendon, 1964), 1: 350, 361.

12 John Keats, *Keats' Poetry and Prose*, Jeffrey Cox (ed.) (New York and London: Norton, 2009), p. 51.

13 Ibid., p. 51.

14 For Smith's borrowing and reworking of her earlier works in "Beachy Head," see Anderson, "Beachy Head," 547–74; Donelle Ruwe, "Charlotte Smith's Sublime: Feminine Poetics, Botany, and *Beachy Head*," *Prism(s): Essays in Romanticism* 7 (1999): 117–32; and Dahlia Porter, "From Nosegay to Specimen Cabinet: Charlotte Smith and the Labour of Collecting," *Charlotte Smith in British Romanticism*, Jacqueline Labbe (ed.) (London: Pickering & Chatto, 2008), pp. 29–44.

15 Jacqueline Labbe, *Charlotte Smith: Romanticism, Poetry and the Cultural of Gender* (Manchester: Manchester University Press, 2003), pp. 152, 179. Smith's mastery and control of the landscape in the poem depends on the prospect view, a position, as Tim Fulford has shown, associated with aristocratic ownership, masculine breadth of vision, and political authority. Tim Fulford, *Landscape, Liberty, and Authority: Poetry, Criticism and Politics from Thomson to Wordsworth* (Cambridge: Cambridge University Press, 1996), pp. 2–5.

16 Charlotte Smith to Cadell and Davies [August 1805], *Collected Letters*, p. 705.

17 Smith, *Beachy Head*, p. 39.

18 Curran, *Poetic Form*, p. 190.

19 Porter, "From Nosegay to Specimen Cabinet," pp. 42–44.

20 As I have argued, this practice in turn created a poetic afterlife for 1790s fiction that carried across the nineteenth century; see Dahlia Porter, "The Spectral Iamb: The Poetic Afterlives of the Late Eighteenth-Century Novel," *The Afterlives of Eighteenth-Century Fiction*, Daniel Cook and Nicholas Seager (eds.) (Cambridge: Cambridge University Press, 2015), pp. 153–73.

21 Gilbert White, *The Natural History and Antiquities of Selborne* (London, 1789), pp. 68–70.

22 Charlotte Smith, *Desmond, A Novel*, 2nd ed. (London, 1792), pp. 125–26, 131, 134–35.

23 For a discussion of the poems in Radcliffe's *Udolpho* as sites of sympathetic communication that give respite from gothic terror, see Horrocks, "Remembering Poetry," 507–27.

24 Prosimetrical was briefly introduced into English in the mid-seventeenth century in "hard word" dictionaries such as Thomas Blount's *Glossographia* (1656) and Elisha Coles's *English Dictionary* (1676), but the usage didn't persist.

25 John Thelwall, *The Peripatetic*, Judith Thompson (ed.) (Detroit: Wayne State University Press, 2001), pp. 71–72.

26 Ibid., p. 123.

27 Ibid., p. 121, emphasis in the original.

28 Ibid., pp. 109–10.

29 John Thelwall, *Political Lectures (No. II.): Sketches of the History of Prosecutions for Political Opinion* (London, 1794), p. 14.

30 Both his *Ode to Science* (1791) and *An Essay towards a Definition of Animal Vitality* (1793), presented at the Guy's Hospital Physical Society that year, reveal Thelwall's familiarity with contemporary scientific debates and methods of investigation. He casts the narrator of *The Peripatetic* as having a "strong thirst for philosophy" but doomed to "struggle unassisted along the thorny paths of science" while his mind made "painful efforts against the prejudices of education." Thelwall, *Peripatetic* [2001], pp. 80, 108.

31 "sylva, *n*. 2," *Oxford English Dictionary*, 2nd ed., 1989, OED Online, Oxford University Press, http://dictionary.oed.com.proxy.library.vanderbilt.edu/cgi/entry/50244999, 20 October 2010.

32 Bacon, *Advancement*, p. 405.

33 Quoted in Alastair Fowler, "The *Silva* Tradition in Jonson's *The Forrest*," *Poetic Traditions of the English Renaissance*, Maynard Mack and George deForest Lord (eds.) (New Haven, CT and London: Yale University Press, 1982), p. 166.

34 De Bruyn, "The Classical Silva," 366.

35 Ibid., 349.

36 Ibid., 366.

37 Francis Bacon, *Sylva Sylvarum; Or, a Natural History in Ten Centuries*, 10th ed., William Rawley (ed.) (London: Thomas Lee, 1676).

38 Judith Thompson, Introduction to *The Peripatetic; or Sketches of the Heart* by John Thelwall (Detroit: Wayne State University Press, 2001), p. 38.

39 Thelwall, *Peripatetic* [2001], p. 279.

PART II

Making Minds
Poetry in Prose

CHAPTER 4

Methodizing the Mind
Experimental Education and the Poetic Excerpt

In 1802, Richard Lovell Edgeworth (RLE, as he designated himself in the prefaces to his daughter's pedagogical fictions) – a long-time friend of Erasmus Darwin and fellow member of the Lunar Society – published a remarkable little book, *Poetry Explained for the Use of Young People*.[1] In the Preface, he complained that current pedagogical methods and educational books, and especially miscellaneous collections of verse, tended to muddle pupils' minds by forcing them to memorize and recite poetry they couldn't understand. An education of this sort, as he later remarked of one of his daughters, filled the student's head with romantic ideas and poetic images instead of a clear, precise, rational arrangement of thoughts.[2] Like Darwin, RLE had accepted the dichotomy, developed in the seventeenth-century debates over the authority of experimental science, between the precise language and logical sequences of philosophical prose and the chaos of imaginative literature, especially poetry. Unlike Darwin, who attempted to simultaneously maintain and bridge this divide in *The Botanic Garden*, RLE wanted nothing to do with poetry. His book was intended as a stopgap measure, a temporary fix to a widespread problem in educational practice. In time, he imagined, practice would catch up with theory and there would be no need for publications such as *Poetry Explained*.

Like many late eighteenth-century educationalists, RLE was a proponent of precepts derived from John Locke's *Essay concerning Human Understanding* (1690) and *Some Thoughts concerning Education* (1693). After Locke, Bacon's inductive method became a central component in theories of education, and by the end of the century "methodizing" one's thoughts through an accretive process of observation, fact collecting, comparison, distinction, linking by analogy, and synthesis demarcated the rational mind.[3] Concluding RLE's *Memoirs* after his death, Maria Edgeworth claimed that her father was "the first to recommend, both by example and by precept, what Bacon would call the experimental method in education."[4] The foundation for RLE's method was laid by his second wife, Honora Sneyd Edgeworth, who recorded her observations of child behavior in the late 1770s. Drawing on Honora Edgeworth's collections of observations, RLE and Maria Edgeworth formulated an educational program that followed the inductive method of experimental philosophy and Lockean empiricism, the substance of which they put forward in *Practical Education* (1798). To support their observation-based pedagogy, Maria Edgeworth wrote a series of popular children's books beginning with *The Parent's Assistant* (1796) and *Early Lessons* (1801). While encapsulating the ideas she and her father articulated in *Practical Education*, these stories also pick up on a new trend in educational publishing, fictional narratives for young readers.[5]

As Alan Richardson notes, the 1780s saw a host of changes in education, including a surge in feminist critiques of educational practice and the appearance of new forms of "didactic 'popular' fiction" and instructional children's literature.[6] Anna Barbauld's innovative series of *Lessons for Children* (1778–79) spurred an outpouring of such didactic fictions, including Thomas Day's *The History of Sandford and Merton* (1783–1789, written at the instigation of Richard Lovell Edgeworth), Wollstonecraft's *Original Stories from Real Life* (1788), Barbauld's popular *Evenings at Home* (6 vols., 1792–1796, written with her brother John Aikin), Charlotte Smith's *Rural Walks* (1795), *Rambles Farther* (1796), and *Minor Morals* (1798), as well as Maria Edgeworth's *Early Lessons* and its sequels, *Continuation of Early Lessons* (1814), *Rosamond: A Sequel to Early Lessons* (1821), *Frank: A Sequel to Early Lessons* (1822), and *Harry and Lucy Concluded* (1825). Taking their cue from Barbauld, these fictions develop narrative and character in tandem: the narrative trajectory follows the progressive formation – or, more often, amelioration – of the character's (and implicitly, the reader's) mind and taste. Maria Edgeworth took this parallel plotting a step further than her contemporaries. In her children's books, sequential plot development and scientific subjects combine to posit an intrinsic connection between narrative continuity and a mind trained to observe, collect, arrange, compare, distinguish, and combine – a mind plotted according to the steps of inductive method.

This chapter considers the material, theoretical, and generic implications of Barbauld's innovations in books by Maria Edgeworth and Charlotte Smith. I begin with a discussion of calls for educational reform at the turn of the century, specifically the idea that a rational mind could only be produced by reading specific kinds of texts, the "strong meat" (as More put it) of logic and philosophy (*SFE*, 168). This concept, I argue, stems from the parallel development of educational theory and children's book publishing in the second half of the eighteenth century, culminating in Barbauld's *Lessons*. By embedding cognitive processes in the physical layout of the page and the sequence of the lessons, Barbauld's series equates textual and cognitive development. This innovation drove Edgeworth's and Smith's subsequent plotting of the fictional text's structure and progression as coincident with the acquisition of a series of mental operations. The Edgeworths' pedagogical theory, however, promoted an explicit rejection of poetry from the educational canon – a radical gesture, considering that miscellaneous collections of verse were the most popular and widely used educational genre of the period. For the Edgeworths, the application of inductive method to cognitive development elevated one form over others – specifically, as Richard Lovell Edgeworth's *Poetry Explained* makes abundantly clear, it consolidated a preference for the logical sequences of prose narrative over and above the fanciful associations of excerpted verse arranged in miscellaneous collections. In her books for young women and children, Smith attempted to combine two popular educational genres, the poetic miscellany and the developmental narrative. Smith's educational books promote poetry – and specifically poetic excerpts embedded in prose narrative – as a tool for inculcating inductive method. For Smith, the verse–prose composite promotes a balance of literary sensibility and rational thought, but grasping this depends not on the reader's capacities but on the author's skill in disposing and linking detached pieces of verse through the connective tissue of prose.

In this chapter, I use the phrase "cognitive development" in a historically specific way to signal the goals of educationalists working in the lineage of Locke's *Essay*. My approach thus diverges from that of Lisa Zunshine, who has analyzed the "cognitive foundations" of specific notions put forward in Barbauld's *Hymns in Prose*, among other texts. For Zunshine, Barbauld's text exploits "certain contingencies in our [evolved] cognitive architecture" that developed over the brain's "million-years-old evolutionary history," during which "it learned to privilege certain ways of processing information and interpreting its environment."[7] Zunshine concludes that "[f]rom the perspective of cognitive analysis, Barbauld in *Hymns* does the opposite of what she thinks she is doing": while Barbauld posits the child as a Lockean blank slate in her Preface and Advertisement, the text itself is "grounded in our cognitive predisposition for conceptualizing living beings differently from artifacts. Barbauld's 'message' makes sense on what we may call an intuitive level precisely because her young reader's mind is *not* a blank slate."[8] While I remain intrigued by Zunshine's argument, this chapter focuses on how Barbauld – and those who adopted her approach to writing children's books – understood and attempted to control the cognitive effect of texts. While they may not have been aware of all the potential cognitive ramifications of their practices, these authors formulated a specific relationship between the formal attributes of a text and the processes of forming the mind. Eighteenth-century empiricist theories of cognition lent themselves to material instantiation, a literalization of Locke's metaphor of the mind as a "white paper, void of all characters" that could be "inscribed."[9] If the mind was literally a text being written, texts could (and inevitably would) script the mind's procedure of knowing. These authors believed that what children read – and most importantly the text's form and structure – would order or disorder the mind, with far-reaching, life-defining consequences. It is no surprise that educationalists writing in this tradition took staunch positions on form, or that some authors were frustrated by the disconnect between educational theory and the economic imperatives of the publishing market. In what follows, I detail how these authors negotiated the philosophical and formal pitfalls of employing inductive method as a script for writing the rational mind.

The Forms of Cognition

My argument in this chapter begins with the 1790s debate over reforming women's education. This debate concentrated and distilled current educational theories, and claims about the form and format of educational books were made more explicit in discussions of women, whose education (it was argued) was inimical to the development of a "methodized" mind. In the 1790s, educational reformers as diverse as Wollstonecraft and More drew on a vast body of eighteenth-century Lockean educational theory to argue for radical changes in the methods and content of education. While they shared a common ground in Locke, More situated *Strictures on Female Education* (1799) as a response to Wollstonecraft's politicization of women's education in *Vindication of the Rights of Woman* (1792). More objected to grounding claims for women's education in "rights," ostensibly because this idea was calculated "to excite in their hearts an impious discontent with the post which God has assigned them in this world" (*SFE*, 179). More's position was an eminently practical one. By 1799, the discourse of rights had become indelibly tied to French revolutionary politics, and in Britain's conservative political climate the term functioned more as a detriment than an aid to reform initiatives.[10] More strategically distances her platform from this rhetoric, but the changes she advocates owe much to Wollstonecraft's educational writings. Like most of their contemporaries, both writers lodge a woman's need for rational education in her ability to fulfill her domestic duties, and both denounce the "present erroneous system" of cultivating accomplishments and excessive sentiment at the expense of "serious study"

(*SFE*, 146, 168). An education in which "feeling is indulged to the exclusion or reason and examination," More argues, "blinds the judgment as much as it misleads the conduct" and unfits women for "the practical purposes of life" (*SFE*, 209, 172).

Excess sentiment, however, was only one part of a larger problem. "Many are the causes," Wollstonecraft argues, "that contribute to enslave women by cramping their understandings and sharpening their senses," and foremost among them is that women "generally speaking, receive only a disorderly kind of education."[11] While men are "from their infancy broken into method," the knowledge women acquire is "of a more desultory kind."[12] For both Wollstonecraft and More, women's piecemeal education produces disjunction while men's more orderly education begets the ability to organize their thoughts. For More, the remedy for a woman's disorderly education was to cultivate "a habit of cool investigation and inquiry" which would "enable her to regulate her own mind" (*SFE*, 209). For this purpose, she recommends the "strong meat" of "Watts's or Duncan's little book of Logic, some parts of Mr. Locke's Essay on the Human Understanding, and Bishop Butler's Analogy" along with other such "sober studies" (*SFE*, 168–69). Such reading would, she argued,

> lead [a woman] to be intent on realities; will give precision to her ideas; will make an exact mind; every study which, instead of stimulating her sensibility, will chastise it; which will give her definite notions; will bring the imagination under dominion; will lead her to think, to compare, to combine, to methodise. (SFE, 168, 172–73)

The figure of "strong meat" was a common and long-standing metaphor for the educational force of inductive method. Abraham Cowley's "To the Royal Society" (1667), for example, suggests that Bacon "boldly undertook the injur'd Pupils caus [*sic*]" when he substituted "solid meats" of inductive method for a philosophy fed "with the Desserts of Poetry."[13] More's reading recommendations thus situate *Strictures* in the lineage of empiricist adaptations of inductive method to pedagogy, and her list of mental operations closely replicates Locke's series of mental faculties in *An Essay concerning Human Understanding*.[14] As detailed in Chapter 1, Locke's *Essay* outlines the faculties "whereby [the mind] makes a further progress toward knowledge": Beginning with observation and accumulation, the mind proceeds to contemplation, discerning or distinguishing, comparing, combination, composition, and finally abstracting.[15] These "operations of the mind, which it makes use of in understanding" replicate the steps Bacon had proposed to guide the understanding to knowledge of nature.[16] With Locke, in other words, the procedure intended to guide the mind had been internalized as a series of mental "operations." In *Strictures*, More replicates this conflation in her plan for forming the rational mind. By reading texts that follow an inductive method of inquiry, the reader will be led to develop the mental faculties that allow her to "compare, combine and methodize."

More may have drawn this parallel from another of her recommended readings, Isaac Watts's *Logick; or The Right Use of Reason* (1725). Watts advises furnishing oneself with a "rich variety of ideas" because this

> general Acquaintance with things ... will assist the Use of Reason in all its following Operations; it will teach you to *judge* of Things *aright*, to *argue justly*, and to *methodize* your Thoughts with *Accuracy*. When you shall find several Things a-kin to each other, and several different from each other, agreeing in some Part of their Idea, and disagreeing in other Parts, you will range your Ideas in better Order, you will be more easily led into a distinct Knowledge of Things, and will obtain a rich Store of proper Thoughts and Arguments upon all Occasions.[17]

Watts describes a process of methodizing one's mind in a series of steps patterned, like Locke's developmental model, on Bacon's inductive method. For Watts and Locke, this process depends on exercising the mind as one would in a scientific enquiry. Following Bacon's directive to apply induction to all areas of knowledge, Watts insists that the "right Use of our Reason ... is not only necessary in order to attain any competent Knowledge in the Sciences, or the Affairs of Learning, but to govern both the greater and meaner *Actions of Life*."[18] For Watts, induction was both the procedure of legitimate science and a template for forming the whole person. Hence More's desire to cultivate in women "that sort of experimental logic, if I may so speak, compounded of observation and reflection, which makes up the moral science of life and manners" (*SFE*, 227–28).

Like the texts it cites, *Strictures* translates a process for understanding external nature into one that seeks to comprehend the human mind and its processes of cognition. Following Locke and Watts, More adopts the "experimental logic" of natural and moral philosophy to reconfigure women's sphere of domestic life and manners as a science.[19] As the conflation of text and mind suggests, More advocates the "strong meat" of the philosophical treatise or book of logic for more than just its content. As a genre, the treatise was particularly suited for training women to methodize their minds because the subject matter – method itself – would teach the precepts of natural and moral philosophy while the carefully plotted arguments would model methodical thought. In this, More follows William

Duncan's *The Elements of Logick* by defining "method" as the "Disposal or Arrangement of our Thoughts, when we endeavor so to put them together, as that their mutual Connection and Dependence may be clearly seen."[20] The key for More was the disposition of thoughts into orderly patterns: if the text followed a logical progression, the person who read it would, as a consequence, have their mind methodized.

More's preference for the treatise correlates with her antipathy to less orderly educational genres, especially the most widely used educational books of the period, miscellaneous collections of excerpts. She complained,

> The Swarms of Abridgements, Beauties, and Compendiums, which form a too considerable part of a young lady's library, may be considered in many instances as an infallible recipe for making a superficial mind … A few fine passages from the poets (passages perhaps which derived their chief beauty from their position and connection) are huddled together by some extract maker, whose brief and disconnected patches of broken and discordant materials, while they inflame young readers with the vanity of reciting, neither fill the mind nor form the taste. (*SFE*, 166–67)

For More, the problem with such collections lay in the lack of connection: the disjointed form of the miscellany replicates itself in the student's mind, creating a veneer of knowledge over a jumble of ideas. In such "crippled mutilations," readers see "nothing of that just proportion of parts, that skillful arrangement of the plan, and that artful distribution of the subject, which, while they prove the master hand of the writer, serve also to form the taste of the reader" (*SFE*, 192). For More and many of her contemporaries, including Coleridge and Richard Lovell Edgeworth, poetic miscellanies were not just incapable of generating patterns of rational thought – they were inimical to this project.

Wollstonecraft was less convinced by this generic requirement than More and RLE. She advocated methodizing women's desultory education, but also published a pedagogical collection of excerpts. To justify the miscellaneous content of *The Female Reader* (1789), she suggests,

> In the present volume, which is principally intended for the improvement of females, the subjects are not only arranged in separate books, but are carefully *disposed* in a series that tends to make them illustrate each other; linking the detached pieces seemed to give an interest to the whole, which even the slightest connection will not fail to produce.[21]

Wollstonecraft asserts that the value of the miscellaneous collection – its interest as well as utility – lies in the acts of disposition and linking. In making the collection, she claims to have begun by arranging and

sequencing the extracts "carefully," but the book remains a conglomera-
tion of "detached pieces," a characteristic reinforced by the opening section, "Select Desultory Thoughts."[22] Wollstonecraft's work as a compiler
was to arrange disjointed pieces in such a way that the reader could grasp
the connections between them and see how they illustrate each other. The
reader, however, would still need to work at bridging the gaps between
separate textual units.

In adopting this form, Wollstonecraft joined a group of compilers who
made claims for the pedagogical efficacy of careful arrangement in miscellaneous collections. Oliver Goldsmith, for example, labeled his *Beauties of
English Poesy* (1767) a "guide to direct [the reader's] application," and suggested that if a collection is "compiled with any share of judgment, it may
at once unite precept and example, shew [readers] what is beautiful, and
inform them why it is so."[23] The most popular educational collection of the
later eighteenth century, compiled by William Enfield, announces much
the same editorial credo in its title, *The Speaker; or Miscellaneous Pieces
selected from the Best English Authors and disposed under Proper Heads, with
a view to facilitate the Improvement of Youth* (1774). Like More, Enfield and
Wollstonecraft emphasize the importance of disposition, but rather than
the text supplying links between ideas, the reader's improvement relies on
the editor's proper selection, arrangement, and disposal of the extracts.

This debate in late-eighteenth-century pedagogical theory about what
kind of text would best inculcate orderly, rational thought was spurred
by earlier innovations in the form and format of books specifically mar-
keted to children. Under the sway of Lockean theories of cognition, midcentury publishers began to recast existing genres, including the reading
primer, the elocutionary collection, and the parent's guidebook. For example, the mid-century publisher John Newbery promoted an explicitly Lockean pedagogy in his *A Little Pretty Pocket-Book* (1744), and his *History
of Little Goody Two Shoes* (1765) is often lauded by critics for replacing
the desultory primer with a story that has a coherent narrative.[24] In the
final decades of the eighteenth century, Newbery's innovations were consolidated by Barbauld, whose series of *Lessons for Children* (1778–79) was
explicitly cast in a Lockean mold and followed associationist theories pop-
ularized in Joseph Priestley's abridgement of David Hartley's *Observations
on Man*.[25] Barbauld's series had a wide distribution in Britain and America, and it established the parameters for the emergence of the novelistic
children's book that became popular in the following decades. William
McCarthy notes that Barbauld's contemporaries credited her series with
introducing the "style of familiar conversation" into the children's reading

book or primer, a concept she may have drawn from reading Daniel Defoe's *Family Instructor* (1715).[26] Barbauld's *Lessons*, however, forego the aphoristic phrases and moral lessons of Defoe's fictionalized conduct book; they also omit the word lists and rhymed couplets that dominated conventional primers. Instead, she extends the formal implications of *Goody Two Shoes* by introducing a model of the child's linguistic and mental development that follows the steps of inductive method from a catalog of discontinuous observations to sequential narrative. As Alan Richardson succinctly puts it, Barbauld's books literalized Locke's metaphor of the mind as white paper by reconceptualizing the child *as* a kind of text.[27]

The first volume of the series, *Lessons for Children, from two to three years old* (1778), offers a mixture of direction, admonishment, and facts gleaned from observation. The young student, Charles, learns that Puss can't talk; that bread is made of corn and corn grows in fields; that snow becomes water when put close to the fire.[28] He also learns the names of colors, how to count to ten, and the uses of different writing implements (ink, pencil, sealing wax). Each lesson corresponds to a part of one day, and subsequently part of a year, with each typographically distinct section adding to the series – breakfast, supper, dinner, summer, winter, spring. The brief sections are keyed to teaching careful observation and good behavior as complements to each other, with Mamma's directing voice as the sole element of stability and connection in the panoply of thoughts and subjects. This is not, however, the discontinuity of a miscellany. The objects and ideas are recorded in the text as they are perceived by the child character. For example, take this scene in the garden:

> There is a pretty butterfly.
> Come, shall we catch it.
> Butterfly, where are you going?
> It is flown over the hedge.
> He will not let us catch him.
> There is a bee sucking the flowers.
> Will the bee sting Charles?
> No, it will not sting you if you let it alone.
> Bees make wax and honey.
> Honey is sweet.
> Charles shall have some honey and bread for supper.
> Caterpillars eat cabbages.
> Here is a poor little snail crawling up the wall.
> Touch him with your little finger.
> Ah, the snail is crept into his shell.[29]

In this segment, Charles observes different insects, but his ability to more closely examine one but not the others provides insight into the qualities that distinguish them (pretty but difficult to catch, stings if bothered and makes honey, crawls on walls and shrinks into shell when touched). Charles lacks a differentiated voice – in the context of other sections, it is likely the questions and answers signal dialogue, rephrased by the mother–teacher – but the sequence presents his mind engaged in observing and accumulating information. Mamma's short declarative sentences direct this process. As Sarah Robbins suggests, the mother–teacher manages the environment by selecting and arranging the circumstances of Charles's learning.[30] Format enhances the empirical basis and direction of the lesson. Each insect is introduced spatially (there, there, here), forming them into a group of like things while also marking the shift in Charles's attention from one object to the next. This strategy, as Joanna Wharton argues of Barbauld's *Hymns in Prose*, "shapes the text as a sensible object in order to forge lasting connections in the mind of the child": snails and their shells are distinguished from bees by our capacity to touch them as we touch the printed page of the book.[31] By carefully managing the lesson's content, format, and material presentation, Barbauld ensures that the text models and enacts the process of storing the mind with a set of clear and precise ideas grounded in empirical observation.

McCarthy notes that the "progressive method" of *Lessons* as a series is designed to "secure Charles's understanding of each step before going on to the next."[32] This point bears further analysis. The next book in the series, *Lessons for Children, of three years old* (1778), opens with the promise "now you and I will tell stories," signaling a formal shift.[33] The short sections continue to be descriptive and the passages remain typographically and conceptually discontinuous, but Charles advances on the path to methodizing his mind. The initial passages teach Charles to compare (April to May to June), a skill he must use in the next section where the repeated question of How many legs does *x* have? pushes him to distinguish between people, mammals, birds, and fish. In Part II, his lessons become more explicitly "scientific" in content in accordance with his increasing ability to arrange his thoughts. He learns to use the sun's position in the sky to determine direction, and then must apply this new knowledge to determine which way the wind blows. Finally, he learns to reason by analogy. When they have tea outside, Mama notes the absence of a table and asks,

> What must we do? O, here is a large round stump of a tree, it will do very well for a table. But we have no chairs. Here is a seat of turf, and a bank

almost covered with violets; we shall sit here, and you and Billy may lie on the carpet. The carpet is in the parlour. Yes, there is a carpet in the parlour, but there is a carpet here too. What is it? Grass is the carpet out of doors.[34]

In a precursor to Darwin's wooly fern, Mamma's careful rhetorical overlaying has forged a conceptual link: she has taught the basis for understanding analogy as likeness of function (grass is to the ground as carpet is to the parlor). Thus, over the course of three volumes, Barbauld has led her young reader through the precise steps of inductive method. Charles has learned, as More phrased it, "the faculty of comparing, combining, analyzing, and separating" the ideas gleaned from observation (*SFE*, 182).

Having graduated from observation and fact gathering to comparing, separating, distinguishing, and thinking analogically, Charles is now ready to combine his ideas and draw conclusions from analogy and example – he is, in other words, ready for narrative. The third book, *Lessons for Children from three to four years old* (1779), shifts from description conveyed in declarative sentences to examples. It opens with Mother (not Mamma) addressing Charles:

> Charles, here are more stories for you, – stories about good boys, and naughty boys, and silly boys, for you know what it is to be good now. And there is a story about two foolish Cocks that were always quarrelling, which is very naughty. Do you quarrel? No. I am glad of it; but if you see any little boys that quarrel you may tell them the story of the Two Cocks.[35]

Up to this point, Charles has drawn his knowledge from the occurrences that fall under his immediate sensory observation (the cat, his food, household items, insects, snow, etc.). In the third book, he has advanced far enough towards methodical thought to unravel how fiction can be applied to real life. People are different from animals, but the anthropomorphic and obviously fictional story of the Cocks, Mother tells him, can also supply observations that are directly relevant to situations one might encounter in the world. Charles's education in methodizing his mind has equipped him to understand a story as allegory.

There are several theoretical positions arising from Barbauld's series of developmentally plotted books that would be important for authors who adopted her innovations. As critics have noted, Barbauld's books demonstrate the teacher's "near absolute control" over the formation of the pupil's mind, a control that is extended to the text itself.[36] By joining the books' form and format to the development of a specific way of apprehending the world, Barbauld suggests that discontinuous form can be used to instill the tools of reason – but having done so, is eventually displaced by a sequential narrative. Inductive method, in other words, engenders formal coherence, and coherent, progressive narrative appears as the inevitable endpoint of using induction to inscribe rational thought processes in a child's mind. In addition, Barbauld's shift to storytelling and allegory in the third volume of *Lessons* "dramatize[s] how written materials could, in effect, substitute for human examples."[37] This substitution was a characteristic of the eighteenth-century conduct book tradition, but it was also fundamental to how induction was deployed in eighteenth-century moral philosophy. As detailed in Chapter 1, Hume's "Science of Man" lacked a fundamental condition for induction, a databank of observations and examples. Hume resolved this problem by rethinking what might constitute his raw materials: He replaced observations and experiments with the ready-made archive of biography, history, and poetry. When Barbauld presents Charles with the story of the Cocks in volume 3 of *Lessons*, she has performed the same transposition, replacing observed phenomena with fictional narrative. Barbauld's endpoint in coherent, sequential narrative thus authorizes a form of educational book that teaches by example rather than direct observation – one in which literary texts can stand in for lived experience.

Barbauld's *Lessons* exerted immense influence on succeeding generations of readers and writers and the subsequent development of children's books. The theory of cognition implicit in her practice led Richard Lovell Edgeworth to extol her books above all others on the market at the time; many authors (including Wollstonecraft, Maria Edgeworth, and Charlotte Smith) explicitly cite Barbauld as the model for their own contributions to the field of children's literature. Well into the nineteenth century, Charles Lamb lamented the effect of Barbauld's *Lessons*: "*Goody Two-Shoes* is almost out of print. Mrs. Barbauld's stuff has banished all the old classics of the nursery... Science has succeeded to Poetry no less in the little walks of children than with men."[38] Profiting from hindsight, Lamb puts his finger on the demonstrable effect of the educational paradigms implicit in Barbauld's children's books. In equating a specific form – sequential narrative – with production of a methodized mind, Barbauld set the stage for an elevation of certain forms, genres, and subjects above others within pedagogical literature. For Richard Lovell Edgeworth and Maria Edgeworth, education as a field of inquiry needed to be reduced to an experimental science, and the established forms and subject matter of experimental science were essential to this project. By conflating method, subject matter, and form, the Edgeworths raised persistent questions about the educational value of poetry, how it should be presented to readers, and what kinds of verse, if any, might forward an educational program that plotted the rational mind according to the steps of induction.

Fiction Methodized

The implicit tie between narrative continuity, methodized thought, and observation-based knowledge in Barbauld's lesson books finds its most explicit articulation in the work of Richard Lovell Edgeworth and Maria Edgeworth. In addition to ten novels and four collections of tales, between 1796 and 1825 Maria Edgeworth published six sets of stories for children – *The Parent's Assistant* (1796), *Early Lessons* (1801), *Continuation of Early Lessons* (1814), *Rosamond: A Sequel* (1821), *Frank: A Sequel* (1822), and *Harry and Lucy Concluded* (1825) – and, in collaboration with her father, the influential pedagogical manual for parents, *Practical Education* (1798).[39] The prefaces to these works (written by Richard Lovell Edgeworth and signed RLE) lay out the Edgeworths' pedagogical program, a practical, hands-on approach rooted in Locke's application of Baconian induction to investigations of the human mind. The Preface to *Practical Education* establishes their position: "to make progress in the art of education," RLE writes, "it must be patiently reduced to an experimental science."[40] The first step toward this end is amassing a collection of particular instances. Following Locke's recommendations in *Some Thoughts concerning Education* (1692), the Edgeworths load their essays with examples of children's behavior gleaned from the notebooks of Honora Sneyd Edgeworth and their own observations of RLE's numerous children.

In his Preface to *The Parent's Assistant* (1796), RLE quotes the Scottish moral philosopher Thomas Reid's *An Inquiry into the Human Mind* (1764) to suggest that Honora Edgeworth's notebooks constitute "a treasure of natural history" because they lay out "a distinct and full history of all that hath passed in the mind of a child from the beginning of life and sensation till it grows to the use of reason."[41] On this subject, Reid bluntly states that "it is in vain to wish for what nature has not put within the reach of our power"; RLE disagrees, insisting that Honora's notes achieve this end by providing "a collection of experiments upon a subject which has been hitherto treated theoretically."[42] In recording her observations of children's behavior – a practice Maria Edgeworth revived many years after Honora's death – Honora Edgeworth had compiled what Hume lacked and Reid thought impossible, a natural history of the child's mind. As RLE argued in a letter explaining her innovation,

> She had observed the advantage of Experiments in many branches of phi-
> losophy and was surprised to find that systems [of] Education were sup-
> ported upon uncertain Theories and Speculation and were contradictory
> and capricious as the diversity of Tastes and the wildness of the imagination
> could invent – She thought if proper Experiments were made upon differ-
> ent Children from their earliest years, if these Experiments were registered,
> if the answers & questions of children at different ages, Capacities and Edu-
> cations were preserved and compared ... some knowledge of the effects
> of different instruction might be acquired, their apparent might be distin-
> guished from their real proficiency, and the success or failure of different
> Experiments might lead to some certainty upon a Subject of such extensive
> importance.[43]

For RLE, Honora Edgeworth's record books were the first step in reducing
education to an experimental science. In them, she collected data on which
to perform the succeeding steps of comparison and distinction. Honora's
collection of observations and experiments thus became fodder for *Practical Education*, and snatches of dialogue from her notebook appear in various chapters in support of the Edgeworths' pedagogical principles. For
example, a specimen of apparent selfishness recorded in Honora's 1778
notebook – "Mo[ther]. Don't you wish your sister to have what she wants?
Ho[nora]. Mother if I say that I don't wish it so, will you give it to me?" –
figures in the chapter "On Sympathy and Sensibility" to exemplify the
"simplicity" of a child educated without "affectation."[44] In a second passage
from the same notebook, Honora records how

> Ho[nora] – about 9 months old when she first began to observe the hardness
> of bodies was slapping her hand upon the table when a cat came under her
> hand as it fell upon the cats head she was very much horrified to feel it so
> soft, & could not be prevailed upon to touch anything of the same [...] till
> near 4 yrs old, tho every gentle means was used to conquer her antipathy –
> her having a wooden cat which was covered with fur corrected it at last.[45]

This observation and its experimental cure for the child's aversion appears
(with minor revisions) in the chapter on "Temper" in a series of examples for curing children of "imaginary apprehensions."[46] As these instances
suggest, in *Practical Education* Honora Edgeworth's collection of piecemeal
observations is conjoined with similar instances and organized into essays
on specific topics. RLE could thus claim that the book was composed
according to "a regular plan": the authors had *not*, RLE assures parents,
"written without method, or ... thrown before them a heap of desultory
remarks and experiments, which lead to no general conclusions, and which
tend to the establishment of no useful principles."[47] Like Wollstonecraft,

RLE fixes the disposal of textual excerpts in a connected chain as the selling point of the work, but like More and Duncan, he credits the authors, not the reader, with drawing principles from the collection. Reducing education to an experimental science, in other words, was an exercise in composing a text inductively; *Practical Education* reflects the authors' practice of arranging, comparing, and connecting observations and experiments to formulate the principles of educational practice.

During the same period when Honora began recording her observations, she and RLE co-wrote what would become the template for Maria Edgeworth's fictional children's stories.[48] The story of Harry and Lucy was originally composed in 1779 and an emended version appeared in Edgeworth's second collection of stories, *Early Lessons* (1801).[49] While ostensibly introduced to explain difficult words used in the short text, the "glossary" between Parts I and II of "Harry and Lucy" in *Early Lessons* comprises a hymn to experimental philosophy. In addition to terms often used in didactic fiction to prescribe good behavior (honest, neatly, trust, and truth), the glossary lists the crucial steps of Baconian induction (associate, collected, compared, examining, experiment, joined, and observed); underscores the book's empiricist ethos (attention, care, distinctly, exactly, habit, purposely, and useful); and, for good measure, explains the instruments (kiln, lever, microscope, orrery, thermometer, barometer), objects (cylinder, globes, fluid, particles, steam), and processes (evaporate, fill, melted, mixed) of experimental science.[50] Writing after her father's death, Edgeworth positions all her pedagogical stories in the lineage of "Harry and Lucy" and *Practical Education*: "I have endeavored to pursue, in this Conclusion of Early Lessons, my father's object in their commencement – to exercise the powers of attention, observation, reasoning, and invention."[51] If *Practical Education* provided parents with principles generated inductively, Maria Edgeworth's children's stories enacted this process in fiction. By seeing themselves in the place of the fictional children Harry, Lucy, Rosamond, and Frank, child readers learned the steps of method that would guide them to rational thought.[52]

As Marilyn Butler has shown, RLE and Honora Edgeworth's story of Harry and Lucy took its philosophical cue from Lockean and associationist models of the mind and drew its formal paradigm from Barbauld's *Lessons for Children*, which RLE read in 1778 and commended – in a 70 page letter to the author – as an exemplary pedagogical text.[53] To display children's minds in the process of formation, Honora and RLE adopt Barbauld's focus on subjects of children's daily lives and immediate observations, and the descriptive third person narrative of "Harry and Lucy" is gradually replaced

by dialogue between the children and their parents. Maria Edgeworth's stories in *Early Lessons* follow this pattern, with each story recording dialogues
between the young pupil and a guiding adult or older sibling. These dialogues, as with Barbauld's *Lessons*, explicitly strive to methodize the character's and reader's mind simultaneously. For example, in "The Purple Jar" –
the first and best-known story in Edgeworth's *Rosamond* series – the young
heroine learns the importance of precise observation and investigation, a
foundational lesson she reminds herself (and the reader) of in later chapters.
Confronted with "a great variety of different sorts of things," Rosamond
desires them all indiscriminately (*EL*, 115). When she finally focuses on one
item, a purple vase, her mother suggests she "examine it" and discern its
use before deciding to purchase it (*EL*, 116). At this moment, Rosamond
is the picture of the "volatile geniuses" described in the chapter on "Attention" in *Practical Education*: these children show quickness and vivacity but
cannot connect their observations – their "associations are strong and various; [but] their thoughts branch off into a thousand beautiful, but useless
ramifications."[54] When Rosamond must choose between new shoes and
the vase, her mother reiterates, "you cannot be sure [the shoes will fit] till
you have tried them on, any more than you can be quite sure you should
like the purple vase *exceedingly*, till you have examined it more attentively"
(*EL*, 117). Rosamond fails to heed this advice, and after buying the vase she
quickly finds the liquid within, not the glass itself, to have been the cause of
the striking color. The story's lesson turns on the centrality of observation,
the first step in induction, which enacts a less-than-subtle critique of the
distractions of modern consumerism.

Rosamond, as critics have noted, is "punished'" for choosing beauty over
practicality (she cannot go on an outing with her father because her shoes
are too shabby), thus making an example of her for the book's child readers.
Rosamond's choice, as critics have argued, may be a triumph of aesthetics
over practicality, but it is also the victory of confusion and chaos over the
orderly progression of reasoned judgment.[55] Considered in this light, the
story manifests what Richard Barney has called "*narrative emplotment*," a
"pedagogical process as ideological 'plot.'"[56] If Rosamond had followed the
narrative path plotted by the progression of the text – if she had examined,
ordered, compared, and distinguished the heaps of "roses, and boxes, and
buckles, and purple flower-pots, and everything" littering the shops and
her mind – she would have certainly, the story implies, bought the shoes
(*EL*, 116). Rosamond violates what for Edgeworth is a basic *formal* premise
of the method of experimental philosophy and empiricist pedagogy: You
must examine, arrange, and connect *before* you can draw conclusions and

make decisions. Rational thought demands linear narrative progression: you should not double back to get the vase once you've already arrived at the shoes.

Peopled with slightly older (Rosamond is seven) and more willful children than Barbauld's Charles, the stories in Edgeworth's *Early Lessons* repeatedly enact this joint development of character and plot. As with Barbauld's *Lessons*, the arc of the *Rosamond* stories mirrors the character's gradual progress through the steps of inductive method. If her failure teaches careful observation in "The Purple Jar," in the next story Rosamond learns the value of order and arrangement. Having imbibed the first steps of method, she then must use them to curb her unruly passions and impulsive desires — for example, her longing for another beautiful purple object, a stone plum, which she examines very carefully before deciding she would rather have the practical, red leather holder for her sewing needles (*EL*, 121). After exchanging impetuous desire for domestic self-control, Rosamond is then asked to try an "experiment" on herself to see if time passes more quickly when she is occupied, and later to use an "exact history" of her brother's past experience to select and arrange the plants in her garden (*EL*, 124, 152). Together, these lessons instill a series of mental operations while driving the plot; her story is the process and she the product of imbibing methodized thought. Edgeworth's *Continuation of Early Lessons* (1814) and *Rosamond: A Sequel* (1821) extend this pattern. As Rosamond grows up, she moves from observing, examining, and ordering to more advanced skills. A visit to a cotton mill, for example, culminates in a demonstration of her ability to recollect, arrange, and connect facts in a logical series, showing she has learned to "command [her] attention, and turn it to observe real things."[57] Edgeworth thus translates the pedagogical objective of teaching method into a structural paradigm that conveys the lessons of direct experience through the medium of fiction.

This strategy works because Edgeworth's characters — and especially the young children of *Early Lessons* — are more or less Lockean white paper that can be gradually inscribed with observations and ideas as well as the procedure of arranging and connecting them. According to this pedagogical paradigm, children learn from experience, and therefore the characters should grow from experience, not by precepts delivered in histories, allegories, or fables.[58] Edgeworth's approach pushes empiricist pedagogy to its logical conclusion: Teaching by example requires character and plot development to be identical, and, if the goal is to instill the process of methodical thinking, the plot must record the progression of mental development shared by character and reader. Reducing education to an experimental science meant exchanging the discontinuity of children's perceptions for what Mitzi Myers called "dramatic, child-centered plots" that stress "learning to think, act and judge, [by focusing] on connecting causes and sequences."[59] What critics have celebrated in Edgeworth's children's fiction – the realism and vitality of her child characters – is thus a direct result of Edgeworth's use of form and structure to replicate in fiction the progressive development of mental faculties. Considered in this light, Edgeworth's lively child characters are in fact more circumscribed, more rigorously controlled, than their flatter, more typological counterparts in earlier fictions.

In their formal logic, Edgeworth's children's books replicate the reasoned arguments of treatises on the human mind and understanding – More's books of logic – but Edgeworth also binds her theory of cognitive development to the subject matter of experimental science. While Rosamond's lessons are more domestic at the outset, the continuations of *Rosamond*, *Frank*, and *Harry and Lucy Concluded* develop mental processes in tandem with explicitly scientific content. To take one of many examples, in the *Continuation of Early Lessons* (1815), Lucy and her brother Harry engage in experiments that teach them how a barometer works. Building on this scene, *Harry and Lucy Concluded* (1825) begins by measuring Lucy's educational progress by how much time has passed since she learned about the barometer.[60] The narrative then moves forward by setting Lucy's powers of observation to the task of identifying a barometer hidden in a walking stick. Lucy acquires this knowledge as part of the plot, and her knowledge of the barometer's construction and function in turn determines the trajectory and development of the story. For Edgeworth, the inductive procedures of experimental science take on a multivalent role as the lesson's subject matter, the pedagogical objective, and the formal principle by which the narrative develops.

An unpublished manuscript plan for *Harry and Lucy Concluded* lays out the compositional procedures that underwrite this overlap in matter, method, and lesson. Edgeworth begins with a statement of the book's educational aims:

> This book should not attempt to teach any particular science. It is intended to show how children may be brought to a taste for science & literature and how their memories – reasoning faculties and inventive power may be trained to the habits which will give them the best chance of succeeding in any science to which they may in afterlife apply.[61]

Here, Edgeworth follows Gerard's *Essay on Genius* in suggesting that science and literature stem from the same processes, those habits of mind that cultivate reason and inventiveness.[62] She goes on to lay down the book's pedagogical approach: "By examining and analyzing some inventions we may find out what ideas are necessary to them & in what order these must be placed to produce the effect desired – & *pointing out the steps the mind takes* we may diminish the sense of difficulty and dispel the notion that invention is a sort of magical process – or a gift confined to a few favored from their birth."[63] Here, Edgeworth points to the consonance between her compositional method and the book's pedagogical objective: the characters' cognitive development through a series of steps conforms to her process of composing the book's episodes, which examine and analyze a series of scientific and technological inventions. *Harry and Lucy Concluded* functions as a meta-reflection on Edgeworth's own process of invention. Her literary works arise from the same series of mental procedures as a barometer or air pump, and both instrument and text carry the mark of their making in their structure and form.

For both Maria Edgeworth and her father, the author's inductive method is manifested in the text's structure and form, which is transferred onto the child's mind through the act of reading. It is thus not the scientific content of books that is important, RLE argues, but the kind of thinking one encounters in books about science. While he cautions against giving children treatises on any specific science too early, REL's "Address to Mothers" in *Continuation of Early Lessons* (1814) recommends that mothers supply their daughters with a copy of "Mrs. Marcet's Chemical Dialogues"

> for the clear and easy reasoning, by which the reader is led from one proposition to another. I speak from experience: one of my children had early acquired such an eager taste for reading, as had filled her mind with a multitude of facts, and images, and words, which prevented her from patient investigation, and from those habits of thinking, and that logical induction, without which, no science, nor any series of truths, can be taught. The "Chemical Dialogues" succeeded in giving a turn to the thoughts of my pupil, which has produced the most salutary effects in her education. Romantic ideas, poetic images, and some disdain of common occupations, seemed to clear away from her young mind; and the chaos of her thoughts formed a new and rational arrangement.[64]

Much as More would replace "enervating or absurd books" of "English Sentiment" and "Italian Poetry" with the "strong meat" of philosophy and logic (*SFE*, 168), RLE advises exchanging poetry for chemistry. Like More, he aligns women's desultory education with romance, poetry, and sensibility, and sets it against the patient investigation and skill in arrangement cultivated in the pursuit of experimental science. The mind is best formed in the image of experimental science, not (as More put it) by activities that fall "under description of polite letters" and "the denomination of taste" in which "women are excellent" (*SFE*, 181), The structure and formal presentation of information characteristic of a specific, implicitly masculine prose genre will effectively plot the mind according to inductive method, defending it from the corrupting influence of Romantic ideas and poetic images.

Maria Edgeworth's fictions for children often thematize this problem, especially in the later books when the children are slightly older. For example, *Harry and Lucy Concluded* opens with Lucy asking her mother why her studies have changed from chemical experiments to arithmetic, drawing, dancing, and music. In the time elapsed since the previous book, Lucy's education has diverged from her brother's and she has taken up conventional female accomplishments that cultivate the "looser analogies" (as Darwin put it) of poetry. In this chapter, Lucy learns the difference between poetry and science: while she recites and revels in lines lifted from Darwin's *The Economy of Vegetation*, her brother Harry provokingly "finds out that similes are not exact." Her mother suggests that this is because his scientific studies reveal "at every step the use, the necessity of exactness. He could not go on without it in measuring or in reasoning."[65] The project of *Harry and Lucy Concluded*, however, is to reintroduce Lucy to experimental science and its chains of inductive reasoning by restricting poetry to a tightly circumscribed role in her education. When Lucy repeats some "pretty lines" from Darwin's *Economy* – "You charmed, indulgent sylphs, their learned toil/And crowned with fame your Torricell and Boyle" – her uncle says she "repeated them well" but Harry objects to the name of the inventor being shortened from Torricelli to Toricell "for the sake of the line."[66] Disregarding this objection, Lucy continues reciting until her uncle chides, "I am sure you cannot understand [the lines], as you are not yet acquainted with the airpump."[67] The prose makes it clear that Lucy has reeled off a long section of Darwin's poem, but Edgeworth admits only the two offending lines into her text as an embedded quotation. These are enough to show, both conceptually and in the material aspect of the printed page, that prosody has derailed truth and confounded Lucy's understanding. Edgeworth reinforces this point several chapters later: when Lucy asks if Boyle or Torricelli invented the air pump, Harry replies, "Neither ... it was that poetry you repeated, which put that mistake into your head. And when once one has got any thing wrong in one's head there is no getting it out again."[68] Poetry is the enemy of methodical thought, and Lucy must stop reciting fanciful verse so she can instead focus her attention on Harry's detailed explanations of the construction, use, and purposes of the hygrometer, air pump, and steam engine. Edgeworth thus uses an embedded quotation and its disruptive potential to negotiate the conventional division between the gendered spheres of knowledge and taste, allowing (or forcing, as the case may be) Lucy and the young reader to reap the cognitive benefits that only, the book implies, scientific study is capable of inculcating.[69]

Poetry, it would seem, was fundamentally inimical to the Edgeworths' pedagogical agenda, which makes it all the more striking that Maria Edgeworth's fictions work very deliberately, over a thirty-year period, to recuperate verse and insert it, materially, into the fabric of her prose. Further, against her father's explicit and repeated insistence that poetry derails methodical thought, a good number of Edgeworth's embedded quotations are *not* designed to put the disjunctive cognitive effects of poetry on display. Indeed, quite the opposite: like Charlotte Smith, whose pedagogical fictions I discuss in the final section of this chapter, Edgeworth attempts to counteract the disruptive potential of embedded verse by making it conform to the inductive method plotted in her prose narratives.

Poetry Explained, Methodically

For RLE, whatever pleasures or plights it might inspire in adults, verse was particularly pernicious when it was used as an educational tool for the young. As he argues in the Preface to *Poetry Explained for the Use of Young People* (1802), reading poetry tends to instill in children "the habit of repeating words to which they affix no distinct ideas, or of admiring melodious sounds which are to them destitute of meaning" (*PE*, iii). Because they don't understand what they read, poetry "is likely to habituate [their] minds to admire without choice or discrimination" – it creates "veneration independent of reason, which disposes the young student to admire and imitate, without instructing him how to analyze and combine" (*PE*, v–vi). Teaching children poetry was likely to result in the very opposite of a mind scripted by inductive method.

Poetry, as the very existence of RLE's *Poetry Explained* suggests, was not easily cast aside – it was the staple of eighteenth- and early-nineteenth-century educational publishing and practice. As RLE acknowledges (with, we might imagine, a heavy sigh),

> It is not to be supposed, that preceptors can be prevailed upon immediately to change their usual practice; nor can it be expected that parents, although convinced of the error of putting fine poetry too early into the hands of children, should have sufficient strength of mind to let their pupils appear ignorant of what others the same age are taught. It is therefore probable, that

the practice of teaching young people a certain quantity of poetry by rote
will long prevail, both in schools and in private families. – With this belief,
the author has endeavoured to render a few popular poems intelligible to
young readers. (*PE*, xiv–xv)

Parents and preceptors will continue to insist on teaching poetry, and all
that remains is to publish a book that hopes, by careful explanation, to
make certain poems comprehensible. The Preface to his second book in this
vein, *Readings in Poetry* (1816), explains, "The poems and passages selected
for explanation have been chosen chiefly from '*Enfield's Speaker*,' because
we are informed that this is an established school-book, and we see in private families that it is in every body's hands."[70] RLE intended his book
as a companion to one of the most widely used pedagogical collections
of its day, William Enfield's *The Speaker; or, Miscellaneous Pieces, Selected
from the Best English Writers, and Disposed under Proper Heads*, first published in 1774 and reissued in at least 25 editions out of six cities from eight
different publishers or printers by 1801. (Enfield's was only the most popular of many similar compilations of extracts, including Vicesimus Knox's
Elegant Extracts series, which had similar market saturation.) RLE's assessment – that poetry produces a "habit of repeating words to which [chil-
dren] affix no distinct ideas" – replays More's criticism of miscellaneous
collection that merely "inflame the young readers with the vanity of reciting, [but] neither fill the mind nor form the taste" (*SFE*, 166–67). RLE's
objection to poetry, in other words, was as much about the medium as
the poems themselves: if children can be led to reason by carefully crafted
narrative sequences, excerpts of verse delivered piecemeal in a compilation
will induce desultory reading antithetical to logic and reason. From within
a pedagogical paradigm that equates rational thought with sequential narrative, poetry delivered in an educational miscellany can only be a disabling
form of digression, discontinuity, and disjunction.

    RLE proposes two solutions to this problem, the ideal and the prac-
tical. In the Preface to *Poetry Explained*, he suggests how to prepare the
mind for reading poetry. First, the pupil's attention must be directed to the
sublime and beautiful in nature, and then he or she should sample selections from the Old Testament or natural histories such as Gilbert White's
Natural History and Antiquities of Selborne, only afterwards advancing to
Anna Barbauld's *Hymns in Prose*. Only after this – and a crash course in
classical mythology – would the student be ready to read and understand
verse. Gradual preparation of this sort, however, must yield to expediency
and "*the existing circumstances*," and therefore RLE offers instead "detailed
explanations of lines" in his book (*PE*, xiii–xv). He chooses Thomas Gray's

"Elegy Written in a Country Churchyard" as a "proper piece to begin with," it being "one of the most popular poems that we know of" and pleasing to "all ranks and ages" (*PE*, 11). He summarizes the opening scene in prose, quotes the first four lines of verse, then provides a key to individual words: "curfew" requires an historical and etymological explanation, "knell" a definition, "parting day" an analogy to a more familiar phrase, and so on (*PE*, 12–13). In this way, the student comes to understand the literal content and melancholy tone of the opening lines, but may still be perplexed by the fourth line – "And leaves the world to darkness and to me" – as RLE makes no mention of the poem's speaker or why he remains on the lea after curfew (*PE*, 12). As this suggests, it is the *words*, their signification and connection to each other, he seeks to explain, not the complexities of lyric subjectivity or anything else that might introduce interpretive ambiguity. While Darwin amplifies the capricious and fanciful in poetry to distinguish it from scientific prose, RLE would reduce poetry to a "philosophical language." As *Practical Education* advises, "a man who attempts to teach will find it necessary to select his terms with care, to define them with accuracy, and to abide by them with steadfastness; thus he will make a philosophical vocabulary for himself."[71] With an accurate understanding of select words, the pupil will grasp the sense of the verse instead of merely being allured by the sound.

With its adamant pursuit of sense, RLE's procedure founders on the rocky shores of poetic imagery. While the glossary-like structure conjoins verse to prose, the entries for specific words often deviate into commentary on various topics, ranging from how the use of epithets differs in prose and verse to a critique of Gray for introducing ambiguity into his poems (*PE*, 18, 31). While recording RLE's preference for the accuracy of prose over the elusiveness of poetic imagery, the effect of these digressions is to infuse prose with the disorienting qualities of verse. For example, in explicating lines from stanza three of Gray's "Elegy" – "Save that from yonder ivy-mantled tower,/The moping owl does to the moon complain" – RLE gives a definition of "moping" as "to seem stupefied by melancholy," which, he argues, might describe the owl during the day but not at twilight when the poem takes place (*PE*, 17, 19). He then adds that the owl is far from stupid, and in fact was considered the favorite of Minerva, "but whether this bird were her favourite as goddess of wisdom, or of war, is doubtful" (*PE*, 19). He concludes it is more likely that because the owl catches prey at night, she was "considered as an emblem of military stratagem," but then adds a quotation from Darwin that explains anatomically why the owl appears to give objects greater attention and thus is considered a bird of wisdom (*PE*, 19–20). Initially, RLE's remarks run against Gray's use of "moping," implicitly criticizing the propriety of the epithet as applied to the owl, but he quickly becomes entangled in the larger question of what the owl signifies in itself and how the poetic owl might align with the owl as a zoological specimen.

When he comes to the second half of the line – "does to the moon complain" – RLE finds himself again caught between figure and fact: "the complaining notes of the owl seem to be addressed to the moon, as there is no other striking *general* object, to which the owl might be supposed to address herself. Probably the notes of the owl are littered to call her companions" (*PE*, 21). Gray has distorted reality – owls don't mope, in the world or in literature, nor do they address themselves to the moon – a problem of figuration that clearly disturbs RLE. How can one explicate something that doesn't accord with what has been observed or recorded – something that, in a word, doesn't make any sense in the first place? RLE can find no other solution but to turn to literary history and its established tropes. The explanation of Gray's line concludes,

> Dogs are also supposed to howl at the moon.
> > 'Nor watchful dogs bark at the silent moon,'
> is a line of Dryden's.
> > 'I'd rather be a dog, and bay the moon,
> > 'Than such a Roman.' SHAKSPEARE. (*PE*, 21)

Here, the physical layout of the text – the variations in font size, italics, all caps, and indentation of quoted material – reproduces the breakdown of the larger interpretive framework and RLE's pedagogical agenda (Fig. 9). It is fair to say that RLE has left his young pupil in a morass of indeterminacy: Do owls howl at the moon? Do dogs mope? Are they wise? Does the word "nor" indicate that *watchful* dogs do or don't bark at the moon? Is baying the same as barking? What Roman? The printed page materializes the cognitive disorientation introduced by embedded quotations, and the novice poetry reader ends up in the condition of Wordsworth's Johnny, who can only report of his nighttime adventure that "The cocks did crow to-whoo, to-whoo,/And the sun did shine so cold."[72]

In his attempts to render Gray's poetic images transparent, RLE has exposed why he objects to poetry in the first place. As in Darwin's *Loves*, he has landed in the realm of fancy, a place where the associative leap from moping owls to howling dogs is par for the course. He can explain, technically, what epithets are and state that the beauty of verse depends on

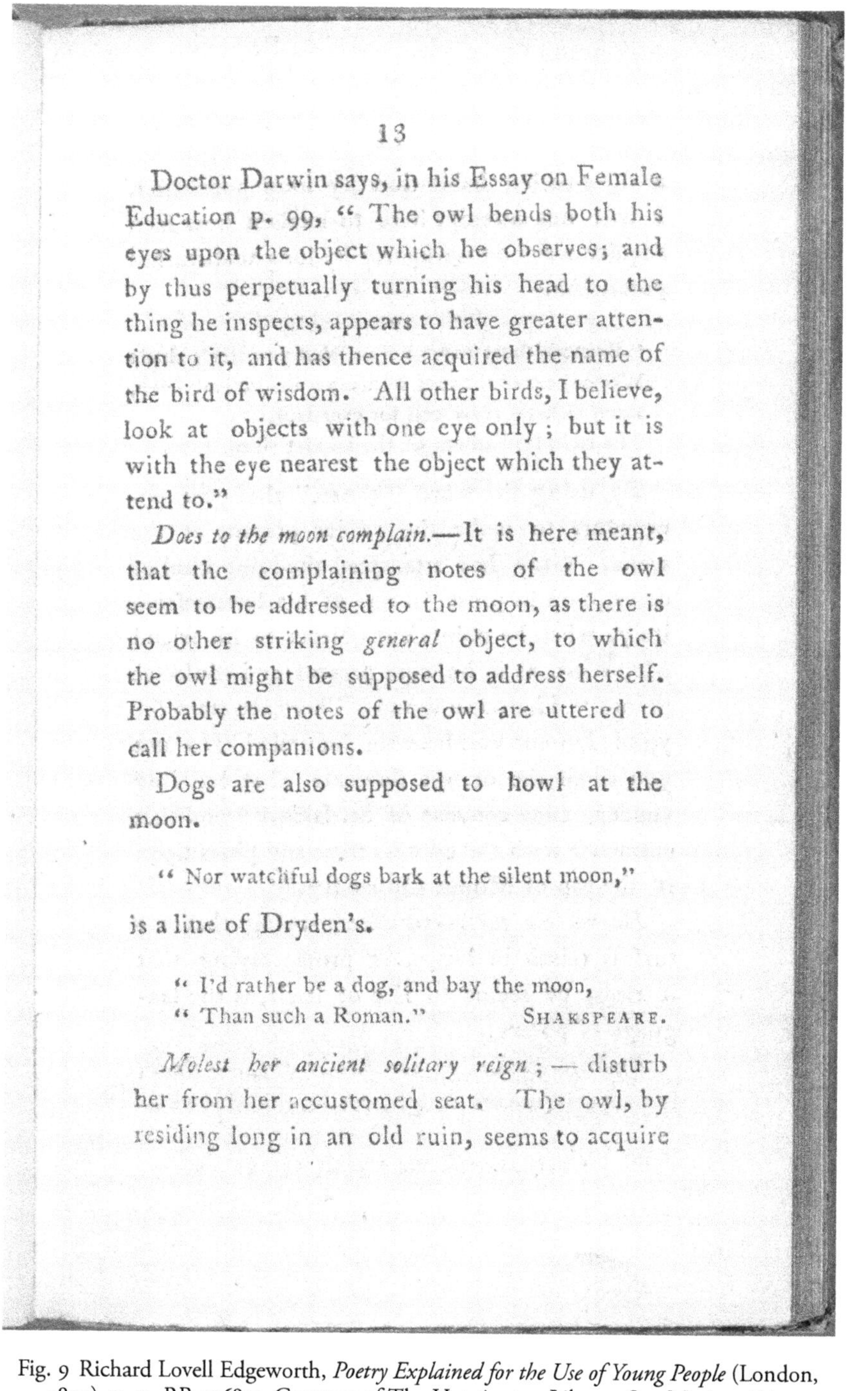

13

Doctor Darwin says, in his Essay on Female Education p. 99, "The owl bends both his eyes upon the object which he observes; and by thus perpetually turning his head to the thing he inspects, appears to have greater attention to it, and has thence acquired the name of the bird of wisdom. All other birds, I believe, look at objects with one eye only ; but it is with the eye nearest the object which they attend to."

Does to the moon complain.—It is here meant, that the complaining notes of the owl seem to be addressed to the moon, as there is no other striking *general* object, to which the owl might be supposed to address herself. Probably the notes of the owl are uttered to call her companions.

Dogs are also supposed to howl at the moon.

" Nor watchful dogs bark at the silent moon,"

is a line of Dryden's.

" I'd rather be a dog, and bay the moon,
" Than such a Roman."   SHAKSPEARE.

Molest her ancient solitary reign ; — disturb her from her accustomed seat. The owl, by residing long in an old ruin, seems to acquire

Fig. 9 Richard Lovell Edgeworth, *Poetry Explained for the Use of Young People* (London, 1802), p. 13. RB 426819. Courtesy of The Huntington Library, San Marino, CA.

their propriety, but it is much harder to pin down signification because figures contain so much beyond themselves. As he inadvertently discovers to
his reader, in poetry an owl is not merely an owl – it is a carrier of historical,
literary, cultural, environmental, and anatomical significations, often contradictory and always multivalent. The embedded quotations from Dryden
and Shakespeare thus heighten rather than tamp down poetry's potential
to jumble up fanciful images, the very thing RLE aims to counter with
his explanations. Excerpted verse rehearses, formally and materially, the
cognitive consequences of introducing poetry into an educational agenda
grounded in inductive method. When he resorts to quotation, RLE points
to the problem of induction, the possibility that attentive observation, careful selection, and accurate arrangement will not, in the end, methodize the
mind. (The problem RLE confronts would become one of Coleridge's most
vexing philosophical conundrums and most potent compositional strategies in his "Essays on Method," examined in the next chapter.)

In *Continuation of Early Lessons* (1814), Maria Edgeworth devotes a chapter of Rosamond's narrative to the problems posed by poetic language, creating a scenario that rewrites RLE's difficulties in *Poetry Explained*. In dialogue with their mother and father, Rosamond and her brother Godfrey
hear about a young factory worker who was reading a story in "Harry and
Lucy" about a girl who was stung by a bee. The complexity of this situation – the reader of Edgeworth's 1814 book reads a story about two children hearing a story about a girl who read another of Edgeworth's stories –
indicates the advanced age and capacities of the imagined audience. The
intertextual reference – Lucy is stung by a bee in Part I of *Early Lessons*
(1801) – draws attention to the factory girl's educational fodder: when
asked what a bee is like, the factory girl asks if it is like a cow. The girl
has learned (or not learned, as the case may be) to read using a primer
like *The Royal Primer; or, an Easy and Pleasant Guide to the Art of Reading*
(Fig. 10). As their father explains to Rosamond and Godfrey, "the sound of
the letter, which is pronounced like the name of the insect, *bee*, was joined
in the child's mind with the idea, or picture of a bull or cow."[73] Having
memorized the letter "b" phonetically, the woodcut has confounded her
comprehension. The girl's confusion was likely exacerbated by the problems of scale: In the primer, the egg might contain the dog, and the lion
and mouse appear quite companionable. The effect of such inaccurate representations in prints of animals, according to *Practical Education*, must
"give children false ideas" and fill the imagination with chimeras.[74] But
this hardly compares to the "defects of language" that Edgeworth draws

Fig. 10 *The Royal Primer* (Brentford: P. Norbury, 1770), p. 8. By permission of the British Library, General Reference Collection 905.a.8.(1.).

attention to: the primer has led the child to form a "capricious analogy" not unlike RLE's owl–dog conjunction, an arbitrary association with no foundation in reality.[75] In its reliance on rhetoric – b is for bull, but also (in other primers) book, bird, ball – the primer runs counter to the Edgeworths' insistence on accurate and careful observation as the foundation of a sound education. Godfrey's ridicule of the poor girl – "She must have been an idiot" or at least "uncommonly silly" – should, the story implies, be applied to the primer and its faulty pedagogy, not to the child who has been forced to memorize something she has not observed and therefore cannot understand.[76]

Rosamond and Godfrey come out of this discussion feeling quite superior to the factory girl, until they begin to examine how well they understand the poetry they have memorized. Rosamond can explain "The Robin's Petition," a first person narrative that is quoted in full, but (unsurprisingly) she gets hung up on the first line of Gray's "Elegy Written in a Country Churchyard" – and the first line is all Edgeworth quotes from the poem. Godfrey takes pains to expose Rosamond's ignorance by quoting phrases she cannot explain, but he fares equally poorly, making it through some lines of Pope's *Homer* and the opening stanza of Gray's "The Bard." Edgeworth allows that "Fortunately for Godfrey, he had carefully read certain notes of Mason's to this poem," but he loses face when he comes to the end of the third stanza, "where historical notes gave him no assistance."[77] Godfrey "could not make any sense of this passage; he did not know who wept – who slept – who the grisly band were – what dreadful harmony they joined, or what they wove with bloody hands."[78] Edgeworth does not attempt to explain the lines, but rather makes explicit what Godfrey (and presumably the reader) does not understand – certainly a safer route than the one pursued by RLE. In this passage, her focus remains on the cognitive limits and development of the pupil, not the intricacies of the verse.

After these demonstrations, Rosamond concludes she should stop memorizing poetry that is beyond her grasp, reiterating a now familiar maxim that it is "foolish to learn mere words, or merely pretty sounds."[79] Her father concurs, but also suggests that a clear and accurate understanding of a topic will make verse both comprehensible and pleasurable. Rosamond's visit to the cotton mill in the previous volume – and the work of observing, collecting, and arranging facts in her mind she has done on this excursion – has prepared her to understand, and truly enjoy, Darwin's lines in *The Loves of the Plants* describing the spinning Jenny, which her father proceeds to recite:

> With wiry teeth, revolving cards release
> The tangled knots, and smooth the ravell'd fleece:
> Next moves the iron hand, with fingers fine,
> Combs the wide card, and forms th'eternal line;
> Slow, with soft lips the whirling can acquires
> The tender skein, and wraps in rising spires;[80]

The child reader who has experienced the mill vicariously through Rosamond, the text implies, will also be able to comprehend these lines – even without the benefit of direct experience and observation. Accurate description in prose, coupled with a carefully plotted sequence of mental operations, is thus offered as the prerequisite for poetic pleasure. Rosamond's taste for realities has secured her from following pretty words to capricious analogies, but Edgeworth's prose allows the child reader to likewise surmount the epistemological pitfalls of poetic language.

Harry and Lucy Concluded performs a similar substitution to rescue poetry from its degraded position. Having established Darwin's "pretty lines" as the enemy of methodical thought in the book's first chapter, Edgeworth plots Lucy's gradual acquisition of the technical and philosophical knowledge necessary to understand a series of inventions. After sixty pages of prose dialogue on the air pump, ten lines from Darwin's poem appear in full, with Lucy (in two lines of interjected prose) differentiating lines referring to the barometer from those describing the air pump[81] (Fig. 11). The inventions are no longer "jumbled in her head" because she reads poetry as a much condensed iteration of the preceding prose narrative.[82] Harry sets about memorizing the lines, which affirms the pedagogical value of Darwin's verse – but only because he and the child reader have been prepared to digest it by a diet of methodical prose. This is confirmed when, after another forty pages of dialogue extending a reference to "'gelid vapour' and 'misty dew drops'" in the quoted lines, Lucy successfully explains the steam engine to their father and both children are rewarded with a series of quotations from Darwin, recited by their father, that describe the "wonders performed by the expansive powers of steam."[83] Edgeworth has made an implicit argument for how poetic excerpts can support an empiricist pedagogy: some little obscurity in the verse might spur the next step in the inductive reasoning plotted in the prose. As Lucy comments of Harry's method of teaching her (which is also, of course, a self-reflexive comment on the structure of Edgeworth's text), "he brought me up to the steam engine by degrees ... I did not know what he was about when he began ... but I saw plainly afterwards, when I found out where I was."[84] Substitute poetry for the steam engine, and Edgeworth's technique for nullifying

"That is true," said Lucy, "but it is pretty well over now. What did you ask me?"

"I asked you what caused that kind of sucking in of your hand into the exhausted receiver?"

She thought for an instant, and answered,

"I believe it was the pressure of the outer air, which was trying to get in at that hole, to fill the vacuum, and which was prevented by the palm of my hand, which it then drove in as much as it could. Well, now I am sure I have *felt* 'the pressure of the viewless air'; and now you must let me repeat the line,

"'The spring and pressure of the viewless air.'"

Harry repeated it after her, declaring it was a very pretty line, besides, it had some common sense in it. Lucy had said it quite at the right time, when it did not interrupt him, or any thing that was going on. He was so much pleased with it, that he begged of her to repeat all those lines

again for him; and when they went out to their garden soon afterwards, instead of beginning to dig, he desired her to say the lines once more, for that he must learn them by heart. Thus he learnt from her some of her taste for poetry, while she acquired from him some of his love of science.

In repeating these lines, Lucy observed which of them alluded to the barometer, and which to the air pump. When she had first learned them by rote, barometer and air pump had been so jumbled in her head, that she could not understand them.

"How my exhausted tubes bright currents flow
Of liquid silver from the lake below;
Weigh the long column of th' incumbent skies,
And with the changeful moment fall or rise—"

she now knew described the barometer, and the succeeding lines the air pump:

"How, as in brazen pumps the pistons move,
The membranic valve sustains the weight above;
Stroke follows stroke, the gelid vapour falls,
And misty dew-drops dim the chrystal walls;
Rare and more rare expands the fluid thin,
And silence dwells with vacancy within."

Fig. 11 Maria Edgeworth, *Harry and Lucy Concluded*, 4 vols. (London, 1825), 1: 132–33. Courtesy of University of Glasgow Library, Special Collections.

poetry's disruptive effects comes into focus. (One might even claim that Edgeworth's prose narrative was built on and around excerpts from Darwin's poems, a point I return to in the final section of this chapter.) Poetry is explained by molding the mind to chains of inductive reasoning, and as a reiteration of prose that plots the steps of induction, embedded verse no longer presents a threat to the development of rational thought.

By leaving Rosamond and Godfrey in the dark while rewarding Lucy with lines from Darwin, Edgeworth's corpus of children's books implies that some verse is less disruptive because it conforms to empirical observation. Conventional anthology pieces generate confusion, while verse that accurately renders experience can, if appropriately employed, approach the clarity of philosophical prose and the model of cognitive development prose plots and teaches. This was not a new development in Edgeworth's late fictions: she had lauded poetry of this kind in her first publication, *Letters to Literary Ladies* (1796). Here, Edgeworth argues that while "formerly the fair sex was kept in Turkish ignorance," now

> writers must offer their discoveries to the public in distinct terms, which every body may understand; ... and the art of teaching has been carried to such perfection, that a degree of knowledge may now with ease be acquired in the course of few years, which formerly was the business of a life to attain. All this is much in favour of female literature. Ladies have become ambitious to superintend the education of their children, and hence have been induced to instruct themselves ... The mother, who now aspires to be the esteemed and beloved instructress of her children, must have a considerable portion of knowledge. Science has of late *"been enlisted under the banners of imagination,"* by the irresistible charms of genius; by the same power, her votaries will be led *"from the looser analogies which dress out the imagery of poetry to the stricter ones which form the ratiocination of philosophy."* Botany has become fashionable; in time it may become useful, if it be not already so.[85]

The passage grounds women's literary authority and access to knowledge in their role as mothers and educators, an argument common in reform-oriented educational writing of the period. Quoting the Advertisement of Darwin's *The Loves of the Plants*, Edgeworth displays her approbation of the stated pedagogical aims of his verse – using poetry to introduce readers to the ratiocination of philosophy – one shared and imitated by numerous female writers of the period, including Charlotte Smith.[86] Rather than her later practice of making poetry comprehensible, in this early essay Edgeworth suggests that the cause of distinctness and the art of teaching might be advanced if ratiocination were taught *through* poetic imagery. This possibility grounds Smith's pedagogical texts, which employ excerpts of poetry explicitly to inculcate the precepts and processes of inductive method.

Poetry Methodized

Most of Charlotte Smith's pedagogical works were published before Edgeworth's *Early Lessons* series began, and they belong to a slightly different strand of the genre's development in the 1790s. Smith's first children's book, *Rural Walks: in Dialogues. Intended for the use of Young Persons* (1795), resembles Wollstonecraft's *Original Stories from Real Life, with Conversations Calculated to Regulate the Affections, and Form the Mind to Truth and Goodness* (1788) more than the developmental narratives of Barbauld and Edgeworth. As Wollstonecraft suggests in her Preface to *Original Stories*, this type of book is "accommodated to the present state of society" because it offers "medicines" to correct existing bad habits in its pupils.[87] Rather than Lockean blank slates waiting to be inscribed by experience, Smith and Wollstonecraft portray older, flawed characters who have already imbibed undesirable traits through an introduction into fashionable society. In the opening pages of *Rural Walks*, for example, Smith's Caroline Cecil arrives at her aunt's rural cottage looking dejected, dressed "in the extremity of fashion," and carrying herself with "an air of haughty superiority, mingled with something of concealed disdain."[88] In the first scene, Caroline literally performs the result of her flawed education. The book opens with a stage direction – "DIALOGUE I [CAROLINE CECIL, going to the window of her Bedchamber]" – followed by Caroline's opening soliloquy (*RW*, 7).[89] With occasional interjections and location changes orchestrated by an omniscient narrator, the book pursues a series of dramatic dialogues, the trajectory of which often swerves from one topic to another according to what any member of the group sees as they perambulate through the countryside. In this peripatetic approach, Smith accommodates Barbauld's empiricist approach in *Lessons* to the capacities of older and considerably more jaded pupils.

From the outset, Smith identifies Caroline's most pressing problem as her disparaging, superficial view of nature. Dialogue I opens with Caroline deploring her miserable condition: "Oh! merciful Heaven, what a dreary place! – Good God! what will become of me! – To be buried alive in such a place as this! A wide wide common, with nothing in sight but those miserable cottages yonder, or a few clumps of mournful fir trees!" (*RW*, 7). A visit to a poor laborer's cottage soon reveals that Caroline is selfish and callous to the misery of others, but this opening passage connects her moral failings to her way of seeing. Rather than a picturesque winter scene – and the "wide wide" breadth of the laborer's economic independence, common land – Caroline sees only cottages, clumps, and her own mournful misery.[90] She has no taste for rural beauty because she perceives the external world as a mirror of her internal state. The appropriately named Mrs. Woodfield has yet to awaken in Caroline the "habit of reflection" that will allow her to grasp the relation between the cottagers and the landscape (*RW*, 11).

Cultivating the "habit of reflection" must begin with the act of close observation. Mrs. Woodfield is explicit in her instruction. In Dialogue II, Caroline stands by as Mrs. Woodfield teaches her younger daughter Henrietta how to make accurate observations: when Henrietta remarks on "a plant ... full of deep red blossoms," her mother replies with its colloquial name, mezerion, and its taxonomic designation – "it is of the same species of plant as that beautiful Daphné Cneorum, or garland Daphné, that we all knelt down to smell when we saw it in Mrs. Bridgeport's garden" (*RW*, 17). With this lesson in taxonomy, Mrs. Woodfield shows her daughters and niece how careful observation allows one to make comparisons across varieties. When Henrietta looks at the red blossoms with her mother's suggestions in mind, she connects their shared memory to the example before her: "So it is Mama; I declare now I recollect they are very much alike" (*RW*, 17). Modeling the correct procedure for Caroline and the book's reader, Henrietta exercises her memory to absorb scientific classifications while simultaneously learning to bring order and connection to her thoughts.

Botanizing passages of this ilk, as Judith Pascoe notes, partake of a broader trend in female education that "singled out [botany] from the other natural sciences as the scientific pursuit most conducive to female character building."[91] In *Rural Walks*, Mrs. Woodfield is clearly an authority on botanical science – she supplies Latin names, common names, characteristics, related species, geographical distribution, commercial and medicinal uses of plants off the top of her head – and her pedagogy trades on the late eighteenth-century interest in botany and natural history in Britain and its colonies.[92] Criticism of botany as an educational pursuit – most famously Richard Polwhele's *Unsex'd Females* (1798) – accused women of "neglecting the demands of propriety in their pursuit of botanical knowledge," a reference to the explicitly sexual nature of Linnaean taxonomy.[93] Smith employs Caroline to represent this objection when she decries women who "torment the world" with "something about petals, and styles, and filaments, and I know not what jargon" (*RW*, 47). In response, Mrs. Woodfield chastises women who talk scientifically "in the hope of being thought wise," recasting Polwhele's objection of immodesty as a problem of the ostentatious display of knowledge. As with Edgeworth's caution against presumptuous, ill-informed "scientific ladies" at the beginning of *Harry and Lucy Concluded*, Smith uses the book's main characters to voice and counter potential objections to the text's pedagogical agenda.[94]

Smith returns to this question of the ostentatious display of knowledge in her third children's book, *Minor Morals, Interspersed with Sketches of Natural History, Historical Anecdotes, and Original Stories* (1798), a series of lectures framed as dialogues between four girls aged seven to twelve and their aunt, Mrs. Belmour. The maternal pedagogue remarks to one of her charges, "I wish you to learn the names of all the trees, shrubs, flowers, and vegetables, which are every day before your eyes, and, without professedly studying botany, to have delight in being acquainted with the indigenous or native plants of the country you live in."[95] As a budding female naturalist, Mary should not openly avow her intention to study natural history, but rather "delight" in the rational amusement of learning the names of plants – the goal of taxonomic science. For this purpose, Mrs. Belmour has "contrived ... a sort of Kalendar of Flora in verse" for Mary and her sisters in which she aims "less to make the poetry fine than comprehensible."[96] As with Edgeworth's proposed use of Darwin's verse to advance female education in *Letters to Literary Ladies*, Smith employs botanical verse to temper the imagination through the production of catalogs and calendars, descriptive lists of specimens that teach young women to observe, compare, connect – to methodize their minds.

As in *Minor Morals*, rather than opposing poetry to orderly thought processes, *Rural Walks* employs verse to cultivate the student's skill of precise, accurate observation. In Dialogue VI, for example, a walk through Wolfs Wood incites Mrs. Woodfield to read – from a volume she carries in her workbag – an excerpt from William Cowper's *The Task* that catalogs Britain's native trees "with their various attributes" (*RW*, 49) (Fig. 12). The poem informs the oblivious Catherine and Smith's readers that ash and beech have smooth grey trunks, the poplar's leaves are streaked with silver lines, and the oak is of a deeper green than the elm (*RW*, 49). In the passage, Cowper's embedded verse functions taxonomically – drawing distinctions between types of trees – rather than as poetry per se. The typographically offset lines do not generate figurative play inimical to the plain style of experimental philosophy; rather, the poetic excerpt collects, compares, and distinguishes between species, teaching the reader how to tell one from another. Smith's use of embedded verse implies that Cowper's own: or of one who deals in dreams and omens;

"Talks all the nonsense you can think of;
"Tells you how Jacky had the chin-cough;
"How Jowler bark'd; and what a fright
"She had with dreams the other night."

Oh, believe me, such conversation as Mrs. Tansy's is an absolute treat to me, compared with all these. Besides, though she does not know quite so much of the matter as the fancies she does, she knows enough to instruct in some plain and simple matters. For example, Caroline, she could tell you, what I do not believe you know, the names of those beautiful trees under which we are going to walk.

Caroline. Indeed I do know; they are almost all beech trees.

Mrs. Woodfield. Pardon me; round the borders of the wood there are many

many other sorts. But come, our constant companion Cowper will give us the best list of these majestic plants, with their various attributes. I have the volume in my work bag, and we will seat ourselves on this fallen tree, and refer to it:

"Nor less attractive is the woodland scene,
"Diversified with trees of every growth,
"Alike, yet various. Here the grey
   "smooth trunks
"Of ash, or lime, or beech distinctly shine;
"Within the twilight of their distant
   "shades;
"There, lost behind a rising ground, the
   "wood
"Seems sunk, and shorten'd to its topmost
   "boughs.
"No tree in all the grove but has its
   "charms,
"Though each its hue peculiar; paler
   "some,
"And of a wannish grey: The willow such,
"And poplar, that with silver lines his
   "leaf,   "And

N 6

Fig. 12 Charlotte Smith, *Rural Walks, in Dialogues, Intended for the Use of Young Persons*, 2 vols. (London, 1795), I: 154–55. Courtesy of University of Glasgow Library, Special Collections.

lines replicate and even stand in for direct observations of nature, just as Edgeworth would claim for sequential prose. Cast as a botanically accurate representation of observed nature, poetry no longer threatens to jumble the mind in romantic flights of fancy; it forwards rather than retards Caroline's progress toward rational thought.

As this makes clear, Smith's children's books reject the opposition between capricious verse and rational prose later codified in More's *Strictures* and RLE's Prefaces to Edgeworth's fictions. While maintaining a similar emphasis on observation, Smith uses verse as a medium for conveying accurate knowledge of nature and as an integral part of inculcating inductive reasoning in the character's and reader's mind. Smith's embrace of the poetic excerpt was forecast by her innovative combination of genres. Pitching *Rural Walks* to her publisher William Davies, Smith described her work as "less desultory than Mrs. Barbauld's 'Evenings at Home' (which have had & still have an amazing sale) & calculated for young persons three or four years older."[97] She expands on this in the work's preface, claiming she sought to "unite the interest of the novel, [with] the instruction of the schoolbook, by throwing the latter into dialogue, mingled with narrative" (*RW*, 3). Smith refers here to the schoolbooks or miscellaneous collections of poetic excerpts so deplored by her contemporaries, specifically Enfield's *Speaker*, which she quotes in *Rural Walks* when Mrs. Woodfield praises Henrietta for repeating a long passage from Cowper "not only with *'good emphasis and discretion,'* but as if you understood it" (*RW*, 44, original emphasis). Breaking into a market dominated by educational miscellanies, conduct books, and collections of unconnected moral stories like Barbauld and John Aikin's *Evenings at Home, or The Juvenile Budget Opened* (1792–96), Smith sought to retain familiar elements – poetry for recitation and forming the taste, anecdotes for instilling moral sensibility – while also cashing in on the new trend in character-driven, developmental narratives.[98]

Verse thus serves two conjoined purposes in Smith's children's books: it inculcates inductive method by training the student in accurate observation, comparison, distinction, and linking by analogy; and it fosters correct taste through elocutionary exercises. Smith fuses these aims in the final pages of Dialogue V in *Rural Walks*, which breaks abruptly from a discussion of the preceding night's ball, and proceeds, physically, into the garden. After a detour through a slew of other subjects – including the tiresome affectation of trembling sensibility and the banality of studied worldliness – Mrs. Woodfield asks Henrietta to recite lines 150–77 from Book VI of Cowper's *Task*, which appears typographically set off in quotation marks across the next two pages (*RW*, 138–40). This feat of memorization (which, Smith implies, should also be undertaken by the reader) in turn introduces an excerpt from Darwin's *The Botanic Garden* (also quoted at length) that – we are told to imagine – Henrietta and Elizabeth sing to piano accompaniment by Caroline. At the close of a chapter describing the superficial accomplishments flaunted by affected, fashionable girls, these performances suture sound poetic taste to useful botanical knowledge. As excerpts to be memorized and recited, they also provide Smith's readers with the tools to cultivate these admirable qualities in themselves. By embedding a poetic miscellany within a novelistic narrative, Smith thus merges two existing pedagogical models. Developmental narrative cultivates patterns of inductive reasoning, giving structure and continuity to the miscellaneous collection, while embedded poems allow for the simultaneous cultivation of scientific knowledge, literary taste, and appropriately sensibility.

In the final sections of *Rural Walks*, Caroline embodies the educational outcome of formal and generic mixture. Caroline's character has been transformed by her lessons. At the outset she failed to see anything in the clumps of firs, but by Dialogue XI, "the good sense and taste that nature had given her, had now room to display itself; and even the dull and grey skies, the almost dismantled woods, and cheerless aspect, which every object wore around her, failed not to awaken in her mind poetical recollections" (*RW*, 92). A dreary day now reflects a quite different internal state – a mind taught to observe, reason, reflect, and make connections. The new and improved Caroline reinforces this assessment by spontaneously quoting, from memory, "a description of scenery extremely resembling the landscape before her" from Anna Seward's 1784 *Louisa, A Poetical Novel* (*RW*, 92). Firmly lodging her poetic excursion in an empiricist analogy between what she observes and what she has read, Caroline first recalls an accurate description of a winter storm that "strips the oaks of their last lingering leaves," which then turns to a scene of sensibility: to the speaker's "tearful eyes, grief's faded form / sits on a cloud, and sighs amid the storm" (*RW*, 93). Caroline is not, however, feeling sorry for herself as she did at the book's outset. Smith's narrator explicitly recalls Caroline's failure to manifest compassion for the sick cottager in Dialogue I, and points out that "so much was her character changed by the pains Mrs. Woodfield had taken to teach her to reflect . . . that her temper was now more likely to be injured by extreme sensibility than to want it" (*RW*, 74). Caroline's recitation of descriptive, sentimental verse thus confirms her transformation into a person capable of clear, precise chains of reasoning, a skill that allows her to benefit from the cultivation of poetic sensibility without becoming mired in romantic fancies.[99]

Smith's fourth children's book, *Conversations Introducing Poetry, Chiefly on Subjects of Natural History* (1804), extends the role of poetry in training the mind in inductive method. To a large degree, this change is a function of another generic innovation. As her letters show, Smith originally conceived of *Conversations* as strictly a "School book of Poetry to exercise the memories of Children" – that is, a miscellaneous collection of poems patterned on Enfield's or Knox's popular compilations.[100] In the Preface to *Conversations*, Smith outlines her compositional process. With the "purpose of teaching a child to repeat them," she began by collecting poems from various sources, including published works by Cowley, Cowper, Gray, William Broome, and Joseph Wharton; she then added poems from her own published works and the portfolio of her sister, Catherine Ann Dorset. After having arranged the poems in a sequence, she "sent [the manuscript] up to be printed."[101] When her new publisher Joseph Johnson returned the manuscript because it was too short, instead of writing 40 additional pages of poetry Smith "undertook to enlarge the book by Conversations," writing the prose around the series of poems.[102] Framed as an apology for the "trespass" of borrowing, Smith's Preface emphasizes that she ordered the poems and only afterwards wrote the prose narrative corresponding to that sequence, thereby making it impossible to remove the borrowed pieces (*CIP*, 61). While they appear quite similar, *Rural Walks* is a fictional work with poetry embedded in it, while *Conversations* is a poetic miscellany with the prose narrative written around and through an existing sequence of poems.

By laying out her compositional process in the Preface, Smith reorients the reader's sense of what a "schoolbook" of poetry might look like and, more importantly, of its function as a pedagogical text. Embedded poems feel tangential to the plot of *Rural Walks*, *Rambles Farther*, and *Minor Morals* because they, more often than not, have very little to do with the ostensible topic of the prose dialogues. To return to the example above, the choral adaptation of Darwin's *The Botanic Garden* may model rational female accomplishments, but its subject – a panegyric to the Goddess of Spring – is not clearly relevant to the discussion directly preceding it, which centers on travelers who, "having been four or five years on the Continent ... affected foreign manners on their return" (*RW*, 43). In *Conversations*, by contrast, the poems determine both moral lesson and narrative trajectory. The book begins with George exclaiming, "Look," and directing his sister Emily's attention to this beautiful shining insect, which has almost hid itself in this white rose, on your favorite tree. – It is shaped very like those brownish chafers which you desired me to take away from the gardener's children yesterday, because you thought they were going to torment and hurt them; but it is not so big, and is much prettier. See what little tassels it has on its horns; the wings shine like some part of the peacock's feathers. (*CIP*, 65)

These children have already learned to observe, compare, and draw connections on the basis of shared attributes, in this case identifying two varieties of the same species and analogically linking the iridescence of insect wings to that of bird feathers. They have also already imbibed aesthetic appreciation of nature – the insect is beautiful, like a peacock, more so than the one they found yesterday – and have taken to heart its moral lessons (i.e., do not torment living creatures). George and Emily, in other words, have already attained the endpoint of Caroline's educational process. They have been habituated to think inductively, and along with their methodized minds they have acquired aesthetic judgment, taste, and ethical sensibility. Upon entering the garden, their mother Mrs. Talbot details the different types of chafers, their appearance and habits, and why it would be unwise to keep this insect. As an alternative to "contriving the captivity of the chafer," Mrs. Talbot recommends they "address a little poem to it," which Emily is assigned to inscribe in her notebook, memorize, and recite the following day (*CIP*, 66). The book's first poem, "To a Green-Chafer, on a White Rose," follows directly, and in the succeeding prose Mrs. Talbot clarifies difficult words before the scene shifts – signaled typographically with a double line – to a new subject and poem on the lady-bird. Unlike those in her earlier books, the poems embedded in *Conversations* are the prose's *raison d'être*, a claim that could also be made for the narrative sequences leading up to Darwin's lines in Edgeworth's *Harry and Lucy Concluded*. In the reverse image of Darwin's or Southey's long poems, which take their cue from the materials gathered up in the prose notes, Smith's prose is conditioned and scripted by the poems embedded in it. The prose sets up, contextualizes, and springs off from the verse, but the book is fundamentally anchored in the poems themselves and their arrangement in a sequence.

Conversations Introducing Poetry – like Wordsworth and Coleridge's *Lyrical Ballads* (1798) and Mary Robinson's *Lyrical Tales* (1800) – actively fosters and draws attention to itself as a composite of distinct generic and formal types. Smith arranged the poems, as she claims in the Preface, with "attention to variety of cadence" and in order of increasing formal and conceptual difficulty (*CIP*, 62). For example, the poem about the green chafer in the first Conversation is written in an uneven ballad meter, consisting of four-line stanzas rhyming a-b-a-b with lines of seven or eight syllables; "The Glow-Worm" of the second Conversation is a Shakespearean sonnet; the "poetical collection" of "Wild Flowers" in the fourth Conversation is composed of nine stanzas, each made up of four lines of iambic tetrameter rhymed a-b-a-b followed by a rhyming couplet in iambic pentameter and hexameter. The final poem of the ninth Conversation, "Studies by the Sea," stretches to thirteen stanzas rhyming a-b-a-b-b-c-b-c-d-d (the final couplet extends the conventional nine-line Spenserian stanza to ten lines). Vocabulary and syntax also intensify as the formal stakes go up. The resulting work plots a different kind of development than Barbauld's or Edgeworth's fictions. In place of a narrative that paces the steps of induction, Smith's book follows a trajectory from simple to complex poetic form, structure, language, and figuration. The compilation of the poetic collection structures George and Emily's education; their minds are forged in the mold of the miscellany.

This miscellany, however, refuses the miscellaneous. The prose narrative frames and bridges the topical gaps between the poems, and the verse–prose composite teaches habits of inductive reasoning; historical, geographical, and botanical knowledge; and aesthetic sensibility and literary taste as all mutually dependent on each other. The chafer poem, for example, resembles an entry in a natural history, describing where it lives ("on a white rose"), how to identify it visually ("green and gold" with a "corselet, of the ruby's hue"), and its defining characteristics (its "fringed feet" and "filmy wings") (*CIP*, 67). The poem ends with a relatively simple moral message, but one that requires the student to reason analogically from insect to human behavior: Just as the chafer should "not wound the flower so fair / That shelters you in sweet repose," the poem chastises a person "who dares / On pity's bosom to intrude / And then that gentle bosom tears / With baseness and ingratitude" (*CIP*, 67). After Emily records the poem – which she is to memorize and recite the next day – Mrs. Talbot prods the children to say what they do not understand. Their admissions prompt her to explain several technical terms, including "shard" ("the outward wings of beetles" that are hard and case-like) and "corselet" (a word "taken from the French word for armour, which was worn to cover the body in battle") (*CIP*, 67). The poem itself leads the pupils through the steps of induction, while the prose dialogue seeks to render the poem comprehensible to the reader. Most of the verse–prose segments in *Conversations* work in a similar fashion. To take a more complicated example, "The Heath" in the seventh Conversation is written (as Mrs. Talbot tells her charges) in blank verse and opens with an exemplary Miltonic periodic sentence: "Even the wide Heath, where the unequal ground / Has never on its rugged surface felt / The hand of Industry, though wild and rough, / Is not without its beauty" (*CIP*, 174). Having discussed perspective and picturesque aesthetics in the dialogue preceding the poem, Mrs. Talbot follows the poem with a prose explanation of how to compose blank verse by "varying the pauses," how to identify chats and linnets, and the propriety of her comparison in the poem between the dodder – a parasitical plant that winds itself around other plants like a wire – and people who see themselves rejected by the world but allow a "self-consoling passion" or vanity to entwine itself around their hearts (*CIP*, 173–77). In both the verse and prose, observation, arrangement, comparison, and distinction are succeeded by analogical linking though personification, which in turn generates a truth of human nature. The prose with which Smith "enlarged" the collection binds the formally diverse poems together, supplying the connections that critics found lacking in conventional educational miscellanies. But the prose also underscores how the poems are designed to work: regardless of their formal complexity, most of the poems follow the same structural pattern of inductive reasoning. Prose frames the verse, contextualizing and explicating it, but the verse itself teaches induction. In *Conversations*, Smith's compositional method of collecting pieces of poetry and stitching them together with prose narrative promotes embedded verse as the very core of empiricist pedagogy. The poetic miscellany, the presumed enemy of methodical thought, is for Smith its enabler and source.

Smith's attachment to the "schoolbook" as an educational genre was likely spurred by the value she assigned poetry above other genres. As she wrote to Thomas Cadell in 1805, "it is on the Poetry I have written that I trust for the little reputation I may hereafter have."[103] Her verse–prose composites challenge the assumptions about the cognitive effects of poetry being codified in the works of her contemporaries – and *Conversations* does this more emphatically than *Rural Walks, Rambles Farther*, or *Minor Morals* because of Smith's compositional process and the central place it gives to poetry. While necessity may have been the mother of invention in *Conversations*, Smith refused to cast poetry as debilitating to the objectives of empirically grounded education. Rather, she merged existing educational genres but also crafted poems that would – individually through their structure and in aggregate as a collection – instill the sequential steps of induction in her readers while explicitly cultivating their taste for poetry and ability to recall and recite it. The poems' subject matter in *Conversations* suggests that Smith concurred with Edgeworth's assessment in *Letters to Literary Ladies*: poems on scientific subjects were more likely to instill the steps of inductive method than conventional anthology pieces. But for Smith, poetry of any variety could just as easily inculcate as thwart the Edgeworths' ideal of "patient investigation" and "logical induction." As the emphasis on compositional process in her Preface suggests, for Smith the function of the embedded poem and its relationship to the prose narrative would be determined by the author. As with miscellany makers such as Enfield or Wollstonecraft, who claimed that the pedagogical value of their texts resided in the disposition of excerpts, Smith's texts invest value in the arrangement of the poems in a series. Unlike a miscellany that relied on readers to supply the connections between quoted passages, *Conversations* links the excerpts with a novelistic narrative of George and Emily's education. While this aligns with Edgeworth's approach in her fictions, unlike that of *Rosamond* or *Harry and Lucy Concluded*, Smith's prose is not the primary vehicle for inductive reasoning in the text. Edgeworth worried over and attempted to mollify the disruptive potential of embedded verse; Smith crafted a composite that replays the steps of induction at two levels, within each individual poem and in the arrangement and linking of poems in the book.

The tension I have developed in this chapter as a whole – between poetry as a record of mental order or, alternatively, of cognitive disorder – defines Coleridge's struggle in the "Essays on Method" in *The Friend* (1818). Coleridge's "Essays" explicitly seek to rescue Baconian induction from its misuses in philosophical materialism and empiricist moral philosophy by insisting that it is first and foremost a property of poets and poetry. In the "Essays," Coleridge employs excerpts from Shakespeare's plays to exemplify inductive method and its opposite, a deficiency of textual and mental arrangement. Shakespeare's own inductive method, Coleridge claims, allowed him to produce texts and characters that make palpable both the lack of methodical thought and the "habit of method" that defines the man of education (*F*, 1: 455). As with Smith's prose–verse composite, the author's ordering and synthesizing imagination produces a unified text and conveys general principles to the reader – but there is always the threat that mental order will be derailed by textual excrescences, those bits of textual evidence that refuse, finally, to cohere. In what follows, I detail Coleridge's strategies for bridging the gap in inductive method – strategies that rest on the synthetic potential of the excerpt itself.

NOTES

1 Richard Lovell Edgeworth, *Poetry Explained for the Use of Young People* (1802), new ed. (London: R. Hunter, 1821), p. iii. Subsequently cited in text as *PE*. Since the central author addressed in this chapter is Maria Edgeworth, to avoid confusion I will grant their shared surname to her and refer to her father by his full name or his initials, RLE, with which he often signed his contributions to their collaborative works.

2 Richard Lovell Edgeworth, "Address to Mothers," in *Continuation of Early Lessons*, 3rd ed., by Maria Edgeworth (London: R. Hunter, 1816), pp. xii, xvii–xviii.

3 In the following discussion of Barbauld, Edgeworth, and Smith, references to "rational thought" (which is firmly lodged in an empiricist approach where knowledge arises from observation and experience) should not be confused with rationalist philosophy, which holds that knowledge depends on *a priori* ideas. As I discuss in the next chapter, Coleridge sets out to mesh empiricist induction and rationalist idealism by aligning Bacon with Plato in his "Essays on Method" (1818).

4 Richard Lovell Edgeworth and Maria Edgeworth, *Memoirs of Richard Lovell Edgeworth, Esq.*, Vol. 2 (London: R. Hunter, 1820), p. 186.

5 Edgeworth also deployed the tenets of experimentally grounded education in her novels of the same period. James Chandler has shown that Edgeworth's *Belinda* is structured by a "Lunar-like interdisciplinary commitment to experiment and practical observation" introduced through various "experimental engagements" both scientific and moral. James Chandler, "Edgeworth and the Lunar Enlightenment," *Eighteenth-Century Studies* 45.1 (2011): 94.

6 Alan Richardson, *Literature, Education, and Romanticism* (Cambridge: Cambridge University Press, 1994), p. 3. J. Paul Hunter notes that criticism of women's faulty education was widespread in late-seventeenth- and eighteenth-century Britain, but while some concerns remained constant (particularly the danger posed to children by mothers trained to care more for dressing their bodies than cultivating their minds), earlier guides were on the whole less radical in their reading recommendations and politics than their 1790s counterparts. J. Paul Hunter, *Before Novels: The Cultural Contexts of Eighteenth-Century English Fiction* (New York: Norton, 1990), pp. 268–70.

7 Lisa Zunshine, "Rhetoric, Cognition, and Ideology in A. L. Barbauld's *Hymns in Prose for Children* (1781)," *Poetics Today* 23.1 (2002): 127.

8 Ibid., 135.

9 Locke, *Essay*, p. 109.

10 For a cogent account of the early nineteenth-century backlash against women educationalists' claim to "natural rights" in the 1790s, see Alan Richardson, *Literature, Education, and Romanticism*, pp. 174–81.

11 Wollstonecraft, *A Vindication of the Rights of Woman*, p. 91.

12 Ibid., pp. 91–92.

13 Abraham Cowley, "To the Royal Society," in *History of the Royal Society*, by Thomas Sprat (London, 1667), n.p..

14 For Bacon's description of inductive method, see the Introduction. More recommends philosophical treatises in her reading list, but the educational works of Locke and Watts – *Some Thoughts concerning Education* (1693) and *A Treatise on the Education of Children and Youth* (1769), respectively – would have also been familiar to her.

15 Locke, *Essay*, pp. 119, 147, 148, 152, 154, 155.

16 Ibid., p. 157.

17 Isaac Watts, *Logick: or, The Right Use of Reason in the Enquiry after Truth* (London, 1725), pp. 110–11, Eighteenth Century Collections Online, http://galenet .galegroup.com.proxy.library.vanderbilt.edu/servlet/ECCO, 5 Sept. 2010.

18 Ibid., p. 2.

19 Richardson's summary of the scholarship on Romantic-era female education underscores the extent to which domestic ideology could be both confining and empowering to women writers; see especially Richardson, *Literature, Education, and Romanticism*, pp. 167–70.

20 William Duncan, *The Elements of Logick* (London, 1748), pp. 269–70, Eighteenth Century Collections Online, http://galenet.galegroup.com.proxy .library.vanderbilt.edu/servlet/ECCO, 5 Sept. 2010. Duncan's treatise was first published as Book VII of J. Dodsley's *The Preceptor: containing a general course of education* (London, 1748).

21 Mary Wollstonecraft, *The Female Reader*, in Vol. 4 of *The Works of Mary Wollstonecraft*, Janet Todd and Marilyn Butler (eds.) (New York: New York University Press, 1989), p. 55; emphasis mine.

22 Ibid., pp. 55, 67.

23 Oliver Goldsmith, *Beauties of English Poesy* (London, 1767), pp. i–ii, Eighteenth Century Collections Online, http://galenet.galegroup.com.proxy .library.vanderbilt.edu/servlet/ECCO, 10 October 2010.

24 Critics have set *Goody Two-Shoes* apart from other midcentury children's books on the basis of its formal coherence. Mary Thwaite argues that "there had been homilies, fragments, fables, short tales, and medleys, but nothing, not even [Sarah Fielding's] *The Governess*, had the charm or continuity of this long complete tale about Margery Meanwell." Mary Thwaite, *From Primer to Pleasure in Reading* (Boston: The Horn Book, 1972), p. 50. In contrast, criticism of Newbery's *A Little Pretty Pocket-Book* turns on its formal fragmentation. As J. Paul Hunter argues, educational guides such as the *Pocket-Book* were often composed of shorter pieces "strung together," and even if common themes ran through the chapters or sections, "the organization and visual format in fact encouraged piecemeal reading." Hunter, *Before Novels*, pp. 297, 300.

25 See Marilyn Butler, *Maria Edgeworth: A Literary Biography* (Oxford: Oxford University Press, 1972), p. 62.

26 William McCarthy, *Anna Letitia Barbauld: Voice of the Enlightenment* (Baltimore: Johns Hopkins University Press, 2008), p. 194.

27 Richardson, *Literature, Education, and Romanticism*, p. 128.

28 Anna Letitia Barbauld, *Lessons for Children, from two to three years old* (London: J. Johnson, 1787), pp. 8, 10, Eighteenth Century Collections Online, http://galenet.galegroup.com.proxy.library.vanderbilt.edu/servlet/ECCO, 5 Sept. 2010.

29 Ibid., pp. 18–20.

30 Sarah Robbins, "Lessons for Children and Teaching Mothers: Mrs. Barbauld's Primer for the Textual Construction of Middle-Class Domestic Pedagogy," *The Lion and the Unicorn* 17.2 (1993): 142.

31 Joanna Wharton, "Inscribing on the Mind: Anna Letitia Barbauld's 'Sensible Objects,'" *Journal for Eighteenth-Century Studies* 35.4 (2012): 535.

32 McCarthy, *Barbauld*, p. 199. Robbins makes a similar observation: "Barbauld's pedagogy of controlled, incremental progress is replicated throughout the several volumes of the *Lessons*, each of which is composed for a reader of a particular age. She carefully sequences her content to move from the simplest, most concrete vocabulary set within very short sentences to increased detail and complexity in word choice and sentence structure." Robbins, "Lessons," 140.

33 Anna Letitia Barbauld, *Lessons for Children of three years old*, 2 Parts (London: J. Johnson, 1788), 1: 4, Eighteenth Century Collections Online, http://galenet.galegroup.com.proxy.library.vanderbilt.edu/servlet/ECCO, 5 Sept. 2010.

34 Ibid., 2: 16–17.

35 Anna Letitia Barbauld, *Lessons for Children, from three to four years old* (London: J. Johnson, 1788), pp. 3–5, Eighteenth Century Collections Online, http://galenet.galegroup.com.proxy.library.vanderbilt.edu/servlet/ECCO, 5 Sept. 2010.

36 Alan Richardson, *Literature, Education, and Romanticism*, p. 129. This condition has led some critics to view the books as ideologically oppressive; see Zunshine, "Rhetoric, Cognition, and Ideology" and Robbins, "Lessons."

37 Hunter, *Before Novels*, p. 282.

38 Quoted in F. J. Harvey Darton, *Children's Books in England*, 3rd ed. (London: British Library, 1999), p. 129. The extensive scientific and technological content of *Evenings at Home, or The Juvenile Budget Opened, consisting of variety of Miscellaneous Pieces, for the Instruction and Amusement of Young Persons* (1792), a collaboration between Barbauld and her brother John Aikin, may have contributed to Lamb's perception. Both Edgeworth and Smith explicitly cite *Evenings at Home* as a model for their own children's books.

39 Critics of Maria Edgeworth's novels and educational works have discussed at length the question of her father's role in her literary productions. Rather than attempting to determine influence – negative or positive – I follow Marilyn Butler's biography in noting that Edgeworth garnered materials for her novels and the stories in her lesson books from various sources, including her father, her stepmothers, the Ruxtons, and many friends and acquaintances. *Practical Education* was a collaborative effort, with chapters written by both father and

daughter, as well as other members of the family. Of the prefaces I quote below, Maria Edgeworth only wrote those published after RLE's death. When asked to rewrite them for a new edition of her works in 1847, she refused, commenting that "in truth I have nothing to say of [these works] but what my dear father has said for me in his prefaces to each of them as they came out. These sufficiently explain the moral design … and I have nothing personal to add." Quoted in Elizabeth Harden, *Maria Edgeworth* (Boston: Twayne, 1984), p. 23.

40 Richard Lovell Edgeworth, Preface, *Practical Education* by Maria Edgeworth, *The Novels and Selected Works of Maria Edgeworth*, Vol. 11, Susan Manly (ed.) (London: Pickering & Chatto, 2003), p. 5.

41 Richard Lovell Edgeworth, "Preface, Addressed to Parents," *The Parent's Assistant* by Maria Edgeworth, *The Novels and Selected Works of Maria Edgeworth*, Vol. 10, Elizabeth Eger and Clíona ÓGallchoir (eds.) (London: Pickering & Chatto, 2003), p. 2.

42 Ibid.

43 Richard Lovell Edgeworth, draft letter to the *Gentlemen's Magazine*, n.d. [1780–1781], quoted in Butler, *Maria Edgeworth*, p. 65.

44 Notebook compiled by Mrs. Honora Edgeworth [1778], Edgeworth Papers, MS. Eng. misc. e. 1459, Bodleian Library, Oxford. Maria Edgeworth, *Practical Education*, in *The Novels and Selected Works of Maria Edgeworth*, Vol. 2, Susan Manly (ed.) (London: Pickering & Chatto, 2003), p. 169. The child referred to here is Honora Sneyd Edgeworth's daughter, also named Honora.

45 Notebook, Eng. misc. e. 1459, Edgeworth Papers, Bodleian Library, Oxford.

46 Maria Edgeworth, *Practical Education*, pp. 94–95.

47 Richard Lovell Edgeworth, Preface, *Practical Education*, p. 6.

48 Butler cites the Preface to the original Harry and Lucy story as "the manifesto not of a single book, but of the whole series of *Early Lessons* completed between 1801 and 1825 by Maria Edgeworth." Butler, *Maria Edgeworth*, p. 64.

49 *Early Lessons* included "Harry and Lucy" (parts I and II), "Rosamond" (parts III–V), "Frank" (parts VI–IX), and three additional stories, "The Little Dog Trusty," "The Orange Man," and "The Cherry Orchard" (part X). Two of these stories and the first and most famous Rosamond story, "The Purple Jar," originally appeared in *The Parent's Assistant*, but were removed in the second edition of 1800 and republished in *Early Lessons* in 1801.

50 Maria Edgeworth, *Early Lessons,* in *The Novels and Selected Works of Maria Edgeworth*, Vol. 12, Elizabeth Eger, Clíona ÓGallchoir, and Marilyn Butler (eds.) (London: Pickering & Chatto, 2003), pp. 83–91. Subsequently cited in text as *EL*.

51 Maria Edgeworth, *Harry and Lucy Concluded* (London: Hunter, 1825), p. vi.

52 Mitzi Myers argued persuasively that Edgeworth's children's stories "are clearly indebted to her educational ideology" and further, "the work's ideological content … empowers [Edgeworth's] achievement, both formally and thematically." Mitzi Myers, "Socializing Rosamond: Educational Ideology and

Fictional Form," *Children's Literature Association Quarterly* 14.2 (1989): 54. While Myers suggests the structure of Edgeworth's stories reflect her pedagogical theory, she focuses on the way Edgeworth's plots mimic life rather than on the inductive procedure I outline below.

53 Butler, *Maria Edgeworth*, p. 61.
54 Maria Edgeworth, *Practical Education*, p. 63.
55 Myers, "Socializing," pp. 52–58.
56 Richard Barney argues that Lockean educational theory pushed eighteenth-century novelists to rehearse "competing agendas of individual interiority versus disciplinary surveillance with the aim of containing them – without complete resolution – within the parameters of *narrative emplotment.*" Richard Barney, *Plots of Enlightenment: Education and the Novel in Eighteenth-Century England* (Stanford, CA: Stanford University Press, 1999), p. 32. Edgeworth's practice in her children's fiction fits this model. The result of Rosamond's emplotment in "The Purple Jar" is inevitable, but it is Rosamond's subjectivity that generates narrative continuity across the stories, thus enabling the plot that constrains her.
57 Maria Edgeworth, *Continuation of Early Lessons*, 3rd ed., 2 vols. (London: R. Hunter, 1816), 1: 272–73, 258. This passage serves up a paean to industry: The mill has "plenty of fresh air, and but little dust; nor were the faces of the men, women, or children, who were at work, pale or miserable; on the contrary, they had a healthy colour, and were lively and cheerful." Edgeworth, *Continuation*, p. 259.
58 Edgeworth very rarely uses long inset stories, and the few exceptions are striking. For instance, in Part II of "Rosamond" in *Early Lessons*, Rosamond's sister Laura reads a fairy story, "Rivuletta." The story, written by Honora Edgeworth (1774–1790, Maria Edgeworth's half-sister by Honora Sneyd Edgeworth, 1753–1780), was used as proof by RLE in *Practical Education* that "an early acquaintance with the accuracy of mathematical demonstration does not, within our experience, contract the powers of the imagination" (*PE*, 448). In "Rosamond," Honora's story is followed by Edgeworth's obviously personal and painful reflection on the young author: "she is no more – Her parents lost her when she was but fifteen" (*EL*, 141). With this emotionally charged subtext, Edgeworth presses the reader into sympathizing with the *author* of a story – an author who stands as proof that one can educate a girl to reason without destroying her natural propensity to imaginative and literary pursuits. In other words, the inset points to Honora, rather than the content of the story, as the substance of the lesson.
59 Myers, "Socializing," 54–55.
60 Maria Edgeworth, *Harry and Lucy Concluded*, 4 vols. (London, 1825), I:I.
61 Maria Edgeworth, Notes, drafts and fair copies of published stories and educational works, Edgeworth Papers MS. Eng. misc. c. 896 (fol. 96v), Bodleian Library, Oxford.
62 For Gerard's take on the methodological consonance and divergence of science and literature, see Chapter 1.

63 Maria Edgewroth, Notes, drafts , and fair copies fol. 96v–97v, my emphasis. Edgeworth's published Preface retreats from this democratic position by asking readers to accept Harry's abilities and knowledge as a mark of "natural genius." Edgeworth, *Harry and Lucy Concluded*, p. xiii.

64 Richard Lovell Edgeworth, "Address to Mothers," pp. xii, xvii–xviii.

65 Maria Edgeworth, *Harry and Lucy Concluded*, p. 5.

66 Ibid., p. 66.

67 Ibid., p. 67.

68 Ibid., p. 116.

69 In a letter to Walter Scott, Edgeworth substantiates this gendered division (thereby denying the overlap between her compositional procedure and the inductive method of experimental science), commenting that her part in the *Early Lessons* series was "merely to spread amusement through it, while [RLE] furnished the solid knowledge and accurate principles of science. The toil, difficulty, mortification I have gone through in finishing these last volumes [of *Harry and Lucy Concluded*] without him cannot be described ... I have no science; and, as to accuracy, can compare myself only to the sailor who 'would never quarrel for a handful of degrees.'" Quoted in Butler, *Maria Edgeworth*, p. 167. Edgeworth reuses the quoted phrase to describe Lucy in the Preface to *Harry and Lucy Concluded*, further claiming that her "faults produce the nonsense and the action necessary to relieve the reader's attention." Edgeworth, *Harry and Lucy Concluded*, p. xiv.

70 Richard Lovell Edgeworth and Maria Edgeworth, *Readings in Poetry*, 2nd ed. (London: R. Hunter, 1816), p. vi.

71 Maria Edgeworth, *Practical Education*, p. 52.

72 William Wordsworth, "The Idiot Boy," in Coleridge and Wordsworth, *Lyrical Ballads* (1798), p. 179.

73 Maria Edgeworth, *Continuation of Early Lessons*, 2: 6.

74 Maria Edgeworth, *Practical Education*, pp. 17–18.

75 Ibid., p. 52.

76 Maria Edgeworth, *Continuation of Early Lessons*, 2: 1, 6.

77 Maria Edgeworth, *Continuation of Early Lessons*, 2: 12–17. William Mason was Gray's friend, literary executor, and biographer; his notes to Gray's poems appeared in *The Poems of Mr. Gray. To which are prefixed Memoirs of his life and writings by W. Mason, M.A.* (London, 1775).

78 Maria Edgeworth, *Continuation of Early Lessons*, 2: 17.

79 Ibid., 2: 20.

80 Ibid., 2: 21–22.

81 Maria Edgeworth, *Harry and Lucy Concluded*, p. 133.

82 Ibid., p. 133.

83 Ibid., pp. 134, 174–75.

84 Ibid., p. 172.

85 Maria Edgeworth, *Letters to Literary Ladies* (London, 1795), pp. 64–66.

86 For women poets' reactions to Darwin's poem, see Judith Pascoe, "Female Botanists and the Poetry of Charlotte Smith," *Re-Visioning Romanticism:*

British Women Writers, 1776–1837, Carol Shiner Wilson and Joel Haefner (eds.) (Philadelphia: University of Pennsylvania Press, 1994), pp. 193–209.

87 Mary Wollstonecraft, *Original Stories from Real Life* (London, 1796), in *The Works of Mary Wollstonecraft*, Vol. 4, Janet Todd and Marilyn Butler (eds.) (New York: New York University Press, 1989), p. 359.

88 Charlotte Smith, *Rural Walks,* in *The Works of Charlotte Smith*, Vol. 12, Elizabeth Dolan (ed.) (London: Pickering & Chatto, 2007), p. 6. Subsequently cited in text as *RW*.

89 Smith's *Conversations Introducing Poetry* also takes up this explicitly dramatic form – including divisions between scenes, all-capital lists of the characters, brief set descriptions in italics, and italic stage directions to explain the ongoing action – thus heightening the discontinuity of text through generic mixture.

90 In her third children's book, *Minor Morals* (1798), Smith explicitly articulates her "view" of common land: Responding to Sophia's opinion that "a common is a very ugly thing," the aunt and teacher Mrs. Belmour counters that they are important nonetheless because "many of these rude places afford subsistence to the poor ... the grass of these wild extents of land serves to pasture a great number of sheep; and in some places the poor are allowed to keep cows upon them, and in others to rear geese." Charlotte Smith, *Minor Morals,* in *The Works of Charlotte Smith*, Vol. 12, Elizabeth Dolan (ed.) (London: Pickering & Chatto, 2007), p. 242.

91 Pascoe, "Female Botanists," p. 198.

92 In contrast to Edgeworth's stories, in which fathers or brothers supply scientific information, in Smith's books women are the authorities on all subjects, scientific, historical, literary, and moral. They do not defer to male counterparts, whom in fact they entirely lack, as Smith did for much of her adult life.

93 Pascoe, "Female Botanists," p. 200.

94 Maria Edgeworth, *Harry and Lucy Concluded*, p. 7.

95 Charlotte Smith, *Minor Morals*, p. 242.

96 Ibid., p. 242.

97 Charlotte Smith, *Collected Letters*, p. 131.

98 Benedict argues that pedagogical collections sought to train readers' aesthetic sensibility and moral compass, a project often concomitant with cultivating a national literary taste. Benedict, *Modern Reader*, p. 198. *Rural Walks* replicates the miscellany's concern with moral improvement as well as cultivating an appreciation for the best of English verse through excerpts from Shakespeare, Drayton, Milton, Prior, Pope, Thomson, Collins, Cowper, Burns, Darwin, William Leslie Bowles, and, of course, Charlotte Smith herself.

99 For a discussion of the elocutionary movement in Britain and its simultaneous cultivation of artifice and true feeling, see Jacqueline George, "Public Reading and Lyric Pleasure: Eighteenth Century Elocutionary Debates and Poetic Practices," *ELH* 76.2 (2009): 371–97.

100 Charlotte Smith, *Collected Letters*, p. 503.
101 Charlotte Smith, *Conversations Introducing Poetry*, in *The Works of Charlotte Smith*, vol. 13, Judith Pascoe (ed.) (London: Pickering & Chatto, 2007), p. 61. Subsequently cited in text as *CIP*.
102 Smith proposes "a plan which would give room for a great deal of other information & serve as a vehicle for the Poetry." Charlotte Smith, *Collected Letters*, p. 610. For an extended discussion of Smith's relations and negotiations with her various publishers, see Judith Stanton, "Charlotte Smith's 'Literary Business': Income, Patronage, and Indigence," *The Age of Johnson* 1 (1987): 375–401.
103 Charlotte Smith, *Collected Letters*, p. 705.

CHAPTER 5

Coleridge and Literary Criticism
The Pains of Induction

What is it that first strikes us, and strikes us at once, in a man of education? . . . It is the unpremeditated and evidently habitual *arrangement*
of his words, grounded on the habit of foreseeing, in each integral
part, or (more plainly) in every sentence, the whole that he intends
to communicate. However irregular and desultory his talk, there is
method in the fragments.

— Samuel Taylor Coleridge, *The Friend*, 1818

Like his contemporaries working in educational reform and pedagogical
theory, Coleridge thought extensively about the effect of disorderly texts
on people's minds. His disparaging comments on the "reading of the reading Public" are strikingly similar to those of Hannah More.[1] As discussed
in the previous chapter, More argues that the "Swarms of Abridgements,
Beauties, and Compendiums" in a young lady's library act like "an infallible recipe for making a superficial mind"; these "crippled mutilations"
erase "that just proportion of parts, that skillful arrangement of the plan,
and that artful distribution of the subject" found in the original work
(*SFE*, 166). In the *Biographia Literaria*, Coleridge similarly argues that periodicals and collections of extracts work like "Anti-Mnemonics, or weaken-
ers of the memory," inspiring in readers a "sort of beggarly day-dreaming"
(*BL*, 1: 48–49). In a long footnote to this observation, Coleridge explains
the content of the reading public's mass dream: "the whole *materiel* and
imagery of the doze," he argues, is supplied by a "sort of mental *camera obscura* manufactured at the printing office, which *pro tempore* fixes,
reflects, and transmits the moving phantasms of one man's delirium, so as
to people the barrenness of a hundred other brains afflicted with the same
trance or suspension of all common sense and all definite purpose" (*BL*, 1:
48). As with More, Coleridge's comments reflect the writerly anxiety, common to many of their contemporaries, about the increase in the number
of readers and the corresponding proliferation of popular printed material
in the later eighteenth century. Coleridge's figurative play also indicates

a pointed critique of texts stitched together from bits and pieces of other texts that fill the mind with shadowy phantasms, producing a kind of mass delusion accompanied by listlessness and loss of common sense. As with Austen's Catherine Morland, reading collections of excerpts will spawn a nation of minds patterned on the gothic novel.

My epigraph indicates Coleridge's cure for this disease, the "man of education" who opens the "Essays on Method" in the revised and expanded version of *The Friend* (1818). Here, Coleridge presents the antithesis of the excerpt-reading public, the man whose conversation, however seemingly irregular and desultory, is carefully arranged to convey a sense of the whole. Like Wollstonecraft and More, Coleridge argues that a "well-disciplined understanding" will become accustomed to methodizing its thoughts, and will as a consequence "contemplate not *things* only, or for their own sake alone, but likewise and chiefly the *relations* of things" (*F*, 1: 451). Once cultivated, the "habit of Method" – a habit explicitly patterned on the steps of Baconian induction – will bring "things the most remote and diverse in time, place and outward circumstance" into "mental contiguity and succession" (*F*, 1: 455). The "Essays" themselves are a textual actuation of this theory of arrangement. Before they appeared as volume 3 of *The Friend* in 1818, these essays comprised the "General Introduction; or, Preliminary Treatise of Method" Coleridge wrote as an introduction for Rest Fenner and Thomas Curtis's *Encyclopædia Metropolitana*. Coleridge claimed to have spent "four months in the *mere* arrangement" of this introduction, but in the hands of John Stoddart (who revised Coleridge's text for Fenner and Curtis), the published "Treatise on Method" had become "a heterogeneous mixture of *Contraries* . . . a compleat Huddle of Paragraphs, without sub- or co-ordination" (*CL*, 4: 820–21).[2] While the words and concepts are largely the same in both texts, Stoddart's "Treatise" maps a historical arc: "Method" found initial expression in classical sources, was taken up and reconfigured by seventeenth-century experimental science, and subsequently became available for the purposes of literary criticism in the eighteenth century. In rewriting Stoddart's revision,[3] Coleridge reverses this argumentative trajectory. In the "Essays," method in literature comes before – structurally and as a conceptual prerequisite for – the development of induction as a tool of scientific enquiry.

As this summary indicates, the "Essays on Method" are concerned with defining and illustrating "method" as a philosophical, scientific, and literary-critical principle, while also attempting, like the educational fictions discussed in the previous chapter, to methodize the reader's mind through the structure and arrangement of the text. While already quite complex, this agenda does not fully explain the function of the "Essays" within the larger work. In *The Friend* (1818), the "Essays" stand as the endpoint to a series of deferrals and digressions, pauses for diversion, and discussions of practically every conceivable subject. As the culmination of a seemingly disorderly text first published in periodical format, the "Essays" are the moment of philosophical reckoning for *The Friend* – the moment when Coleridge reveals the whole that has underwritten his seemingly desultory text. This revelation takes the form of a reconciliation of figureheads – Shakespeare and Davy, Plato and Bacon – and the opposed traditions they represent, imaginative literature and experimental science, philosophical idealism and experimental philosophy. These successive realignments enable Coleridge to reconnect science to metaphysics, religion to morality, and finally Man to Nature and God, the objective and final endpoint of both the "Essays" and *The Friend.* The reconciliation passages in the "Essays" stand as the structural culmination and philosophical payoff of Coleridge's project.

While critics have examined the famous chiasmus between Shakespeare and Davy as evidence for Coleridge's understanding of the relationship between science and literature, it has been little remarked that both passages of reconciliation in the "Essays" are composed of clearly demarcated quotations.[4] The extensive use of quotations in the "Essays" aligns them with many of Coleridge's published works, from *Omniana*, the collection of quotations and commentary that he produced with Robert Southey in 1812, to the *Aids to Reflection* (1825), a series of theological aphorisms and comments that began as a collection of "beauties" extracted from the works of Archbishop Robert Leighton. Even a cursory scan of the physical layout of the pages of the *Biographia* and *The Friend* reveals the centrality of quotations to Coleridge's most renowned and widely discussed literary-critical and philosophical projects. Beyond this, in the "Essays" quotations provide the evidentiary ground for Coleridge's progression to the ultimate and final principle.

Coleridge was, like his friend and collaborator Robert Southey, an inveterate collector of textual scraps – excerpts litter his notebooks, ground his marginalia, and provide him with a litany of obscure chapter mottos running across the pages of his published prose works.[5] Scholarly interest in Coleridge's omnivorous reading and habits of recording has increased in recent years since the publication of the fat volumes of his *Marginalia* and *Notebooks.*[6] But for many decades – indeed most of the nineteenth and twentieth centuries – this topic had been inextricable from questions about what materials Coleridge "borrowed" from other works. In an extended discussion of Coleridge's "plagiarisms," Thomas McFarland famously confessed, "Coleridge's borrowings are not only real, but so honeycomb his work as to form virtually a mode of composition."[7] Stepping off from this observation, Jerome Christensen illustrates what he calls the *Biographia*'s "Marginal Method": To write his literary life, Coleridge "annexes a body of thought – Maass's text, Macintosh's lectures – into his manuscript to supply a sustaining text that he can cover with marginalia: notes, interpolations, and revisions."[8] This method, according to Christensen, produces an "apparent progression that goes nowhere, a dispersion of the author's moral and ontological integrity through the compulsive, unacknowledged use of other's ideas and words."[9]

In contrast to this focus on "unacknowledged" borrowing, critics have recently begun to consider Coleridge's stockpiling of quotations in relation to the commonplace tradition and various strategies for information management developed in the sixteenth, seventeenth, and eighteenth centuries. As Anthony Harding suggests, Coleridge recognized that "the material form of the notebook not only forces 'stray thoughts' into a particular shape, but acts as a stimulus to thinking in certain ways."[10] Jillian Hess elaborates on this idea in her discussion of the notebooks, investigating how for Coleridge "a particular structure for organizing information . . . mirrors particular structures of thought in its very form."[11] By underscoring the relationship between Coleridge's notebooks and the commonplace books kept by Josiah Wedgwood and Humphry Davy, Hess suggests that the seeming jumble of quotes, observations, experiments, commentary, and reflection in Coleridge's notebooks may actually reflect a shared epistemic model in which the individual produces knowledge by working through raw materials.[12] The episteme Hess describes is grounded in the "fresh examination of particulars" recommended by Baconian induction, the very procedure Coleridge seeks to reclaim from "mere empiricism" and philosophical materialism in the "Essays on Method." As I argue below, even more than Coleridge's notebooks, the text of the "Essays" seeks to instantiate – to embody and materialize on the page – the practice and principle it describes. This happens through the strategic use of quotations.

Hess's claim about the notebooks does not seem so far afield when one considers late-eighteenth- and early-nineteenth-century projects such as Novalis's *Das Allgemeine Brouillon* [*Notes for a Romantic Encyclopedia*], but it does bump up against Coleridge's disparaging comments on collections of extracts. This disjunction becomes even more pronounced when applied to Coleridge's published works. If piecemeal texts are a kind of mass delirium generator, what guarantees that Coleridge's collections of stitched together quotes, observations, reflections, and commentary will habituate a reader's mind to method? Further, what proves that a seemingly jumbled work is itself the product of the unifying processes of a methodized mind, rather than an immethodical miscellany produced by the mechanical pull of the printing press? Coleridge's project in the "Essays on Method" is to solve this conundrum as it manifests as both a practical and a philosophical problem. Following James McKusick, I show that Coleridge is fundamentally an inductive critic: regardless of the order of presentation, he formulated his literary-critical, philosophical, and theological principles by way of analysis of and commentary on particular textual instances. The manipulation of a textual archive – compiling, arranging, comparing, distinguishing, and synthesizing quotes and excerpts – defines his method of philosophical disquisition. To reinvigorate inductive method, as he sought to do in the "Essays," was thus to legitimate his own method of composition and to confirm the palliative effect of his seemingly disjointed text on the minds of his readers. This explains why Coleridge sets out to reclaim induction from Bacon's philosophical progeny – empiricists and philosophical materialists from Locke to Hume to Hartley – in the *Biographia* and again in the "Essays on Method." In both texts, Coleridge does this by turning to Shakespeare as the epitome of the creative imagination, an author whose works reveal the "unity of principle through all the diversity of forms" (*F*, 1: 470). The relationship of Shakespeare's texts to his synthetic imagination provides Coleridge with a bridge from the accumulation of particular instances to the formulation of universal principles.

Coleridge's treatment of *Hamlet* in the opening pages of the "Essays" reveals, starkly, the practical problem with this solution. Textual examples designed to illustrate method exceed the principle they are intended to embody, instead exposing the difficulty of turning a heap of excerpts into an expression of general truth. As the foundation for a "science of relations," the character of Hamlet emblematizes, rather than solves, the problem of induction. Hamlet, of course, also mirrors what Coleridge chastises himself for over and over in his notebooks, letters, and published works – the "fault" of "eternally pursuing the likenesses" until "my illustrations swallow up my thesis."[13] Fittingly, this Darwinian chain of analogies provides Coleridge with a way to stop the gap in induction. As critics have noted in passing, Coleridge reused and recycled the same bits of text over and over; this practice allowed the excerpts to accrue meaning as they resurfaced again and again in his notebooks, marginal notes, lectures, and published works, or moved between, within, and through various publications. Coleridge mobilizes this accumulation of signification in his strategic reuse of quotations in *The Friend*. Through the iterative structure of *The Friend*, the reader's mind is forced into method not by logical progression or narrative continuity, but a kind of self-reflection – a sustained attentiveness to the movements of the mind itself – modeled on the action of retroactively tracing the accumulated meanings of specific, reused quotations. In effect, Coleridge solves the conundrum of the unwieldy excerpt by turning quotations into *sententiae*, undoing their evidentiary status to make excerpts into the voice of principle.

Reclaiming Induction

Coleridge's early rejection of empiricism has long been noted in critical accounts of the development of his philosophical thought. By most accounts, the series of philosophical letters he wrote to Josiah Wedgwood in 1801 on Locke and Descartes signal his break with the empiricist tradition; this rupture is forecast in his more familiar letter to Thelwall of October 1797, quoted in my Introduction. In this earlier missive, Coleridge dismally reflected that "all the knowledge, that can be acquired, child's play – the universe itself – what but an immense heap of *little* things? – I can contemplate nothing but parts, & parts are all *little* – ! – My mind feels as if it ached to behold & know something *great* – something *one* & *indivisible*" (*CL*, I: 349). Here Coleridge registers a central concern of this study, the disjunction between an ever-growing heap of particular instances and the synthetic principles promised by Bacon's inductive method. As his seventeenth-century adherents understood it, a fundamental component of Baconian induction was its refusal to rely on a unifying theory in the early stages of collecting observations and experiments. The project of undifferentiated accumulation produced disorderly collections epitomized by the *Philosophical Transactions of the Royal Society*, in which "observations" or "reports" on Saturn's satellites, luminous arches, geologic strata in Ireland, human respiration, Tabasheer, children with two heads, and sugar ants had been piling up – by the time Coleridge voiced his complaint – for over 130 years.[14] From his early letters to the "Essays on Method," Coleridge's reaction against empiricism is bound up with a critique of this use of induction – a question that matters deeply to him because of its consequences for his own philosophical and compositional method.

The drive to heap up examples in seventeenth-century experimental science irked Coleridge, and in the "Essays" he lays out his objections to it in comments on Robert Hooke, the Royal Society's first Curator of Experiments. The inanity of Hooke's "philosophical life" is emblematized in the "appalling catalogue of preliminaries" a naturalist must become conversant with "before he can form 'even a foundation upon which any thing like a sound and stable *Theory* can be constituted'" (*F*, 1: 484). The problem is not solely variety, but the way arrangement forges arbitrary connections between ideas. A consecutive history of "schoolmasters, writing-masters, printers, book-binders, stage-players, dancing-masters, and vaulters, *apothecaries, chirurgeons, seamsters, butchers, barbers, laundresses*, and *cosmetics!*" creates chaos out of order: if placing vaulters and apothecaries side by side was not bad enough (being completely void of connection), the relation between the surgeon, seamster, and butcher as occupations involving cutting constitutes a "comical caricature" of the application of Bacon's method to the organization of knowledge (*F*, 1: 483). For Coleridge, contemporary science reveals the outcome of Hooke's legacy. Until the end of the eighteenth century, zoology remained "weighed down and crushed, as it were, by the inordinate number and manifoldness of facts and phænomena apparently separate, without evincing the least promise of systematizing itself by any inward combination, any vital interdependence of its parts" (*F*, 1: 473). Likewise, botany was "little more than an enormous nomenclature; a huge catalogue, *bien arrangè*, yearly and monthly augmented . . . a mass enlarging by endless appositions, but without a nerve that oscillates, or a pulse that throbs, in sign of *growth* or inward sympathy" (*F*, 1: 469). Without an infusion of vitality from speculative thinkers like Erasmus Darwin and John Hunter, science grounded in mere arrangement would merely repeat, Coleridge lamented, the "blind and guideless industry of ages" (*F*, 1: 470).

Perhaps unsurprisingly, the "strong meat" Hannah More recommended for impressing inductive method on the mind – books of logic by Locke and Isaac Watts – is for Coleridge moral philosophy's counterpart to Hooke and his legacy. Watts's directions for "the improvement of the mind" consist of acquainting oneself with "*things* ancient and modern; *things* natural, civil, and religious; *things* of your native land, and of foreign countries; *things* domestic and national; *things* present, past, and future" and so on up to God and yourself – a project of infinite accumulation without synthesis that Coleridge finds equally ludicrous but even more dangerous than Hooke's litany of professions (*F*, 1: 484, original emphasis). In the "Essays," Coleridge explicitly plots cognitive development as a history parallel to that of the sciences: "in the growth of the sciences and in the mind of a rightly-educated individual" "aimless activity and unregulated accumulation" will give way to "a period of orderliness, of circumspection, of discipline, in which we purify, separate, define, select, arrange," which in turn *should* lead to "the attainment of a scientific METHOD" (*F*, 1: 499). However, without a crucial element – something to guide the processes of accumulation and arrangement – the entire process will result in a turn to the sensual. Like the varnished and overcivilized youth of early nineteenth-century Britain, past societies that "determined to shape their convictions and deduce their knowledge from without, by exclusive observation of outward and sensible things as the only realities" became "great masters of the AGREEABLE" and "idolaters" of the "material elements" (*F*, 1: 501–02). As this suggests, experimental science and empiricist moral philosophy share the same fundamental problem: in heaping up an enormous databank of examples, these approaches spawned philosophical materialism, a position that discounts both human agency and divine will.

In *The Friend*, Hooke and Watts function as representatives of "mere empiricism" or "naïve Baconianism," the belief that indiscriminate collecting would eventually lead to the formation of principles.[15] The "common notion of Lord Bacon," Coleridge scoffs in an 1819 lecture on the history of philosophy, is that "you watch everything without having a reason for so doing, and that after you have collected the facts that belong to any subject . . . you may proceed to the theory."[16] My ellipses register the problem of induction, the difficulty of translating a well-arranged heap of facts into general truths or principles, dating back to Bacon's formulation of inductive method in the *Novum Organum*.[17] For Coleridge, the solution to the gap between observed phenomena and synthetic principle rests with a "mental Initiative" or "leading thought" that precedes and enables induction (*F*, 1: 466, 455). There must be an idea provided by the mind to guide collecting, arrangement, and experiment – otherwise, these activities will generate nothing more than vast catalogs. This "pre-cogitation," Coleridge makes clear, is not a hypothesis or a theory built on generalization from particular instances of experience or sense perception, but something supplied by (and already existing in) the mind (*F*, 1: 476). As he puts it in his critique of Locke in the *Biographia*, "How can we make bricks without straw? Or build without cement? We learn all things indeed by *occasion* of experience; but the very facts so learnt force us inward on the antecedents, that must be pre-supposed in order to render experience itself possible" (*BL*, 1: 142). There must exist something to do the experiencing, and to synthesize experience – the mind cannot be at once the builder and the edifice of knowledge.

The "Essays on Method" set out to address this problem by reclaiming induction from two centuries of abuse by Bacon's philosophical progeny. Coleridge performs this task in "Essay IX" by realigning the epitomes of experimental and idealist philosophy, Bacon and Plato. He also assigns this moment a central place in the larger philosophical project of *The Friend*. Coleridge begins "Essay IX" with the assertion that the following discussion will "recapitulate the substance of the doctrines asserted and vindicated in the preceding pages," and the essay concludes by asserting, "we can now, as men furnished with fit and respectable credentials, proceed to the historic importance and practical application of METHOD" (*F*, 1: 488, 493). More than a restatement, the essay will "unite into one" the essence of the preceding arguments, and by doing so will act as a "letter of reference" entitling Coleridge to apply the principle of method to the history and progress of society in "Essay X" and the ontological problem of Being in "Essay XI."[18] "Essay IX" is explicitly marked as an evidentiary pivot, drawing together what has come before and underwriting what comes after. As he claims at the end of "Essay VIII," "in collating the philosophical works of Lord Bacon with those of Plato . . . we shall not only extract that from each, which is for all ages, and which constitutes their true systems of philosophy, but shall convince ourselves that they are radically one and the same system: in that, namely, which is of universal and imperishable worth! – the science of Method, and the grounds and conditions of the science of Method" (*F*, 1: 487).

To effect this crucial and much touted collation, Coleridge offers "a brief statement of our renowned countryman's own principles of Method, conveyed for the greater part in his own words" (*F*, 1: 488). What follows and comprises the substance of the essay is akin to a close reading: Coleridge quotes from Bacon's works in Latin, and proceeds to give the "clear and evident" meaning of the passages in English for his reader (*F*, 1: 489). To bring Bacon into step with Platonic idealism, Coleridge needed to prove that, for Bacon, there is in every rational being "the pure reason, the spirit, lumen siccum, νοῦς, φῶς νοερόν, intellectual intuition, &c. &c.; and that in this are to be found the indispensible conditions of all science, and scientific research" (*F*, 1: 491). To support this claim, Coleridge collapses two of Bacon's aphorisms, effectively equating "ideas of the divine mind" with "true and intrinsic signatures and impressions of things just as they are found by sound Reason and the dry light that for teaching's sake we are in the habit of calling the interpretation of nature" (*F*, 1: 492 n.1). In this stitched-together quotation, "sound Reason" – by which Bacon means knowledge built up through induction from particular instances to general principles – becomes "pure reason," knowledge existing *prior* to sense perception. With a sleight of pen, Coleridge makes the forefather of Lockean empiricism speak as one convinced of the necessity of *a priori* ideas.[19]

Considering that Bacon's "true and intrinsic signatures" are the *product* of method, Coleridge effectively argues that method must be its own antecedent – it must exist in the mind as law even as it guides the mind toward the formation of laws. As detailed in Chapter 1, this is not surprising. Coleridge's splicing accurately reflects the historical process by which the steps of Baconian method were adapted into late-eighteenth-century theories of mind. Even so, in rehearsing this historical process Coleridge plays fast and loose with his source. The next two quotations in his discussion of Bacon go further, effectively rewriting Bacon's text. In the first instance, Coleridge adds a clause in Latin to the end of a quotation from the *Novum Organum* to reinforce his reading; in the second, he begins the sentence with "According to Lord Bacon . . . an idea would be defined as – " and then inserts a statement of his own manufacture in Latin, without quotation marks (*F*, I: 492 n. 3, 493 n. 2). An attentive reader well versed in Bacon's works may have noticed this divergence from Bacon's "own words," but it is more likely that Coleridge's substitution would have passed unnoticed. Either way, the absence of quotation marks releases him from strict adherence to the source, even if it lessens the evidentiary punch of his statement.

The procedure Coleridge follows in "Essay IX" is not unique to his corpus, nor does it reflect a recent development in his thought about empiricism. The 1801 letters to Josiah Wedgwood on Locke and Descartes follow a similar process. In this series of letters, Coleridge first narrates his decision to take "Locke from my Landlord's Shelf & read it attentively," and then accuses Locke (as he would also do to Bacon) of misrepresenting the originality of his system. As evidence of this, Coleridge provides quotations from four authors: The first, in Greek, he "extracted from Diog. Laert. in the Life of PLATO; the second [in Latin] from Daniel Sennertus, an adherent of the Aristotelian Philosophy who wrote the passage about the year 1620"; the third from Locke's *An Essay concerning Human Understanding*; and the fourth from Descartes's *Meditations* (*CL*, 2: 684). This series of passages, which closes the body of the first letter, establishes (as Coleridge claims at the beginning of his second letter) that Locke and Descartes "held precisely the same opinions concerning the original Sources of our Ideas" and their shared opinion was also "a Tenet, common to all the Philosophers before them" (*CL*, 2: 685–86). When he sets out to align Bacon with Plato in *The Friend*, Coleridge thus resorts to a familiar strategy for dealing with empiricist moral philosophy: he heaps up textual examples and – by juxtaposition, minor modifications, substitutions, and analysis of specific aspects of language and construction – bends them into the service of his larger project of establishing universal principles supposedly shared by philosophers whose works, by all conventional accounts, radically diverged.[20]

In pointing to these instances, I do not intend to take Coleridge to task for misuse of sources. Rather, I'm interested in how he tackles a knotty philosophical problem by quoting and analyzing specific textual instances, which he then compounds and modifies to fit his argument. As many critics have noted, Coleridge's compositional process is not merely aggregative: "borrowed materials are constantly transformed and combined in new ways" in his literary and philosophical works.[21] Recalling that induction is fundamentally a procedure applied to a body of textual snippets, we can see that Coleridge has plotted both his letters to Wedgwood and "Essay IX" on the model of inductive method. He has collected and carefully arranged a set of textual instances and preceded to compare, distinguish, combine, and finally synthesize them into the expression of a principle. His procedure, however, reveals the problem of induction on a micro-level. Confronted with passages that don't quite coalesce, he is forced to add something of his own invention to bridge that gap between particulars and principle. One might, of course, put this another way: Coleridge has already decided on the principle he wants to establish, thus making his procedure in Essay IX more rightly a performance of induction than a strict adherence to Bacon's method. In this, his practice fits with that of his contemporaries working in botany, chemistry, zoology, and moral philosophy (including Darwin, Davy, and Hunter), most of whom claimed adherence to Baconianism even as they practiced a more hypothesis-based or speculative approach to knowledge production.[22]

In locating Coleridge's procedure of textual excerpting as a performance of induction, I am also making a pointed claim about the importance of induction in his philosophical system. Coleridge is driven to rescue inductive method from its associations with philosophical materialism because it forms the core of his analytical procedure. As the letters to Wedgwood make clear, this procedure involved an imaginative leap from quoted passages to stated principles. The physical separation onto different sheets of paper and temporal distance between the composition and delivery of the letters covers over the uncertain movement from the four quotations that conclude the first letter to Wedgwood to the general claim that begins the second letter. Thus the "problem of induction" is manifested in the material conditions of writing: Coleridge's strategy of using quotations in his letters and the "Essays on Method" reveals and covers over the difficulty of arriving at a synthetic statement of general truths by way of the process of collection, arrangement, comparison, and distinction. "Essay IX" is of especial importance in this regard. By adding his own words to the series of quotations from Bacon, Coleridge indicates the crucial role of a "*leading Thought*" or mental "Initiative" in the reconciliation of philosophical positions; as he suggests early in the "Essays," "where the habit of Method is present and effective, things most remote and diverse in time, place, and outward circumstance, are brought into mental congruity and succession" (*F*, 1: 455). Rather than a violation of the integrity of his source text, Coleridge's addition of material reiterates *in practice* a basic tenet of method as it is conceptualized in the "Essays": to avoid becoming interred in a heap of particulars, induction requires the addition of a guiding thought from the author's mind – and in the case of "Essay IX," that mind is Coleridge's.

The Critic's Method

Coleridge's project in the "Essays on Method" thus generates a twofold approach: He is simultaneously establishing method as a philosophical principle, and demonstrating that principle in his critical engagement with textual excerpts. In making this claim, I am entering a long-standing debate over how Coleridge's philosophical and aesthetic principles connect – or fail to connect – to his "practical criticism" (*BL*, 2: 19). As recent studies establish, twentieth-century efforts to divorce Coleridge's practice of textual analysis from his theoretical statements ended in contradictory claims. The New Critics, for example, claimed that his preoccupation with German idealism made it impossible for him to attend to the specifics of poetic language while also asserting that he was a great critic because of his attention to linguistic particulars.[23] In contrast, critics from Richard Fogle in the early 1960s to James McKusick in the mid-1980s insisted that Coleridge's formulation of principles is inextricable from his critical practice. In *Coleridge's Philosophy of Language*, McKusick suggests that Coleridge's practice of desynonymization underscores the link between his linguistic speculations and his attention to the specificity of language in his criticism. Coleridge's theory of organic form, he argues, developed in tandem with his practical treatment of Shakespeare's poetic language, which resists representational transparency by foregrounding its own verbal texture and inner logic. McKusick's carefully plotted interplay of principle and practice maintains a sense of directionality, and his chapter concludes with the claim that "as a critic, Coleridge works inductively from the facts of literary experience rather than deductively from metaphysical axioms."[24]

As I am arguing, Coleridge's inductive approach to textual analysis was calculated: the "technical *process* of philosophy" – the way we can "obtain adequate notions of any truth" (*BL*, 2: 11) – derives from Baconian induction. Here, I want to extend McKusick's insight further by considering the relationship between Coleridge's inductive method of practical criticism and his attempt to establish induction as a philosophical principle in the "Essays on Method." This project is carried out by positing the author's synthetic mind as a "cure" for the "problem of induction" – a position supported by the strategic manipulation of specific textual excerpts, most obviously quotations from Shakespeare's plays.

To establish a backdrop for his project in the "Essays," I'll first consider Coleridge's critical practice vis-à-vis his formulation of principles in earlier works that rely on readings of Shakespeare. In Chapter 14 of the *Biographia Literaria* (the first chapter of the second volume), he begins his distinction between poetry and prose by introducing a definition of the process of philosophical disquisition, distinction followed by synthesis. This process allows Coleridge to establish principles; the succeeding chapters, he claims, will be an "application of these principles to the purposes of practical criticism," specifically in the discussion of Shakespeare's sonnets and "Venus and Adonis" in Chapter 15 (*BL*, 2: 19) (Fig. 4). Structurally, textual excerpts function as proofs or "credentials" of already established principles. Having detailed what makes a "legitimate" poem in Chapter 14, Coleridge precedes in Chapter 15 to "discover" the "qualities" in Shakespeare's poems that are "promises and specific symptoms of poetic power" (*BL*, 2: 19). The definition of the legitimate poem in Chapter 14 was similarly "anticipated" by the philosophical distinction between fancy and imagination in Chapter 13 – to know what makes a poem is the same as knowing what constitutes the poet's genius. The distinction between the superficial and legitimate forms of the poem is nested within and built upon the distinction between the mental processes of fancy and imagination.

Chapter 13, however, famously founders on the rocks of its own methodology, and the interpolated "letter from a friend" likens the effect of philosophical disquisition to that of entering a gloomy cathedral full of "fantastic shapes yet all decked with holy insignia and mystic symbols" (*BL*, 1: 300–301). Chapter 14 offers an implicit explanation for what has gone awry: the poet's "synthetic and magical power" of imagination "reveals itself in the balance or reconciliation of opposite or discordant qualities" – a revelation impossible to grasp without recourse to the text (*BL*, 2: 16). When divested of its foundation in particular textual instances, as it is in Chapter 13, the formulation of principles becomes a journey into gothic romance.

Coleridge's struggle in Chapters 13–15 of the *Biographia* arises from having reversed the order of inductive method: He has attempted to formulate philosophical principles without previously building up the collection of textual instances requisite for any induction. Coleridge may claim to treat textual excerpts as "credentials," but by the time he set to work on the *Biographia*, he had been building the concepts of poetry, the poet, genius, fancy, and imagination from particular textual instances for many years in his notebooks and his lectures on literature from 1808 to 1814. Many of these lectures center on Shakespeare's poems and plays, and in lectures on other topics Shakespeare is a continual point of reference, contrast, qualification, and amplification. In the early lectures, the myriad-minded bard embodies the principle of imagination, but his works are the fountains from which this principle emanates. For example, in an 1808 lecture on the principles of poetry (recorded in his notebooks), Coleridge describes fancy and imagination by way of Shakespeare's "Venus and Adonis," the same text he chose as the ostensible focus of Chapter 15 of the *Biographia*. In the lecture notes, he begins by pointing out that the lines beginning "Full gently now" exemplify Fancy's aggregative power and its work of bringing together dissimilar images (*LL*, 1: 67). He contrasts this with the imagination's power to modify and combine "many circumstances into one moment of thought to produce that ultimate end of human Thought, and human Feeling, Unity," reminding himself parenthetically to "Quote the passage p. 28 *before this* observation" (*LL*, 1: 68, original emphasis). Whether he stuck to this order in the lecture or not, Coleridge's notes suggest a conceptual trajectory from passage to principle. The textual examples do not merely function as proofs of already established principles; they are the materials on which the philosophical distinction between imagination and fancy is established. While the 1808 lectures, taken as a series, move from a physiological discussion of taste and a historical comparison of modern and ancient drama (Lectures 1 and 2) to readings of Shakespeare's plays (Lectures 3 and 4), the foundational principles of fancy and imagination arise out of textual examples.

As with the fancy–imagination distinction, Coleridge also began developing his argument about Shakespeare's synthetic mind in his lectures on literature. In Lecture 7 of the 1811–1812 series, for example, Coleridge distinguishes characters in *Romeo and Juliet* according to how their passions and habits of mind are drawn in the play.[25] He first identifies Tybalt and Capulet as examples of passion "drawn truly but not individualized" (*LL*, 1: 304). Capulet is marked by an impatience of character reflective of his age and rank, as when he chastises Tybalt in Act I scene v:

> Go to, go to;
> You are a saucy boy: – Is't so, indeed? –
> This trick may chance to scathe you; – I know what.
> You must contrary me! marry, 'tis time –
> Well said, my hearts: – You are a princox; go:
> Be quiet, or – More light, more light! For shame!
> I'll make you quiet; What! – Cheerly, my hearts.[26]

In Coleridge's reading, this passage shows Capulet's anger moving from one object to another: he is reproving Tybalt and threatening him with the loss of his legacy, but "seeing the lights burn dimly Capulet turns his anger ag.ᵗ the servants" (*LL*, 1: 306). The result, Coleridge argues, is "that no one passion is to [sic] predominant but that it always includes all the parts of the character," an effect achieved by the Poet calling forth the sensibilities of nature as if "had the 100 arms of the Polypus, thrown out in all directions to catch the predominant feeling" (*LL*, 1: 305–06). Later in the same lecture, Coleridge marks the Nurse's uncultivated mind by her propensity toward coincidental images: "'Tis since the earthquake now eleven years; / And she was wean'd, – I never shall forget it, – / . . . For I had then laid wormwood to my dug, / Sitting in the sun under the dove-house wall."[27] While the Nurse's character is conditioned by observation of outward circumstances, Coleridge argues that she is also an "admirable generalization" produced by Shakespeare's meditative genius: the passage shows that "more in fact was brought into one portrait here than any single observation could have given & nothing incongruous to the whole was introduced" (*LL*, 1: 309). In this lecture, Coleridge has effectively argued for unified, congruous characters – characters who are essential components of the play's overarching unity – by analyzing what seem like unimportant, throwaway passages. The more disjointed and jumbled the utterance – the more opaque the quoted passage – the more fitted it appears to be for Coleridge's purpose of revealing the poet's synthetic mind and the unity of his work.

This odd condition of Coleridge's practical criticism can be explained, I believe, by drilling further into the relationship between the textual excerpt and the formulation of principles in the lectures. As Matthew Scott notes, Coleridge's lectures on literature "are at once acts of close reading, a revelation or evocation of the matter of art and literature" and "difficult, occasionally straining exercises in the divination of aesthetic principles" contiguous "with other (largely German) Romantic hopes of discovering a universal key in art to questions of taste, pleasure and moral sense."[28] I want to push this point further and suggest that Coleridge's critical practice combines aspects of late-eighteenth-century British criticism of

Shakespeare with concepts from turn-of-the-century German criticism, especially the work of Shakespeare's German editors, August Wilhelm Schlegel and Caroline Schlegel. Coleridge's debts to A. W. Schlegel have long been a source of controversy, as detailed in R. A. Foakes's Introduction to the Bollingen edition of Coleridge's *Lectures 1808–1819: On Literature*.[29] Coleridge's ideas about the unity and harmoniousness of Shakespeare's plays – and specifically the bard's ability to connect various parts into a unity of total impression – correlate with points developed in the Schlegels' essay on *Romeo and Juliet*, published first in *Die Horen* (1797) republished in *Charakteristiken und Kritiken* (1801) and again in A. W. Schlegel's later *Ueber dramatische Kunst und Literatur* (1809; translated into English as *A Course of Lectures on Dramatic Art and Literature* by John Black in 1815), which Coleridge read in 1811. In *A Course of Lectures*, A. W. Schlegel notes that English critics "extol the beauty and sublimity of [Shakespeare's] separate descriptions, images, and expressions. This last is the most superficial and cheap mode of criticising works of art."[30] Instead of chopping the plays up into "a mere accumulation of dead parts," he recommends "penetrating to the central point and viewing all the parts as so many irradiations from it," which will allow the critic to "elevate himself to the comprehensive contemplation of a work of art."[31] Coleridge would wholeheartedly agree with this goal, but his critical *practice* diverges from that of Schlegel. In practice, Schlegel rarely quotes lines from the plays and he does not engage in the close analysis of the texture of language that defines Coleridge's practical criticism. In *A Course of Lectures*, Schlegel describes the scenes and characters in detail to prove that they are all necessary parts of the unified play; Coleridge quotes and analyzes passages to attain the same end.

Where Coleridge diverges from his German contemporaries in his attention to specific passages, he replicates the format, if not the goals, of late-eighteenth-century criticism of Shakespeare published in Britain. As Jean Marsden argues, Shakespeare criticism underwent a sea change in the second half of the eighteenth century: "as morality becomes an aspect of the text, the plot becomes irrelevant, and instruction, that composite effect long separated from the specifics of poetic language, in the end becomes an outgrowth of specific passages, its genius located in a grouping of words and dependent on textual interpretation."[32] This "new reliance of careful textual scrutiny" stands behind critical works such as William Richardson's *A Philosophical Analysis and Illustration of some of Shakespeare's Remarkable Characters* (1774), Maurice Morgan's *An Essay on the Dramatic Character of Sir John Falstaff* (1777), and Walter Whiter's *A Specimen of the Commentary on Shakespeare* (1794), among others.[33] Whether or not he was familiar with these works, Coleridge's analysis of the language and structure of specific passages – which he quotes in his text – partakes of the critical conventions followed by these authors.[34] These conventions were in turn grounded in an inductive approach to literary criticism promoted, if not practiced, by Scottish Enlightenment rhetoricians. Adam Smith, James Beattie, and Hugh Blair, among others, plant the "science of Criticism" (as Beattie called it) firmly in experience, observation, and close study of writers' practices; they also – like their contemporaries in the natural sciences – reject the "mere classification" and lists of terms typical of earlier treatments of rhetoric.[35] Blair, for example, argues that the "rules of Criticism . . . are not formed by a train of abstract reasoning, independent of facts and observations. Criticism is an art founded wholly on experience"; further, principles such as Aristotle's unities "were not rules first discovered by logical reasoning and then applied to poetry; but they were drawn from the practice of Homer and Sophocles."[36] In accordance with these views, Blair dedicates a series of his *Lectures on Rhetoric* to an extended, sentence-by-sentence analysis of Addison's *Spectator* papers on the "Pleasures of the Imagination." Although Blair has already established his standards of judgment earlier in the *Lectures* and his criticism of Addison aims solely at showing why certain passages are stylistically beautiful and others are not, his use of quotations *suggests* that he is formulating tenets of aesthetic appreciation from his analysis of the text.

William Richardson's *Philosophical Analysis and Illustration of some of Shakespeare's Remarkable Characters* carries this approach considerably further, to the point of engaging in a largely inductive critical practice. His book opens by isolating the problem of analyzing the seeming "anarchy and confusion" of human thoughts, feelings, and affections, and asserts (in the tradition begun by Hume) that the "difficulty of making just experiments is the principal reason why knowledge of human nature is retarded."[37] After a lengthy explanation of why moral philosophers cannot perform adequate experiments on themselves or other people, Richardson suggests that the "class of poetical writers that excel in imitating the passions, might contribute . . . to rectify and enlarge the sentiments of philosophers."[38] Specifically, he argues that "the genius of Shakespeare is unlimited. Possessing extreme sensibility, and uncommonly susceptible, he is the Proteus of the drama; he changes himself into every character, and enters easily into every condition of human nature." Therefore, Richardson concludes, Shakespeare's *texts* provide an ideal platform for "tracing the principles of human conduct."[39] In the analyses of specific characters that follow, Richardson is not interested in judging Shakespeare's works according to pre-established rules or in establishing the poetic justice or morality of the plays. Rather, as his comments on a sequence of extracted passages from *Macbeth* indicate, he sought to establish the motions of a character's mind as a specific passion – in this case ambition – increases in violence.[40] As in Coleridge's lectures on literature, passages from the plays are introduced into Richardson's critical text as the objects of analysis, and they provide the foundation for the critic's claims about the unity and coherence of character. Quotations are the material ground on which principles can be built.

Despite the similarities in format, analysis of passages, and treatment of character, Coleridge's criticism has loftier goals than Richardson's. As Marsden notes, one consequence of the new text-based criticism of Shakespeare was that "the literary text disintegrated into smaller and smaller fragments . . . [and] critics applied an increasingly fragmented view of the literary work."[41] This claim is reinforced by the clear correlation between late-eighteenth-century critical treatments of Shakespeare and collections of *sententiae* and maxims such as Elizabeth Griffith's *The Morality of Shakespeare's Drama* (1775). Griffith's aims are more in line with the pedagogical miscellanies of the day. Her commentary points out the lessons conveyed by quoted passages and gives no attention to character or the play as a whole. However, her practice of chopping the plays up into easily digestible tidbits accords with Richardson's critical practice; the way quotations appear on the printed page suggests criticism defined by an accumulation of dead parts, the practice so vehemently objected to by A. W. Schlegel. Even as Coleridge adopted the text-based, inductive approach of late-eighteenth-century empiricist criticism of Shakespeare, his larger critical goals were explicitly antagonistic to the fragmentation of the text. Like the Schlegels, Coleridge was dedicated to establishing the unity of character, of the plays, and of Shakespeare's artistic vision in the plays. Unlike the Schlegels, he set himself up to elucidate this unity by way of a detailed analysis of quoted passages.

Coleridge's mode of practical criticism can be identified in his early lectures on literature, but the project of tying textual analysis to the formulation of principles is more fully played out in the *Biographia*. In the aftermath of the unhappy result of Chapters 13–15, he takes up the project once again in the "Essays on Method" in *The Friend*. In what follows, I suggest how Coleridge's use of excerpts from Shakespeare binds his critical practice to his reclamation of induction as a philosophical principle in the "Essays." The result, however, is yet again not entirely satisfactory, primarily because to employ Hamlet as a figurehead for "method" brings the textual excerpt into conflict with the principle it is intended to generate.

As Coleridge acknowledges, character analysis pursued by way of the careful orchestration of quotations might undermine rather than support his claims for Shakespeare's meditative genius and, by implication, dissolve the "mental initiative" that was to bridge the gap between particular instances and general truths.

The Poet's Genius

Unlike the revised text that appeared in the *Encyclopædia Metropolitana*, which opens with a definition of "method" as exemplified in the sciences, the revised "Essays on Method" in *The Friend* open with quotations from Shakespeare's plays. Contrasting these excerpts yields the "principles" that can also be, Coleridge claims two essays later, "proved from the most familiar of the SCIENCES" (*F*, 1: 466). Coleridge's strategic reordering of the text may be traced to the problems he encountered in the *Biographia*: putting the principles before particulars did not work the first time, so he was loath to try it again. In the "Essays," quotations from Shakespeare identify the lack or presence of method as a mental construct, a procedure for mental sorting, arrangement, and most importantly, connection. Thus, in her exchange with Falstaff from *Henry IV, Part II*, "Mrs. Quickley" (as Coleridge denominates her) reveals the absence of method, a lack "occasioned by an habitual submission of the understanding to mere events and images as such, and independent of any power in the mind to classify or appropriate them" (*F*, 1: 450–51). Hamlet, by contrast, exemplifies the "well-disciplined" mind, one "accustomed to contemplate not *things* only, or for their own sake alone, but likewise and chiefly the *relations* of things" (*F*, 1: 451, 455). Coleridge's definition of the imagination in another 1808 lecture draws a similar distinction: the imagination "acts chiefly by producing out of many things, as it would have appeared in the description of an ordinary mind, described slowly & in unimpassioned succession, a oneness" (*LL*, 1: 81). Hamlet's methodical mind and its activity of thought prepares the way for imaginative unity, while the antithesis to imagination – the "unimpassioned succession" of the ordinary mind – is captured neatly in Mrs. Quickley's immethodical talk.[42]

To be clear: Mrs. Quickley is not a purveyor of Fancy's aggregative and associative power, as described in the lectures and the *Biographia*. Fancy is a mode of memory and thus remains bound to the laws of association, but it is also "emancipated from time and space" (*BL*, 1: 294). Mrs. Quickley's speech is a litany of things orchestrated by the memory of a specific event. In the text quoted by Coleridge, her narrative jumps from parcel-gilt goblet, to dolphin chamber, to sea-coal fire, to wound, to mess of vinegar, to dish of prawns, and is thus less a progression than an inventory – a heap of things existing in a particular space at a particular time. In this aspect, Mrs. Quickley's talk instantiates the problem Coleridge recurs to throughout the "Essays on Method," the formal condition shared by Linnaean botany, Hooke's list of professions, and Watts's catalog of knowledge: she produces a sequence of artificial associations based on time, space, number, or name. Put another way, Mrs. Quickley is an empiricist of the worst kind, guided solely by observation and compilation; like the Nurse in *Romeo and Juliet*,

> in all her recollections she entirely assists herself by a remembrance of visual circumstances. The great difference between the cultivated and uncultivated mind was this [–] that the cultivated mind would be found to recal the past by certain regular trains of cause & effect whereas with the ~~who~~ uncultivated it was wholly done by a coincidence of images or circumstances which happened at the same time. (*LL*, 1: 308)

The result of her immethodical thought, as Hooke is made to demonstrate later in the "Essays," is a heap of particulars whose connective tissue amounts to little more than "&c &c. &c." (*F*, 1: 451, 484).

In an 1811 lecture on *Love's Labour's Lost*, Coleridge describes the literary equivalent of Mrs. Quickley, the modern "pleasures" poem. Such works are made by "heaping together a certain number of images" and "then merely tying [them] together with a string as if it had [been] bought at a penny the yard" (*LL*, 1: 272). Coleridge's metaphor is telling: Like the "slight festoon of ribbons" that structures Darwin's *The Loves of the Plants* or Southey's patchwork stitchery in *Thalaba the Destroyer*, sewing is a sign of a text pulling apart at the seams – one in which parts refuse to coalesce into a larger whole. Such heaping was explicitly connected to women's desultory education in accomplishments. As Coleridge comments on Darwin's *The Botanic Garden*, "it was written with all the industry of a Milliner or tradesman, who was anxious to dress up his ideas in silks & satins ~~and~~ by collecting all the sonorous & handsome looking words" (*LL*, 1: 207). The consequence of such literary stitchery, Coleridge continues, is a visible cognitive gap:

> When the artist had come to the end of one thought, another must arise between which there was not the least connection of mind, or even of logic (which was the least connection of a poet) or of passions frequently acting by contrast, but always justifying themselves – no, there was no such connection, but a full pause ensues & the reader must begin again. 'Oh Hope! likewise' &c. (*LL*, 1: 272)

Works of this type exhibit the flaw of old women, seventeenth-century experimental philosophers, and eighteenth-century empiricist moral philosophy, a "want of concatenation" that barred Southey from the title of imaginative poet in Coleridge's estimation (*CH*, 92).[43]

In opening pages of the "Essays on Method," Coleridge sets these odd bedfellows – Mrs. Quickley and her attendants Hooke, Linnaeus, Watts, and the rest – against the cultivated intellect of the "man of education," Hamlet (a character whose discourse evinces the result of a mind trained in method), and Shakespeare himself, a poet capable of "passing into all forms of human character & passion" while "reducing [this] multitude into unity of effect" (*LL*, 1: 244, 249). This triumvirate allows Coleridge to uphold the central point of the "Essays": The goal of method – universal laws – cannot be attained without "a principle of connection given by the mind," a guiding idea that foresees the whole in each integral part (*F*, 1: 471, 448). As my epigraph to this chapter indicates, while his talk may seem fragmentary, the man of education arranges his words so that each sentence forecasts the whole he intends to communicate. Likewise, Shakespeare may appear to be a "mere child of nature" with an "irregular mind" (as early-eighteenth-century critics had argued), but his works actually exhibit "that union and interpenetration of the universal and the particular, which ever must pervade all works of decided genius and true science" (*LL*, 1: 208; *F*, 1: 457). In opening the "Essays" with this assertion, Coleridge posits an analogical relation between the arrangement of a text (words, sentences, lines, scenes, etc.) and the inductive method of scientific enquiry, and gives the mind precedence in both activities. The mind's capacity to unify and synthesize – its habits of methodizing and powers of imagination – can resolve the problems posed by the discursive heaping up of disconnected ideas, images, facts, experiments, or things, whether these emanate from Mrs. Quickley, pleasures poems, Linnaeus, or the Royal Society's *Philosophical Transactions*.

Structurally, then, the "Essays on Method" begin with the analysis of quotations from Shakespeare's plays to prefigure and ground Coleridge's reclamation of Baconian induction later in the series, but the process does not come off without a hitch. After opening with the quote from Mrs. Quickley that exemplifies immethodical thought, Coleridge contrasts it with an example of method in a speech by Hamlet. In this passage, not one of the circumstances "could have been omitted without injury to the intelligibility of the whole process," thus evidencing the bard's ability to make a whole from parts (*F*, 1: 452). However, it also shows Hamlet's own mind to be "meditative to excess," a characteristic that, Coleridge argues, "with due abatement and reduction, is distinctive of every powerful and methodizing intellect" (*F*, 1: 452). After quoting another long passage from the same exchange between Horatio and Hamlet in Act 5 of the play, Coleridge admits that if we overlooked the difference in content and "considered the *form* alone, we should find both *immethodical*; Hamlet from the excess, Mrs. Quickley from the want, of reflection and generalization" (*F*, 1: 453). This condition of his textual examples generates several more pages of repetition, qualification, and elaboration. The problem, as Coleridge concludes halfway through this morass, is that a meditative mind might be "stretched into despotism" by an "undue preponderance" of method and produce not unity but "the grotesque or the fantastical" (*F*, 1: 455). In a reversal of the problems he encountered in Chapter 13 of the *Biographia*, opening with textual examples has yet again landed Coleridge amid the fantastic shapes of gothic ornament.

Coleridge's critical practice of working inductively from textual instances to guiding principles has, in this instance, suggested that the mind's capacity to forge unity from a mass of particular instances is illusory, or at least highly fallible. Further, Hamlet's excesses raise the specter of Shakespeare's own. How does one distinguish between immethodical discourse produced by the poet's method – his ability to bring diverse things into congruity "the more striking as the less expected" – and a textual manifestation of the poet's own excrescences of thought? When employed as the foundation for philosophical disquisition, literature had already proven itself an unmanageable databank, one apt to pile up contradictory instances akin to those that populate Darwin's scientific or Southey's historical annotations. As detailed in Chapter 1, Burke had run up against this problem in his use of passages in *A Philosophical Enquiry into the Origin of Our Ideas of the Sublime and Beautiful*: when made to stand in for mental processes, the vast field of textual examples actively controverts the very principles of mind it was meant to secure. Similarly, Coleridge's tangle of passages in the opening pages of the "Essays" does more to dismantle the guiding light of "mental Initiative" than to uphold it as a necessary corrective for sight-bound science or, by extension, the moral compass of the nation.

The opening essay in the series thus exposes a similar crux to what Christensen calls the "grand chiasmus" of the *Biographia Literaria*: "that the text is unified because it is the product of an integral consciousness and that consciousness is unified because it produces integral texts."[44] Christensen extends this point in his reading of the Hamlet passages in *The Friend*. As a result of quoting Shakespeare's plays, Coleridge's textual examples "devour his thesis" and "the chiasmus with which he figures method wantons with the antithetical division between true philosophy and specious rhetoric" established in the preceding essay on the sophists in ancient Greece.[45] As a consequence, for Christensen method appears as little more than a rhetorical effect. I am making a different point here. The condition of Coleridge's writing "where the Illustration swallows up or out-dazzles the Proposition" (as he put it) is itself a *methodological* problem, the result of building philosophical principles from a databank of textual excerpts (*LL*, 1: 64). It is, in other words, the problem of induction – the very problem Shakespeare's unifying, meditative consciousness is intended to counter and assuage in the "Essays."

Unlike Burke, Coleridge recognized that the limits of a unifying authorial consciousness would surface as textual excess. Commenting on Shakespeare's sonnets, he notes that they "have been strangely jumbled & misplaced, I doubt not; but remove all the light & less worthy ones, & confine the attention to the connected suite, (forming a sort of poetic conjunction disjunctive, a divine Holomery, all making one Whole, and yet each component Stanza a Whole of itself)."[46] To grasp the whole, one must remove the slight and unworthy, the excrescences of text that prevent the balance of parts and whole and impede the procedure by which we "distinguish subtly in order that we then be able to assimilate truly" (*LL*, 1: 202). Thus, while the chiasmus is indeed an important figure in Coleridge's resolution of opposites, the two terms are never self-contained; there is always an excess of quotation, an excerpt that creeps onto the tightrope and topples the carefully orchestrated rhetorical balancing of any seeming binary. Such instabilities were, as I have argued, characteristic of Coleridge's large-scale literary-critical and philosophical projects in the *Biographia* and *The Friend* – an effect of his life as a "library-cormorant" greedily consuming everything from duodecimos to folios (*CL*, 1: 260). Like his contemporaries, Coleridge's compositional procedure rests on amassing, arranging, comparing, and distinguishing bits and pieces of other people's texts. However, as I argue below, Coleridge eventually found a cure for his gluttony in the disease itself: his practice of textual excerpting, recycling, and reusing resuscitates both the poet's integral consciousness and his inductive method. The particular's excess becomes the principle's saving grace.

Disciplining the Excerpt

In 1827 Coleridge observed, "I have a smack of Hamlet myself," referring to the central trait of Hamlet's character, "the prevalence of the abstracting and generalizing habit over the practical."[47] As with Hamlet, an excess of

generalization often got in the way of Coleridge making himself understood. He isolates the problem in the opening pages of the "Essays on
Method": "in attending too exclusively to the relations which the past or
passing events and objects bear to general truth, and the moods of his own
Thought, the most intelligent man is sometimes in danger of overlook-
ing that other relation, in which [the events and objects] are likewise to
be placed to the apprehension and sympathies of his hearers" (*F*, 1: 454).
The subject of the passage is Hamlet, but Coleridge is certainly thinking
of himself. Like his publications from "The Ancyent Marinere" to *The
Friend*, Coleridge's lectures on literature drew charges of disorganization
and obscurity, even to the point of incomprehensibility.[48] In a letter to
Catherine Clarkson about Coleridge's 1808 lectures, Henry Crabbe Robinson quipped, "I have only two lectures to speak about and shall not pretend
to speak of them in the order in which Coleridge spoke, since there was no
order in his speaking" (quoted in *LL* 1: 114). After listening to Lecture 3
of the 1811–1812 series on Shakespeare and Milton, William Hazlitt commented that Coleridge "had no capability of attending to one object [but
rather] he was constantly endeavoring to push matters to the furthest till he
became obscure to every body but himself" (quoted in *LL*, 1: 233). Having
heard Lecture 6 in the same series, Charles Lamb scoffed, "[t]his is not so
much amiss. Coleridge said in his advertisement he would speak about the
nurse in *Romeo and Juliet*, and so he is delivering the lecture in the character of the nurse" (quoted in *LL*, 1: 283). Whether the problem was too
much reflection – pushing matters to the farthest like Hamlet – or replicating the Nurse's complete lack of reflection, the effect was the same: To
his audience, Coleridge's talk was immethodical.

Long before he commenced lecturing, Coleridge had pinpointed his
propensity to pile up ideas and pursue endless strings of connections.
In an astonishing notebook passage from December 1804, he applies the
philosophical procedure of distinction to himself. There are "two sorts of
talkative fellows," he proposes, those who use 500 words to express an idea
and those who

> use five hundred more ideas, images, reasons &c than there is any need of to
> arrive at their object/till the only object arrived at is the ~~readers~~ mind's eye
> of the bye-stander is dazzled with colors succeeding so rapidly as to leave
> one vague impression that there has been a great Blaze of colours all about
> something. Now this is my case – & a grievous fault it is/my illustrations
> swallow up my thesis – I feel too intensely the omnipresence of all in each,
> platonically speaking – or psychologically my brain-fibers, or the spiritual
> Light which abides in ~~that~~ brain marrow as visible Light appears to do

in sundry rotten mackerel & and other *smashy* matters, is of too general affinity with all things/and tho' it perceives the *difference* of things, yet is eternally pursuing the likenessnesses, or rather that which is common/bring me two things that seem the very same, & then I am quick enough to shew the difference, even to hair-splitting – but to go on from circle to circle till I break against the shore of my Hearer's patience, or have my Concentricals dashed to nothing by a Snore – that is my ordinary mishap.[49]

With its affinity to decomposing fish – in which distinct organs have lique-fied and become smashy – his mind refuses to keep things asunder, hound-ing instead after likenesses. The effect on the listener resembles that of Southey's *The Curse of Kehama*, which dazzles the reader with "colours of superlative brilliancy [on] a canvas of endless extent" but fails to convey a clear message (*CH*, 146). It is no wonder Darwin's *The Botanic Garden* nau-seated Coleridge – in its web of associations and analogies, looping back on themselves without progression or development, it presents the scientific and literary mirror of Coleridge's mind.[50]

In drawing these comparisons to Southey and Darwin, I'm suggesting that Coleridge's immethodical talk in the lectures was as much a product of his method of constructing texts as of his unique "brain marrow." As Chris-tensen suggests, Coleridge's compositional practice of using other texts to construct his own introduces "promiscuities" and "errancies," moments of textual instability that niggle the possibility of a unified book and its counterpart, a unified life. Rather than unifying genius, the reader of the *Biographia* "tracks a writer who becomes entangled in the intricacies of his composition."[51] I could read the opening of the "Essays on Method," as Christensen does, as more of the same: Coleridge is just repeating the same cycle, undoing the synthetic power of mind in the moment of its formula-tion. But perhaps this is also a moment of recognition, of exposure – this is what the mind makes after it has been stuffed with texts, and any attempt to methodize its excesses is bound to end in a tangle. (It is no coincidence that the passage Coleridge analyzes contains Hamlet's explanation of the text of a letter and how he rewrote it, reusing its linguistic forms while revising its message.) In the first of the "Essays on Method," then, Coleridge proposes a second, underlying subject for the "Essays" and *The Friend* as a whole. While he explicitly sets out to reclaim Baconian induction and make it fit for the work of scientific and moral enquiry, the "Essays on Method" are equally concerned with resuscitating induction as a compositional practice, a way of making texts out of other texts.

Coleridge had been thinking about *The Friend* in this way – as a med-itation on how texts are made – from its earliest incarnation. In the 1808

Prospectus, he avows (speaking to an anonymous correspondent), "I have employed almost the whole of my Life in acquiring, or endeavoring to acquire, useful Knowledge by Study, Reflection, Observation" while "at different Periods of my Life I have not only planned, but collected the Materials for, many Works on various and important Subjects" (*F*, 2: 16). Regrettably, he continues, he had compiled materials for "so many [works] indeed, that the Number of my unrealized Schemes, and the Mass of my miscellaneous Fragments, have often furnished my Friends with a Subject of Raillery, and sometimes Regret and Reproof" (*F*, 2: 16). Like Southey, Coleridge underscores that the storehouse of materials – excerpts and fragments collected in commonplace books – is merely "dead stock" until they have been "worked up" into a saleable commodity (*LC*, 413). Coleridge accounts for his failure to produce such a commodity by a Hamlet-like "Over-activity of Thought, modified by a constitutional Indolence" that made it "more pleasant to me to continue acquiring, than to reduce what I had acquired to a regular Form" (*F*, 2: 16). But this was not the worst of his trouble. Coleridge also had a smack of Hooke and Watts about him: as he wrote, while

> almost daily throwing off my Notices or Reflections in desultory Fragments, I was still tempted onward by an increasing Sense of the Imperfection of my Knowledge, and by the Conviction, that, in Order fully to comprehend and develope any one Subject, it was necessary that I should make myself Master of some other, which again as regularly involved a third, and so on, with an ever-widening Horizon. (*F*, 2: 16)

Here, Coleridge subjects himself to the same critique he would aim at seventeenth-century empiricism and eighteenth-century empiricist models of education: you could spend an eternity building the foundation for a more perfect induction without making any progress toward a principle – or a book.

There was, however, one saving grace in his piling propensity, according to the Prospectus. The habit "of daily noting down, in my Memorandum or Common-place Books, both Incidents and Observations; whatever had occurred to me from without, and all the Flux and Reflux of my Mind within itself" could be turned to advantage because

> the Number of these Notices, and their Tendency, miscellaneous as they were, to one common end (*"quid sumus et quid futuri gignimur," what we are and what we are born to become; and thus from the End of our Being to deduce its proper Objects*) first encouraged me to undertake the Weekly Essay, of which you will consider this Letter as the Prospectus. (*F*, 2: 16–17)

To rescue the compiler from his presumed lassitude, Coleridge first conjoins the storehouse of study – textual excerpts – with accumulated experience and reflections. His collections are useful because they combine
different kinds of knowledge, including materials gathered by direct observation of the external world and the workings of his own mind. This
statement underscores Hess's observation that Romantic-era commonplace
books were not understood simply as a repository for received knowledge;
rather, they "embraced a transcendent epistemology that focused on the
workings of the mind itself."[52] Further, in emphasizing the mind's motions,
Coleridge engages in a distinction akin to Burke's parsing of textual examples from observed behaviors and passions: human "compositions" constitute a more manageable databank, being of a less "complex texture" than
passages taken from poets.[53] An embodied essentialism underwrites both
accounts: for Burke, passions in the mind are effects of a "violent emotion of the nerves," while for Coleridge, the mind's fluxes and observations
record "what we are and what we are born to become."[54] But where Burke
would draw a strict boundary, Coleridge cannot. Reused and recycled for
centuries, the perfect fodder for the commonplace, a line quoted from Persius's *Satires* transforms the miscellany into the end of our being.[55] The
essence of identity – the mental prerequisite for its empirical foundation –
can only be expressed by a *sententia*.

This is not, I would argue, a case of Coleridge reverting all truth to
rhetoric, as Christensen suggests. Rather, the Prospectus opens the question
The Friend would pursue beginning in 1809 and culminating in the "Essays
on Method": How does one get from the endlessly proliferating databank
of particulars to laws of nature or principles of moral and social order? This
is the avowed problem addressed in the "Essays on Method," and it is a difficulty replicated in Coleridge's analytical and critical procedures as well as
his compositional method. The solution to this multifaceted problem, the
Prospectus suggests, lies in the problem itself. If the materials of induction
always exceed the procedure's capacity for synthesis – if the example would
inevitably swallow up the thesis, derail the process, dislodge the principle –
then the materials themselves must hold the answer. Put another way,
Coleridge's practice of reiterative quoting implies that the way to stop the
gap in induction is to turn the excerpt into an aphorism, a *sententia* that
signifies beyond itself through the power of accumulated meaning.

Moments of requoting constitute alternative threads or byways through
Coleridge's works, connecting passages and topics that are quite literally
"most remote and diverse in time, place and outward circumstance" and
bringing them into "mental contiguity" (*F*, 1: 455). Spread across hundreds

of pages of multiple works, both published and unpublished, such reiterated quotations bind the "Essays on Method" to the revised and reconcep-
tualized *The Friend*. They also promote a nonlinear form of reading that has
much in common with the composite nature and structure of Coleridge's
notebooks. In my assessment, Coleridge's practice of quoting and requoting suggests that to generate principles, inductive method requires not just
a "guiding thought" from the mind, but also a mind attuned to its own
propensities and failings – a mind both conditioned by method but also
continually made into the object of scientific enquiry.

Between the opening examples of Hamlet's meditative excesses of reflection in the "Essays" and the moment of philosophical reckoning in Bacon's
"own words" with which I began this chapter, Coleridge conjoins art and
science by linking Shakespeare's method to that of the figureheads of contemporary chemistry, Humphry Davy, William Wollaston, and Charles
Hatchett. This famous chiasmus of science and literature turns on terms
familiar from the Prospectus, the lectures on literature, and the distinction between Mrs. Quickley and Hamlet that opens the "Essays." Shakespeare's "profound yet observant meditation" produces "nature idealized
into poetry" while the "meditative observation" of Davy and his contemporaries yields "poetry, as it were, substantiated and realized in nature" (*F*,
1: 471). The practitioners of experimental science might begin with observation while the imaginative poet starts with meditation or reflection –
Davy looks at the world, Shakespeare delves into himself – but each must
be modified (adjectivally) by the other, distinct in their likeness.

This careful balancing act is twice interrupted, first by a typographically set off excerpt from *Paradise Lost* (which appears in quotation marks
in the 1818 edition) and again by an italicized line in Latin from Thomas
Gale's edition of Joannes Scotus Erigena's *De divisione naturae* (1681). Both
quoted passages qualify and modify Coleridge's definition of the chemists'
inductive method: It is through their "meditative observation" that

> By some connatural force,
> Powerful at greatest distance to unite
> With secret amity things of like kind'

> we find poetry, as it were, substantiated and realized in nature: yea, nature
> itself disclosed to us, GEMINAM *istam naturam, quæ fit et facit, et creat et
> creatur*, as at once the poet and the poem! (*F*, 1: 471)

Coleridge quotes Milton extensively in *The Friend*, beginning in the first
essay with Book I, line 27 of *Paradise Lost*, and ending with this quote
from Book X, lines 246–48. While he does double back occasionally, as the

reader proceeds through Coleridge's book, he or she also proceeds through Milton's epic, finally reaching these lines in which Death speaks to Sin as both are drawn toward Paradise at the moment of the fall. Milton's "connatural force" figures the interpenetration of Shakespeare's method and the method of chemical philosophy by poetically revealing "the unity of nature in substances most unlike" (*NO*, 120). Inductive method in the sciences ought to function like the poet's methodical mind – like Milton discovering to us the affinity between Sin, Death, and the newly fallen human world. The offset quotation thus serves to textually infuse the chemist's method with its literary counterpart while staking a claim for inductive method as a "connatural," an innate property of a particular cast of mind.[56]

Quoting *Paradise Lost* here thus upholds Coleridge's earlier use of Shakespeare to introduce and promote "mental Initiative" as the prerequisite to inductive method in the sciences. The lines, however, carry the baggage of their context. In choosing the description of the moment when Death and Sin are drawn to the fallen world – the instant when opposites suddenly agree in their nature, and human sexuality and mortality is born of their likeness – Coleridge suggests how the "meditative observation" of chemistry substantiates and realizes poetry. Chemical philosophy makes poetry palpable, imbues it with solidity. If Wordsworth was waiting for science to put on a form of flesh and blood (as he suggested in the revised 1802 Preface to *Lyrical Ballads*), then Coleridge implies that science remakes poetry into substance, embodying it, or, in a more telling definition, demonstrating it and verifying it with evidence.[57] Chemistry realizes poetry, authorizing Milton's lines and revealing their truth to nature, but this is not a happy affair, since death is the inevitable result. Something of Milton's sublime mind is lost here, destroyed by the empirical base of scientific enquiry.

But the matter doesn't end here. The chiasmus built around Milton concludes with a colon, inviting the reader to go on. What follows might provide further explanation or, read another way, the chiasmus has merely prepared the reader for what succeeds the colon, the actual substance of the thought. Coleridge begins with an affirmation, "yea," but immediately turns the idea on its head: rather than poetry realized in nature we find nature disclosed to us "as at once the poet and the poem" (*F*, 1: 471). The Latin quotation is the mechanism through which this discovery is made; it is that which uncovers and unfolds what has been hidden, the secret affinity of nature and poetry. The quotation, in other words, replaces the method of experimental science – the chemists' "meditative observation" and its power to authorize and materialize poetry – with something else entirely, a definition of "the divine nature, which made and is making, both creates and is created" (F, 1: 146n.). As Coleridge noted of this passage in 1803 when he copied it into one of his notebooks, Erigena explains the created universe "as only a manifestation of the unity of God in forms."[58] Both made and making, creating and created, nature (like the poet–poem conjunction) is unified by what it manifests, that which creates but is not created. The third term outside the chiasmus, God, forms the conduit between nature and the poet, unifying both world and work.

This third term is precisely where the "Essays on Method" inevitably conclude. The final, long "Essay XI" proclaims that if he is ever to "reduce Phænomena to Principles," man must "learn to comprehend nature in himself, and its laws in the ground of his own existence" (F, 1: 511). The problem is that we may doubt "whether the Knowing of the Mind has its correlative in the Being of Nature" (F, 1: 512). To resolve these doubts requires raising the mind to the consideration of existence, but again we are stopped short: "Not TO BE, then, is impossible: TO BE, incomprehensible" – and this is the "intuition of absolute existence," something we bear witness to in our own minds, a truth that "manifests itself" as revelation and whose source is God (F, 1: 514–16). The revelation of the final cause, as Coleridge makes clear, is not something we can derive from the "organs of sense: for these supply only surfaces, undulations, phantoms"; in fact, to arrive at revelation, we must move out of "the confused multiplicity of seeing with which 'the films of corruption' bewilder us, and out of the unsubstantial shows of existence, which, like the shadow of an eclipse, or the chasms in the sun's atmosphere, are but *negations* of sight," and into "that *singleness of eye*, with which '*the whole body shall be full of light*'" (F, 1: 512). The senses, and particularly the eyes, are unreliable, likely to be deceived by natural phenomena, those facts taken for wonders. Coleridge thus returns, via the Gospel of Matthew, to empiricism's fatal flaw: no amount of meditation can rectify the sight-bound approach of Lockean empiricism. But to throw away the world of sight would not do either. Even an awakened soul, Coleridge explains by way of an intricate organic metaphor, cannot neglect the "outward and conditional causes of her growth" without which "its own productivity would have remained forever hidden from itself" (F, 1: 513–14). Without sensation, without sight of the created forms of nature, the inner eye cannot see the truth of God. Without the ground laid by the chiasmus of meditation and observation, Shakespeare and Davy, art and science, religious revelation – as the progression of the "Essays" attests – is not possible.

It would appear that Coleridge, at the end of *The Friend*, leaves his readers in the same irresolvable quandary manifested in Darwin's *The Botanic*

Garden. The mechanism of observation – the means by which instances, facts, and observations are accumulated – obscures the path to law, principle, truth, but at the same time the senses are indispensable to the process of discovery. Coleridge had, however, prepared a way around this impasse, a route paved by recycled quotations. Erigena's string of linked nouns and verbs had already appeared in *The Friend* in the first "Landing Place, or Essays interposed for Amusement, Retrospect and Preparation" (*F*, 1: 127). Here, Coleridge explains Luther's theory of apparitions, itself spun off from a story of Luther having thrown an ink-stand at the Devil while imprisoned in Wartburg castle. Coleridge argues that in one of those "rapid alterations of the sleeping with the half-waking state," Luther may have had in his mind a "full view of the Room in which he was sitting, of his writing Table and all the Implements of Study, as they really existed, and at the same time a brain-image of the Devil, vivid enough to have acquired apparent *Outness*" (*F*, 1: 140). Such a situation – in which the half-wakening mind and fluttering eyelids reproduce the sensory world while shaping and condensing "mere *thoughts* . . . into *things*, into realities" – accounts for Luther's act of hurling the ink pot at the wall, the mark of which (Coleridge claims) can still be seen there (*F*, 1: 142). The mind has written on the world with indelible ink, but this was an effect, Coleridge argues, not of a supernatural occurrence but of optical illusion, a trick played by the collusion of eye and mind.

All this would seem to confirm the unreliability of the senses, their tendency to lead us astray into delusive dream world of phantasms, a reiteration of the fantastic gothic interior of the *Biographia*'s Chapter 14. Luther was as great a Poet as ever lived, "but his poetic images were so vivid that they mastered the Poet's own mind" – like Hamlet, "he was *possessed* with them" (*F*, 1: 140). Coleridge, on the other hand, reports that he has long been in the habit of practicing such optical illusions on himself, one of which he details at length in the opening of the next essay. Not only this, but he had compiled a "whole memorandum book filled with records of these Phænomena" which would provide "facts and data for Psychology" or materials for a "theory of perception and its dependence on memory and imagination" (*F*, 1: 146). As he notes, "for persons not accustomed to these subtle notices of self observation" it would appear incredible "what small and remote resemblances . . . will suffice to make a vivid thought consubstantiate with the real object, and derive from it an outward perceptibility" (*F*, 1: 145–46). To draw out this difference, Coleridge turns to his late friend Tom Wedgwood, with whom he spent hours "watching and instantly recording these experiences of the world within us, of the

'gemina natura, quæ fit et facit, et creat et creatur!'" (*F*, 1: 146). Here, Erigena's divine nature appears as the flip side of "mere empiricism"; it is the
phantasmatic experience of the mind's play registered by the eye, an experience that can itself be carefully observed and recorded. The solution to the
quandary of sensory deception, Coleridge intimates, can be found in that
space between waking and dream, the state of half-closed eyelids where the
mind meets the world, where the eye sees what the mind makes, where
thoughts are substantiated and ghosts write on walls. Here, observation
and mediation merge, and experience can grasp the third term, the incomprehensible, God.

Coleridge locates the solution to the problem of induction – that gap
between particular facts and general principles – in human psychology,
in the mind observing the tricks it plays on itself. Self-awareness generated through self-experimentation – the very approach rejected by Hume
and Burke in preference for a textual archive – supplies the necessary
ground by which the mind can attest to the unity of things most unlike.
A number of other critics have argued for the centrality of Coleridge's self-
experimentation and his conversations with Tom Wedgwood about human
psychology in the development of his later philosophical thought. Gavin
Budge suggests that Tom Wedgwood supplied Coleridge with a "vitalist
account of the mind's activity in perception as a process of quasi-organic
assimilation of sense data."[59] Along similar lines, Noel Jackson argues that,
like many writers of the period, Coleridge considered "self-reflection as
an activity designed to reveal general, even universal laws of mankind,"
which accounts for his "self-experimental approach"; the "multitude of little experiments on sensations and my own senses" he conducted establishes
him "as at once the transcendental subject and empirical object of knowledge."[60] Coleridge's account of Tom Wedgwood in *The Friend* accords with
these assessments. Tom Wedgwood already embodied, at this early moment
in *The Friend*, the chiasmus of Shakespeare and Davy, Bacon and Plato.
He combined a "fine and ever-wakeful sense of beauty" with "the most
patient accuracy in experimental Philosophy and the profounder researches
of metaphysical science," and he "united all the spring and play of fancy
with the subtlest discrimination and an inexorable judgement" (*F*, 1: 147).
Through Tom, Coleridge indicates that the limitations of the empirical
chemist can be overcome by a mind watching itself, recording its own
motions; further, with self-analysis, the poet (or critic) can identify and
quash those excrescences of thought that might derail method's capacity
for synthesis. The active, reflective mind corrects both the eye and itself.

The particular instance of recycled quotation I've discussed here hardly
stands alone in Coleridge's vast body of writing. It is, however, a particularly

illuminating example because it occurs at a crucial moment in Coleridge's attempt to instantiate his version of induction and to argue for the centrality of the mind to the true application of Bacon's method. Coleridge's solution to the problem of induction is inextricable from the path he asks readers to follow in order to grasp the purport of the chiasmus between Davy and Shakespeare. The reader of *The Friend* only arrives at the essential component of mental self-experiment and self-reflection by unraveling the thread of quotations from Shakespeare and the chemists to Coleridge's eulogy for Tom Wedgwood two volumes and many hundred pages earlier. As with his letters to Josiah Wedgwood on Locke and empiricism, the physical separation and distance traveled between the first quotation and its reincarnation works a kind of magic, transforming a snippet of Erigena's text into a vehicle for metaphysical resolution.[61]

To be clear: Coleridge has not actually reached a resolution. Rather, he has supplied the reader with the answer before formulating the question. Tom Wedgwood is the real-world exemplar of the outcome of the chiasmus – although, of course, he is no longer among the living. In effect, Coleridge's thread of quotation leads to a solution as ghostly, as ephemeral, as the problem it purports to solve. Perhaps there is no escape from the gothic – and perhaps that is precisely the point. It is only through repeated encounters with the excesses of gothic ornament – those excrescences of smashy matter, the mind's phosphorescence – that one becomes able to grasp what would otherwise elude us, that final step in which the heap of particulars coalesces into the one. Like the Ancyent Marinere, readers need the elfish light of the coiling water-snakes, those richly attired containers of accumulated meaning which break the phantasmagoric spell – and like the Ancyent Marinere, we must be carried forward by the journey itself, a journey Coleridge describes as the "motion of a serpent, which the Egyptians made the emblem of intellectual power . . . at every step he pauses and half recedes; and from the retrogressive movement collects the force which again carries him onward. Precipitandus est *liber* spiritus, says Petronius Arbiter most happily" (*BL* 2: 14). And so on, backward and onward, snipping and quoting, *ad infinitum*.

NOTES

1 Samuel Taylor Coleridge, *Biographia Literaria*, 2 vols., James Engell and W. Jackson Bate (eds.), vol. 7 of *The Collected Works of Samuel Taylor Coleridge* (Princeton: Princeton University Press, 1986), 1: 48. Cited subsequently in text.
2 Coleridge's ire was directed more at his publishers than at Stoddart, but he did note that Stoddart's revision was characteristic of his approach to editing: "Had the Paradise Lost been presented to him in Mss, [Stoddart] would have given

the same opinion, & pulled it piecemeal & rejoined it in the same manner"
(*CL*, 4: 821).

3 Coleridge pleaded at length with Fenner to return his manuscript of the introductory essay, but when he finally extricated it from the publisher in April 1818,
he found it had been "cut up into snips so as to make it almost useless." See
CL, 4: 821, 823, 825, 860. Apparently, Stoddart's editorial method included a
literal dismemberment of the text.

4 See in particular Trevor Levere, *Poetry Realized in Nature: Samuel Taylor
Coleridge and Early Nineteenth-Century Science* (Cambridge: Cambridge University Press, 1981), which takes its title from the famous chiasmus.

5 As Christensen has argued of the *Biographia*, Coleridge needed a "*body of
thought*" on which to hang his philosophical disquisitions, "a sustaining text he
[could] cover with marginalia." Jerome Christensen, *Coleridge's Blessed Machine
of Language* (Ithaca, NY and London: Cornell University Press, 1981), p. 104.

6 As noted in Chapter 3 and discussed below, Coleridge's notebooks, like
Southey's, partake of the long-standing commonplace tradition. Editorial decisions about titles, and especially the 1850 publication of *Southey's Common-place
Book* and the edition of Coleridge's *Notebooks* (Princeton, 1957–2002), have
obscured this connection.

7 Thomas McFarland, *Coleridge and the Pantheist Tradition* (London: Oxford
University Press, 1969), p. 28.

8 Christensen, *Blessed Machine*, p. 104.

9 Ibid., pp. 120–21.

10 Anthony Harding, "Coleridge's Notebooks: Manuscript to Print to Database,"
The Coleridge Bulletin, New Series 24 (2004): 7.

11 Jillian Hess, "Coleridge's Fly-Catchers: Adapting Commonplace-Book Form,"
Journal of the History of Ideas 73.3 (2012): 465.

12 Ibid., 470–73.

13 Samuel Taylor Coleridge, *Notebooks*, 5 vols., Kathleen Colburn (ed.) (London:
Routledge, 1957–2002), 2: 2372.

14 This particular series of topics appears in *Philosophical Transactions of the Royal
Society of London* 80 (1 Jan. 1790): v–vi, iii–iv. Tabasheer is a translucent substance extracted from the joints of bamboo.

15 Levere, *Poetry Realized*, pp. 15, 86–87; Jonathan Smith, *Fact and Feeling*, p. 16.

16 Samuel Taylor Coleridge, *Lectures 1818–1819; On the History of Philosophy*,
2 vols., J. R. de J. Jackson (ed.), vol. 8 of *The Collected Works of Samuel Taylor
Coleridge* (Princeton, NJ: Princeton University Press, 2000), 2: 489. As Jackson notes, much of this section on Bacon in Lecture 11 paraphrases material
included in *The Friend*.

17 Poovey, *Modern Fact*, p. 15.

18 "recapitulate," *v.* 1a, *Oxford English Dictionary Online*, 3rd ed., Oxford University Press, http://www.oed.com.proxy.library.vanderbilt.edu/Entry/159360,
5 March 2011.

19 Despite Locke's obvious links to seventeenth-century experimental philosophy, early-nineteenth-century accounts of Bacon explicitly distanced him from

Locke's empiricist philosophy; Bacon may have given a "splendid impulse to Empiricism," but he was not an empiricist himself. It was not until the mid-nineteenth century – amid critiques leveled at inductive method as detrimental to the advance of the physical sciences – that Bacon took on the title of empiricist. See Aarsleff, *Locke to Saussure*, pp. 143, 126, and Pérez-Ramos, *Idea of Science*, pp. 25–26.

20 This strategy replicates Hume's approach when he supplies a curiously diverse lineage of philosophers who have applied induction to moral questions in the opening pages of *A Treatise of Human Nature*. See Chapter 1.

21 Jonathan Bate, *Shakespeare and the English Romantic Imagination* (Oxford: Clarendon, 1986), p. 24. Bate builds on observations made in Thomas McFarland's *Coleridge and the Pantheist Tradition*.

22 Pérez-Ramos, *Idea of Science*, p. 22.

23 For an astute analysis of the New Critical take on Coleridge's criticism, see James McKusick, *Coleridge's Philosophy of Language* (New Haven, CT: Yale University Press, 1986), p. 88. McKusick extends and irrigates critical ground laid by Paul Hamilton, *Coleridge's Poetics* (Stanford, CA: Stanford University Press, 1983).

24 McKusick, *Coleridge's Philosophy*, p. 117.

25 The 1811–1812 lectures on Shakespeare and Milton revisit and expand on the topics Coleridge had treated in the "Lectures on the Principles of Poetry" (1808), as evinced by parallel passages in Lecture 3 of 1808 and Lecture 2 of 1811 (*LL*, 1: 65, 201–03) and Lecture 3 of 1808 and Lecture 4 of 1811 (*LL*, 1: 66–69, 241–43). While little is known about the content of 1808 Lectures 5–20, a substantive record of the 1811–1812 series exists through John Collier's extensive shorthand notes. For a discussion of Collier's transcriptions and the other extant records of this series, see *LL*, 1: 159–72.

26 William Shakespeare, *Romeo and Juliet*, in *The Plays of William Shakespeare*, Vol. 20 (London, 1803), pp. 69–70. Coleridge used this heavily annotated edition of Shakespeare's plays for his 1811–1812 series of lectures; for a discussion of the critical opinions contained in the notes to this edition, see R. A. Foakes, Introduction to *Lectures 1808–1819: On Literature*, 2 vols., by Samuel Taylor Coleridge (Princeton, NJ: Princeton University Press, and London: Routledge & Kegan Paul, 1987), p. lxvii.

27 Shakespeare, *Romeo and Juliet*, p. 38.

28 Matthew Scott, "Coleridge's Lectures 1808–1819: On Literature," *The Oxford Handbook of Samuel Taylor Coleridge*, Frederick Burwick (ed.) (London: Oxford University Press, 2009), p. 190.

29 Foakes, Introduction to *Lectures 1808–1819: On Literature*, pp. liii–lxvii and 172–75. While providing a blow-by-blow description of the debate over what Coleridge "plundered" from Schlegel in his lectures, Foakes discounts the importance of similarities between Coleridge's criticism and that of late eighteenth-century critics of Shakespeare such as William Richardson, Thomas Whatley, Maurice Morgann, and Walter Whiter. Foakes asserts, "there is no reason to think that Coleridge worked his way through the lesser known

criticism of this century, but he was certainly familiar with the main picture, if not with the shadings and unusual features we now see." Ibid., pp. lxvi–lxvii.

30 Augustus William Schlegel, *A Course of Lectures on Dramatic Art and Literature*, John Black (trans.) (London: Henry G. Bohn, 1846), p. 360.

31 Ibid., p. 360. It is striking how closely Schlegel's critical approach correlates with Joshua Reynolds's advice to budding visual artists in his *Discourses on Art*; see Chapter 1.

32 Jean Marsden, *Re-imagined Text: Shakespeare, Adaptation, and Eighteenth-Century Literary Theory* (Lexington: University Press of Kentucky, 1995), p. 134.

33 Ibid., p. 128.

34 One might argue that Coleridge's practice of quoting and analyzing passages also replicates the structure of contemporary periodical reviews published in *The Monthly Magazine* and *The Critical Review*, which Coleridge contributed to in the 1790s and early 1800s. On the whole, however, periodical reviews of this period do not explicitly connect their critical assessments of particular works to the passages quoted. As discussed in Chapter 1, reviews often quote passages as exemplary "beauties" even when the review has little good to say about the work as a whole. In Coleridge's own review of Matthew Lewis's *The Monk*, for example, he levels a long, detailed, scathing critique of the novel's incapacity to evoke pleasure or to inculcate any moral truth, but concludes the review by quoting Lewis's poem "The Exile" in full as an example of an "exquisitely tender elegy." Samuel Taylor Coleridge, Review of *The Monk*, by Matthew Lewis, *Critical Review* (Feb. 1797): 194–200. Reprinting original poems from novels was a common practice in periodical reviews of the period; see Porter, "The Spectral Iamb," pp. 153–73.

35 James Engell, "The New Rhetoric and Romantic Poetics," *Rhetorical Traditions and British Romantic Literature*, Don Bialostosky and Lawrence Needham (eds.) (Bloomington: Indiana University Press, 1995), pp. 218–19.

36 Blair, *Lectures on Rhetoric*, I: 46–47. Blair's assertion is a familiar one at midcentury: as Johnson argued in the *Rambler* 158 (21 September 1751), "we owe few of the rules of writing to the acuteness of those by whom they are delivered . . . practice has introduced rules, rather than rules have directed practice." Samuel Johnson, *The Rambler*, vol. 5 (London: J. Payne, 1752), p. 189. This position is reiterated by Wordsworth and Coleridge in the Advertisement to the 1798 *Lyrical Ballads*, which argues poetry can be on any subject that interests the human mind, a fact evidenced "not in the writings of Critics, but in those of Poets themselves." Coleridge and Wordsworth, *Lyrical Ballads* (1798), p. i.

37 William Richardson, *A Philosophical Analysis and Illustration of Some of Shakespeare's Remarkable Characters*, 2nd ed. (London: Murray, 1774), p. 14. See Chapter 1 for a discussion of Hume's substitution of textual evidence for observations of human behavior as the data on which to perform induction.

38 Ibid., p. 24.

39 Ibid., pp. 24, 38, 41.

40 In his focus on character and the development of passions, Richardson's analysis of Shakespeare forms part of the critical context for Joanna Baillie's *A Series of Plays: In which it is Attempted to Delineate the Stronger Passions of the Mind*

(1798), as well as Coleridge's own *Remorse* (1813), originally drafted as *Osorio* in 1797.

41 Marsden, *Re-imagined Text*, p. 128.

42 Coleridge makes a similar distinction between modes of thought in his debate with Wordsworth's Preface to *Lyrical Ballads* in Chapter 17 of the *Biographia*: Mrs. Quickley fits the portrait of "the rustic, [who] from the more imperfect development of his faculties, and from the lower state of their cultivation, aims almost solely to convey *insulated facts* ... while the educated man chiefly seeks to discover and express those *connections* of things, or those relative *bearings* of fact to fact, from which some more or less general law is deducible" (*BL*, 2: 52–53).

43 For Coleridge's early assessment of Southey as a poet, see Chapter 4; in the *Biographia*, Coleridge expressly casts Southey as a poet of fancy (*BL*, 1: 63–64).

44 Christensen, *Blessed Machine*, p. 121.

45 Jerome Christensen, "The Method of *The Friend*," *Rhetorical Traditions and British Romantic Literature*, Don Bialostosky and Lawrence Needham (eds.) (Bloomington: Indiana University Press, 1995), p. 12. For an earlier and longer version of this argument, see Christensen, *Blessed Machine*, pp. 235–58.

46 Samuel Taylor Coleridge, *Marginalia*, Part 4, H. J. Jackson and George Whalley (eds.), Vol. 12 of the *Collected Works of Samuel Taylor Coleridge* (Princeton, NJ: Princeton University Press, 1998), p. 466.

47 Samuel Taylor Coleridge, *Specimens of the Table Talk of the late Samuel Taylor Coleridge*, Vol. 1 (London: John Murray, 1835), pp. 68–69.

48 Southey's review of *Lyrical Ballads* (1798) in the *Critical Review* tasks the "Ancyent Marinere" for having stanzas "laboriously beautiful; but in connection they are absurd and unintelligible." Robert Southey, Review of *Lyrical Ballads, with a few other poems* in *The Critical Review* 24 (Oct. 1798): 200. In a prepublication review of the *Statesman's Manual* in 1816, Hazlitt observed that *The Friend* was "so obscure, that it has been supposed to be written in cipher, and that it is necessary to read it upwards and downwards, or backwards and forwards, as it happens, to make head or tail of it. The effect is exceedingly like the qualms produced by the heaving of a ship becalmed at sea; the motion is so tedious, improgressive, and sickening." Quoted in Barbara E. Rooke, Introduction to *The Friend* by Samuel Taylor Coleridge, 2 vols. (Princeton, NJ: Princeton University Press, and London: Routledge & Kegan Paul, 1969), I: lxxx.

49 Coleridge, *Notebooks*, 2: 2372.

50 Coleridge famously ends his 13 May 1796 letter to John Thelwall with the phrase, "I absolutely nauseate Darwin's Poem," a judgment that arises from remarks on the use of adjectives in poetry (*CL*, 1: 216). Coleridge objects to the want of harmony in Darwin's verse, a condition of its decorative (rather than substantive) associations.

51 Christensen, *Blessed Machine*, pp. 168–69.

52 Hess, "Coleridge's Fly-Catchers," 465.

53 Burke, *Philosophical Enquiry*, pp. 53–54.

54 Ibid., p. 162.

55 Nineteenth-century editors of Persius had established the long legacy of this
    line, including appearances in Augustin, John of Salisbury, and Barthius; see
    Arthur John Macleane (ed.), *Decii Junii Juvenalis et A. Persii Flacci Satirae*, 2nd
    ed. rev. (London: Whittaker & Co., 1867), p. 403.
56 Seamus Perry makes a similar claim about Coleridge's use of Milton in his liter-
    ary criticism: for Coleridge, Milton's role is to "represent the sublime possibility
    of an entirely internal kind of poetic creativity." Seamus Perry, *Coleridge and
    the Uses of Division* (Oxford: Clarendon Press, 1999), p. 214.
57 "substantiate," v., *Oxford English Dictionary Online*, 2nd ed. (1989), http://www
    .oed.com.proxy.library.vanderbilt.edu/view/Entry/193058, 23 Nov. 2011.
58 Coleridge, *Notebooks*, 1: 1382.
59 Gavin Budge, "Indigestion and Imagination in Coleridge's Critical Thought,"
    Romantic Empiricism: Poetics and the Philosophy of Common Sense, 1780–1830,
    Gavin Budge (ed.) (Cranbury, NJ: Associated University Presses, 2007), p. 142.
    Budge builds on work by Alan Barnes on the importance of Tom Wedgwood's
    ideas to Coleridge's later philosophical positions. See Alan Barnes, "Coleridge,
    Tom Wedgwood, and the Relationship between Time and Space in Midlands
    Enlightenment Thought," *British Journal for Eighteenth-Century Studies* 30
    (2007): 243–60.
60 Noel Jackson, *Science and Sensation in Romantic Poetry* (Cambridge: Cam-
    bridge University Press, 2008), pp. 105, 107–08.
61 Neil Vickers develops the connection between Coleridge's philosophical letters
    to Josiah Wedgwood in 1801 and Tom Wedgwood's experiments with vision
    at greater length; see Neil Vickers, "Coleridge's Abstruse Researches," *Samuel
    Taylor Coleridge and the Sciences of Life*, Nicholas Roe (ed.), (Oxford: Oxford
    University Press, 2001), pp. 160–65.

The Final Landing Place
The Composite Incarnate

By the second and third decades of the nineteenth century, the literary composite had become both self-referential and historical. As the tenets of synthetic genius and organic growth were trumpeted by Wordsworth and Coleridge and then Hazlitt and De Quincey, authors were still hyperconscious of their compositional method and its roots in experimental science. This is obvious in Coleridge's chiasmus of Shakespeare and Davy in the "Essays on Method," and here, as in many things, he has his finger on the pulse of the times. Induction became more, not less, of a cultural force in the first half of the nineteenth century, and it was explicitly associated with the practice of quotation. In 1830, John Herschel equated Bacon's method with legitimate science, a characterization William Whewell follows in his 1840 proclamation: Bacon was "not only one of the Founders, but the supreme Legislator of the modern Republic of Science."[1] This moment in Whewell's text is telling. Before considering the value of Bacon's method for the physical sciences, Whewell notes that Bacon's aphorisms are "frequently quoted by metaphysical, ethical, and even theological writers," those who deal "with mind, with manners, with morals, with polity."[2] (Indeed, Whewell, too, had put his finger on something: Authors regularly claimed to be applying Bacon's inductive method to quotations from scripture in the heated theological debates of the 1820s to 1850s.)[3] Standing as the hallmark of legitimate scientific enquiry in the early nineteenth century, induction was also an established procedure for making knowledge from a textual archive in moral philosophy, theology, ethics, aesthetics, education, criticism, and literature. And it was then, as it is today, a response to an endless stream of print, increasing daily, monthly, yearly with the adoption of the stream press, the rolling press, stereotype printing, and a host of other technological shifts.[4]

Early-nineteenth-century authors were certainly aware of the history of inductive method, its cultural and epistemological sway, and its procedure for dealing with textual excess. They were also aware of the composite's literary history. For many authors, quoting and embedding typographically offset poems in prose or lining pages with a barge of annotation immediately raised the specter of the mixed genre texts of the previous decades, especially the experimental forms of the politically radical 1790s. The composite carried the philosophical, political, and aesthetic baggage of another time, a time when hope ran high and change was nigh. Fraught as it was even in that heady decade, the prose–verse composite was redeployed in the teens and twenties, as Coleridge and Maria Edgeworth clearly demonstrate, for quite different political and social ends: to stabilize church and state, to temper enthusiasm with hard facts. But if Keats represents the din of information overload subsiding into a "pleasing chime," others were more interested in the threat once posed by the composite. As I pointed out in the Interlude, Percy Shelley considered the annotated poem (when stripped of its material disjunctiveness) a fit container for the radical politics of *Queen Mab*, and Scott saw its potential for promoting an anti-imperialist Scottish cultural nationalism. The composite's radical leanings may have been tamped down, rolled back, covered over in the nineteenth century – but they were still there, materially, on the pages of books printed as the century turned. And those pages were a potent reminder of what had been and what had changed.

As many critics have noted, Victor Frankenstein's creature has an education lifted from Mary Shelley's own reading; his mental landscape is produced by yoking Milton's Christian verse epic, Johann Wolfgang von Goethe's sentimental prose fiction, Plutarch's prose biographies, and Volney's philosophical travel narrative. Shelley's 1831 Preface to the novel famously advertises it as her "hideous progeny," pointing to the consonance between the creature's manufacture and her own compositional process. The novel is a composite of her reading that in turn becomes the template for the creature's education. But even before his bookish education commences, the creature's mind is forged according to the steps of induction. As he records in the opening pages of his narrative, he at first experiences sensations but has "no distinct ideas" until he begins to "distinguish," to "observe with great accuracy," to "examine," reflect, and discover causes.[5] The creature starts as the quintessential Lockean blank slate, waiting to be inscribed by experience and education. As with Barbauld's Charles, the creature graduates from observation and reflection to narrative, and Victor's experiment journal provides him with a fragmentary text to annotate and fill out with the select passages from the (very limited) textual archive he acquires in his travels.

The creature's origin myth emerges from Victor's procedures of knowledge-making as recorded in his experiment book and conveyed to Walton through an extended narrative analepsis. Committing himself to chemistry, Victor reads books, attends lectures, and cultivates conversation, compiling information that he calls the "first steps towards knowledge."[6] He then decides to specialize in physiology, which leads him to fix his attention on the progress of decay, "examining and analyzing all the minutia of causation . . . until from the midst of this darkness a sudden light broke in upon me" and he discovers the cause of life.[7] As Shelley's verbs indicate, Victor has followed a slow, steady path of inductive method and his "stages of discovery were distinct and probable" yet "some miracle might have produced" his sudden epiphany. After his discovery, "all the steps by which I had been progressively led to it were obliterated, and I beheld only the result."[8] Tracing Victor's process, Shelley has described the problem of induction: The steps of collecting data, observing, examining, comparing, analyzing build up Victor's knowledge, but the leap to a synthetic principle of life requires a miracle. His discovery never, Shelley implies, should have happened.

If the creature's philosophical origins are firmly inductive, his physical body arises from Victor's application of induction to the imaginative work of composition. His imagination "exalted" by discovery and the "first enthusiasm of success," Victor begins by "collecting and arranging" his materials to construct the creature. Rather than the steady stages of his research, here Shelley focuses our attention on Victor's inner propulsion, his "breathless eagerness" and the "resistless, and almost frantic impulse" he follows until he has lost "all soul and sensation but for this one pursuit."[9] Victor is an enthusiast, a dedicatee of Baconian induction whose "extreme empiricism" generates the unremitting, monomaniacal pursuit of a single object.[10] Victor's mental state manifests in the creature's physical structure: He embodies a malignant, diseased induction, one conformable to an overactive imagination enthralled by its own power. Coleridge's assessment of Hamlet's immethodical talk pertains equally to Victor's material composition: An "undue preponderance" of method produces something "grotesque and fantastical" (*F* 1: 455).

The creature thus seems triply destined for misery. His mind is a miscellany, his philosophical origin an irresolvable "problem," his body the bastardization of empiricism. And yet there is more: The creature's knowledge base mirrors Shelley's reading, but as with Southey's footnotes or Smith's embedded poems, *how* the creature stitches textual excerpts together determines their effect on his mind. When he acquires the three books that together form his entire textual archive, he "continually studied and exercised my mind upon these histories."[11] As with Victor's study of alchemy, the creature's undirected reading propels him down the perilous path of untoward conjunctions. He adopts Werter's inflated notions of sensibility, sutures it to the condition of Milton's all-too-attractive Satan, and acts against Plutarch's history by adopting Volney's revolutionary politics and rejection of social hierarchy. To exemplify: The creature is stronger than man, can endure more physical hardship, but quickly reaches the limit of his emotional endurance. The creature conceives of an emotional breaking point because he has learned about it from Goethe: Werter argues that human nature

> has its limits. It is able to endure a certain degree of joy, sorrow, and pain, but collapses as soon as this is exceeded. The question, therefore, is, not whether a man is strong or weak, but whether he is able to endure the measure of his suffering, moral or physical . . . Observe a man in his natural, confined condition; consider how ideas work upon him, and how impressions affect him, till at length a violent passion seizes him, destroys all his powers of calm reflection, and utterly ruins him.[12]

For the creature, Werter is "a more divine being than I had ever beheld or imagined," one whose opinions he takes as a pattern for his own response to suffering and isolation. But unlike Werter, the creature does not (at first) choose suicide but rather seeks revenge on his maker, trading the cult of sensibility for Hegel's master–slave dialectic. This he adopts from Milton, whose Satan who alternately rages and almost repents, teetering between self-righteous indignation and self-loathing, but always returning to revenge at the sight of "pleasure not for him ordain'd" because "within him Hell / He brings, and round about him, nor from Hell / One step, no more than from himself can fly."[13] As with all his reading, the creature applies this internal hell "personally to my own feelings and condition": rejecting Adam, "I considered Satan as a fitter emblem of my condition; for often, like him, when I viewed the bliss of my protectors, the bitter gall of envy rose within me."[14] Having imbibed Satan's rage and envy, the creature directs it via Volney's portrait of the "strange system of human society" from which "when I heard details of vice and bloodshed . . . I turned away with disgust and loathing."[15] By selecting, compiling, and arranging bits of texts and comparing them with the record of his origins and his experience of the world, the creature teaches himself to resent his emotional isolation and to see it as an effect of the historical *longue durée* of injustice and inequality, what man has made of man. The mental and physical hell into which Victor and the creature descend in volume 3 of the novel is the result of truths arrived at by textual splicing, a process of linking by analogy so natural yet so dangerous to the infant mind. *Frankenstein* thus demonstrates the result of a mind patterned on formal mixture, where the gaps between bits of texts are stitched up by imaginative leaps and fanciful likenesses.

All of this is to say: Shelley's target in her most famous novel is the compositional method I have investigated throughout this book. Whether we consider the creature misguided or devious, Victor as clueless or callous, their twined fate prods readers to consider the consequences of induction as a procedure for both scientific enquiry and cognitive development. Inductive method, it would seem, produces monstrosity of mind and matter. Victor's methodological miracle combines with his frantic, myopic creative process to generate the creature; the creature's firmly empirical education coupled with his textual practices of selection and stitchery propels his epic fall from innocence. It would appear that Shelley rejects the composite both as a compositional process and as a formal condition of the printed book. That said, the novel clearly encourages a sympathetic response to the creature's first-person narrative, itself embedded in Victor's story as told to Walton. The embodied composite may be a threat to Victor (psychologically, physically, narratively), but the creature is not unambiguously demonized in the novel as a whole. His education is faulty because he was abandoned by his creator, and Victor's flight from the laboratory enables the creature's eventual imaginative alignment with Satan instead of Adam. Further, like the naïve Catherine Morland in *Northanger Abbey*, the creature's views on injustice, class hierarchy, and social inequality may be skewed and misapplied, but they are not wrong. Shelley's novel supports this conclusion through multiple subplots: the injustice of Justine's trial and execution, Theodore De Lacey's betrayal by Safie's father, Victor's own imprisonment for the murder of Clerval. In the novel, the composite creature is dangerous to a specific knowledge maker, one who, like Victor, creates composites and afterward abandons them without considering the consequences. It is not the composite text, but authors like Victor, that Shelley takes aim at with her moral tale. The question remains: What or who is the real-world target for Shelley's barbed critique?

After his "escape" from the grinning creature on that dreary night in November, Victor walks the streets of Ingolstadt, "impelled to hurry on" but "without any clear conception of where I was, or what I was doing." In this confused state, Victor falls into quotation: he feels

> Like one, that on a lonely road
>   Doth walk in fear and dread,
> And having once turn'd round, walks on
>   And turns no more his head:
> Because he knows, a frightful fiend
>   Doth close behind him tread.[16]

Shelley likens Victor's condition to that of the eponymous "hero" of Coleridge's "The Rime of the Ancyent Marinere," the first poem in Wordsworth and Coleridge's collaborative volume *Lyrical Ballads and a few other poems* (1798). Hurried on through a sequence of surreal, hallucinatory scenes – unable to determine where the ship is going or what is happening on it – readers certainly, as the Advertisement to the volume claimed they would, struggled with "feelings of strangeness and aukwardness."[17] This struggle was provoked by the poem's rapid shifts in form, speaker, and setting, special effects Coleridge borrowed from the fabricated narrative gaps and antiquated language of recovered or translated ballads such as those collected in Thomas Percy's *Reliques of Ancient English Poetry* (1765). The poem's formal dislocations mirror the Marinere's fate, hurried along but unable to escape the consequences of his actions. The embedded quotation thus foretells Victor's fate in the concluding chapters of Shelley's novel. Chasing and chased by the creature, Victor has become the pursuer and the frightful fiend that doth behind him tread. But the typographically offset lines of verse early in the narrative also point to the dangers of a specific compositional practice (Fig. 13). What made Coleridge's poem so disconcerting – its mixed measures, its narrative fissures, its unanchored dialogues that interrupt narrative progression, and eventually, in 1817, its marginal annotations – will haunt and hunt Victor, materialized in the form of his creature. It is the *materiality* of mixture, the intrusion of verse into prose, which Shelley uses to signal the composite's threat to its creator.

Directly after the quotation from Coleridge's "Ancyent Marinere," Victor encounters Clerval, who nurses him back to health and reawakens Victor's appreciation of nature's bounty and beauty. In contrast to the creature's sublime environs, Victor associates Clerval with "the 'very poetry of nature,'" a quotation lifted from Leigh Hunt's *Story of Rimini* (as Shelley indicated in a footnote). This reflection comes later in the novel, as Victor travels homeward after being cleared of Clerval's murder. After quoting Hunt, Victor completes his eulogy on his departed friend by quoting the final poem in the 1798 *Lyrical Ballads*, Wordsworth's "Lines written a few miles above Tintern Abbey, upon revisiting the banks of the Wye during a Tour, July 13, 1798." Victor reminisces,

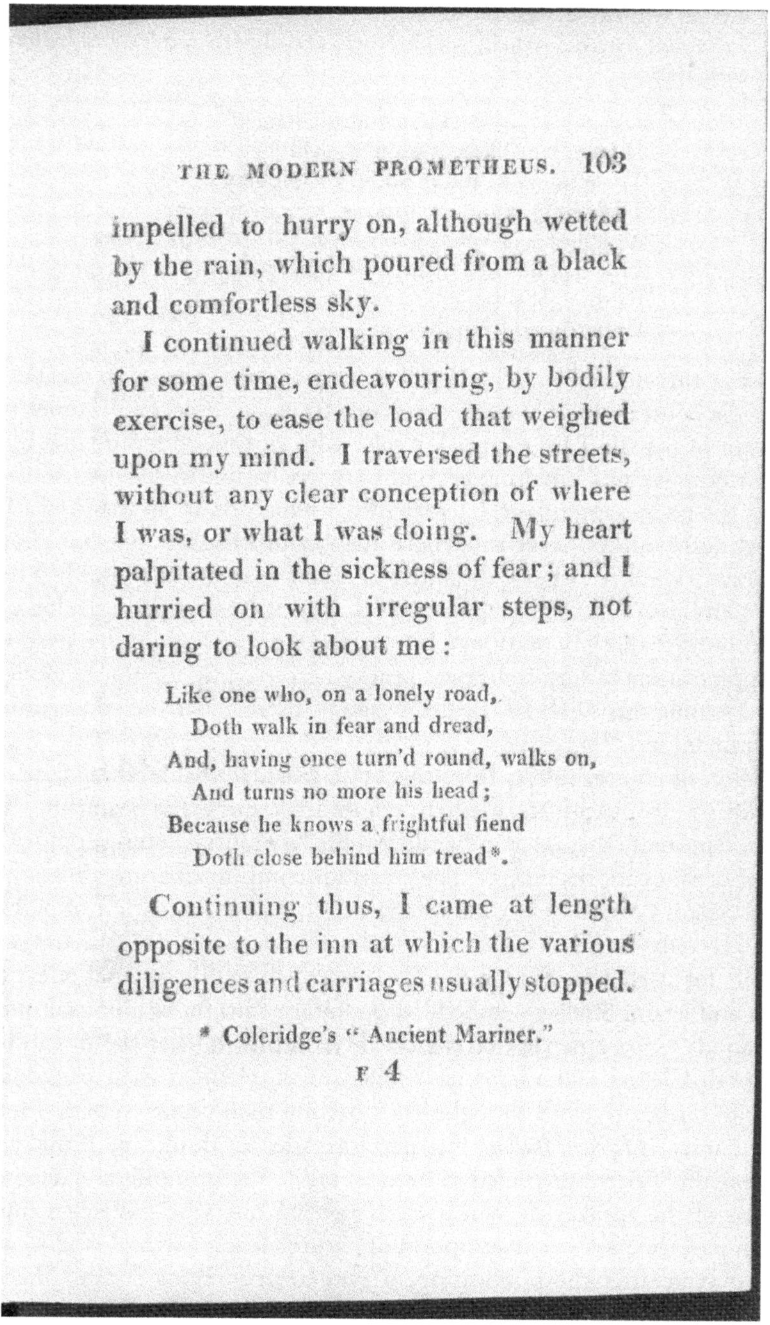

THE MODERN PROMETHEUS. 103

impelled to hurry on, although wetted by the rain, which poured from a black and comfortless sky.

I continued walking in this manner for some time, endeavouring, by bodily exercise, to ease the load that weighed upon my mind. I traversed the streets, without any clear conception of where I was, or what I was doing. My heart palpitated in the sickness of fear; and I hurried on with irregular steps, not daring to look about me :

> Like one who, on a lonely road,
>   Doth walk in fear and dread,
> And, having once turn'd round, walks on,
>   And turns no more his head;
> Because he knows a frightful fiend
>   Doth close behind him tread*.

Continuing thus, I came at length opposite to the inn at which the various diligences and carriages usually stopped.

* Coleridge's " Ancient Mariner."

F 4

Fig. 13 Mary Shelley, *Frankenstein, or the Modern Prometheus*, 3 vols. (London, 1818), 1: 103. Courtesy of University of Glasgow Library, Special Collections.

human sympathies were not sufficient to satisfy [Clerval's] eager mind. The
scenery of external nature, which others regard with admiration, he loved
with ardor:

> ———————— The sounding cataract
> Haunted me like a passion: the tall rock,
> The mountain, and the deep and gloomy wood,
> Their colours and their forms, were then to me
> An appetite: a feeling and a love,
> That had no need of a remoter charm,
> By thought supplied, or any interest
> Unborrowed from the eye.[18]

By using this quotation, Victor places Clerval's attachment to nature in
a specific context. Like Dorothy in William's poem, Clerval occupies the
position of the speaker's former self, one who consumed nature like food
but without seeking anything beyond what was visible to the eye. According to the poem's argument, Clerval always remained as "in the hour / Of
thoughtless youth," never to achieve the power of reflection that allows
the poem's speaker to hear "the still, sad music of humanity" and feel that
"sense sublime / Of something far more deeply interfused."[19] In the logic of
the recontextualized quotation, Clerval stands for the unthinking, passionate appreciation of surface beauty, beauty perceived by the senses alone –
the very thing that raises an "insurmountable barrier" between the creature
and humankind.[20]

Victor, of course, suffers from this same malady, unable to see past the
creature's hideous features. He had "selected his features as beautiful," but
insists repeatedly that once imbued with life "no mortal could support the
horror of that countenance."[21] The creature's composite nature – the product of Victor's careful selection, arrangement, and combination of parts –
provokes only fear and loathing, and he abandons his hideous progeny
to shift for itself in a human world that replicates this original rejection
again and again. Shelley's embedded quotation thus raises a crucial question about sensory perception and beauty, and introduces the possibility
that both Clerval and Victor have failed to supplement their passionate
appetite for beauty with thought, thus barring their access to basic forms
of humanity. If Lyrical Ballads instructs its reader to "think, and think, and
think again," Victor has failed to heed its call.[22] Victor stands as a debased
version of the speaker in Wordsworth's poem, one who has never quite
gotten past the passive consumption of nature's lovely forms.

Two years after the publication of Frankenstein, Percy Bysshe Shelley
would take up the problem of our perception of the beautiful and hideous

in "The Sensitive Plant" (1820), a poem that contrasts the artificial beauty of a botanic garden with the putrid, noisome, "monstrous undergrowth" that sprouts up in its ruins.[23] As the lovely "rare blossoms from every clime" rot and decay after their beautiful Lady-curator dies, "agarics and fungi with mildew and mold / Started like mist from the wet ground cold; / Pale, fleshy, – as if the decaying dead / With a spirit of growth had been animated!"[24] Like Victor's creature, these seemingly reanimated plants are heaped with disgusting imagery, forming a lurid contrast to the sensual beauty celebrated in the first and second parts of the poem. We might be liable to reject these foul animations as Mary Shelley's characters do the hideous creature, if it were not for the poem's conclusion. In the final stanza, PBS suggests that even though repulsive, leprous, filthy life forms have replaced the lovely flowers, "For love, and beauty, and delight / There is no death nor change: their might / Exceeds our organs – which endure / No light – being themselves obscure."[25] In "The Sensitive Plant," the light of truth lies beyond our faulty organs in that "something far more deeply interfused,' an understanding of nature as an interconnected totality rather merely the changeable surface of beautiful colors and forms celebrated in Victor's eulogy for Clerval.[26] Alongside PBS's later poem, we might read the embedded quotation from "Tintern Abbey" in *Frankenstein* as a pointed critique of Victor's embrace of this eye-bound aesthetic. By letting his organs of sight triumph over his "human sympathies" – by rejecting the creature because of his hideous aspect – Victor has perpetrated ruin, death, and destruction for everyone he loves. The moral for Victor as creator? Once you have made a composite, there is no going back, no matter how frightful it might appear. It, too, is love and beauty and delight.

With this observation, I'm reading these embedded quotations from "The Rime of the Ancyent Marinere" and "Tintern Abbey" as Mary Shelley's critique of the authors of the 1798 volume, and specifically a critique of their retreat from the formal and political tenets expressed in the 1798 *Lyrical Ballads* as a book. The volume's explicitly stated experimental ethos; its challenge to "our own pre-established codes of decision"; its ties to Joseph and Amos Cottle, Thomas Beddoes, Humphry Davy, John Prior Estlin, and the larger Bristol culture of radical science and social reform; its representation of social outcasts from beggars and idiots to children and abandoned mothers – all of the things that made it attractive to the politically radical Shelleys – were bound up with the book's dedication to formal mixture, its pervasive mingling of ballad and lyric, new and old, supernatural and everyday, prose and verse. Recognizing that "the strangeness of ["The Ancyent Marinere" may have] deterred readers from going on," in 1800 Wordsworth scaled back the volume's commitment to disjunction by moving "The Rime" (retitled "The Ancient Mariner, A Poet's Reverie") to the second to last position and putting "in its place some little things which would be more likely to suit the common taste."[27] By 1816–1817, when Mary Shelley was drafting *Frankenstein*, the formal and social commitments of *Lyrical Ballads* must have seemed thoroughly retracted and retrenched, supplanted by the taxonomic structure of *Poems in two volumes* (1815) and the dull morality of *The Excursion* (1814). (After reading the latter, she wrote of Wordsworth, "He is a slave."[28]) In July 1818, Mary Shelley wrote to Maria Gisborne that she would be "indignant" to hear that Coleridge was writing for "the most detestable of all papers – the Courier" and that Wordsworth had turned "ministerial" in his *Two Addresses to the Freeholders of Westmorland* (1818).[29] Promoting the conventional view of the Lake Poets' fall into reactionary conservatism, Shelley suggests that Coleridge and Wordsworth had lost, or actively eschewed, the political, social, and aesthetic ethos of experimental mixture announced and materialized in the 1798 *Lyrical Ballads*. In their retreat from the composite order, Coleridge and Wordsworth had betrayed the fight against inequality, injustice, hegemony, authoritarianism, slavery, imperialism, bloodshed, and war in pursuit of popularity, prosperity, and posterity.

What, then, did the composite mean in 1818–1825, the endpoint of this study? For Maria Edgeworth, Mary Shelley, Percy Shelley, Scott, Hemans, Thewall, Byron, Southey, Coleridge, and many others, it still posed a threat, still provoked anxiety over its potential to disrupt progress and derail thought, its propensity to conjoin and sever, to expose the maker's method. But it also held out a promise of revolution, resistance, revolt – the promise that one could still mobilize the printed page for pedagogical, political, theological, social, and aesthetic ends. And in the same way that Bacon's method stuck because it was flexible and adaptable to whatever ideological position the author might seek to support, the Romantic's snip and splice model of knowledge making lives on in our digital culture of cut and paste. Its lesson: Use your power wisely.

NOTES

1 Herschel, *Preliminary Discourse*, p. 104, and Whewell, *Inductive Sciences*, 2: 389.
2 Whewell, *Inductive Sciences*, 2: 390–91.
3 See, for example, the debate over the validity of inductive method between a reviewer for the *British Critic, Quarterly Theological Review, and Ecclesiastical Record*, Vol. 3 (London, 1828), pp. 326–63, and the author of *The Nature and Extent of Christian Dispensation with Reference to the Salvability of the Heathen*

(1827), Edward William Grinfield, who prints a reply to the article. At the midcentury, John Brande Morris enters the "Ignorantist controversy" by insisting that "reason can make an induction from a number of texts" to prove that Christ had knowledge of God's plan for man's salvation, while F. D. Maurice accuses his opponent, the Rev. Dr. Richard Jelf of Kings College Cambridge, of relying on prejudices to guide his induction from scriptural passages. John Brande Morris, *Jesus the Son of Mary: Or, The Doctrine of the Catholic Church* (London, 1851), pp. 283–85, and Frederick Denison Maurice, *The Word "Eternal" and the Punishment of the Wicked* (Cambridge, 1854), p. 10.

4 The common wooden platen press could print about 250 sheets per hour. In 1811, Friedrich Konig produced a steam-driven flatbed cylinder press which could print eight hundred copies an hour on one side. Two of Konig's presses were purchased by *The Times* of London in 1814, making it (the editors claimed) the "first newspaper printed by steam." By 1866, *The Times*'s Waller rotary steam press was pumping out twenty-five thousand sheets per hour, printed on both sides. D. C. Greetham, *Textual Scholarship: An Introduction* (New York: Garland, 1994), p. 145. For reactions to the massive uptake in printed matter, see "Proliferation" in The Multigraph Collective, *Interacting with Print*.

5 Mary Shelley, *Frankenstein, or the Modern Prometheus* [1818], 3rd ed., D. L. Macdonald and Kathleen Scherf (eds.) (Peterborough: Broadview Press, 2012), pp. 121–22.

6 Ibid., p. 77.

7 Ibid., pp. 78–79.

8 Ibid., pp. 78–79.

9 Ibid., pp. 80–81.

10 Victor's overly enthusiastic pursuit of scientific knowledge could have been patterned on a host of historical figures, as was commonly remarked in the period. For a discussion of this condition in the infamous case of the prison reformer John Howard, see Gabriel Cervantes and Dahlia Porter, "Extreme Empiricism: John Howard, Poetry, and the Thermometrics of Reform," *The Eighteenth-Century: Theory and Interpretation* 57.1 (2016): 109–13.

11 Mary Shelley, *Frankenstein*, p. 142.

12 Johann Wolfgang von Goethe, *The Sorrows of Young Werther*, trans. Victor Lange and Judith Ryan (New York: Suhrkamp, 1988), pp. 33–34.

13 John Milton, *Paradise Lost, a Poem written in Ten Books* (London, 1667), Book 8, ll. 470 and Book 4, ll. 20–23. *Historical Texts*, 9 May 2017.

14 Mary Shelley, *Frankenstein*, p. 144.

15 Ibid., p. 135.

16 Ibid., p. 85.

17 Coleridge and Wordsworth, *Lyrical Ballads* (1798), p. ii. Reviewers complained the poem was "a Dutch attempt at German sublimity," "a dark enigma," a "rhapsody of unintelligible wildness and incoherence." See "Reviews of the 1798 volume" in Samuel Taylor Coleridge and William Wordsworth, *Lyrical Ballads 1798 and 1800*, Michael Gamer and Dahlia Porter (eds.) (Peterborough: Broadview, 2008), pp. 149, 154, 158.

18 Mary Shelley, *Frankenstein*, pp. 166–67.

19 Coleridge and Wordsworth, *Lyrical Ballads* (1798), pp. 206–07.

20 Ibid., p. 156.

21 Ibid., pp. 83–84.

22 "Lines written in early spring," in Coleridge and Wordsworth, *Lyrical Ballads* (1798), p. 115.

23 Percy Shelley, "The Sensitive Plant," in *Shelley's Poetry and Prose*, 2nd ed., Donald Reiman and Neil Fraistat (eds.) (New York: Norton, 2002), p. 293, ll. 59.

24 Ibid., p. 293, ll. 62–65.

25 Ibid., p. 295, ll. 21–24.

26 Wordsworth, "Lines Written a Few Miles above Tintern Abbey," in Coleridge and Wordsworth, *Lyrical Ballads* (1798), p. 207.

27 William Wordsworth to Joseph Cottle, *The Letters of William and Dorothy Wordsworth, Vol. 1: The Early Years: 1787–1805*, Ernest De Selincourt and Chester L. Shaver (eds.) (Oxford: Oxford University Press, 1967), p. 264.

28 Mary Shelley, *The Journals of Mary Shelley*, Paula Feldman and Diana Scot-Kilvert (eds.) (Baltimore: Johns Hopkins University Press, 1987), p. 25.

29 Mary Shelley, *Letters of Mary Wollstonecraft Shelley*, vol. 1, Betty Bennett (ed.) (Baltimore: Johns Hopkins University Press, 1980), p. 75.

Bibliography

Aarsleff, Hans, *From Locke to Saussure*, Minneapolis: University of Minnesota Press, 1982

Abrams, M. H., *The Mirror and the Lamp: Romantic Theory and the Critical Tradition*, New York: Norton, 1958

Addison, Joseph, *Notes upon the twelve books of Paradise lost. Collected from the Spectator*, London, 1719, *Eighteenth Century Collections Online*, http://galenet. galegroup.com.proxy.library.vanderbilt.edu/servlet/ECCO, 12 Sept. 2010

Adolph, Robert, *The Rise of Modern Prose Style*, Cambridge, MA: MIT Press, 1968

Allan, David, *Commonplace Books and Reading in Georgian England*, Cambridge: Cambridge University Press, 2010

Anderson, John M., "'Beachy Head': The Romantic Fragment Poem as Mosaic," *Huntington Library Quarterly* 63.4 (2000): 547–74

Bacon, Francis, *The Advancement of Learning*, in vol. 3 of *The Works of Francis Bacon*, James Spedding, Robert Leslie Ellis, and Douglas Denon Heath (eds.), London: Longman et al., 1857

    The Great Instauration and the New Organon, in vol. 4 of *The Works of Francis Bacon: Translations of the Philosophical Works*, James Spedding, Robert Leslie Ellis, and Douglas Denon Heath (eds.), London: Longman et al., 1858.

    Sylva Sylvarum; or, a Natural History in Ten Centuries, 10th ed., William Rawley (ed.), London: Thomas Lee, 1676

    Of the Wisdom of the Ancients, in vol. 4 of *The Works of Francis Bacon*, James Spedding, Robert Leslie Ellis, and Douglas Denon Heath (eds.), London: Longman et al., 1857–74; Facsimile. Stuttgart–Bad Cannstatt: F. Frommann Verlag G. Holzboog, 1961–63

Baillie, Joanna, *A Series of Plays: In which it is Attempted to Delineate the Stronger Passions of the Mind*, London, 1798

Barchas, Janine, *Graphic Design, Print Culture, and the Eighteenth-Century Novel*, Cambridge: Cambridge University Press, 2003

Barbauld, Anna Letitia, *Lessons for Children, from two to three years old*, London: J. Johnson, 1787, *Eighteenth Century Collections Online*, http://galenet .galegroup.com.proxy.library.vanderbilt.edu/servlet/ECCO, 5 Sept. 2010

    Lessons for Children, of three years old, 2 Parts, London: J. Johnson, 1788, *Eighteenth Century Collections Online*, http://galenet.galegroup.com.proxy.library .vanderbilt.edu/servlet/ECCO, 5 Sept. 2010

Lessons for Children, from three to four years old, London: J. Johnson, 1788, *Eighteenth Century Collections Online*, http://galenet.galegroup.com.proxy.library .vanderbilt.edu/servlet/ECCO, 5 Sept. 2010

Barnaby, Andrew, and Lisa Schnell, *Literate Experience: The Work of Knowing in Seventeenth-Century English Writing*, New York: Palgrave Macmillan, 2002

Barnes, Alan, "Coleridge, Tom Wedgwood, and the Relationship between Time and Space in Midlands Enlightenment Thought," *British Journal for Eighteenth-Century Studies* 30 (2007): 242–60.

Barney, Richard, *Plots of Enlightenment: Education and the Novel in Eighteenth-Century England*, Stanford, CA: Stanford University Press, 1999

Bate, Jonathan, *Shakespeare and the English Romantic Imagination*, Oxford: Clarendon, 1986

Beal, Peter, "Notions in Garrison: The Seventeenth-Century Commonplace Book," *New Ways of Looking at Old Texts: Papers of the Renaissance English Text Society, 1985–1991*, W. Speed Hill (ed.), Binghamton, NY: Renaissance English Text Society, 1993

Beckford, William, "A Letter from Geneva, May 22, 1778," Beckfordiana: The William Beckford website, www.beckford.c18.net/wbgenevaletter.html, 15 August 2010

Behler, Ernst, *German Romantic Literary Theory*, Cambridge: Cambridge University Press, 1993

Bell's Common-place Book, for the pocket; form'd generally upon the principles recommended and practised by Mr. Locke, London, 1770

Benedict, Barbara, *Making the Modern Reader: Cultural Mediation in Early Modern Literary Anthologies*, Princeton, NJ: Princeton University Press, 1996

"The Paradox of the Anthology: Collecting and *Différence* in Eighteenth-Century Britain," *New Literary History* 34.2 (2003): 231–56

Berry, Christopher, *Social Theory of the Scottish Enlightenment*, Edinburgh: Edinburgh University Press, 1997

Bervin, Jen, *Nets*, New York: Ugly Duckling Presse, 2003

Bewell, Alan, "Erasmus Darwin's Cosmopolitan Nature," *ELH* 76.1 (2009): 19–48

"'Jacobin Plants': Botany as Social Theory in the 1790s," *Wordsworth Circle* 20.3 (1989): 132–39

Wordsworth and the Enlightenment: Nature, Man, and Society in the Experimental Poetry, New Haven, CT: Yale University Press, 1989

Birkerts, Sven, "The Millennial Warp," *Readings*, Saint Paul, MN: Graywolf Press, 1999

Blair, Ann, *Too Much to Know: Managing Scholarly Information before the Modern Age*, New Haven, CT and London: Yale University Press, 2010

Blair, Hugh, *Lectures on Rhetoric and Belles Lettres*, 2 vols., Edinburgh, 1783

Bolton, Carol, *Writing the Empire: Robert Southey and Romantic Colonialism*, London: Pickering & Chatto, 2007

"*Thalaba the Destroyer*: Southey's Nationalist 'Romance,'" *Romanticism on the Net* 32–33 (Nov. 2003–Feb. 2004): n.p., www.erudit.org/revue/ron/2003/v/ n32-33/009260ar.html, 19 Sept. 2010

Braudy, Leo, *Narrative Form in History and Fiction*, Princeton, NJ: Princeton University Press, 1970

British Critic, Quarterly Theological Review, and Ecclesiastical Record, vol. 3, London, 1828

Brown, Marshall, "Poetry and the Novel," *The Cambridge Companion to Fiction in the Romantic Period*, Richard Maxwell and Katie Trumpener (eds.), Cambridge: Cambridge University Press, 2008

Budge, Gavin, "Indigestion and Imagination in Coleridge's Critical Thought," *Romantic Empiricism: Poetics and the Philosophy of Common Sense, 1780–1830*, Gavin Budge (ed.), Cranbury, NJ: Associated University Presses, 2007

Buffon, Georges-Louis Leclerc, Comte de, *L'Histoire Naturelle, générale et particulière* (1744–88), www.buffon.cnrs.fr, 17 April 2011

Burke, Edmund, *A Philosophical Enquiry into the Sublime and Beautiful and Other Pre-Revolutionary Writings*, David Womersley (ed.), London and New York: Penguin, 1998

Burns, Robert, "On the late Captain Grose's Perigrinations thro' Scotland, Collecting the Antiquities of the Kingdom," *Poems, chiefly in the Scottish Dialect*, 2 vols., Edinburgh, 1793

Burroughs, William S., "Origin and Theory of the Tape Cut-Ups," *Break Through in Grey Room*, Sub Rosa Records, 2001

Butler, Marilyn, *Maria Edgeworth: A Literary Biography*, Oxford: Oxford University Press, 1972

Byron, George Gordon, *Childe Harold's Pilgrimage, A Romaunt: and Other Poems*, 3rd ed., London: John Murray, 1812

English Bards and Scotch Reviewers; A Satire, London: James Cawthorn, 1810

Calè, Luisa, *Fuseli's Milton Gallery: "Turning Readers into Spectators,"* Oxford: Oxford University Press, 2006

Carr, Nicholas, "Is Google Making Us Stupid? What the Internet Is Doing to Our Brains," *The Atlantic* (July/August 2008), www.theatlantic.com/magazine/archive/2008/07/is-google-making-us-stupid/306868/, 14 September 2014

Castle, Terry, *The Female Thermometer: Eighteenth-Century Culture and the Invention of the Uncanny*, New York and Oxford: Oxford University Press, 1995

Cervantes, Gabriel, and Dahlia Porter, "Extreme Empiricism: John Howard, Poetry, and the Thermometrics of Reform," *The Eighteenth-Century: Theory and Interpretation* 57.1 (2016): 95–119

Chandler, James, "Edgeworth and the Lunar Enlightenment," *Eighteenth-Century Studies* 45.1 (2011): 87–104

Christensen, Jerome, *Coleridge's Blessed Machine of Language*, Ithaca, NY: Cornell University Press, 1981

"The Method of *The Friend*," *Rhetorical Traditions and British Romantic Literature*, Don Bialostosky and Lawrence Needham (eds.), Bloomington: Indiana University Press, 1995

Cohen, Ralph, "On the Interrelations of Eighteenth-Century Literary Forms," *New Approaches to Eighteenth-Century Literature*, Phillip Harth (ed.), New York: Columbia University Press, 1974

Coleridge, Samuel Taylor, *Biographia Literaria, or Biographical Sketches of my Literary Life and Opinions*, 2 vols., London, 1816

  Biographia Literaria, 2 vols., James Engell and W. Jackson Bate (eds.), vol. 7 of *The Collected Works of Samuel Taylor Coleridge*, Princeton, NJ: Princeton University Press, 1983

  Collected Letters of Samuel Taylor Coleridge, 6 vols., Earl Leslie Griggs (ed.), Oxford: Clarendon Press, 1956–71

  The Friend, 2 vols., Barbara E. Rooke (ed.), vol. 4 of *The Collected Works of Samuel Taylor Coleridge*, Princeton, NJ: Princeton University Press, 1969

  Lectures 1818–1819: On the History of Philosophy, 2 vols., J.R. de J. Jackson (ed.), vol. 8 of *The Collected Works of Samuel Taylor Coleridge*, Princeton, NJ: Princeton University Press, 2000

  Lectures 1808–1819: On Literature, 2 vols., R. A. Foakes (ed.), vol. 5 of *The Collected Works of Samuel Taylor Coleridge*, Princeton, NJ: Princeton University Press and London: Routledge, 1987

  Marginalia, Part 4, H. J. Jackson and George Whalley (eds.), vol. 12 of the *Collected Works of Samuel Taylor Coleridge*, Princeton, NJ: Princeton University Press, 1998

  Notebooks, 5 vols., Kathleen Colburn (ed.), London: Routledge, 1957–2002

  "Review of *The Monk*, by Matthew Lewis," *Critical Review*, Feb. 1797

  Specimens of the Table Talk of the late Samuel Taylor Coleridge, vol. 1, London: John Murray, 1835

Coleridge, Samuel Taylor, and William Wordsworth, *Lyrical Ballads: An Electronic Scholarly Edition*, Bruce Graver and Ronald Tetreault (eds.), Romantic Circles Electronic Editions, original HTML format, August 2003

  Lyrical Ballads 1798 and 1800, Michael Gamer and Dahlia Porter (eds.), Peterborough, ON: Broadview Press, 2008

Cosgrove, Peter, "Undermining the Text: Edward Gibbon, Alexander Pope and the Anti-authenticating Footnote," *Annotation and Its Texts*, Stephen Barney (ed.), New York: Oxford University Press, 1991

Cowley, Abraham, "To the Royal Society," in *History of the Royal Society*, by Thomas Sprat, London, 1667

Crary, Jonathan, *Techniques of the Observer: On Vision and Modernity in the Nineteenth Century*, Cambridge, MA: MIT Press, 1990

Curran, Stuart, *Poetic Form and British Romanticism*, New York: Oxford University Press, 1986

d'Alembert, Jean Le Rond, *Preliminary Discourse to the Encyclopedia of Diderot*, Richard Schwab (trans.), Chicago: Chicago University Press, 1995

Darnton, Robert, *A Case for Books*, New York: Public Affairs, 2009

Darton, F. J. Harvey, *Children's Books in England*, 3rd ed., London: British Library, 1999

Darwin, Erasmus, *The Botanic Garden; A Poem, in two parts. Part I. Containing The Economy of Vegetation. Part II. Loves of the Plants. With Philosophical Notes*, London: J. Johnson, 1791

  The Botanic Garden, Part II. Containing The Loves of the Plants, A Poem with Philosophical Notes, Lichfield: J. Johnson, 1789

Collected Letters of Erasmus Darwin, Desmond King-Hele (ed.), Cambridge: Cambridge University Press, 2007

The Temple of Nature; or The Origin of Society, a Poem with Philosophical Notes (London, 1803), Martin Priestman (ed.), Romantic Circles Electronic Editions, www.rc.umd.edu/editions/darwin_temple/addnotes/addnote15 .html, August 2010

Zoonomia; or, the laws of organic life, 2 vols., London, 1794–96

Daston, Lorraine, "Baconian Facts, Academic Civility, and the Prehistory of Objectivity," *Annals of Scholarship* 8 (1991): 337–64

"Historical Epistemology," *Questions of Evidence: Proof Practice and Persuasion across the Disciplines*, James Chandler, Arnold L. Davidson, and Harry D. Harootunian (eds.), Chicago: Chicago University Press, 1995

"Marvelous Facts and Miraculous Evidence in Early Modern Europe," *Questions of Evidence: Proof Practice and Persuasion across the Disciplines*, James Chandler, Arnold L. Davidson, and Harry D. Harootunian (eds.), Chicago: Chicago University Press, 1995

Daston, Lorraine, and Peter Galison, *Objectivity*, New York: Zone Books, 2007

Davy, Humphry, *The Collected Works of Sir Humphry Davy*, John Davy (ed.), 9 vols., London, 1839–40

Dear, Peter, *Discipline and Experience: The Mathematical Way in the Scientific Revolution*, Chicago: Chicago University Press, 1995

Dear, Peter (ed.), *The Literary Structure of Scientific Argument*, Philadelphia: University of Philadelphia Press, 1991

De Bruyn, Frans, "The Classical Silva and the Generic Development of Scientific Writing in Seventeenth Century England," *New Literary History* 32.2 (2001): 347–73

de Grazia, Margreta, "Shakespeare in Quotation Marks," *The Appropriation of Shakespeare: Post-Renaissance Reconstructions of the Works and the Myth*, Jean I. Marsden (ed.), New York: St. Martin's Press, 1992

Derrida, Jacques, *Of Grammatology*, Gayatri Chakravorty-Spivak (trans.), Baltimore: Johns Hopkins University Press, 1976

"White Mythology: Metaphor in the Text of Philosophy," *Margins of Philosophy*, Alan Bass (trans.), Chicago: University of Chicago Press, 1982

DiMaria, Robert, *Samuel Johnson and the Life of Reading*, Baltimore: Johns Hopkins University Press, 1997

Drucker, Johanna, "Letterpress Language: Typography as a Medium for the Visual Representation of Language," *Leonardo* 17.1 (1984): 66–74

The Visible Word: Experimental Typography and Modern Art, 1909–1923, Chicago: University of Chicago Press, 1994

Duff, David, *Romanticism and the Uses of Genre*, Oxford: Oxford University Press, 2013

Duncan, William, *The Elements of Logick*, London, 1748, *Eighteenth Century Collections Online*, http://galenet.galegroup.com.proxy.library.vanderbilt.edu/servlet/ECCO, 20 Sept. 2010

Eddy, Matthew Daniel, "The Shape of Knowledge: Children and the Visual Culture of Literacy and Numeracy," *Science in Context* 26.2 (2013): 215–45

Edgeworth, Honora, Notebook compiled by Mrs. Honora Edgeworth, 1778, Edgeworth Papers, MS. Eng. misc. e. 1459, Bodleian Library, Oxford

Edgeworth, Maria, *Continuation of Early Lessons*, 2 vols., 3rd ed., London: R. Hunter, 1816

Early Lessons, in *The Novels and Selected Works of Maria Edgeworth*, vol. 12, Elizabeth Eger, Clíona ÓGallchoir, and Marilyn Butler (eds.), London: Pickering & Chatto, 2003

Harry and Lucy Concluded, London: Hunter, 1825

Letters to Literary Ladies, London, 1795

Notes, drafts and fair copies of published stories and educational works, Edgeworth Papers MS. Eng. misc. c. 896, Bodleian Library, Oxford, UK: n.d.

Practical Education, in *The Novels and Selected Works of Maria Edgeworth*, vol. 2, Susan Manly (ed.), London: Pickering & Chatto, 2003

Rosamond, A Sequel, London: R. Hunter, 1821

Edgeworth, Richard Lovell, "Address to Mothers," in *Continuation of Early Lessons*, 3rd ed., by Maria Edgeworth, London: R. Hunter, 1816

Poetry Explained for the Use of Young People (1802), new ed., London: R. Hunter, 1821

"Preface, Addressed to Parents," in *The Parent's Assistant* by Maria Edgeworth, *The Novels and Selected Works of Maria Edgeworth*, Elizabeth Eger and Clíona ÓGallchoir (eds.), vol. 10, London: Pickering & Chatto, 2003

Preface to *Practical Education* by Maria Edgeworth, *The Novels and Selected Works of Maria Edgeworth*, Susan Manly (ed.), vol. 11, London: Pickering & Chatto, 2003

Readings in Poetry, 2nd ed., London: R. Hunter, 1816

Edgeworth, Richard Lovell, and Maria Edgeworth, *Memoirs of Richard Lovell Edgeworth, Esq.*, vol. 2, London: R. Hunter, 1820

Ellison, Julie, "The Politics of Fancy in the Age of Sensibility," *Re-visioning Romanticism: British Women Writers, 1776–1837*, Carol Shiner Wilson and Joel Haefner (eds.), Philadelphia: University of Philadelphia Press, 1994

Enfield, William, *The Speaker: or, Miscellaneous Pieces, selected from the best English writers*, London: Joseph Johnson, 1774, *Eighteenth Century Collections Online*, http://galenet.galegroup.com.proxy.library.vanderbilt.edu/servlet/ECCO, 10 October 2010

Engell, James, *The Creative Imagination: Enlightenment to Romanticism*, Cambridge, MA: Harvard University Press, 1981

"The New Rhetoric and Romantic Poetics," *Rhetorical Traditions and British Romantic Literature*, Don Bialostosky and Lawrence Needham (eds.), Bloomington: Indiana University Press, 1995

Fairer, David, *Organising Poetry: The Coleridge Circle, 1790–1798*, Oxford: Oxford University Press, 2009

Favret, Mary, "Telling Tales about Genre: Poetry in the Romantic Novel," *Studies in the Novel* 26.2 (1994): 153–72

Ferguson, Adam, *An Essay on the History of Civil Society*, Edinburgh, 1767, *Eighteenth Century Collections Online*, http://galenet.galegroup.com.proxy.library.vanderbilt.edu/servlet/ECCO, 10 October 2010

Ferris, Ina, and Paul Keen, "Introduction: Towards a Bookish Literary History," *Bookish Histories: Books, Literature, and Commercial Modernity, 1700–1900*, Ina Ferris and Paul Keen (eds.), New York: Palgrave Macmillan, 2009

Ferris, Ina, "Antiquarian Authorship: D'Israeli's Miscellany of Literary Curiosity and the Question of Secondary Genres" *Studies in Romanticism* 45.4 (2006): 523–42

Fielding, Henry, *The History of the Adventures of Joseph Andrews*, Edinburgh, 1767
   The History of Tom Jones, a Foundling, 4 vols., London, 1749

Foakes, R. A., Introduction to *Lectures 1808–1819: On Literature* by Samuel Taylor Coleridge, 2 vols., Princeton, NJ: Princeton University Press and London: Routledge & Kegan Paul, 1987

Foucault, Michel, *The Order of Things: An Archaeology of the Human Sciences*, New York: Routledge, 1994

Fowler, Alastair, *Kinds of Literature: An Introduction to the Theory of Genres and Modes*, Oxford: Oxford University Press, 1985
   "The Silva Tradition in Jonson's *The Forrest*," *Poetic Traditions of the English Renaissance*, Maynard Mack and George deForest Lord (eds.), New Haven, CT and London: Yale University Press, 1982

Fraistat, Neil, "The Material Shelley: Who Gets the Finger in Queen Mab?" *Wordsworth Circle* 33.1 (2002), 33–36

Fulford, Tim, "Coleridge, Darwin, Linnaeus: The Sexual Politics of Botany," *Wordsworth Circle* 28 (1997): 124–30
   "Heroic Voyages and Superstitious Natives: Southey's Imperialist Ideology," *Studies in Travel Writing* 2.1 (1998): 46–64
   Landscape, Liberty, and Authority: Poetry, Criticism and Politics from Thomson to Wordsworth, Cambridge: Cambridge University Press, 1996
   "Pagodas and Pregnant Throes: Orientalism, Millenarianism and Robert Southey," *Romanticism and Millenarianism*, Tim Fulford (ed.), New York: Palgrave, 2002

Fuseli, Henry, *The Nightmare* (1781), Detroit: Detroit Institute of Arts

Gamer, Michael, "Laureate Policy," *Wordsworth Circle* 42.1 (2011): 42–45

Gaskell, Philip, *A New Introduction to Bibliography*, New Castle, DE: Oak Knoll Press, 1995

Genette, Gerard, *Paratexts: Thresholds of Interpretation*, Cambridge: Cambridge University Press, 1987

George, Jacqueline, "Public Reading and Lyric Pleasure: Eighteenth Century Elocutionary Debates and Poetic Practices," *ELH* 76.2 (2009): 371–97

Gerard, Alexander, *An Essay on Genius*, London, 1774

Gigante, Denise, *Life: Organic Form and Romanticism*, New Haven, CT: Yale University Press, 2009

Gilmore, John, Introduction to *The Poetics of Empire: A Study of James Grainger's* The Sugar-Cane *(1764)*, London: Athlone Press, 2000

Goethe, Johann Wolfgang von, *The Sorrows of Young Werther*, Victor Lange and Judith Ryan (trans.), New York: Suhrkamp, 1988

Goldsmith, Oliver, *Beauties of English Poesy*, London, 1767
   History of the Earth and Animated Nature, London, 1774

Golinski, Jan, *British Weather and the Climate of Enlightenment*, Chicago and London: University of Chicago Press, 2007

Grafton, Anthony, *The Footnote: A Curious History*, Cambridge, MA: Harvard University Press, 1997

Grainger, James, *The Sugar Cane: A Poem in Four Books, with notes*, London: R. and J. Dodsley, 1764

Gray, Thomas, *Poems, a new edition*, London: J. Dodsley, 1768

Gray, Thomas, *The Poems of Mr. Gray. To which are prefixed Memoirs of his life and writings by W. Mason, M.A.*, London, 1775

Greetham, D. C., *Textual Scholarship: An Introduction*, New York: Garland, 1994

Groom, Nick, *The Making of Percy's Reliques*, Oxford: Oxford University Press, 1999

Hackel, Heidi Brayman, *Reading Material in Early Modern England: Print, Gender, and Literacy*, Cambridge: Cambridge University Press, 2005

Hamilton, Paul, *Coleridge's Poetics*, Stanford, CA: Stanford University Press, 1983

Harden, Elizabeth, *Maria Edgeworth*, Boston: Twayne, 1984

Hardie, Philip R., *The Epic Successors of Virgil: A Study in the Dynamics of a Tradition*, Cambridge: Cambridge University Press, 1993

Harding, Anthony, "Coleridge's Notebooks: Manuscript to Print to Database," *The Coleridge Bulletin*, New Series 24 (2004): 1–10

Haskell, Yasmin, "Religion and Enlightenment in the Neo-Latin Reception of Lucretius," *The Cambridge Companion to Lucretius*, Stuart Gillespie and Philip Hardie (eds.), Cambridge: Cambridge University Press, 2007, www.cambridge.org/core/what-we-publish/collections/cambridge-companions, 31 July 2010

Havens, Earle (ed.), *"Of Common Places, or Memorial Books: A Seventeenth-Century Manuscript from the James Marshall and Marie-Louise Osborn Collection,"* New Haven, CT: Yale University Press, 2001

Heringman, Noah, *Romantic Rocks, Aesthetic Geology*, Ithaca, NY: Cornell University Press, 2004

Heringman, Noah (ed.), *Romantic Science: The Literary Forms of Natural History*, Albany: State University of New York, 2003

Herschel, John Frederick William, *Preliminary Discourse on the Study of Natural Philosophy*, London, 1833

Hess, Jillian, "Coleridge's Fly-Catchers: Adapting Commonplace-Book Form," *Journal of the History of Ideas* 73.3 (2012): 463–83

Horace, *Q. Horatius Flaccus, ex recensione & cum notis atque emendationibus Richardi Bentleii*, Richard Bentley (ed.), Cambridge, 1711

Horrocks, Ingrid, "'Her Ideas Arranged Themselves': Re-membering Poetry in Radcliffe," *Studies in Romanticism* 47.4 (2008): 507–27

Hume, David, *An Enquiry concerning Human Understanding*, 1772, Tom L. Beauchamp (ed.), Oxford: Oxford University Press, 1999

   A Treatise of Human Nature: Being an Attempt to Introduce the Experimental Method of Reasoning into Moral Subjects, 3 vols., London, 1739–40

Hunter, J. Paul, *Before Novels: The Cultural Contexts of Eighteenth-Century English Fiction*, New York: Norton, 1990

Jackson, J. R. de J. (ed.), *Coleridge: The Critical Heritage*, London: Routledge & K. Paul, 1970

Jackson, Noel, "Rhyme and Reason: Erasmus Darwin's Romanticism," *Modern Language Quarterly: A Journal of Literary History* 70.2 (2009): 171–94

  Science and Sensation in Romantic Poetry, Cambridge: Cambridge University Press, 2008

James, Josh, "How Much Data Is Created Every Minute?" 8 June 2012, DOMO, www.domo.com/blog/2012/06/how-much-data-is-created-every-minute/, 10 October 2014

Johns, Adrian, *The Nature of the Book: Print and Knowledge in the Making*, Chicago: University of Chicago Press, 2000

Johnson, Samuel, *The Lives of the Most Eminent English Poets; with Critical Observations on their Works*, vol. 1 of 4, London, 1781, *Eighteenth Century Collections Online*, http://galenet.galegroup.com.proxy.library.vanderbilt.edu/servlet/ECCO, 11 May 2011

  "Preface to Pope," vol. 7 of *Prefaces, Biographical and Critical, to the Works of the English Poets*, London: J. Nichols, 1781, *Eighteenth Century Collections Online*, http://find.galegroup.com.proxy.library.vanderbilt.edu/ecco, 15 April 2011

  The Rambler, 6 vols., London: J. Payne, 1752

Jones, Richard Foster, "Science and English Prose Style in the Third Quarter of the Seventeenth Century," *The Seventeenth Century: Studies in the History of English Thought and Literature from Bacon to Pope*, Stanford, CA: Stanford University Press, 1951

Jones, William, *The Works of Sir William Jones*, 6 vols., London: G. G. and J. Robinson, 1799

Jordanova, Ludmilla, *Sexual Visions: Images of Gender in Science and Medicine between the Eighteenth and Twentieth Centuries*, Madison: University of Wisconsin Press, 1989

Kames, Henry Home, Lord, *Elements of Criticism*, 2 vols., 3rd ed., Edinburgh, 1765

Keats, John, *Keats' Poetry and Prose*, Jeffrey Cox (ed.), New York and London: Norton, 2009

Kelley, Theresa, *Reinventing Allegory*, Cambridge: Cambridge University Press, 1997

King-Hele, Desmond, *Doctor of Revolution: The Life and Genius of Erasmus Darwin*, New York: Faber & Faber, 1977

  Erasmus Darwin and the Romantic Poets, New York: St. Martin's Press, 1986

Kirkley, Harriet, *A Biographer at Work: Samuel Johnson's Notes for the "Life of Pope,"* Lewisburg: Bucknell University Press, 2002

Klancher, Jon, *Transfiguring the Arts and Sciences: Knowledge and Cultural Institutions in the Romantic Age*, Cambridge: Cambridge University Press, 2014

  "Wild Bibliography: The Rise and Fall of Book History in Nineteenth-Century Britain," *Bookish Histories: Books, Literature, and Commercial Modernity,*

1700–1900, Ina Ferris and Paul Keen (eds.), New York: Palgrave Macmillan, 2009

Knox, Vicesimus, *Elegant Extracts in Prose, a new edition*, London, 1784

Labbe, Jacqueline, *Charlotte Smith: Romanticism, Poetry and the Culture of Gender*, Manchester: Manchester University Press, 2003

Law, Jules David, *The Rhetoric of Empiricism: Languages and Perception from Locke to I. A. Richards*, Ithaca, NY: Cornell University Press, 1993

Leask, Nigel, *British Romantic Writers and the East*, Cambridge: Cambridge University Press, 1992

Levere, Trevor H., *Poetry Realized in Nature: Samuel Taylor Coleridge and Early Nineteenth-Century Science*, Cambridge: Cambridge University Press, 2002

Levine, Joseph, *Humanism and History: Origins of Modern English Historiography*, Ithaca, NY: Cornell University Press, 1987

Levinson, Marjorie, *The Romantic Fragment Poem: A Critique of Form*, Chapel Hill, NC and London: University of North Carolina Press, 1986

Linné, Carl von, *A System of Vegetables, according to their classes genera orders species with their characters and differences*, Botanical Society at Lichfield (trans.), 2 vols., Lichfield, 1783, *Eighteenth Century Collections Online*, http://galenet .galegroup.com.proxy.library.vanderbilt.edu/servlet/ECCO, 5 Aug. 2010

Lipking, Lawrence, *Ordering of the Arts in Eighteenth-Century England*, Princeton, NJ: Princeton University Press, 1970

Llana, James, "Natural History and the *Encyclopédie*," *Journal of the History of Biology* 33.1 (2000): 1–25

Locke, John, *An Essay concerning Human Understanding*, Roger Woolhouse (ed.), New York: Penguin, 1997

Logan, James Venable, *The Poetry and Aesthetics of Erasmus Darwin*, Princeton, NJ: Princeton University Press, 1936

Lyon, John and Phillip R. Sloan (eds. and trans.), *From Natural History to the History of Nature: Readings from Buffon and His Critics*, Notre Dame, IN and London: University of Notre Dame Press, 1981

Mack, Ruth, "Horace Walpole and the Objects of Literary History," *ELH* 75.2 (2008): 367–87

Mackey, Nathaniel, "Sight-Specific, Sound-Specific," in *Paracritical Hinge: Essays, Talks, Notes, Interviews*, Madison: University of Wisconsin Press, 2005

Macleane, Arthur John (ed.), *Decii Junii Juvenalis et A. Persii Flacci Satirae*, 2nd ed. rev., London: Whittaker & Co., 1867

Madden, Lionel (ed.), *Robert Southey: The Critical Heritage*, New York: Routledge, 1995

Majeed, Javed, *Ungoverned Imaginings: James Mill's* The History of British India *and Orientalism*, Oxford: Clarendon, 1992

Manning, Susan, "Antiquarianism, the Scottish Science of Man, and the Emergence of Modern Disciplinarity," *Scotland and the Borders of Romanticism*, Leith Davis, Ian Duncan, and Janet Sorensen (eds.), Cambridge: Cambridge University Press, 2004

Markley, Robert, *Fallen Languages: Crises of Representation in Newtonian England, 1660–1740*, Ithaca, NY: Cornell University Press, 1993

Marsden, Jean, *The Re-imagined Text: Shakespeare, Adaptation, and Eighteenth-Century Literary Theory*, Lexington: University Press of Kentucky, 1995.

Maurice, Frederick Denison, *The Word "Eternal" and the Punishment of the Wicked*, Cambridge, 1854

McCarthy, William, *Anna Letitia Barbauld: Voice of the Enlightenment*, Baltimore: Johns Hopkins University Press, 2008

McFarland, Thomas, *Coleridge and the Pantheist Tradition*, Oxford: Clarendon, 1969

  Romanticism and the Forms of Ruin: Coleridge, Wordsworth and the Modalities of Fragmentation, Princeton, NJ: Princeton University Press, 1981

McGann, Jerome, "How to Read a Book," *The Textual Condition*, Princeton, NJ: Princeton University Press, 1991

McKenzie, D. F., "Typography and Meaning: The Case of William Congreve," *Making Meaning: "Printers of the Mind" and Other Essays*, Peter D. McDonald and Michael F. Suarez, S. J. (eds.), Amherst: University of Massachusetts Press, 2002

McKusick, James, *Coleridge's Philosophy of Language*, New Haven, CT: Yale University Press, 1986

McNeil, Maureen, *Under the Banner of Science: Erasmus Darwin and His Age*, Manchester: Manchester University Press, 1987

Merchant, Carolyn, *The Death of Nature: Women, Ecology and the Scientific Revolution*, New York: Harper Collins, 1980

Merleau-Ponty, Maurice, *Prose of the World*, Claude Lefort (ed.), John O'Neill (trans.), Evanston: Northwestern University Press, 1973

Millgate, Jane, "Scott's Lay of the Last Minstrel: The History of a Book," *European Romantic Review* 13.3 (2002): 225–38

Milton, John, *Paradise Lost, a Poem written in Ten Books*, London, 1667, historicaltexts.jisc.ac.uk, 9 May 2017

Momigliano, Arnaldo, "Gibbon's Contribution to Historical Method," *Contributo alla storia degli studi classici*, Rome, 1955

More, Hannah, *Strictures on the Modern System of Female Education*, 1799, in *Selected Writings of Hannah More*, Robert Hole (ed.), London: William Pickering, 1996

Morgan, J., *A Complete History of Algiers*, 2 vols., London, 1728

Morris, John Brande, *Jesus the Son of Mary: Or, The Doctrine of the Catholic Church*, London, 1851

Multigraph Collective, *Interacting with Print: Elements of Reading in the Era of Print Saturation*, Chicago: University of Chicago Press, 2018

Myers, Mitzi, "Socializing Rosamond: Educational Ideology and Fictional Form," *Children's Literature Association Quarterly* 14.2 (1989): 52–58

Newbery, John, *The History of Little Goody Two-Shoes*, London: T. Carnan and J. Newbery, 1772, *Eighteenth Century Collections Online*, http://galenet.galegroup.com.proxy.library.vanderbilt.edu/servlet/ECCO, 5 Sept. 2010

A Little Pretty Pocket-Book, Intended for the Instruction and Amusement of Little Master Tommy, and Pretty Miss Polly, 10th ed., London: J. Newbery, 1760

New Commonplace Book, A, London, 1799

Novalis, *Notes for a Romantic Encyclopedia*, David Wood (trans. and ed.), Albany: State University of New York Press, 2007

Ong, Walter, *Orality and Literacy: The Technologizing of the Word*, London and New York: Routledge, 2002

Oxford English Dictionary, 2nd ed., 1989, Oxford: Oxford University Press, public. oed.com/page-tags/oed-online/

Packham, Catherine, "The Science and Poetry of Animation: Personification, Analogy, and Erasmus Darwin's *Loves of the Plants*," *Romanticism* 10 (2004): 191–208

Parker, David Reed, *The Commonplace Book in Tudor England*, Lannam, MD: University Press of America, 1998

Pascoe, Judith, "Female Botanists and the Poetry of Charlotte Smith," *Re-Visioning Romanticism: British Women Writers, 1776–1837*, Carol Shiner Wilson and Joel Haefner (eds.), Philadelphia: University of Pennsylvania Press, 1994

The Hummingbird Cabinet, Ithaca, NY: Cornell University Press, 2006

Peacock, Thomas, "The Four Ages of Poetry," in *Peacock's Four Ages of Poetry, Shelley's Defense of Poetry, Browning's Essay on Shelley*, H. F. B. Brett-Smith (ed.), Boston: Houghton Mifflin, 1921

Percy, Thomas, *Reliques of Ancient English Poetry*, 3 vols., London: Dodsley, 1765

Pérez-Ramos, Antonio, "Bacon's Forms and the Maker's Knowledge Tradition," *Cambridge Companion to Bacon*, Markku Peltonen (ed.), Cambridge: Cambridge University Press, 1996

Francis Bacon's Idea of Science and the Maker's Knowledge Tradition, Oxford and New York: Clarendon, Oxford University Press, 1988

Perry, Seamus, *Coleridge and the Uses of Division*, Oxford: Clarendon Press, 1999

Philosophical Transactions, of the Royal Society of London 80 (1 Jan. 1790)

Pickering, Samuel, *John Locke and Children's Books in Eighteenth-Century England*, Knoxville: University of Tennessee Press, 1981

Piggott, Stuart, *Ancient Britons and the Antiquarian Imagination*, New York: Thames and Hudson, 1989

Piper, Andrew, *Book Was There: Reading in Electronic Times*, Chicago: University of Chicago Press, 2012

Dreaming in Books: The Making of the Bibliographic Imagination in the Romantic Age, Chicago: University of Chicago Press, 2009

Pocock, J. G. A., "Enthusiasm: The Antiself of Enlightenment," *The Certainty of Doubt*, Miles Fairburn and W. H. Oliver (eds.), Wellington: Victoria University Press, 1996

Poovey, Mary, *A History of the Modern Fact: Problems of Knowledge in the Sciences of Wealth and Society*, Chicago: University of Chicago Press, 1998

Pope, Alexander, *The Dunciad Variorum*, London: A Dod, 1729

An Essay on Man, Enlarged and improved by the author. With notes by William Warburton, M.A., London, 1745

The Rape of the Lock: A Herio-Comical Poem, London, 1714

Porter, Dahlia, "From Nosegay to Specimen Cabinet: Charlotte Smith and the Labour of Collecting," *Charlotte Smith in British Romanticism*, Jacqueline Labbe (ed.), London: Pickering & Chatto, 2008, 29–44

"The Spectral Iamb: The Poetic Afterlives of the Late Eighteenth-Century Novel," *The Afterlives of Eighteenth-Century Fiction*, Daniel Cook and Nicholas Seager (eds.), Cambridge: Cambridge University Press, 2015

Pratt, Lynda, "Revising the National Epic: Coleridge, Southey and Madoc," *Romanticism: The Journal of Romantic Culture and Criticism* 2.2 (1996): 149–62

Priestman, Martin, Introduction, *The Temple of Nature; or the Origin of Society*, by Erasmus Darwin, Romantic Circles Electronic Editions, 2006, Section 8, www.rc.umd.edu/editions/darwin_temple/intro.html, 15 August 2010

Price, Leah, *The Anthology and the Rise of the Novel*, Cambridge: Cambridge University Press, 2000

Primer, Irwin, "Erasmus Darwin's *Temple of Nature*: Progress, Evolution, and the Eleusinian Mysteries," *Journal of the History of Ideas* 25.1 (1964): 58–76

Q. Horatius Flaccus, Ex Recensione et cum Notis Atque Emendationibus Richardi Bentlii, Leipzig, 1826

Radcliffe, Ann, *The Mysteries of Udolpho, A Romance, Interspersed with some Pieces of Poetry*, 4 vols., London, 1794

Reddick, Alan, *The Making of Johnson's Dictionary, 1746–1773*, Cambridge and New York: Cambridge University Press, 1990

Rajan, Balachandra, "Monstrous Mythologies: Southey and *The Curse of Kehama*," *European Romantic Review* 9.2 (1998): 201–16

Rajan, Tilottama, "The Encyclopedia and the University of Theory: Idealism and the Organization of Knowledge," *Textual Practice* 21.2 (2007): 335–58

"Spirit's Psychoanalysis: Natural History, the History of Nature and Romantic Historiography," *European Romantic Review* 14.2 (2003): 187–96

Reid, Thomas, *Essays on the Intellectual Powers of Man*, Edinburgh, 1785

An Inquiry into the Human Mind, on the Principles of Common Sense, 2nd ed., Edinburgh, 1765

Reiss, Timothy, *Discourse of Modernism*, Ithaca, NY: Cornell University Press, 1982

Reynolds, Joshua, *Discourses on Art*, Robert R. Wark (ed.), New Haven, CT: Yale University Press, 1997

Richardson, Alan, *British Romanticism and the Science of the Mind*, Cambridge: Cambridge University Press, 2001

Literature, Education, and Romanticism, Cambridge: Cambridge University Press, 1994

Richardson, William, *A Philosophical Analysis and Illustration of Some of Shakespeare's Remarkable Characters*, 2nd ed., London: Murray, 1774

Ritterbush, Philip, *Overtures to Biology: The Speculations of Eighteenth-Century Naturalists*, New Haven, CT: Yale University Press, 1964

Robbins, Sarah, "Lessons for Children and Teaching Mothers: Mrs. Barbauld's Primer for the Textual Construction of Middle-Class Domestic Pedagogy," *The Lion and the Unicorn* 17.2 (1993): 135–51

Roberts, Daniel Sanjiv, Introduction to *The Curse of Kehama* by Robert Southey, vol. 4 of *The Poetical Works of Robert Southey*, London: Pickering & Chatto, 2004

Roger, Jacques, *Buffon: A Life in Natural History*, Sarah Lucille Bonnefoi (trans.), Ithaca, NY: Cornell University Press, 1997

Rooke, Barbara E., Introduction to *The Friend* by Samuel Taylor Coleridge, 2 vols., vol. 4 of *The Collected Works of Samuel Taylor Coleridge*, Princeton, NJ: Princeton University Press, 1969

Rowland, Ann Wierda, "Romantic Poetry and the Romantic Novel," *Cambridge Companion to British Romantic Poetry*, James Chandler and Maureen McLane (eds.), Cambridge: Cambridge University Press, 2008

Ruston, Sharon, *Shelley and Vitality*, New York: Palgrave Macmillan, 2005

Ruwe, Donelle, "Charlotte Smith's Sublime: Feminine Poetics, Botany, and *Beachy Head*," *Prism(s): Essays in Romanticism*, 7 (1999): 117–32

Saglia, Diego, "Words and Things: Southey's East and the Materiality of Oriental Discourse," *Robert Southey and the Contexts of English Romanticism*, Lynda Pratt (ed.), Aldershot: Ashgate, 2006

Sargent, Rose-Mary, *The Diffident Naturalist: Robert Boyle and the Philosophy of Experiment*, Chicago: University of Chicago Press, 1995

Schiebinger, Londa, *The Mind Has No Sex? Women in the Origins of Modern Science*, Cambridge, MA: Harvard University Press, 1989

Schildknecht, Christiane, "Experiments with Metaphors: On the Connection between Scientific Method and Literary Form in Francis Bacon," *From a Metaphorical Point of View: A Multidisciplinary Approach to the Cognitive Content of Metaphor*, Zdravko Radman (ed.), Berlin and New York: de Gruyter, 1995

Schlegel, Augustus William, *A Course of Lectures on Dramatic Art and Literature*, John Black (trans.), London: Henry G. Bohn, 1846

Schmidgen, Wolfram, *Exquisite Mixture: The Virtues of Impurity in Early Modern England*, Philadelphia: University of Pennsylvania Press, 2013

Schoenfield, Mark, *British Periodicals and Romantic Identity: The "Literary Lower Empire,"* New York: Palgrave Macmillan, 2009

Schuster, John A., and Richard R. Yeo, Introduction, *The Politics and Rhetoric of Scientific Method*, John A. Schuster and Richard R. Yeo (eds.), Dordrecht: D. Reidel, 1986

Scott, Matthew, "Coleridge's Lectures 1808–1819: On Literature," *The Oxford Handbook of Samuel Taylor Coleridge*, Frederick Burwick (ed.), New York: Oxford University Press, 2009

Seward, Anna, *Letters of Anna Seward: Written between the Years 1784 and 1807*, 6 vols., Edinburgh: Constable, 1811

Sewell, Elizabeth, *The Orphic Voice: Poetry and Natural History*, New Haven, CT: Yale University Press, 1960

Shakespeare, William, *Romeo and Juliet*, vol. 20 of *The Plays of William Shakespeare*, London, 1803

Shapin, Steven, and Simon Schaffer, *Leviathan and the Air-Pump: Hobbes, Boyle, and the Experimental Life*, Princeton, NJ: Princeton University Press, 1985

Sharafuddin, Mohammed, *Islam and Romantic Orientalism: Literary Encounters with the Orient*, London: I. B. Tauris, 1994

Shelley, Mary, *Frankenstein, or the Modern Prometheus*, 3 vols., London, 1818

   Frankenstein, or the Modern Prometheus [1818], 3rd ed., D. L. Macdonald and Kathleen Scherf (eds.), Peterborough, ON: Broadview Press, 2012

   Journals of Mary Shelley, Paula Feldman and Diana Scot-Kilvert (eds.), Baltimore: Johns Hopkins University Press, 1987

   Letters of Mary Wollstonecraft Shelley, vol. 1, Betty Bennett (ed.), Baltimore: Johns Hopkins University Press, 1980

Shelley, Percy, *The Collected Letters of Percy Shelley*, 2 vols., Frederick L. Jones (ed.), Oxford: Clarendon, 1964

   Queen Mab; A Philosophical Poem: with notes, London: P. B. Shelley, 1813

   Shelley's Poetry and Prose, 2nd ed., Donald Reiman and Neil Fraistat (eds.), New York: Norton, 2002

Shteir, Ann, *Cultivating Women, Cultivating Science: Flora's Daughters and Botany in England 1760–1860*, Baltimore: Johns Hopkins University Press, 1996

Simpson, David, *Romanticism, Nationalism and the Revolt against Theory*, Chicago: University of Chicago Press, 1993

Siskin, Clifford, and William Warner, "This Is Enlightenment: An Invitation in the Form of an Argument," *This Is Enlightenment*, Clifford Siskin and William Warner (eds.), Chicago: University of Chicago Press, 2010

Smellie, William, *Natural History, General and Particular, by the Count de Buffon*, Edinburgh, 1780–85

Smith, Charlotte, *Beachy Head: With Other Poems*, London, 1807

   The Collected Letters of Charlotte Smith, Judith Phillips Stanton (ed.), Bloomington: Indiana University Press, 2003

   Conversations Introducing Poetry, in *The Works of Charlotte Smith*, vol. 13, Judith Pascoe (ed.), London: Pickering & Chatto, 2007

   Desmond, A Novel, 2nd ed., London, 1792

   Elegiac Sonnets, 3rd ed., London: Dodsley, Gardnew and Bew, 1786

   Elegiac Sonnets and other essays, 2nd ed., Chichester, 1784

   Minor Morals, in *The Works of Charlotte Smith*, vol. 12, Elizabeth Dolan (ed.), London: Pickering & Chatto, 2007

   Rural Walks, in Dialogues, Intended for the Use of Young Persons, 2 vols., London, 1795

   Rural Walks, in *The Works of Charlotte Smith*, vol. 12, Elizabeth Dolan (ed.), London: Pickering & Chatto, 2007

Smith, Jonathan, *Fact and Feeling: Baconian Science and the Nineteenth-Century Literary Imagination*, Madison: University of Wisconsin Press, 1994

Snyder, Lauren J., "The Mill–Whewell Debate: Much Ado about Induction," *Perspectives on Science* 5.2 (1997): 159–98

Southey, Charles Cuthbert (ed.), *Life and Correspondence of Robert Southey*, New York: Harper & Brothers, 1855

Southey, Robert, *The Collected Letters of Robert Southey, Part III: 1804–1809*, Carol Bolton and Tim Fulford (eds.), Romantic Circles Electronic edition, 2009. www.rc.umd.edu/editions/southey_letters/Part_Three/HTML/letterEEd.26.1134.html, 10 June 2014

The Curse of Kehama. London: Longman et al., 1810.

The Doctor, 2 vols., New York: Harper, 1872

Journals of a Residence in Portugal, 1800–1801 and a Visit to France, 1838: Supplemented by Extracts from his Correspondence, Adolfo Cabral (ed.), Oxford: Clarendon, 1960

Madoc. London: Longman et al, 1805.

New Letters of Robert Southey, Vol. 1: 1792–1810, Kenneth Curry (ed.), New York and London: Columbia, 1965

"Review of Lyrical Ballads, with a few other poems," in *The Critical Review* 24 (Oct. 1798): 200

Southey's Common-place Book, 4 vols., John Wood Warter (ed.), London: Longman, Brown, Green, and Longmans, 1850

Thalaba the Destroyer, London, 1801

Thalaba the Destroyer, Tim Fulford (ed.), vol. 3 of *Robert Southey: Poetical Works, 1793–1810*, London: Pickering & Chatto, 2004

Vindiciæ Ecclesiæ Anglicanæ: Letters to Charles Butler Comprising Essays on the Romish Religion and Vindicating the Book of the Church, London, 1826

KES MG 218 (labeled "Collections for the History of Manners & Literature in England"), n.d.

KES MG 224, Keswick Museum, Keswick, UK, n.d.

KES MG 415 (labeled "Notebook 3"), n.d.

KES MG 420 (labeled "Notebook 17"), n.d.

Southey Papers, Add MS 47887, British Library, n.d.

Sprat, Thomas, *History of the Royal Society*, London, 1667, facs. ed. with introduction and notes by Jackson I. Cope and Harold Whitmore Jones, St. Louis: Washington University Press, 1958

Stanton, Judith, "Charlotte Smith's 'Literary Business': Income, Patronage, and Indigence," *The Age of Johnson* 1 (1987): 375–401

Starr, Gabrielle, *Lyric Generations: Poetry and the Novel in the Long Eighteenth Century*, Baltimore: Johns Hopkins University Press, 2004

Steadman, John, *The Hill and the Labyrinth: Discourse and Certitude in Milton and his Near-Contemporaries*, Berkley: University of California Press, 1984

Stewart, David, *Romantic Magazines and Metropolitan Literary Culture*, New York: Palgrave Macmillan, 2011

Stewart, Dugald, *Elements of the Philosophy of the Human Mind*, vol. 2, Edinburgh: Constable, 1814, *Eighteenth Century Collections Online*, http://galenet.galegroup.com.proxy.library.vanderbilt.edu/servlet/ECCO, 27 August 2010

Stewart, Susan, *Crimes of Writing: Problems in the Containment of Representation*, Oxford: Oxford University Press, 1991

"Notes on Distressed Genres," *Journal of American Folklore* 104.411 (1991): 5–31

Sweet, Rosemary, "Antiquaries and Antiquities in Eighteenth-Century England," *Eighteenth-Century Studies* 34.2 (2001): 181–206

Swift, Jonathan, *Travels into several remote nations of the world. In four parts. By Lemuel Gulliver, first a surgeon, and then a captain of several ships*, 2 vols., London, 1726, *Eighteenth Century Collections Online*, http://galenet.galegroup.com.proxy.library.vanderbilt.edu/servlet/ECCO, 15 August 2010

Teute, Fredrika, "The Loves of the Plants; or, The Cross-Fertilization of Science and Desire at the End of the Eighteenth Century," *Huntington Library Quarterly* 63.3 (2000): 319–45

Thelwall, John, *The Peripatetic; or Sketches of the Heart, of Nature and Society; in a series of Politico-Sentimental Journals, in Verse and Prose, of the Eccentric Excursions of Sylvanus Theophrastus supposed to be written by himself*, 3 vols., Southwark, 1793

The Peripatetic, Judith Thompson (ed.), Detroit: Wayne State University Press, 2001

Political Lectures (No. II.): Sketches of the History of Prosecutions for Political Opinion, London, 1794

Thompson, Judith, Introduction to *The Peripatetic*, by John Thelwall, Detroit: Wayne State University Press, 2001

Thwaite, Mary, *From Primer to Pleasure in Reading*, Boston: The Horn Book, 1972

Trott, Nicola, "Poemets and Poemlings: Robert Southey's Minority Interest," *Robert Southey and the Contexts of English Romanticism*, Lynda Pratt (ed.), Aldershot: Ashgate, 2006

Valenza, Robin, *Literature, Language, and the Rise of the Intellectual Disciplines in Britain, 1680–1820*, Cambridge: Cambridge University Press, 2009

Vickers, Brian, "The Royal Society and English Prose Style: A Reassessment," *Rhetoric and the Pursuit of Truth: Language Change in the Seventeenth and Eighteenth Centuries*, Brian Vickers and Nancy S. Strueve (eds.), Los Angeles: Clark Library, 1985

Vickers, Neil, "Coleridge's Abstruse Researches," *Samuel Taylor Coleridge and the Sciences of Life*, Nicholas Roe (ed.), Oxford: Oxford University Press, 2001

Watts, Isaac, *Logick: or, The Right Use of Reason in the Enquiry after Truth*, London: 1725, *Eighteenth Century Collections Online*, http://galenet.galegroup.com.proxy.library.vanderbilt.edu/servlet/ECCO, 5 Sept. 2010

Wellmon, Chad, *Organizing Enlightenment: Information Overload and the Invention of the Modern Research University*, Baltimore: Johns Hopkins University Press, 2015

"Touching Books: Diderot, Novalis, and the Encyclopedia of the Future," *Representations* 114 (Spring 2011): 65–102

Wendorf, Richard, "Abandoning the Capital in Eighteenth-Century London," *Reading, Society and Politics in Early Modern England*, Kevin Sharpe and Steven N. Zwicker (eds.), Cambridge: Cambridge University Press, 2003

Wharton, Joanna, "Inscribing on the Mind: Anna Letitia Barbauld's 'Sensible Objects,'" *Journal for Eighteenth-Century Studies* 35.4 (2012): 535–50

Whewell, William, *The Philosophy of the Inductive Sciences*, 2 vols., London, 1840

White, Daniel, *Early Romanticism and Religious Dissent*, Cambridge: Cambridge University Press, 2006

White, Gilbert, *The Natural History and Antiquities of Selborne*, London, 1789

White, Patricia, "Black and White and Read All Over: A Meditation on Footnotes," *Text* 5 (1991): 81–90

Wimsatt, William, *Philosophic Words: A Study of Style and Meaning in the* Rambler *and* Dictionary *of Samuel Johnson*, Hamden, CT: Archon Books, 1968

Wollstonecraft, Mary, *The Female Reader*, 1789, in vol. 4 of *The Works of Mary Wollstonecraft*, Janet Todd and Marilyn Butler (eds.), New York: New York University Press, 1989

     Original Stories from Real Life, 1796, *The Works of Mary Wollstonecraft*, Janet Todd and Marilyn Butler (eds.) vol. 4, New York: New York University Press, 1989

     A Vindication of the Rights of Woman, 1792, in vol. 5 of *The Works of Mary Wollstonecraft*, Janet Todd and Marilyn Butler (eds.), New York: New York University Press, 1989

Wood, David, Introduction, *Notes for a Romantic Encyclopedia* by Novalis, Albany: State University of New York Press, 2007

Wordsworth, William, *The Poetical Works of William Wordsworth*, 5 vols., London: Longman, 1827

Wordsworth, William, and Dorothy Wordsworth, *The Letters of William and Dorothy Wordsworth, Vol. 1: The Early Years: 1787–1805*, Ernest De Selincourt and Chester L. Shaver (eds.), Oxford: Oxford University Press, 1967

Yeo, Richard, *Encyclopedic Visions: Scientific Dictionaries and Enlightenment Culture*, Cambridge: Cambridge University Press, 2001

     Notebooks, English Virtuosi, and Early Modern Science, Chicago and London: University of Chicago Press, 2014

Zionkowski, Linda, "Bridging the Gulf Between: The Poet and the Audience in the Work of Gray," *ELH* 58.2 (1991): 331–50

Zunshine, Lisa, "Rhetoric, Cognition, and Ideology in A. L. Barbauld's *Hymns in Prose for Children* (1781)," *Poetics Today* 23.1 (2002): 123–39

Index

287

CAMBRIDGE STUDIES IN ROMANTICISM

General Editor
James Chandler, *University of Chicago*